EVERYMAN'S LIBRARY

EVERYMAN,
I WILL GO WITH THEE,
AND BE THY GUIDE,
IN THY MOST NEED
TO GO BY THY SIDE

JOAN DIDION

I WRITE TO FIND OUT WHAT I AM THINKING

THE YEAR OF MAGICAL THINKING

BLUE NIGHTS

SOUTH AND WEST

LET ME TELL YOU WHAT I MEAN

WITH AN INTRODUCTION
BY GRIFFIN DUNNE

EVERYMAN'S LIBRARY
Alfred A. Knopf   New York   London

432

THIS IS A BORZOI BOOK
PUBLISHED BY ALFRED A. KNOPF

First included in Everyman's Library, 2025
The Year of Magical Thinking Copyright © 2005 by Joan Didion
Blue Nights Copyright © 2011 by Joan Didion
South and West Copyright © 2017 by Joan Didion
Let Me Tell You What I Mean Copyright © 2021 by Joan Didion

Introduction copyright © 2025 by Griffin Dunne
Bibliography and Chronology copyright © 2025 by Everyman's Library

This edition is published in the UK by arrangement with
HarperCollins Publishers Limited.

Permissions credits can be found at the back of this volume.

Penguin Random House values and supports copyright. Copyright fuels creativity, encourages diverse voices, promotes free speech, and creates a vibrant culture. Thank you for buying an authorized edition of this book and for complying with copyright laws by not reproducing, scanning, or distributing any part of it in any form without permission. You are supporting writers and allowing Penguin Random House to continue to publish books for every reader. Please note that no part of this book may be used or reproduced in any manner for the purpose of training artificial intelligence technologies or systems.

Published by Alfred A. Knopf, a division of Penguin Random House LLC, 1745 Broadway, New York, NY 10019. Published in the United Kingdom by Everyman's Library, 50 Albemarle Street, London W1S 4BD and distributed by Penguin Random House UK, One Embassy Gardens, 8 Viaduct Gardens, London SW11 7BW.

Originally published in 2005 (*The Year of Magical Thinking*), 2011 (*Blue Nights*), 2017 (*South and West*), 2021 (*Let Me Tell You What I Mean*) in the United States by Alfred A. Knopf, and in the United Kingdom by Fourth Estate, an imprint of HarperCollins Publishers.

everymanslibrary.com   penguinrandomhouse.com
www.penguin.co.uk/about/publishing-houses/everyman

ISBN: 978-0-593-99221-0 (US)
978-1-84159-432-3 (UK)

Library of Congress Control Number: 2025938108
A CIP catalogue reference for this book is available from the British Library

Typography by Peter B. Willberg
Book design by Barbara de Wilde and Carol Devine Carson
Typeset in the UK by Input Data Services Ltd, Bridgwater, Somerset
Printed and bound in Germany by GGP Media GmbH, Pössneck

The authorized representative in the EU for product safety and compliance is Penguin Random House Ireland, Morrison Chambers, 32 Nassau Street, Dublin D02 YH68, Ireland, https://eu-contact.penguin.ie

CONTENTS

Introduction vii
Select Bibliography xvii
Chronology xviii

The Year of Magical Thinking 1

Blue Nights 155

South and West 279

Let Me Tell You What I Mean 353

Acknowledgments 436

INTRODUCTION

Life changes fast,
Life changes in an instant.
You sit down to dinner and life as you know it ends.
The question of self-pity.

Those were among the first words my aunt, Joan Didion, wrote when she finally returned to her desk on May 20, 2004 after the sudden death by heart attack of her beloved husband of thirty-nine years, John Gregory Dunne, on December 30, 2003. They are also the words that open *The Year of Magical Thinking*.

There had been signs, early indications of impending catastrophe, a dog whistle that John would not live out the year, that even Joan, after decades of marriage, was not attuned to hear.

John had ongoing issues with his "ticker," as he called his heart. He had undergone a procedure in the late 80s for a weak artery and more recently he'd had a pacemaker implanted (a "widow maker," John delighted in quoting his cardiologist). But it was his state of mind in his last days, filled with dread and doom, that Joan didn't take as warning that her husband had an appointment in Samarra.

"*I tell you that I shall not live two days.*" Joan repeats this line of Sir Gawain's in growing self-flagellation, and with every incantation her cat-o'-nine-tails cuts deeper, as if punishment for ignoring what then seemed obvious while writing *The Year of Magical Thinking*.

"I don't think I'm up for this," John said to Joan on their way home from seeing their only daughter Quintana in the ICU of Beth Israel North, where at that moment she was fighting for her life.

"You don't get a choice," Joan replied.

Everything he had done had been worthless, John said hopelessly to Joan the night he died or the night before. His current piece in *The New York Review of Books*—about Gavin Lambert's biography of Natalie Wood—was worthless, he said. He didn't know what he was even doing in New York. "Why did I waste time on a piece about Natalie Wood?" he said, perhaps sensing the precious hours he had left.

"This might not be normal," wrote Joan later, about those hours, "but neither was it normal for a father to see a child beyond his help."

There were other signs Joan would later remember: how John said, either three or twenty-seven hours before he died, that detail she didn't recall, "You were right about Hawaii."

Was he talking about that time in the 70s when she wanted to buy a house in Honolulu, and he didn't? What was driving this sudden regret?

This is one of many memories that haunted Joan that year. And as a journalist, she felt compelled to document her loss, not to make sense to the reader, but to herself, so she might understand how grief could toy with her imagination to the point where she could magically believe that at any moment John might walk through the door after his morning stroll in Central Park.

"See enough and write it down," Joan noted in her essay, "On Keeping a Notebook."

"In time of trouble, I had been trained since childhood," she writes in *The Year of Magical Thinking* thirty-six years later. "Read, learn, work it up, go to the literature. Information was control. Given that grief remained the most general of afflictions its literature seemed remarkably spare."

She explored her grief in a submersible built for one, diving into the journal of C. S. Lewis, pulling quotes from Freud, finding passages in Thomas Mann's *The Magic Mountain*, always looking, but never finding anyone who could articulate what she was feeling.

Describing the journey of her grief in my documentary *The Center Will Not Hold*, Joan said, "The reason I had to write it down, is that no one had ever told me what it was like."

"It's the first book about grief not by a believer," the playwright David Hare correctly points out later in the film.

And who thought that journey would become a bestseller, let alone win the National Book Award or be a finalist for the Pulitzer Prize. Didion was no stranger to bestseller lists, but no one anticipated the sheer volume of sales of *The Year of Magical Thinking*, or the months it would remain aloft.

INTRODUCTION

I was on a movie set almost six months after the book's release. Joan was still on the bestseller list. I noticed a young actress I was working with, nineteen or twenty years old at the most, rush back to her chair and her copy of *The Year of Magical Thinking*. When we wrapped for the day, I casually asked what she thought of the book.

"She's incredible, this lady. My grandmother died last year and I can't talk to anybody about it."

The young actress stopped to look at the book in her hands, gently running a finger over Joan's name.

"Nobody gets it . . . but she does."

When she asked me if I'd ever read it, I nodded and offered nothing more, not wanting to break the spell by telling her of my relationship to the author.

"Do you know," she began, her face a picture of wonder, "if she has ever written anything else before?"

That's the thing about this book. Until *Magical Thinking* Joan had never had such an enormous audience. More importantly, she hadn't had an audience that was as young and hungry to discover all she had written before *Magical Thinking*.

Joan was suddenly next-level famous. It wasn't unusual for people to stop *me* in airports or coffee shops to say in halting voices how much *Magical Thinking* meant to them, that my aunt helped them get over, understand, and accept the loss of their parent, child, or sibling. They somehow knew of my family connection, and by connecting with me could finally express their debt to Joan, even if indirectly.

Every time I shared these encounters with her, Joan would look at me with an expression somewhere between bafflement and wariness. She was not the kind of person to embrace flattery, at least not on the outside, but I suspect that beneath her unreadable and sometimes intimidating expression lived a quiet amazement that her words had brought comfort to so many.

The one wound Joan couldn't heal was her own. No amount of magical thinking could distract her from the cold fact that she had outlived first her husband and then, unimaginably, her daughter. This is the story she tells in *Blue Nights*. Quintana is still alive in *Magical Thinking*, though just barely. She suffered a brain injury from a fall at LAX two days after John's funeral.

She'd planned to return to Malibu with her newlywed husband, Gerry Michael, to relive the happiest moments of her childhood. The brain injury led to complications, each one more dire, until finally, on August 26, 2005, Quintana Roo Dunne died at the age of thirty-nine. Once again, Joan wrote to understand her feelings, but this time, for her next and last book, *Blue Nights*, she wrote to face the unthinkable.

"I very nearly didn't finish it," she once told me, nervously twirling John's wedding ring on a delicate gold chain around her neck, "but I went on."

Her closest friends were dismayed when they read the galley. Earl McGrath, to whom she dedicated *South and West*, also in this Everyman collection, said to me that he told Joan to her face that he "hated" *Blue Nights*. I asked why he would say such a thing.

"Because I love her, and she loved Quintana and was a great mother who didn't deserve the pain she put herself through to write it."

Joan is very tough on herself in *Blue Nights*, and for anyone who loved her, it was—and is—painful to read. She confronts her mortality—she was no longer afraid to die—and her failing health. She relives happy memories of Quintana as a child running on the beach and the blissful day of her wedding to Gerry at St. John the Divine.

"On that wedding day, July 26, 2003, we could see no reason to think that such ordinary blessings would not come their way," Joan writes, but with the caveat: "Do notice: We still counted happiness and health and love and luck and beautiful children as 'ordinary blessings.'"

Other memories accompany the guilt and regret: at the age of five her daughter called Camarillo Mental Institution to ask what she needed to do if she was going crazy. While examining a childhood photo of Quintana, Joan notices the then-unnoticed signs of melancholia, which prompt brutal introspection:

How could I have missed what was so clearly there to be seen?
Was I the problem? Was I always the problem?

For *Blue Nights*, she volunteered for a mission no one asked her to undertake. Rereading the book to write this introduction, I can feel the toll each sentence took on her and the almost

INTRODUCTION

Sisyphean struggle it must have been to finish it. She did it for Q. She did it for herself. She did it because as a child of the West, she was raised with the frontier ethic that you don't leave the dead behind.

*

Joan had a closet in her office where she kept years of rough drafts of articles, books, and screenplays that were developed but never made. (What I wouldn't have given to see the film of her adaptation of Katharine Graham's autobiography or John and Joan's adaptation of his book *Vegas*.) In that closet were also pages and notes for an unfinished piece written during a drive through the South and collected in *South and West*, based on a road trip she and John made in 1970.

Either before, after, or during the time Joan wrote *Play It As It Lays*, she bought a bright banana-colored Corvette Stingray, just like the one Maria, the book's heroine, drove aimlessly through L.A. Like Maria, Joan took long road trips where freeway exits shaped like clovers merged with highway 91 to Riverside, past San Bernardino, and onto Interstate 15 toward Barstow, and back again. John did most of the driving and though they had no destination in mind, the purpose of these excursions was far from aimless. The Vette's two bucket seats were an office that hovered around 80 mph on the open road and freeways and was where the work got done. Joan rode shotgun with a stack of papers and a notebook on her lap, reading John's pages back to him, or making final edits for her own essays, some of which are included in this collection.

In June 1970 Joan and John took the LAX exit off the 405 to board a flight headed south to Louis Armstrong International Airport. "The idea was to start in New Orleans and from there we had no plan," she writes at the beginning of the piece. "We went wherever the day took us. I seem to remember that John drove."

As they were approaching Port Sulphur, Louisiana, in the hour-long drive, Joan notes they ran over three snakes, including "a thick black moccasin already dead, twisted across the one lane." Of course, she notices the snakes, she grew up with them in the West and was taught by her father that if you come across a rattlesnake always kill it to protect the next man on the trail: another lesson in frontier morality. For her avid readers, Didion was to snakes what Ahab was to Moby. So naturally, when crossing the Mississippi line and passing a reptile farm, they have to pull over to see the copperheads. John and Joan got trapped in the reptile house during a downpour and decided to make a run for it to the main building. Joan slipped in the mud and had "an instant of irrational panic that there were snakes in the mud and all around me." Maybe the copperhead was finally getting its revenge for her giving them such a bad name.

Her process on the trip was to jot down overheard conversations, quotes from random strangers, deft descriptions of their appearance, and the conditions of big cities and sleepy small towns they visited along the back roads and blue highways. Then, at day's end, she typed up all that she had seen and heard, most likely with a glass of bourbon and a Pall Mall burning in an ash tray. As Joan noted about herself in the preface to *Slouching Towards Bethlehem*, "My only advantage as a reporter is that I am so physically small, so temperamentally unobtrusive, and so neurotically inarticulate that people tend to forget that my presence runs counter to their best interests."

With no "reportorial imperative to any of the places" they went, she talked to anyone and observed everything: at a beauty parlor she talked to a girl hoping to get her cosmetology license, she attended a Pony League game, and at yet another motel pool observed a boy wrapped in the Confederate flag being called to supper. Curiosity led her to a Mississippi Broadcasters' Convention where she quotes the lieutenant governor saying, shortly after the Kent State shootings, "I have come to think we are living in the era of the demonstrators—unruly, unwashed, uninformed, and sometimes un-American people—disrupting private and public life in this country."

Though George Wallace was governor of Alabama and other white supremacists running for public office were "a totally explicable phenomenon," Joan heard a lot about inclusivity in the "New South." One particularly memorable character is a white owner of an "ethnic station" that plays gospel and soul and hosts a program called *Adventures in Black History*, "to point out the contributions black people have made." He reeks of

INTRODUCTION

open-mindedness when addressing the need to increase school funding for the African-American community but adds, "I'm not saying I'm going to have a black minister come home to dinner tonight, 'cause I'm not."

It was Joan's tactic as a journalist to rarely ask questions and to let the silence do all the work. Invariably, a racist would fill the air with the perfect quote that denies he is one. Were she to return to the South today, she might find those people finally comfortable saying the quiet part out loud.

The last twelve pages of *South and West* are notes, reflections, and historical research about growing up in the West as a fifth-generation Californian. These notes began in 1976 for an unfinished article Jann Wenner commissioned Joan to write for *Rolling Stone* about Patty Hearst, whose California roots extended as far back as her own. But as she began writing about Ms. Hearst, her thoughts strayed inward, uncovering, as she wrote, her own "mixed emotions," evoking memories of a prophecy a high-school yearbook had made about her place in the world, of being a sorority girl at Berkeley, of the darkened silverware and dried flowers in her family's home on 22nd and T Street in Sacramento. She finds a certain kinship with the writer and essayist Gertrude Atherton (1857–1948), whose articles were about politics, feminism, and war, and whose novels were often set in California. Like Joan, Ms. Atherton loathed snakes and would cut them in two with an ax.

She closes the *West* chapter of *South and West* with: "I am at home in the West. The hills of the coast ranges look 'right' to me, the particular flat expanse of the Central Valley comforts my eye. The place names have a ring of real places to me."

Joan never wrote the piece about Patty Hearst, but these notes would find their way into the larger subject of personal history and the history of California in *Where I Was From* (2003). What began as a story about one Californian became a memoir about another, and how growing up in the center of a Pacific state with such a rugged history had shaped her morality, intuition, and the strong convictions we have become so familiar with.

*

JOAN DIDION

The Saturday Evening Post discovered Norman Rockwell and published Jack London's *The Call of the Wild*. The magazine's first edition was in 1897 and it managed to survive two world wars, near-death libel suits, a fickle readership that both climbed and declined, until finally throwing in the towel in 1969. I took the magazine's demise personally.

For me, *The Post*, as we called it around the dinner table, was like a family update. On alternate weeks Joan and John had a column called "Points West" and just below the title was a flattering sketch of their faces gazing at the reader. It was from these essays I learned that their house on Franklin Avenue in Hollywood (a "senseless killing neighborhood" as Joan called it) had been robbed. It was in the essay "On Being Unchosen by the College of One's Choice," included in her 2021 collection of twelve pieces called *Let Me Tell You What I Mean*, that I learned that when Joan was seventeen she received a letter of rejection from Stanford, and was so humiliated she considered swallowing a bottle of codeine tablets. When I read that in 1968, I was a terrible student facing my own humiliation at being held back to repeat the sixth grade. I remember taking comfort that my aunt forgave herself for being rejected by Stanford, and hearing the wisdom she imparted as though she were speaking directly to me: "Of course none of it matters very much at all, none of these early successes, early failures." But it was the last line of the essay that gave me the most hope: "Finding one's role at seventeen is problem enough, without being handed somebody else's script."

"Why I Write" has practically become a handbook for aspiring writers, but what delights me about the collection of essays in *Let Me Tell You What I Mean* is that they have not been revisited since first published in various magazines and are today remembered mostly by readers of a certain age. New readers will find here evidence that Joan's unique vision of American culture and her skepticism towards media consensus predate her more famous essays in *Slouching Towards Bethlehem* and *The White Album*.

Her iconoclasm is on full display in "Everywoman.com," the last piece in this collection, in which she calls out the prevailing misogyny toward Martha Stewart and digs far beneath the media's caricature to find an entrepreneur who threatens men of power.

INTRODUCTION

*

Throughout their marriage, John was Joan's protector, her Irish John Wayne who, though unarmed, would fire off a deadly round of invective toward anyone he felt had maligned his wife. (Pauline Kael would rue the day she took on Joan in a review of *Play It As It Lays*.) When John died, my father took his place, though his approach was less hot-blooded.

When my father died in 2009, it became my turn in the natural order to inherit the role of Joan's protector. What I did not know at the time, or appreciate as much as I do now, was that this familial role would extend beyond her life, becoming a mission I would gratefully carry to the end of mine.

To be the nephew of Joan Didion is a little like being related to one of the chiseled faces on Mount Rushmore. I can feel Joan blush at that hyperbole, in fact I've felt her looking over my shoulder ever since Everyman's Library asked me to write this introduction, but I can't say I mind the company.

Griffin Dunne

GRIFFIN DUNNE has written, directed, produced and acted for film and television. Of all his projects, the documentary he directed for Netflix, *Joan Didion: The Center Will Not Hold*, is the one he is most proud of. His memoir about his family, *The Friday Afternoon Club* was published by Penguin in June 2024.

SELECT BIBLIOGRAPHY

BY JOAN DIDION

The Joan Didion Collection (3-volume boxed set), Library of America, New York, 2024.
Joan Didion: Memoirs and Later Writings, edited by David Ulin, Library of America, New York, 2024.
We Tell Ourselves Stories in Order to Live: Collected Nonfiction, introduced by John Leonard, Everyman's Library, Alfred A. Knopf, New York, 2006.

BIOGRAPHY/BIBLIOGRAPHY

LILI ANOLIK, *Didion & Babitz*, Scribner, New York, 2024.
TRACY DAUGHERTY, *The Last Love Song: A Biography of Joan Didion*, St. Martin's Press, New York, 2015.
SARA DAVIDSON, *The Didion Files: Fifty Years of Friendship with Joan Didion* (self-published), 2023.
KATHERINE U. HENDERSON, *Joan Didion*, Ungar, New York, 1981.
FRED RUE JACOBS, *Joan Didion: Bibliography*, The Loop Press, Keene, CA, 1977.
DONNA OLENDORF, "Joan Didion: A Checklist, 1955–1980," Bulletin of Bibliography 38.1 (Jan–March 1981): 32–44.

CRITICISM

ROBERT S. BOYNTON, *The New New Journalism: Conversations with America's Best Nonfiction Writers on Their Craft*, Vintage, New York, 2005.
SHARON FELTON, ed., *The Critical Response to Joan Didion*, Greenwood Press, Westport, CN, 1994.
ELLEN G. FRIEDMAN, ed., *Joan Didion: Essays and Conversations*, Ontario Review Press, Princeton, NJ, 1984.
EVELYN McDONNELL, *The World According to Joan Didion*, Harper One, New York, 2023.
ALISSA WILKINSON, *We Tell Ourselves Stories: Joan Didion and the American Dream Machine*, Liveright/W. W. Norton, 2025.

CHRONOLOGY

DATE	AUTHOR'S LIFE	LITERARY CONTEXT
		1925 *The New Yorker* is founded by American journalist Harold Ross.
		1929 Woolf: *A Room of One's Own*.
		1932 Hammett: *The Thin Man*.
		1933 Orwell: *Down and Out in Paris and London*.
		N. West: *Miss Lonelyhearts*.
1934	Joan Didion is born at Mercy Hospital, Sacramento, California to Eduene Jerrett Didion and Frank Reese Didion (5 December).	1934 Fitzgerald: *Tender Is the Night*. Miller: *Tropic of Cancer*. Waugh: *A Handful of Dust*; *Ninety-Two Days*.
1935–41	Lives in Sacramento, California.	1935 Lewis: *It Can't Happen Here*.
		1936 Orwell: "Shooting an Elephant."
		1937 Orwell: *The Road to Wigan Pier*.
		1938 Orwell: *Homage to Catalonia*.
		1939 Steinbeck: *The Grapes of Wrath*.
		1940 Hemingway: *For Whom the Bell Tolls*.
		1941 Fitzgerald: *The Last Tycoon*.
1942–43	Lives in Tacoma, Washington; Durham, North Carolina; and Colorado Springs, Colorado, where her father is stationed with Army Air Corps.	1942 Eliot: *Four Quartets*. Camus: *The Stranger*.
		1943 Chandler: *The Lady in the Lake*.
1944	Returns to Sacramento with her mother and brother (father returns in 1945).	1944 Borges: *Ficciones*.
		1945 Orwell: *Animal Farm*.
		1946 Orwell: "A Nice Cup of Tea"; "Decline of the English Murder." Hersey: *Hiroshima* (report).

HISTORICAL EVENTS

1932 La Matanza, massacre in El Salvador by government troops following a peasant rebellion in western part of the country.
1933 Roosevelt announces "New Deal." Hitler becomes German Chancellor.

1936 Outbreak of Spanish Civil War. Hitler and Mussolini form Rome–Berlin Axis. Edward VIII abdicates; George VI crowned in UK. Stalin's "Great Purge" of the Communist Party (to 1938).
1937 Japanese invasion of China.

1938 Germany annexes Austria; Munich crisis.
1939 Nazi–Soviet Pact. Hitler invades Poland; World War II begins.

1940 Churchill becomes Prime Minister in UK. Dunkirk evacuation. Fall of France. Battle of Britain. The Blitz.
1941 Japan attacks Pearl Harbor; US enters war. Germans invade USSR.
1942 Fall of Singapore. Russian troops halt German advance at Stalingrad. North Africa campaign; Battle of El Alamein.

1944 Attempted military coup in Colombia. Normandy landings and liberation of Paris. Red Army reaches Belgrade and Budapest.

1945 Unconditional surrender of Germany; Hitler commits suicide. US drops atomic bombs on Hiroshima and Nagasaki. End of World War II. United Nations founded. Death of Roosevelt; Truman becomes US President.
1946 Nuremberg trials. "Iron Curtain" speech by Churchill.

JOAN DIDION

DATE	AUTHOR'S LIFE	LITERARY CONTEXT
		1947 Warren: *All the King's Men*.
		1948 Mailer: *The Naked and the Dead*.
		1949 Orwell: *Nineteen Eighty-Four*. Beauvoir: *The Second Sex*.
		1950 Lessing: *The Grass Is Singing*.
		1951 Salinger: *The Catcher in the Rye*.
1952	Graduates from C. K. McClatchy High School, Sacramento.	1952 Beckett: *Waiting for Godot*. McCarthy: *The Groves of Academe*.
		1953 Bellow: *The Adventures of Augie March*.
		1954 K. Amis: *Lucky Jim*.
		1955 Nabokov: *Lolita*. Greene: *The Quiet American*. Baldwin: *Notes of a Native Son* (essays). Miller: *A View from the Bridge*.
1956–63	Graduates from the University of California at Berkeley (1956). Lives in New York while working for *Vogue*.	1956 Mahfouz: *The Cairo Trilogy* (to 1957).
		1957 Kerouac: *On the Road*. Pasternak: *Doctor Zhivago*.
		1958 Lampedusa: *The Leopard*. Achebe: *Things Fall Apart*.
		1959 Burroughs: *Naked Lunch*. Bellow: *Henderson the Rain King*. Gellhorn: *The Face of War*. Grass: *The Tin Drum*.
		1960 Updike: *Rabbit, Run*.
		1961 Naipaul: *A House for Mr. Biswas*. Heller: *Catch-22*.
		1962 Lessing: *The Golden Notebook*. Solzhenitsyn: *One Day in the Life of Ivan Denisovich*.
1963	First novel, *Run River*.	1963 *The New York Review of Books* is founded by Robert Silvers, Barbara Epstein and publisher A. Whitney Ellsworth. Arendt: *Eichmann in Jerusalem*. McCarthy: *The Group*. Plath: *The Bell Jar*.

CHRONOLOGY

HISTORICAL EVENTS

1948 Jewish state of Israel comes into existence. Russian blockade of West Berlin. Assassination of Gandhi in India. Apartheid introduced in South Africa.
1949 Communists win Chinese Civil War. North Atlantic Treaty signed.

1950 Korean War (to 1953).

1952 Eisenhower elected US President. Accession of Elizabeth II in UK.

1953 Death of Stalin.

1954 Vietnam War (to 1975).
1955 UN refuses to discontinue discussions on 1952 Cruz Report on apartheid; South Africa withdraws from UN.

1956 Khrushchev delivers "Secret Speech" at 20th Party Congress. Suez crisis in Egypt. California repeals all Alien Land Laws.
1957 Civil Rights Commission established in US to safeguard voting rights.

1959 Castro seizes power in Cuba and forms a Socialist government.

1960 John F. Kennedy wins the US presidency.
1961 Anti-Castro force of Cuban exiles backed by CIA attempts invasion of Cuba at the Bay of Pigs. Yuri Gagarin becomes first man in space. Construction of the Berlin Wall.
1962 Cuban missile crisis.

1963 Assassination of Kennedy; Johnson becomes President.

JOAN DIDION

DATE	AUTHOR'S LIFE	LITERARY CONTEXT
1964	Marries writer John Gregory Dunne at Mission San Juan Bautista, San Benito County, California (30 January). Moves from New York to Portuguese Bend, Los Angeles County, California (June).	1964 Naipaul: *An Area of Darkness*. Bellow: *Herzog*.
		1965 Wolfe: *The Kandy-Kolored Tangerine-Flake Streamline Baby* (essays). Mailer: *An American Dream*. Scott: *The Raj Quartet* (to 1975).
1966	Only child, Quintana Roo Dunne, is born at St. John's Hospital, Santa Monica (3 March). Moves with family from Portuguese Bend to Franklin Avenue in Hollywood.	1966 Sontag: *Against Interpretation* (essays). Gellhorn: *Vietnam: A New Kind of War*. Rhys: *Wide Sargasso Sea*.
		1967 McCarthy: reports on Vietnam from Saigon and Hanoi (to 1968). Styron: *The Confessions of Nat Turner*. Dunne: *Delano*. Márquez: *One Hundred Years of Solitude*.
1968	*Slouching Towards Bethlehem*.	1968 Solzhenitsyn: *Cancer Ward*.
		1969 Hersh: *Vietnam War: My Lai Massacre* (report). Nader: *The Great American Gyp* (report). Dunne: *The Studio*. Sontag: *Styles of Radical Will*. Oates: *Them*.
1970	*Play It As It Lays*.	1970 Bellow: *Mr. Sammler's Planet*. Gordimer: *A Guest of Honour*.
1971	Moves with family to the Pacific Coast Highway in Malibu. *The Panic in Needle Park* is released, starring Al Pacino and Kitty Winn. It is the first motion picture credited to Didion and Dunne, and also first to Pacino.	1971 Updike: *Rabbit Redux*. McCarthy: *Birds of America*. F. O'Connor: *The Complete Stories*. Lessing: *Briefing for a Descent into Hell*.

CHRONOLOGY

HISTORICAL EVENTS

1964 Civil Rights Act prohibits discrimination in the US. Nobel Peace Prize is awarded to Martin Luther King.

1965 Human rights activist Malcolm X is assassinated. President Johnson orders US intervention in the Dominican Republic when civil war breaks out.

1966 Mao launches Cultural Revolution in China. Revolutionary Black nationalist organization the Black Panther Party is founded in Oakland, California.

1967 Six-Day War between Israel and Arab states. Outbreaks of racial violence mount in many US cities; President Johnson appoints a commission to look into causes. 75,000 young people gather at Haight-Ashbury, California for "Summer of Love." Argentinian-born Cuban guerrilla hero Che Guevara is shot dead in Bolivia.

1968 Martin Luther King assassinated in Memphis, Tennessee, triggering violent reaction throughout the US. Czechoslovakia is invaded by Soviet troops seeking to reinstate Communism. Richard Nixon is elected US President.
1969 US troops begin to withdraw from Vietnam. US astronaut Neil Armstrong becomes first man on the moon. Woodstock rock festival, New York State attracts 400,000 fans.

1970 Salvador Allende becomes first Socialist President of Chile in a democratic election. Death of de Gaulle in France.

JOAN DIDION

DATE	AUTHOR'S LIFE	LITERARY CONTEXT
		1972 DeLillo: *End Zone*.
		1973 Pynchon: *Gravity's Rainbow*. Solzhenitsyn: *The Gulag Archipelago* (to 1975).
		1974 Dunne: *Vegas*. Gordimer: *The Conservationist*.
		1975 Bellow: *Humboldt's Gift*. Levi: *The Periodic Table*.
		1976 Gordimer: *Letter from South Africa* (report). Hong Kingston: *The Woman Warrior*.
1977	*A Book of Common Prayer*.	1977 Dunne: *True Confessions*. Morrison: *Song of Solomon*.
1978	Moves with family from Malibu to Brentwood Park. Receives the Morton Dauwen Zabel Award for Fiction from the American Academy of Arts and Letters.	1978 French: *The Woman's Room*. Munro: *The Beggar Maid*.
1979	*The White Album*.	1979 Calvino: *If on a winter's night a traveler*. Mailer: *The Executioner's Story*.
		1980 Hong Kingston: *China Men*. McCarthy: *Cannibals and Missionaries*.
		1981 Vargas Llosa: *The War of the End of the World*. Márquez: *Chronicle of a Death Foretold*. Rushdie: *Midnight's Children*. Updike: *Rabbit Is Rich*.
		1982 Walker: *The Color Purple*. Dunne: *Dutch Shea, Jr*. Allende: *The House of the Spirits*. Levi: *If Not Now, When?*
1983	*Salvador*.	1983 Updike: *Hugging the Shore* (essays). Walker: *In Search of our Mothers' Gardens* (essays).
1984	*Democracy*.	1984 Brookner: *Hotel du Lac*. Barnes: *Flaubert's Parrot*. Naipaul: *Among the Republicans* (report).

CHRONOLOGY

HISTORICAL EVENTS

1972 Strategic Arms Limitation Treaty (SALT I) signed by US and USSR. Eleven Israeli athletes are killed by Arab guerrillas at the Olympic Village near Munich.
1973 US Supreme Court suspends capital punishment (until 1976). Chilean President Allende and at least 2,700 others are killed in a coup led by General Pinochet.
1974 Nixon resigns in wake of Watergate scandal; Ford becomes US President.
1975 Vietnam War ends.

1976 Death of Chairman Mao in China. Jimmy Carter elected US President.

1978 Camp David Agreement between Carter, Egyptian President Sadat and Israeli Prime Minister Begin.

1979 Margaret Thatcher elected first female Prime Minister in UK. Carter and Brezhnev sign SALT II Arms Limitation Treaty. Soviets occupy Afghanistan.
1980 Mariel Boatlift, mass exodus of Cuban refugees to US. Shipyard worker Lech Walsea leads strikes in Gdansk, Poland. Iran–Iraq War begins (to 1988). The Farabundo Martí National Liberation Front established in El Salvador; launches armed struggle against the government. Ronald Reagan elected US President.
1981 Attempted assassination of Reagan in Washington. President Sadat killed by Islamic fundamentalists in Egypt. El Mozote massacre: hundreds of civilians die at hands of Salvadoran armed forces.

1982 Argentina occupies Falkland Islands, resulting in war with Britain.

1983 US troops invade Grenada after the government is overthrown.

1984 Famine in Ethiopia. Indira Gandhi assassinated in India.

JOAN DIDION

DATE	AUTHOR'S LIFE	LITERARY CONTEXT
		1985 Márquez: *Love in the Time of Cholera*.
		1986 Levi: *The Drowned and the Saved*.
		Munro: *The Progress of Love*.
		Atwood: *The Handmaid's Tale*.
1987	*Miami*.	1987 Dunne: *The Red White and Blue*.
		Wolfe: *The Bonfire of the Vanities*.
		Morrison: *Beloved*.
1988	Moves from California to New York.	1988 Rushdie: *The Satanic Verses*.
		Carey: *Oscar and Lucinda*.
		Gellhorn: *A View from the Ground*.
		Carver: *Where I'm Calling From*.
		1989 Márquez: *The General in His Labyrinth*.
		Atwood: *Cat's Eye*.
		Ozick: *The Shawl*.
		Dunne: *Harp*.
		1990 Pynchon: *Vineland*.
		Updike: *Rabbit at Rest*.
		1991 Updike: *Odd Jobs* (essays).
		Jung Chang: *Wild Swans*.
1992	*After Henry*.	1992 Ondaatje: *The English Patient*.
		Oates: *Black Water*.
		1993 Roth: *Operation Shylock*.
		1994 Allende: *Paula*.
		Heller: *Closing Time*.
		Dunne: *Playland*.
		Murakami: *The Wind-Up Bird Chronicle*.
		1995 Guterson: *Snow Falling on Cedars*.
		M. Amis: *The Information*.
1996	*The Last Thing He Wanted*. Receives Edward MacDowell Medal from The MacDowell Colony.	1996 Updike: *In the Beauty of the Lilies*.
		Ozick: *Fame & Folly* (essays).

CHRONOLOGY

HISTORICAL EVENTS

1985 Gorbachev becomes General Secretary in USSR; period of reform begins. South African government declares State of Emergency.
1986 Nuclear explosion at Chernobyl. US bombs Libya. New State of Emergency declared in South Africa. Gorbachev–Reagan summit.

1988 George Bush elected US President. Gorbachev announces significant troop reductions and withdrawal from Afghanistan.

1989 Collapse of Communism in Eastern Europe. Fall of the Berlin Wall. First democratic elections in USSR. Tiananmen Square massacre in China.

1990 Pinochet stands down as President of Chile. End of Communist monopoly in USSR. Yeltsin elected first leader of Russian Federation. Nelson Mandela released from jail after 27 years' imprisonment. John Major becomes Prime Minister in UK.
1991 Gulf War. Bush and Gorbachev sign START arms reduction treaty. Central government in USSR suspended. War begins in former Yugoslavia. End of apartheid in South Africa.
1992 Peace accords signed in El Salvador, signalling end to 12-year civil war. Riots in Los Angeles. Bill Clinton elected US President.

1993 Palestinian leader Arafat and Israeli Prime Minister Rabin sign peace agreement in US. Maastricht Treaty ratified.
1994 Massacres in Rwanda. Mandela leads the ANC to victory in South African elections. Russian military actions against Chechen Republic. IRA ceasefire announced. The Channel Tunnel is opened.

1995 Israeli Prime Minister Rabin assassinated.

1996 President Clinton re-elected.

JOAN DIDION

DATE	AUTHOR'S LIFE	LITERARY CONTEXT
		1997 Dunne: *Monster: Living Off the Big Screen*. Roth: *American Pastoral*. Ozick: *The Puttermesser Papers*. Bellow: *The Actual*. McEwan: *Enduring Love*. 1998 Morrison: *Paradise*. DeLillo: *Underworld*. Roth: *I Married a Communist*. Heller: *Now and Then*. 1999 Sontag: *In America*.
		2000 Bellow: *Ravelstein*. Roth: *The Human Stain*. Atwood: *The Blind Assassin*.
2001	*Political Fictions*; wins George Polk Book Award.	2001 Franzen: *The Corrections*. Munro: *Hateship, Friendship, Courtship, Loveship, Marriage*. 2002 Safran Foer: *Everything Is Illuminated*.
2003	Quintana Roo Dunne marries Gerald Michael at the Cathedral Church of St. John the Divine, New York (26 July). *Where I Was From* (October). John Gregory Dunne dies of cardiac arrest, New York (30 December).	2003 Hersh: *Lunch with the Chairman; Selective Intelligence* (reports). Atwood: *Oryx and Crake*.
		2004 Dunne: *Nothing Lost*. Hersh: *Torture at Abu Ghraib* (report).
2005	Quintana Roo Dunne Michael dies of septic shock, New York (26 August). *The Year of Magical Thinking* (November); wins 2005 National Book Award for Nonfiction.	2005 Mayer: *Outsourcing Terror: The secret history of America's 'extraordinary rendition' program* (report). Safran Foer: *Extremely Loud and Incredibly Close*.
2006	*We Tell Ourselves Stories in Order to Live: Collected Nonfiction*, introduction by John Leonard.	2006 Adichie: *Half of a Yellow Sun*. Atwood: *The Tents*. Munro: *The View from Castle Rock*. Pynchon: *Against the Day*. Updike: *Terrorist*.
2007	*The Year of Magical Thinking*, the one-woman show directed by David Hare, produced by Scott Rudin, written by Didion,	2007 DeLillo: *Falling Man*. Díaz: *The Brief Wondrous Life of Oscar Wao*. McEwan: *On Chesil Beach*.

CHRONOLOGY

HISTORICAL EVENTS

1997 Tony Blair elected Prime Minister in the UK. UK hands sovereignty of Hong Kong to People's Republic of China.

1998 Iraq disarmament crisis. Referendum in Northern Ireland accepts Good Friday Agreement; an assembly is elected. General Pinochet is arrested and detained in UK on an extradition request from Spain. Lewinsky scandal; President Clinton is impeached (acquitted February 1999).
1999 Serbs attack ethnic Albanians in Kosovo; US leads NATO in bombing of Belgrade.
2000 Putin succeeds Yeltsin as Russian President. Further violence in Chechen Republic. Pinochet returns to Chile; Supreme Court rules that he is unfit to stand trial. Milosevic's regime in former Yugoslavia collapses; Kostunica elected President. George W. Bush elected US President.
2001 Al-Qaeda terrorist attacks of 9/11. US and allied military attacks against the Taliban in Afghanistan.

2003 Iraq weapons crisis; American and British troops invade Iraq. Saddam Hussein captured in Iraq by US troops.

2004 Terrorist bombings in Madrid. Beslan school hostage crisis. George W. Bush re-elected as US President. Indian Ocean tsunami.

2005 Blair re-elected as Prime Minister in UK. Terrorist bombings in London. Provisional IRA formally orders an end to its armed campaign (since 1969). First forced evacuation of settlers under Israel Unilateral Disengagement Plan.

2006 Iran joins "nuclear club." Saddam Hussein sentenced to death.

2007 Virginia Tech shooting. Bush reduces US forces in Iraq. Al Gore and UN climate scientists win Nobel Peace Prize. Nancy Pelosi elected first female Speaker of US Congress. Tony Blair resigns; succeeded by Gordon Brown as British Prime Minister. iPhone introduced.

DATE	AUTHOR'S LIFE	LITERARY CONTEXT
2007 cont.	starring Vanessa Redgrave, opens March 29 at the Booth Theatre and runs for 24 weeks. Prix Médecis Essais for *The Year of Magical Thinking* and National Book Foundation's Medal for Distinguished Contribution to American Letters (November).	Russo: *Bridge of Sighs*.
		2008 Auster: *Man in the Dark*. Lahiri: *Unaccustomed Earth*. Oates: *My Sister, My Love*.
2009	Honorary Doctor of Letters from Harvard University (June 4). Vanessa Redgrave reprises her performance in a benefit at the Cathedral of St. John the Divine.	2009 Kingsolver: *The Lacuna*. Moore: *The Gate at the Stairs*. Munro: *Too Much Happiness*. Murakami: *1Q84*. Roth: *The Humbling*.
		2010 Auster: *Sunset Park*. Egan: *A Visit from the Goon Squad*. Franzen: *Freedom*. Roth: *Nemesis*. P. Smith: *Just Kids*.
2011	Honorary Doctor of Letters from Yale University (September). *Blue Nights* (November).	2011 Eugenides: *The Marriage Plot*. Ferrante: *My Brilliant Friend*. Patchett: *State of Wonder*. Wallace: *The Pale King*. 2012 Morrison: *Home*. Munro: *Dear Life*. Robinson: *When I Was a Child I Read Books* (essays). Tyler: *The Beginner's Goodbye*.
2013	Presented with the National Humanities Medal at the White House by President Obama (July). At the annual dinner receives the PEN Center USA's Lifetime Achievement Award (October).	2013 Adichie: *Americanah*. Tartt: *The Goldfinch*.
		2014 M. Amis: *Zone of Interest*. Atwood: *Stone Mattress*. Cusk: *Outline Trilogy* (to 2018). Klein: *This Changes Everything*. Oates: *Lovely, Dark, Deep*. Smiley: *The Last Hundred Years Trilogy* (to 2015).

CHRONOLOGY

HISTORICAL EVENTS

2008 Barack Obama, Democratic Senator from Illinois, elected first Black President of the United States. Collapse of Lehman Brothers triggers world financial crisis.
2009 Ongoing world financial crisis. H1N1 ("swine flu") global pandemic. Barack Obama awarded Nobel Peace Prize.

2010 Healthcare Reform Bill passed by President Obama. Deepwater Horizon (BP rig) oil spill in Gulf of Mexico. US combat mission ends in Iraq. British general election returns a hung parliament. Conservative leader David Cameron forms a coalition government with the Liberal Democrats (to 2015). iPad introduced.
2011 "Arab Spring": protests and rebellions against repressive regimes across Middle East. Syrian Civil War begins. Osama Bin Laden killed by US Navy Seals. US: Occupy Wall Street movement begins. "Don't Ask, Don't Tell" policy repealed. Martin Luther King Jr. Memorial opens to the public.

2012 Obama re-elected US President. Mars Science Laboratory "Curiosity Rover" lands on Mars. Xi Jinping becomes General Secretary of Chinese Communist Party.

2013 Edward Snowden leaks classified documents revealing mass surveillance by the US National Security Agency. Boston Marathon bombing. Black Lives Matter movement begins.

2014 Russia annexes Crimea. ISIS declares Islamic Caliphate.

JOAN DIDION

DATE	AUTHOR'S LIFE	LITERARY CONTEXT
		2015 Franzen: *Purity*. Lee: *Go Set a Watchman*. Morrison: *God Help the Child*. Moshfegh: *Eileen*. Rushdie: *Two Years Eight Months & Twenty-Eight Nights*. P. Smith: *M Train*. Yanagihara: *A Little Life*. 2016 Safran Foer: *Here I Am*. Levy: *Hot Milk*. Whitehead: *The Underground Railroad*.
2017	*South and West: From a Notebook*, foreword by Nathaniel Rich (February). Griffin Dunne's documentary, *Joan Didion: The Center Will Not Hold*, premieres at the New York Film Festival (October).	2017 Auster: *4 3 2 1*. Egan: *Manhattan Beach*. Strout: *Anything Is Possible*.
		2018 Burns: *Milkman*. Moore: *See What Can Be Done* (essays). Moshfegh: *My Year of Rest and Relaxation*. Z. Smith: *Feel Free* (essays). 2019 Atwood: *The Testaments*. Whitehead: *The Nickel Boys*.
		2020 DeLillo: *The Silence*. Offill: *Weather*.
2021	*Let Me Tell You What I Mean*, foreword by Hilton Als (January). Joan Didion dies (December) at the age of 87 in her apartment in New York from the complications of Parkinson's Disease.	2021 Cusk: *Second Place*. Everett: *The Trees*. Franzen: *Crossroads*. Patchett: *These Precious Days* (essays). Whitehead: *Harlem Shuffle*.
2022	*Joan Didion: What She Means* exhibit opens at the Hammer Museum, Los Angeles.	2022 Ozick: *Antiquities*. Diaz: *Trust*. Egan: *The Candy House*. McEwan: *Lessons*. Moshfegh: *Lapvona*. Yanagihara: *To Paradise*.

CHRONOLOGY

HISTORICAL EVENTS

2015 Iran agrees deal on nuclear program with world powers. Paris Climate Accord commits majority of countries to reducing greenhouse gas emissions. Islamic terror attacks in Paris. Refugee crisis in Europe. US Supreme Court rules that all states must recognize same-sex marriage. UK: David Cameron re-elected as Prime Minister.

2016 Trump wins US presidential election. UK referendum on EU membership results in "Leave" vote. David Cameron resigns; Theresa May becomes Prime Minister. Missile and nuclear testing in North Korea. Coup in Turkey fails.

2017 Trump takes up office of President, promising to "make America great again." Xi Jinping granted second term as General Secretary of CCP. North Korean crisis (to 2018). #MeToo movement goes global.

2018 "Trade War"; Trump imposes tariffs on imports from China. Trump announces his intention to withdraw the US from the Iranian nuclear agreement but negotiates with North Korea's Kim Jong-un over denuclearization.

2019 Hong Kong protests (to 2020). President Donald Trump impeached (acquitted 2021). UK: Resignation of May. Boris Johnson becomes Prime Minister (July); wins large majority in general election (Dec) on promise to "get Brexit done." Amazon rainforest wildfires. First COVID-19 case in Wuhan, China.

2020 COVID-19 declared a pandemic by World Health Organization. Climate disasters continue: Australia fire season, US wildfires, droughts and tropical storms. George Floyd killed by police in Minneapolis, triggering worldwide Black Lives Matter protests. Joe Biden elected US President; Kamala Harris elected first Black Vice President of the US.

2021 Trump supporters storm the Capitol building in protest of election results. US commits to rejoin Paris Climate Agreement. COVID-19 vaccine created. Last US troops withdraw from Afghanistan—Taliban take over the country.

2022 Russia invades Ukraine. Roe v Wade overturned by US Supreme Court; constitutional protections for abortion severed. Inflation rises worldwide. Protesters in Iran march against the country's treatment of women. Pakistan flooding crisis. Death of Queen Elizabeth II. Xi Jinping granted a third term as General Secretary of the CCP.

THE YEAR
OF MAGICAL
THINKING

This book is for John and for Quintana

1

Life changes fast.
Life changes in the instant.
You sit down to dinner and life as you know it ends.
The question of self-pity.

Those were the first words I wrote after it happened. The computer dating on the Microsoft Word file ("Notes on change.doc") reads "May 20, 2004, 11:11 p.m.," but that would have been a case of my opening the file and reflexively pressing save when I closed it. I had made no changes to that file in May. I had made no changes to that file since I wrote the words, in January 2004, a day or two or three after the fact.

For a long time I wrote nothing else.
Life changes in the instant.
The ordinary instant.

At some point, in the interest of remembering what seemed most striking about what had happened, I considered adding those words, "the ordinary instant." I saw immediately that there would be no need to add the word "ordinary," because there would be no forgetting it: the word never left my mind. It was in fact the ordinary nature of everything preceding the event that prevented me from truly believing it had happened, absorbing it, incorporating it, getting past it. I recognize now that there was nothing unusual in this: confronted with sudden disaster we all focus on how unremarkable the circumstances were in which the unthinkable occurred, the clear blue sky from which the plane fell, the routine errand that ended on the shoulder with the car in flames, the swings where the children were playing as usual when the rattlesnake struck from the ivy. "He was on his way home from work—happy, successful, healthy—and then, gone," I read in the account of a psychiatric nurse whose husband was killed in a highway accident. In 1966 I happened to interview many people who had been living in Honolulu on the morning of December 7, 1941; without exception, these people began their accounts of Pearl Harbor by telling me what an "ordinary Sunday morning" it had been. "It was just an ordinary beautiful September day," people still say when asked to describe the morning in New York when American Airlines 11 and United Airlines 175 got flown into the World Trade towers. Even the report of the 9/11 Commission opened on this insistently premonitory and yet still dumbstruck narrative note: "Tuesday, September 11, 2001, dawned temperate and nearly cloudless in the eastern United States."

"And then—gone." *In the midst of life we are in death*, Episcopalians say at the graveside. Later I realized that I must have repeated the details of what happened to everyone who came to the house in those first weeks, all those friends and relatives who brought food and made drinks and laid out plates on the dining room table for however many people were around at lunch or dinner time, all those who picked up the plates and froze the leftovers and ran the dishwasher and filled our (I could not yet think *my*) otherwise empty house even after I had gone into the bedroom (our bedroom, the one in which there still lay on a sofa a faded terrycloth XL robe bought in the 1970s at Richard Carroll in Beverly Hills) and shut the door. Those moments when I was abruptly overtaken by exhaustion are what I remember most clearly about the first days and weeks. I have no memory of telling anyone the details, but I must have done so, because everyone seemed to know them. At one point I considered the possibility that they had picked up the details of the story from one another, but immediately rejected it: the story they had was in each instance too accurate to have been passed from hand to hand. It had come from me.

Another reason I knew that the story had come from me was that no version I heard included the details I could not yet face, for example the blood on the living room floor that stayed there until José came in the next morning and cleaned it up.

José. Who was part of our household. Who was supposed to

be flying to Las Vegas later that day, December 31, but never went. José was crying that morning as he cleaned up the blood. When I first told him what had happened he had not understood. Clearly I was not the ideal teller of this story, something about my version had been at once too offhand and too elliptical, something in my tone had failed to convey the central fact in the situation (I would encounter the same failure later when I had to tell Quintana), but by the time José saw the blood he understood.

I had picked up the abandoned syringes and ECG electrodes before he came in that morning but I could not face the blood.

In outline.

It is now, as I begin to write this, the afternoon of October 4, 2004.

Nine months and five days ago, at approximately nine o'clock on the evening of December 30, 2003, my husband, John Gregory Dunne, appeared to (or did) experience, at the table where he and I had just sat down to dinner in the living room of our apartment in New York, a sudden massive coronary event that caused his death. Our only child, Quintana, had been for the previous five nights unconscious in an intensive care unit at Beth Israel Medical Center's Singer Division, at that time a hospital on East End Avenue (it closed in August 2004) more commonly known as "Beth Israel North" or "the old Doctors' Hospital," where what had seemed a case of December flu sufficiently severe to take her to an emergency room on Christmas morning had exploded into pneumonia and septic shock. This is my attempt to make sense of the period that followed, weeks and then months that cut loose any fixed idea I had ever had about death, about illness, about probability and luck, about good fortune and bad, about marriage and children and memory, about grief, about the ways in which people do and do not deal with the fact that life ends, about the shallowness of sanity, about life itself. I have been a writer my entire life. As a writer, even as a child, long before what I wrote began to be published, I developed a sense that meaning itself was resident in the rhythms of words and sentences and paragraphs, a technique for withholding whatever it was I thought or believed behind an increasingly impenetrable polish. The way I write is who I am, or have become, yet this is a case in which I wish I had instead of words and their rhythms a cutting room, equipped with an Avid, a digital editing system on which I could touch a key and collapse the sequence of time, show you simultaneously all the frames of memory that come to me now, let you pick the takes, the marginally different expressions, the variant readings of the same lines. This is a case in which I need more than words to find the meaning. This is a case in which I need whatever it is I think or believe to be penetrable, if only for myself.

2

December 30, 2003, a Tuesday.
We had seen Quintana in the sixth-floor ICU at Beth Israel North.
We had come home.
We had discussed whether to go out for dinner or eat in.
I said I would build a fire, we could eat in.
I built the fire, I started dinner, I asked John if he wanted a drink.
I got him a Scotch and gave it to him in the living room, where he was reading in the chair by the fire where he habitually sat.
The book he was reading was by David Fromkin, a bound galley of *Europe's Last Summer: Who Started the Great War in 1914?*
I finished getting dinner, I set the table in the living room where, when we were home alone, we could eat within sight of the fire. I find myself stressing the fire because fires were important to us. I grew up in California, John and I lived there together for twenty-four years, in California we heated our houses by building fires. We built fires even on summer evenings, because the fog came in. Fires said we were home, we had drawn the circle, we were safe through the night. I lit the candles. John asked for a second drink before sitting down. I gave it to him. We sat down. My attention was on mixing the salad.
John was talking, then he wasn't.
At one point in the seconds or minute before he stopped talking he had asked me if I had used single-malt Scotch for his second drink. I had said no, I used the same Scotch I had used for his first drink. "Good," he had said. "I don't know why but I don't think you should mix them." At another point in those seconds or that minute he had been talking about why World

War One was the critical event from which the entire rest of the twentieth century flowed.

I have no idea which subject we were on, the Scotch or World War One, at the instant he stopped talking.

I only remember looking up. His left hand was raised and he was slumped motionless. At first I thought he was making a failed joke, an attempt to make the difficulty of the day seem manageable.

I remember saying *Don't do that*.

When he did not respond my first thought was that he had started to eat and choked. I remember trying to lift him far enough from the back of the chair to give him the Heimlich. I remember the sense of his weight as he fell forward, first against the table, then to the floor. In the kitchen by the telephone I had taped a card with the New York–Presbyterian ambulance numbers. I had not taped the numbers by the telephone because I anticipated a moment like this. I had taped the numbers by the telephone in case someone in the building needed an ambulance.

Someone else.

I called one of the numbers. A dispatcher asked if he was breathing. I said *Just come*. When the paramedics came I tried to tell them what had happened but before I could finish they had transformed the part of the living room where John lay into an emergency department. One of them (there were three, maybe four, even an hour later I could not have said) was talking to the hospital about the electrocardiogram they seemed already to be transmitting. Another was opening the first or second of what would be many syringes for injection. (Epinephrine? Lidocaine? Procainamide? The names came to mind but I had no idea from where.) I remember saying that he might have choked. This was dismissed with a finger swipe: the airway was clear. They seemed now to be using defibrillating paddles, an attempt to restore a rhythm. They got something that could have been a normal heartbeat (or I thought they did, we had all been silent, there was a sharp jump), then lost it, and started again.

"He's still fibbing," I remember the one on the telephone saying.

"*V*-fibbing," John's cardiologist said the next morning when he called from Nantucket. "They would have said '*V*-fibbing.' V for ventricular."

Maybe they said "V-fibbing" and maybe they did not. Atrial fibrillation did not immediately or necessarily cause cardiac arrest. Ventricular did. Maybe ventricular was the given.

I remember trying to straighten out in my mind what would happen next. Since there was an ambulance crew in the living room, the next logical step would be going to the hospital. It occurred to me that the crew could decide very suddenly to go to the hospital and I would not be ready. I would not have in hand what I needed to take. I would waste time, get left behind. I found my handbag and a set of keys and a summary John's doctor had made of his medical history. When I got back to the living room the paramedics were watching the computer monitor they had set up on the floor. I could not see the monitor so I watched their faces. I remember one glancing at the others. When the decision was made to move it happened very fast. I followed them to the elevator and asked if I could go with them. They said they were taking the gurney down first, I could go in the second ambulance. One of them waited with me for the elevator to come back up. By the time he and I got into the second ambulance the ambulance carrying the gurney was pulling away from the front of the building. The distance from our building to the part of New York–Presbyterian that used to be New York Hospital is six crosstown blocks. I have no memory of sirens. I have no memory of traffic. When we arrived at the emergency entrance to the hospital the gurney was already disappearing into the building. A man was waiting in the driveway. Everyone else in sight was wearing scrubs. He was not. "Is this the wife," he said to the driver, then turned to me. "I'm your social worker," he said, and I guess that is when I must have known.

"I opened the door and I seen the man in the dress greens and I knew. I immediately knew." This was what the mother of a nineteen-year-old killed by a bomb in Kirkuk said on an

HBO documentary quoted by Bob Herbert in *The New York Times* on the morning of November 12, 2004. "But I thought that if, as long as I didn't let him in, he couldn't tell me. And then it—none of that would've happened. So he kept saying, 'Ma'am, I need to come in.' And I kept telling him, 'I'm sorry, but you can't come in.'"

When I read this at breakfast almost eleven months after the night with the ambulance and the social worker I recognized the thinking as my own.

Inside the emergency room I could see the gurney being pushed into a cubicle, propelled by more people in scrubs. Someone told me to wait in the reception area. I did. There was a line for admittance paperwork. Waiting in the line seemed the constructive thing to do. Waiting in the line said that there was still time to deal with this, I had copies of the insurance cards in my handbag, this was not a hospital I had ever negotiated—New York Hospital was the Cornell part of New York–Presbyterian, the part I knew was the Columbia part, Columbia-Presbyterian, at 168th and Broadway, twenty minutes away at best, too far in this kind of emergency—but I could make this unfamiliar hospital work, I could be useful, I could arrange the transfer to Columbia-Presbyterian once he was stabilized. I was fixed on the details of this imminent transfer to Columbia (he would need a bed with telemetry, eventually I could also get Quintana transferred to Columbia, the night she was admitted to Beth Israel North I had written on a card the beeper numbers of several Columbia doctors, one or another of them could make all this happen) when the social worker reappeared and guided me from the paperwork line into an empty room off the reception area. "You can wait here," he said. I waited. The room was cold, or I was. I wondered how much time had passed between the time I called the ambulance and the arrival of the paramedics. It had seemed no time at all (*a mote in the eye of God* was the phrase that came to me in the room off the reception area) but it must have been at the minimum several minutes.

I used to have on a bulletin board in my office, for reasons having to do with a plot point in a movie, a pink index card on which I had typed a sentence from *The Merck Manual* about how long the brain can be deprived of oxygen. The image of the pink index card was coming back to me in the room off the reception area: "Tissue anoxia for > 4 to 6 min. can result in irreversible brain damage or death." I was telling myself that I must be misremembering the sentence when the social worker reappeared. He had with him a man he introduced as "your husband's doctor." There was a silence. "He's dead, isn't he," I heard myself say to the doctor. The doctor looked at the social worker. "It's okay," the social worker said. "She's a pretty cool customer." They took me into the curtained cubicle where John lay, alone now. They asked if I wanted a priest. I said yes. A priest appeared and said the words. I thanked him. They gave me the silver clip in which John kept his driver's license and credit cards. They gave me the cash that had been in his pocket. They gave me his watch. They gave me his cell phone. They gave me a plastic bag in which they said I would find his clothes. I thanked them. The social worker asked if he could do anything more for me. I said he could put me in a taxi. He did. I thanked him. "Do you have money for the fare," he asked. I said I did, the cool customer. When I walked into the apartment and saw John's jacket and scarf still lying on the chair where he had dropped them when we came in from seeing Quintana at Beth Israel North (the red cashmere scarf, the Patagonia windbreaker that had been the crew jacket on *Up Close & Personal*) I wondered what an uncool customer would be allowed to do. Break down? Require sedation? Scream?

I remember thinking that I needed to discuss this with John.

There was nothing I did not discuss with John.

Because we were both writers and both worked at home our days were filled with the sound of each other's voices.

I did not always think he was right nor did he always think I was right but we were each the person the other trusted. There was no separation between our investments or interests in any given situation. Many people assumed that we must be, since sometimes one and sometimes the other would get the better review, the bigger advance, in some way "competitive," that our private life must be a minefield of professional envies and resentments. This was so far from the case that the general insistence on it came to suggest certain lacunae in the popular understanding of marriage.

That had been one more thing we discussed.

What I remember about the apartment the night I came home alone from New York Hospital was its silence.

In the plastic bag I had been given at the hospital there were a pair of corduroy pants, a wool shirt, a belt, and I think nothing else. The legs of the corduroy pants had been slit open, I supposed by the paramedics. There was blood on the shirt. The belt was braided. I remember putting his cell phone in the charger on his desk. I remember putting his silver clip in the box in the bedroom in which we kept passports and birth certificates and proof of jury service. I look now at the clip and see that these were the cards he was carrying: a New York State driver's license, due for renewal on May 25, 2004; a Chase ATM card; an American Express card; a Wells Fargo MasterCard; a Metropolitan Museum card; a Writers Guild of America West card (it was the season before Academy voting, when you could use a WGAW card to see movies free, he must have gone to a movie, I did not remember); a Medicare card; a Metro card; and a card issued by Medtronic with the legend "I have a Kappa 900 SR pacemaker implanted," the serial number of the device, a number to call for the doctor who implanted it, and the notation "Implant Date: 03 Jun 2003." I remember combining the cash that had been in his pocket with the cash in my own bag, smoothing the bills, taking special care to interleaf twenties with twenties, tens with tens, fives and ones with fives and ones. I remember thinking as I did this that he would see that I was handling things.

When I saw him in the curtained cubicle in the emergency room at New York Hospital there was a chip in one of his front teeth, I supposed from the fall, since there were also bruises on his face. When I identified his body the next day at Frank

E. Campbell the bruises were not apparent. It occurred to me that masking the bruises must have been what the undertaker meant when I said no embalming and he said "in that case we'll just clean him up." The part with the undertaker remains remote. I had arrived at Frank E. Campbell so determined to avoid any inappropriate response (tears, anger, helpless laughter at the Oz-like hush) that I had shut down all response. After my mother died the undertaker who picked up her body left in its place on the bed an artificial rose. My brother had told me this, offended to the core. I would be armed against artificial roses. I remember making a brisk decision about a coffin. I remember that in the office where I signed the papers there was a grandfather's clock, not running. John's nephew Tony Dunne, who was with me, mentioned to the undertaker that the clock was not running. The undertaker, as if pleased to elucidate a decorative element, explained that the clock had not run in some years, but was retained as "a kind of memorial" to a previous incarnation of the firm. He seemed to be offering the clock as a lesson. I concentrated on Quintana. I could shut out what the undertaker was saying but I could not shut out the lines I was hearing as I concentrated on Quintana: *Full fathom five thy father lies/Those are pearls that were his eyes.*

Eight months later I asked the manager of our apartment building if he still had the log kept by the doormen for the night of December 30. I knew there was a log, I had been for three years president of the board of the building, the door log was intrinsic to building procedure. The next day the manager sent me the page for December 30. According to the log the doormen that night were Michael Flynn and Vasile Ionescu. I had not remembered that. Vasile Ionescu and John had a routine with which they amused themselves in the elevator, a small game, between an exile from Ceauşescu's Romania and an Irish Catholic from West Hartford, Connecticut, based on a shared appreciation of political posturing. "So where is bin Laden," Vasile would say when John got onto the elevator, the point being to come up with ever more improbable suggestions:

"Could bin Laden be in the penthouse?" "In the maisonette?" "In the fitness room?" When I saw Vasile's name on the log it occurred to me that I could not remember if he had initiated this game when we came in from Beth Israel North in the early evening of December 30. The log for that evening showed only two entries, fewer than usual, even for a time of the year when most people in the building left for more clement venues:

> NOTE: *Paramedics arrived at 9:20 p.m. for Mr. Dunne.*
> *Mr. Dunne was taken to hospital at 10:05 p.m.*
> NOTE: *Lightbulb out on A-B passenger elevator.*

The A-B elevator was our elevator, the elevator on which the paramedics came up at 9:20 p.m., the elevator on which they took John (and me) downstairs to the ambulance at 10:05 p.m., the elevator on which I returned alone to our apartment at a time not noted. I had not noticed a lightbulb being out on the elevator. Nor had I noticed that the paramedics were in the apartment for forty-five minutes. I had always described it as "fifteen or twenty minutes." *If they were here that long does it mean that he was alive?* I put this question to a doctor I knew. "Sometimes they'll work that long," he said. It was a while before I realized that this in no way addressed the question.

The death certificate, when I got it, gave the time of death as 10:18 p.m., December 30, 2003.

I had been asked before I left the hospital if I would authorize an autopsy. I had said yes. I later read that asking a survivor to authorize an autopsy is seen in hospitals as delicate, sensitive, often the most difficult of the routine steps that follow a death. Doctors themselves, according to many studies (for example Katz, J. L., and Gardner, R., "The Intern's Dilemma: The Request for Autopsy Consent," *Psychiatry in Medicine* 3:197–203, 1972), experience considerable anxiety about making the request. They know that autopsy is essential to the learning and teaching of medicine, but they also know that the procedure touches a primitive dread. If whoever it was at New York

Hospital who asked me to authorize an autopsy experienced such anxiety I could have spared him or her: I actively wanted an autopsy. I actively wanted an autopsy even though I had seen some, in the course of doing research. I knew exactly what occurs, the chest open like a chicken in a butcher's case, the face peeled down, the scale in which the organs are weighed. I had seen homicide detectives avert their eyes from an autopsy in progress. I still wanted one. I needed to know how and why and when it had happened. In fact I wanted to be in the room when they did it (I had watched those other autopsies with John, I owed him his own, it was fixed in my mind at that moment that he would be in the room if I were on the table) but I did not trust myself to rationally present the point so I did not ask.

If the ambulance left our building at 10:05 p.m., and death was declared at 10:18 p.m., the thirteen minutes in between were just bookkeeping, bureaucracy, making sure the hospital procedures were observed and the paperwork was done and the appropriate person was on hand to do the sign-off, inform the cool customer.

The sign-off, I later learned, was called the "pronouncement," as in "Pronounced: 10:18 p.m."

I had to believe he was dead all along.

If I did not believe he was dead all along I would have thought I should have been able to save him.

Until I saw the autopsy report I continued to think this anyway, an example of delusionary thinking, the omnipotent variety.

A week or two before he died, when we were having dinner in a restaurant, John asked me to write something in my notebook for him. He always carried cards on which to make notes, three-by-six-inch cards printed with his name that could be slipped into an inside pocket. At dinner he had thought of something he wanted to remember but when he looked in his pockets he found no cards. I need you to write something down, he said. It was, he said, for his new book, not for mine, a point he stressed because I was at the time researching a book that involved sports. This was the note he dictated: "Coaches used to go out after a game and say 'you played great.' Now they go out with state police, as if this were a war and they the military. The militarization of sports." When I gave him the note the next day he said "You can use it if you want to."

What did he mean?

Did he know he would not write the book?

Did he have some apprehension, a shadow? Why had he forgotten to bring note cards to dinner that night? Had he not warned me when I forgot my own notebook that the ability to make a note when something came to mind was the difference between being able to write and not being able to write? Was something telling him that night that the time for being able to write was running out?

One summer when we were living in Brentwood Park we fell into a pattern of stopping work at four in the afternoon and going out to the pool. He would stand in the water reading (he reread *Sophie's Choice* several times that summer, trying to see how it worked) while I worked in the garden. It was a small, even miniature, garden with gravel paths and a rose arbor and beds edged with thyme and santolina and feverfew. I had convinced John a few years before that we should tear out a lawn to plant this garden. To my surprise, since he had shown no previous interest in gardens, he regarded the finished product as an almost mystical gift. Just before five on those summer afternoons we would swim and then go into the library wrapped in towels to watch *Tenko*, a BBC series, then in syndication, about a number of satisfyingly predictable English women (one was immature and selfish, another seemed to have been written with *Mrs. Miniver* in mind) imprisoned by the Japanese in Malaya during World War Two. After each afternoon's *Tenko* segment we would go upstairs and work another hour or two, John in his office at the top of the stairs, me in the glassed-in porch across the hall that had become my office. At seven or seven-thirty we would go out to dinner, many nights at Morton's. Morton's felt right that summer. There was always shrimp quesadilla, chicken with black beans. There was always someone we knew. The room was cool and polished and dark inside but you could see the twilight outside.

John did not like driving at night by then. This was one reason, I later learned, that he wanted to spend more time in New York, a wish that at the time remained mysterious to me. One night that summer he asked me to drive home after dinner at Anthea Sylbert's house on Camino Palmero in Hollywood. I remember thinking how remarkable this was. Anthea lived less than a block from a house on Franklin Avenue in which we had lived from 1967 until 1971, so it was not a question of reconnoitering a new neighborhood. It had occurred to me as I started the ignition that I could count on my fingers the number of times I had driven when John was in the car; the single other time I could remember that night was once spelling him on a drive from Las Vegas to Los Angeles. He had been dozing in the passenger seat of the Corvette we then had. He had opened his eyes. After a moment he had said, very carefully, "I might take it a little slower." I had no sense of unusual speed and glanced at the speedometer: I was doing 120.

Yet.

A drive across the Mojave was one thing. There had been no previous time when he asked me to drive home from dinner in town: this evening on Camino Palmero was unprecedented. So was the fact that at the end of the forty-minute drive to Brentwood Park he pronounced it "well driven."

He mentioned those afternoons with the pool and the garden and *Tenko* several times during the year before he died.

Philippe Ariès, in *The Hour of Our Death*, points out that the essential characteristic of death as it appears in the *Chanson de Roland* is that the death, even if sudden or accidental, "gives advance warning of its arrival." Gawain is asked: "Ah, good my lord, think you then so soon to die?" Gawain answers: "I tell you that I shall not live two days." Ariès notes: "Neither his doctor nor his friends nor the priests (the latter are absent and forgotten) know as much about it as he. Only the dying man can tell how much time he has left."

You sit down to dinner.

"You can use it if you want to," John had said when I gave him the note he had dictated a week or two before.

And then—gone.

Grief, when it comes, is nothing we expect it to be. It was not what I felt when my parents died: my father died a few days short of his eighty-fifth birthday and my mother a month short of her ninety-first, both after some years of increasing debility. What I felt in each instance was sadness, loneliness (the loneliness of the abandoned child of whatever age), regret for time gone by, for things unsaid, for my inability to share or even in any real way to acknowledge, at the end, the pain and helplessness and physical humiliation they each endured. I understood the inevitability of each of their deaths. I had been expecting (fearing, dreading, anticipating) those deaths all my life. They remained, when they did occur, distanced, at a remove from the ongoing dailiness of my life. After my mother died I received a letter from a friend in Chicago, a former Maryknoll priest, who precisely intuited what I felt. The death of a parent, he wrote, "despite our preparation, indeed, despite our age, dislodges things deep in us, sets off reactions that surprise us and that may cut free memories and feelings that we had thought gone to ground long ago. We might, in that indeterminate period they call mourning, be in a submarine, silent on the ocean's bed, aware of the depth charges, now near and now far, buffeting us with recollections."

My father was dead, my mother was dead, I would need for a while to watch for mines, but I would still get up in the morning and send out the laundry.

I would still plan a menu for Easter lunch.

I would still remember to renew my passport.

Grief is different. Grief has no distance. Grief comes in waves, paroxysms, sudden apprehensions that weaken the knees and blind the eyes and obliterate the dailiness of life. Virtually everyone who has ever experienced grief mentions this phenomenon of "waves." Eric Lindemann, who was chief of psychiatry at Massachusetts General Hospital in the 1940s and interviewed many family members of those killed in the 1942 Cocoanut Grove fire, defined the phenomenon with absolute specificity in a famous 1944 study: "sensations of somatic distress occurring in waves lasting from twenty minutes to an hour at a time, a feeling of tightness in the throat, choking with shortness of breath, need for sighing, and an empty feeling in the abdomen, lack of muscular power, and an intense subjective distress described as tension or mental pain."

Tightness in the throat.

Choking, need for sighing.

Such waves began for me on the morning of December 31, 2003, seven or eight hours after the fact, when I woke alone in the apartment. I do not remember crying the night before; I had entered at the moment it happened a kind of shock in which the only thought I allowed myself was that there must be certain things I needed to do. There had been certain things I had needed to do while the ambulance crew was in the living room. I had needed for example to get the copy of John's medical summary, so I could take it with me to the hospital. I had needed for example to bank the fire, because I would be leaving it. There had been certain things I had needed to do at the hospital. I had needed for example to stand in the line. I had needed for example to focus on the bed with telemetry he would need for the transfer to Columbia-Presbyterian.

Once I got back from the hospital there had again been certain things I needed to do. I could not identify all of these things but I did know one of them: I needed, before I did anything else, to tell John's brother Nick. It had seemed too late in the evening to call their older brother Dick on Cape Cod (he went to bed early, his health had not been good, I did not want to wake him with bad news) but I needed to tell Nick. I did not plan how to do this. I just sat on the bed and picked up the phone and dialed the number of his house in Connecticut. He answered. I told him. After I put down the phone, in what I can only describe as a new neural pattern of dialing numbers and saying the words, I picked it up again. I could not call Quintana (she was still where we had left her a few hours before, unconscious in the ICU at Beth Israel North) but I could call Gerry, her husband of five months, and I could call my brother, Jim, who would be at his house in Pebble Beach. Gerry said he would come over. I said there was no need to come over, I would be fine. Jim said he would get a flight. I said there was no need to think about a flight, we would talk in the morning. I was trying to think what to do next when the phone rang. It was John's and my agent, Lynn Nesbit, a friend since I suppose the late sixties. It was not clear to me at the time how she knew but she did (it had something to do with a mutual friend to whom both Nick and Lynn seemed in the last minute to have spoken) and she was calling from a taxi on her way to our apartment. At one level I was relieved (Lynn knew how to manage things, Lynn would know what it was that I was supposed to be doing) and at another I was bewildered: how could I deal at this moment with company? What would we do, would we sit in the living room with the syringes and the ECG electrodes and the blood still on the floor, should I rekindle what was left of the fire, would we have a drink, would she have eaten?

Had I eaten?

The instant in which I asked myself whether I had eaten was the first intimation of what was to come: if I thought of food, I learned that night, I would throw up.

Lynn arrived.

We sat in the part of the living room where the blood and electrodes and syringes were not.

I remember thinking as I was talking to Lynn (this was the part I could not say) that the blood must have come from the fall: he had fallen on his face, there was the chipped tooth I had noticed in the emergency room, the tooth could have cut the inside of his mouth.

Lynn picked up the phone and said that she was calling Christopher.

This was another bewilderment: the Christopher I knew best was Christopher Dickey, but he was in either Paris or Dubai and in any case Lynn would have said Chris, not Christopher. I found my mind veering to the autopsy. It could even be happening as I sat there. Then I realized that the Christopher to whom Lynn was talking was Christopher Lehmann-Haupt, who was the chief obituary writer for *The New York Times*. I remember a sense of shock. I wanted to say *not yet* but my mouth had gone dry. I could deal with "autopsy" but the notion of "obituary" had not occurred to me. "Obituary," unlike "autopsy," which was between me and John and the hospital, meant it had happened. I found myself wondering, with no sense of illogic, if it had also happened in Los Angeles. I was trying to work out what time it had been when he died and whether it was that time yet in Los Angeles. (Was there time to go back? Could we have a different ending on Pacific time?) I recall being seized by a pressing need not to let anyone at the *Los Angeles Times* learn what had happened by reading it in *The New York Times*. I called our closest friend at the *Los Angeles Times*, Tim Rutten. I have no memory of what Lynn and I did then. I remember her saying that she would stay the night, but I said no, I would be fine alone.

And I was.

Until the morning. When, only half awake, I tried to think why I was alone in the bed. There was a leaden feeling. It was the same leaden feeling with which I woke on mornings after John and I had fought. Had we had a fight? What about, how had it started, how could we fix it if I could not remember how it started?

Then I remembered.

For several weeks that would be the way I woke to the day.

I wake and feel the fell of dark, not day.

One of several lines from different poems by Gerard Manley Hopkins that John strung together during the months immediately after his younger brother committed suicide, a kind of improvised rosary.

> *O the mind, mind has mountains; cliffs of fall*
> *Frightful, sheer, no-man-fathomed. Hold them cheap*
> *May who ne'er hung there.*
> *I wake and feel the fell of dark, not day.*
> *And I have asked to be*
> *Where no storms come.*

I see now that my insistence on spending that first night alone was more complicated than it seemed, a primitive instinct. Of course I knew John was dead. Of course I had already delivered the definitive news to his brother and to my brother and to Quintana's husband. *The New York Times* knew. The *Los Angeles Times* knew. Yet I was myself in no way prepared to accept this news as final: there was a level on which I believed that what had happened remained reversible. That was why I needed to be alone.

After that first night I would not be alone for weeks (Jim and his wife Gloria would fly in from California the next day, Nick would come back to town, Tony and his wife Rosemary would come down from Connecticut, José would not go to Las Vegas, our assistant Sharon would come back from skiing, there would never not be people in the house), but I needed that first night to be alone.

I needed to be alone so that he could come back.

This was the beginning of my year of magical thinking.

3

The power of grief to derange the mind has in fact been exhaustively noted. The act of grieving, Freud told us in his 1917 "Mourning and Melancholia," "involves grave departures from the normal attitude to life." Yet, he pointed out, grief remains peculiar among derangements: "It never occurs to us to regard it as a pathological condition and to refer it to medical treatment." We rely instead on "its being overcome after a certain lapse of time." We view "any interference with it as useless and even harmful." Melanie Klein, in her 1940 "Mourning and Its Relation to Manic-Depressive States," made a similar assessment: "The mourner is in fact ill, but because this state of mind is common and seems so natural to us, we do not call mourning an illness. . . . To put my conclusion more precisely: I should say that in mourning the subject goes through a modified and transitory manic-depressive state and overcomes it."

Notice the stress on "overcoming" it.

It was deep into the summer, some months after the night when I needed to be alone so that he could come back, before I recognized that through the winter and spring there had been occasions on which I was incapable of thinking rationally. I was thinking as small children think, as if my thoughts or wishes had the power to reverse the narrative, change the outcome. In my case this disordered thinking had been covert, noticed I think by no one else, hidden even from me, but it had also been, in retrospect, both urgent and constant. In retrospect there had been signs, warning flags I should have noticed. There had been for example the matter of the obituaries. I could not read them. This continued from December 31, when the first obituaries appeared, until February 29, the night of the 2004 Academy Awards, when I saw a photograph of John in the Academy's "In Memoriam" montage. When I saw the photograph I realized for the first time why the obituaries had so disturbed me.

I had allowed other people to think he was dead.

I had allowed him to be buried alive.

Another such flag: there had come a point (late February, early March, after Quintana had left the hospital but before the funeral that had waited on her recovery) when it had occurred to me that I was supposed to give John's clothes away. Many people had mentioned the necessity for giving the clothes away, usually in the well-intentioned but (as it turns out) misguided form of offering to help me do this. I had resisted. I had no idea why. I myself remembered, after my father died, helping my mother separate his clothes into stacks for Goodwill and "better" stacks for the charity thrift shop where my sister-in-law Gloria volunteered. After my mother died Gloria and I and Quintana and Gloria and Jim's daughters had done the same with her clothes. It was part of what people did after a death, part of the ritual, some kind of duty.

I began. I cleared a shelf on which John had stacked sweatshirts, T-shirts, the clothes he wore when we walked in Central Park in the early morning. We walked every morning. We did not always walk together because we liked different routes but we would keep the other's route in mind and intersect before we left the park. The clothes on this shelf were as familiar to me as my own. I closed my mind to this. I set aside certain things (a faded sweatshirt I particularly remembered him wearing, a Canyon Ranch T-shirt Quintana had brought him from Arizona), but I put most of what was on this shelf into bags and took the bags across the street to St. James' Episcopal Church. Emboldened, I opened a closet and filled more bags: New Balance sneakers, all-weather shoes, Brooks Brothers shorts, bag after bag of socks. I took the bags to St. James'. One day a few weeks later I gathered up more bags and took them to John's office, where he had kept his clothes. I was not yet prepared to address the suits and shirts and jackets but I thought I could handle what remained of the shoes, a start.

I stopped at the door to the room.

I could not give away the rest of his shoes.

I stood there for a moment, then realized why: he would need shoes if he was to return.

The recognition of this thought by no means eradicated the thought.

I have still not tried to determine (say, by giving away the shoes) if the thought has lost its power.

On reflection I see the autopsy itself as the first example of this kind of thinking. Whatever else had been in my mind when I so determinedly authorized an autopsy, there was also a level of derangement on which I reasoned that an autopsy could show that what had gone wrong was something simple. It could have been no more than a transitory blockage or arrhythmia. It could have required only a minor adjustment—a change in medication, say, or the resetting of a pacemaker. In this case, the reasoning went, they might still be able to fix it.

I recall being struck by an interview, during the 2004 campaign, in which Teresa Heinz Kerry talked about the sudden death of her first husband. After the plane crash that killed John Heinz, she said in the interview, she had felt very strongly that she "needed" to leave Washington and go back to Pittsburgh.

Of course she "needed" to go back to Pittsburgh.

Pittsburgh, not Washington, was the place to which he might come back.

The autopsy did not in fact take place the night John was declared dead.

The autopsy did not take place until eleven the next morning. I realize now that the autopsy could have taken place only after the man I did not know at New York Hospital made the phone call to me, on the morning of December 31. The man who made the call was not "my social worker," not "my husband's doctor," not, as John and I might have said to each other, our friend from the bridge. "Not our friend from the bridge" was family shorthand, having to do with how his Aunt Harriet Burns described subsequent sightings of recently encountered strangers, for example seeing outside the Friendly's in West Hartford the same Cadillac Seville that had earlier cut her off on the Bulkeley Bridge. "Our friend from the bridge," she would say. I was thinking about John saying "not our friend from the bridge" as I listened to the man on the telephone. I recall expressions of sympathy. I recall offers of assistance. He seemed to be avoiding some point.

He was calling, he said then, to ask if I would donate my husband's organs.

Many things went through my mind at this instant. The first word that went through my mind was "no." Simultaneously I remembered Quintana mentioning at dinner one night that she had identified herself as an organ donor when she renewed her driver's license. She had asked John if he had. He had said no. They had discussed it.

I had changed the subject.

I had been unable to think of either of them dead.

The man on the telephone was still talking. I was thinking: If she were to die today in the ICU at Beth Israel North, would this come up? What would I do? What would I do now?

I heard myself saying to the man on the telephone that my husband's and my daughter was unconscious. I heard myself saying that I did not feel capable of making such a decision before our daughter even knew he was dead. This seemed to me at the time a reasonable response.

Only after I hung up did it occur to me that nothing about it was reasonable. This thought was immediately (and usefully —notice the instant mobilization of cognitive white cells) supplanted by another: there had been in this call something that did not add up. There had been a contradiction in it. This man had been talking about donating organs, but there was no way at this point to do a productive organ harvest: John had not been on life support. He had not been on life support when I saw him in the curtained cubicle in the emergency room. He had not been on life support when the priest came. All organs would have shut down.

Then I remembered: the Miami-Dade Medical Examiner's office. John and I had been there together one morning in 1985 or 1986. There had been someone from the eye bank tagging bodies for cornea removal. Those bodies in the Miami-Dade

Medical Examiner's office had not been on life support. This man from New York Hospital, then, was talking about taking only the corneas, the eyes. *Then why not say so? Why misrepresent this to me? Why make this call and not just say "his eyes"?* I took the silver clip the social worker had given me the night before from the box in the bedroom and looked at the driver's license. *Eyes: BL*, the license read. *Restrictions: Corrective Lenses.*

Why make this call and not just say what you wanted?

His eyes. His blue eyes. His blue imperfect eyes.

>   *and what i want to know is*
> *how do you like your blueeyed boy*
> *Mister Death*

I could not that morning remember who wrote those lines. I thought it was E. E. Cummings but I could not be sure. I did not have a volume of Cummings but found an anthology on a poetry shelf in the bedroom, an old textbook of John's, published in 1949, when he would have been at Portsmouth Priory, the Benedictine boarding school near Newport to which he was sent after his father died.

(*His father's death: sudden, cardiac, in his early fifties, I should have taken that warning.*)

If we happened to be anywhere around Newport John would take me to Portsmouth to hear the Gregorian chant at vespers. It was something that moved him. On the flyleaf of the anthology there was written the name *Dunne*, in small careful handwriting, and then, in the same handwriting, blue ink, fountain-pen blue ink, these guides to study: *1) What is the meaning of the poem and what is the experience? 2) What thought or reflection does the experience lead us to? 3) What <u>mood, feeling, emotion</u> is stirred or created by the poem as a whole?* I put the book back on the shelf. It would be some months before I remembered to confirm that the lines were in fact E. E. Cummings. It would also be some months before it occurred to me that my anger at this unknown caller from New York Hospital reflected another version of the primitive dread that had not for me been awakened by the autopsy question.

What was the meaning and what the experience?
To what thought or reflection did the experience lead us?
How could he come back if they took his organs, how could he come back if he had no shoes?

4

On most surface levels I seemed rational. To the average observer I would have appeared to fully understand that death was irreversible. I had authorized the autopsy. I had arranged for cremation. I had arranged for his ashes to be picked up and taken to the Cathedral of St. John the Divine, where, once Quintana was awake and well enough to be present, they would be placed in the chapel off the main altar where my brother and I had placed our mother's ashes. I had arranged for the marble plate on which her name was cut to be removed and recut to include John's name. Finally, on the 23rd of March, almost three months after his death, I had seen the ashes placed in the wall and the marble plate replaced and a service held.

We had Gregorian chant, for John.

Quintana asked that the chant be in Latin. John too would have asked that.

We had a single soaring trumpet.

We had a Catholic priest and an Episcopal priest.

Calvin Trillin spoke, David Halberstam spoke, Quintana's best friend Susan Traylor spoke. Susanna Moore read a fragment from "East Coker," the part about how "one has only learnt to get the better of words / For the thing one no longer has to say, or the way in which / One is no longer disposed to say it." Nick read Catullus, "On His Brother's Death." Quintana, still weak but her voice steady, standing in a black dress in the same cathedral where she had eight months before been married, read a poem she had written to her father.

I had done it. I had acknowledged that he was dead. I had done this in as public a way as I could conceive.

Yet my thinking on this point remained suspiciously fluid. At dinner in the late spring or early summer I happened to meet a prominent academic theologian. Someone at the table raised a question about faith. The theologian spoke of ritual itself being a form of faith. My reaction was unexpressed but negative, vehement, excessive even to me. Later I realized that my immediate thought had been: *But I did the ritual. I did it all.* I did St. John the Divine, I did the chant in Latin, I did the Catholic priest and the Episcopal priest, I did "For a thousand years in thy sight are but as yesterday when it is past" and I did "*In paradisum deducant angeli.*"

And it still didn't bring him back.

"Bringing him back" had been through those months my hidden focus, a magic trick. By late summer I was beginning to see this clearly. "Seeing it clearly" did not yet allow me to give away the clothes he would need.

In time of trouble, I had been trained since childhood, read, learn, work it up, go to the literature. Information was control. Given that grief remained the most general of afflictions its literature seemed remarkably spare. There was the journal C. S. Lewis kept after the death of his wife, *A Grief Observed*. There was the occasional passage in one or another novel, for example Thomas Mann's description in *The Magic Mountain* of the effect on Hermann Castorp of his wife's death: "His spirit was troubled; he shrank within himself; his benumbed brain made him blunder in his business, so that the firm of Castorp and Son suffered sensible financial losses; and the next spring, while inspecting warehouses on the windy landing-stage, he got inflammation of the lungs. The fever was too much for his shaken heart, and in five days, notwithstanding all Dr. Heidekind's care, he died." There were, in classical ballets, the moments when one or another abandoned lover tries to find and resurrect one or another loved one, the blued light, the white tutus, the *pas de deux* with the loved one that foreshadows the final return to the dead: *la danse des ombres*, the dance of the shades. There were certain poems, in fact many poems. There was a day or two when I relied on Matthew Arnold, "The Forsaken Merman":

> *Children's voices should be dear*
> *(Call once more) to a mother's ear;*
> *Children's voices, wild with pain—*
> *Surely she will come again!*

There were days when I relied on W. H. Auden, the "Funeral Blues" lines from *The Ascent of F6:*

> *Stop all the clocks, cut off the telephone,*
> *Prevent the dog from barking with a juicy bone,*
> *Silence the pianos and with muffled drum*
> *Bring out the coffin, let the mourners come.*

The poems and the dances of the shades seemed the most exact to me.

Beyond or below such abstracted representations of the pains and furies of grieving, there was a body of subliterature, how-to guides for dealing with the condition, some "practical," some "inspirational," most of either useless. (Don't drink too much, don't spend the insurance money redecorating the living room, join a support group.) That left the professional literature, the studies done by the psychiatrists and psychologists and social workers who came after Freud and Melanie Klein, and quite soon it was to this literature that I found myself turning. I learned from it many things I already knew, which at a certain point seemed to promise comfort, validation, an outside opinion that I was not imagining what appeared to be happening. From *Bereavement: Reactions, Consequences, and Care*, compiled in 1984 by the National Academy of Sciences' Institute of Medicine, I learned for example that the most frequent immediate responses to death were shock, numbness, and a sense of disbelief: "Subjectively, survivors may feel like they are wrapped in a cocoon or blanket; to others, they may look as though they are holding up well. Because the reality of death has not yet penetrated awareness, survivors can appear to be quite accepting of the loss."

Here, then, we had the "pretty cool customer" effect.

I read on. Dolphins, I learned from J. William Worden

of the Harvard Child Bereavement Study at Massachusetts General Hospital, had been observed refusing to eat after the death of a mate. Geese had been observed reacting to such a death by flying and calling, searching until they themselves became disoriented and lost. Human beings, I read but did not need to learn, showed similar patterns of response. They searched. They stopped eating. They forgot to breathe. They grew faint from lowered oxygen, they clogged their sinuses with unshed tears and ended up in otolaryngologists' offices with obscure ear infections. They lost concentration. "After a year I could read headlines," I was told by a friend whose husband had died three years before. They lost cognitive ability on all scales. Like Hermann Castorp they blundered in business and suffered sensible financial losses. They forgot their own telephone numbers and showed up at airports without picture ID. They fell sick, they failed, they even, again like Hermann Castorp, died.

This "dying" aspect had been documented, in study after study.

I began carrying identification when I walked in Central Park in the morning, in case it happened to me.

If the telephone rang when I was in the shower I no longer answered it, to avoid falling dead on the tile.

Certain studies, I learned, were famous. They were icons of the literature, benchmarks, referred to in everything I read. There was for example "Young, Benjamin, and Wallis, *The Lancet* 2:454–456, 1963." This study of 4,486 recent widowers in the United Kingdom, followed for five years, showed "significantly higher death rates for widowers in first six months following bereavement than for married." There was "Rees and Lutkins, *British Medical Journal* 4:13–16, 1967." This study of 903 bereaved relatives versus 878 non-bereaved matched controls, followed for six years, showed "significantly higher mortality for bereaved spouses in first year." The functional explanation for such raised mortality rates was laid out in the Institute of Medicine's 1984 compilation: "Research to date has shown that, like many other stressors, grief frequently leads to changes in the endocrine, immune, autonomic nervous, and cardiovascular systems; all of these are fundamentally influenced by brain function and neurotransmitters."

There were, I also learned from this literature, two kinds of grief. The preferred kind, the one associated with "growth" and "development," was "uncomplicated grief," or "normal bereavement." Such uncomplicated grief, according to *The Merck Manual*, 16th Edition, could still typically present with "anxiety symptoms such as initial insomnia, restlessness, and autonomic nervous system hyperactivity," but did "not generally cause clinical depression, except in those persons inclined to mood disorder." The second kind of grief was "complicated grief," which was also known in the literature as "pathological bereavement" and was said to occur in a variety of situations. One situation in which pathological bereavement could occur, I read repeatedly, was that in which the survivor and the deceased had been unusually dependent on one another. "Was the bereaved actually very dependent upon the deceased person for pleasure, support, or esteem?" This was one of the diagnostic criteria suggested by David Peretz, M.D., of the Department of Psychiatry at Columbia University. "Did the bereaved feel helpless without the lost person when enforced separations occurred?"

I considered these questions.

Once in 1968 when I needed unexpectedly to spend the night in San Francisco (I was doing a piece, it was raining, the rain pushed a late-afternoon interview into the next morning), John flew up from Los Angeles so that we could have dinner together. We had dinner at Ernie's. After dinner John took the PSA "Midnight Flyer," a thirteen-dollar amenity of an era in California when it was possible to fly from Los Angeles to San Francisco or Sacramento or San Jose for twenty-six dollars round-trip, back to LAX.

I thought about PSA.

All PSA planes had smiles painted on their noses. The flight attendants were dressed in the style of Rudy Gernreich in hot-pink-and-orange miniskirts. PSA represented a time in our life when most things we did seemed without consequence, no-hands, a mood in which no one thought twice about flying seven hundred miles for dinner. This mood ended in 1978, when a PSA Boeing 727 collided with a Cessna 172 over San Diego, killing one hundred and forty-four.

It occurred to me when this happened that I had overlooked the odds when it came to PSA.

I see now that this error was not confined to PSA.

When Quintana at age two or three flew PSA to Sacramento to see my mother and father she referred to it as "going on the smile." John used to write down the things she said on scraps of paper and put them in a black painted box his mother had given him. This box, which remains with its scraps of paper on a desk in my living room, was painted with an American eagle and the words "E Pluribus Unum." Later he used some of the things she said in a novel, *Dutch Shea, Jr.* He gave them to Dutch Shea's daughter, Cat, who had been killed by an IRA bomb while having dinner with her mother in a restaurant on Charlotte Street in London. This is part of what he wrote:

> "Where you was?" she would say, and "Where did the morning went?" He wrote them all down and crammed them into the tiny secret drawer in the maple desk Barry Stukin had given him and Lee as a wedding present. . . . Cat in her school tartan. Cat who could call her bath a "bathment" and the butterflies for a kindergarten experiment "flybutters." Cat who had made up her first poem at the age of seven: "I'm going to marry / A boy named Harry/ He rides horses / And handles divorces."

> The Broken Man was in that drawer. The Broken Man was what Cat called fear and death and the unknown. I had a bad dream about the Broken Man, she would say. Don't let the Broken Man catch me. If the Broken Man comes, I'll hang onto the fence and won't let him take me. . . . He wondered if the Broken Man had time to frighten Cat before she died.

I see now what I had failed to see in 1982, the year *Dutch Shea, Jr.* was published: this was a novel about grief. The literature would have said that Dutch Shea was undergoing pathological bereavement. The diagnostic signs would have been these: He is obsessed with the moment Cat died. He plays and replays the scene, as if rerunning it could reveal a different ending: the restaurant on Charlotte Street, the endive salad, Cat's lavender espadrilles, the bomb, Cat's head in the dessert trolley. He tortures his ex-wife, Cat's mother, with a single repeated question: why was she in the ladies' room when the bomb went off? Finally she tells him:

> You never gave me much credit for being Cat's mother, but I did raise her. I took care of her the day she got her period the first time and I remember when she was a little girl she called my bedroom her sweet second room and she called spaghetti buzzghetti and she called people who came to the house hellos. She said where you was and where did the morning went and you told Thayer, you son of a bitch, you wanted someone to remember her. So she told me she was pregnant, it was an accident, and she wanted to know what to do and I went into the ladies' room because I knew I was going to cry and I didn't want to cry in front of her and I wanted to get the tears out of the way so I could act sensibly and then I heard the bomb and when I finally got out part of her was in the sherbet and part of her was in the street and you, you son of a bitch, you want someone to remember her.

I believe John would have said that *Dutch Shea, Jr.* was about faith.

When he began the novel he already knew what the last words would be, not only the last words of the novel but the last words thought by Dutch Shea before he shoots himself: "I believe in Cat. I believe in God." *Credo in Deum.* The first words of the Catholic catechism.

Was it about faith or was it about grief?

Were faith and grief the same thing?

Were we unusually dependent on one another the summer we swam and watched *Tenko* and went to dinner at Morton's?

Or were we unusually lucky?

If I were alone could he come back to me on the smile?

Would he say get a table at Ernie's?

PSA and the smile no longer exist, sold to US Airways and then painted off the planes.

Ernie's no longer exists, but was briefly re-created by Alfred Hitchcock, for *Vertigo*. James Stewart first sees Kim Novak at Ernie's. Later she falls from the bell tower (also re-created, an effect) at Mission San Juan Bautista.

We were married at San Juan Bautista.

On a January afternoon when the blossoms were showing in the orchards off 101.

When there were still orchards off 101.

No. The way you got sideswiped was by going back. The blossoms showing in the orchards off 101 was the incorrect track.

For several weeks after it happened I tried to keep myself on the correct track (the narrow track, the track on which there was no going back) by repeating to myself the last two lines of "Rose Aylmer," Walter Savage Landor's 1806 elegy to the memory of a daughter of Lord Aylmer's who had died at age twenty in Calcutta. I had not thought of "Rose Aylmer" since I was an undergraduate at Berkeley, but now I could remember not only the poem but much of what had been said about it in whichever class I had heard it analyzed. "Rose Aylmer" worked, whoever was teaching this class had said, because the overblown and therefore meaningless praise for the deceased in the first four lines ("Ah, what avails the sceptred race! / Ah, what the form divine! / What every virtue, every grace! / Rose Aylmer, all were thine") gets brought into sudden, even shocking relief by "the hard sweet wisdom" of the last two lines, which suggest that mourning has its place but also its limits: "A night of memories and sighs / I consecrate to thee."

" 'A *night* of memories and sighs,' " I remembered the lecturer repeating. "*A night*. One night. It might be all night but he doesn't even say *all night*, he says *a night*, not a matter of a lifetime, a matter of some hours."

Hard sweet wisdom. Clearly, since "Rose Aylmer" had remained embedded in my memory, I believed it as an undergraduate to offer a lesson for survival.

December 30, 2003.

We had seen Quintana in the sixth-floor ICU at Beth Israel North.

Where she would remain for another twenty-four days.

Unusual dependency (is that a way of saying "marriage"? "husband and wife"? "mother and child"? "nuclear family"?) is not the only situation in which complicated or pathological grief can occur. Another, I read in the literature, is one in which the grieving process is interrupted by "circumstantial factors," say by "a delay in the funeral," or by "an illness or second death in the family." I read an explanation, by Vamik D. Volkan, M.D., a professor of psychiatry at the University of Virginia in Charlottesville, of what he called "re-grief therapy," a technique developed at the University of Virginia for the treatment of "established pathological mourners." In such therapy, according to Dr. Volkan, a point occurs at which:

> we help the patient to review the circumstances of the death—how it occurred, the patient's reaction to the news and to viewing the body, the events of the funeral, etc. Anger usually appears at this point if the therapy is going well; it is at first diffused, then directed toward others, and finally directed toward the dead. Abreactions—what Bibring [E. Bibring, 1954, "Psychoanalysis and the Dynamic Psychotherapies," *Journal of the American Psychoanalytic Association* 2:745 ff.] calls "emotional reliving"—may then take place and demonstrate to the patient the actuality of his repressed impulses. Using our understanding of the psychodynamics involved in the patient's need to keep the lost one alive, we can then explain and interpret the relationship that had existed between the patient and the one who died.

But from where exactly did Dr. Volkan and his team in Charlottesville derive their unique understanding of "the psychodynamics involved in the patient's need to keep the lost one alive," their special ability to "explain and interpret the relationship that had existed between the patient and the one who died"? Were you watching *Tenko* with me and "the lost one" in Brentwood Park, did you go to dinner with us at Morton's? Were you with me and "the one who died" at Punchbowl in Honolulu four months before it happened? Did you gather up plumeria blossoms with us and drop them on the graves of the unknown dead from Pearl Harbor? Did you catch cold with us in the rain at the Jardin du Ranelagh in Paris a month before it happened? Did you skip the Monets with us and go to lunch at Conti? Were you with us when we left Conti and bought the thermometer, were you sitting on our bed at the Bristol when neither of us could figure how to convert the thermometer's centigrade reading into Fahrenheit?

Were you there?

No.

You might have been useful with the thermometer but you were not there.

I don't need to "review the circumstances of the death." I was there. I didn't get "the news," I didn't "view" the body. I was there.

I catch myself, I stop.

I realize that I am directing irrational anger toward the entirely unknown Dr. Volkan in Charlottesville.

Persons under the shock of genuine affliction are not only upset mentally but are all unbalanced physically. No matter how calm and controlled they seemingly may be, no one can under such circumstances be normal. Their disturbed circulation makes them cold, their distress makes them unstrung, sleepless. Persons they normally like, they often turn from. No one should ever be forced upon those in grief, and all over-emotional people, no matter how near or dear, should be barred absolutely. Although the knowledge that their friends love them and sorrow for them is a great solace, the nearest afflicted must be protected from any one or anything which is likely to overstrain nerves already at the threatening point, and none have the right to feel hurt if they are told they can neither be of use or be received. At such a time, to some people companionship is a comfort, others shrink from their dearest friends.

That passage is from Emily Post's 1922 book of etiquette, Chapter XXIV, "Funerals," which takes the reader from the moment of death ("As soon as death occurs, someone, the trained nurse usually, draws the blinds in the sick-room and tells a servant to draw all the blinds of the house") through seating instructions for those who attend the funeral: "Enter the church as quietly as possible, and as there are no ushers at a funeral, seat yourself where you approximately belong. Only a very intimate friend should take a position far up on the center aisle. If you are merely an acquaintance you should sit inconspicuously in the rear somewhere, unless the funeral is very small and the church big, in which case you may sit on the end seat of the center aisle toward the back."

This tone, one of unfailing specificity, never flags. The emphasis remains on the practical. The bereaved must be urged to "sit in a sunny room," preferably one with an open fire. Food, but "very little food," may be offered on a tray: tea, coffee, bouillon, a little thin toast, a poached egg. Milk, but only heated milk: "Cold milk is bad for someone who is already over-chilled." As for further nourishment, "The cook may suggest something that appeals usually to their taste—but very little should be offered at a time, for although the stomach may be empty, the palate rejects the thought of food, and digestion is never in best order." The mourner is prompted to practice economy as he or she accommodates the wearing of mourning: most existing garments, including leather shoes and straw hats, will "dye perfectly." Undertaking expenses should be checked in advance. A friend should be left in charge of the house during the funeral. The friend should see that the house is aired and displaced furniture put back where it belongs and a fire lit for the homecoming of the family. "It is also well to prepare a little hot tea or broth," Mrs. Post advised, "and it should be brought them upon their return without their being asked if they would care for it. Those who are in great distress want no food, but if it is handed to them, they will mechanically take it, and something warm to start digestion and stimulate impaired circulation is what they most need."

There was something arresting about the matter-of-fact wisdom here, the instinctive understanding of the physiological disruptions ("changes in the endocrine, immune, autonomic nervous, and cardiovascular systems") later catalogued by the Institute of Medicine. I am unsure what prompted me to look up Emily Post's 1922 book of etiquette (I would guess some memory of my mother, who had given me a copy to read when we were snowbound in a four-room rented house in Colorado Springs during World War Two), but when I found it on the Internet it spoke to me directly. As I read it I remembered how cold I had been at New York Hospital on the night John died. I had thought I was cold because it was December 30 and I had come to the hospital bare-legged, in slippers, wearing only the linen skirt and sweater into which I had changed to get dinner. This was part of it, but I was also cold because nothing in my body was working as it should.

Mrs. Post would have understood that. She wrote in a world in which mourning was still recognized, allowed, not hidden from view. Philippe Ariès, in a series of lectures he delivered at Johns Hopkins in 1973 and later published as *Western Attitudes toward Death: From the Middle Ages to the Present*, noted that beginning about 1930 there had been in most Western countries and particularly in the United States a revolution in accepted attitudes toward death. "Death," he wrote, "so omnipresent in the past that it was familiar, would be effaced, would disappear. It would become shameful and forbidden." The English social anthropologist Geoffrey Gorer, in his 1965 *Death, Grief, and Mourning*, had described this rejection of public mourning as a result of the increasing pressure of a new "ethical duty to enjoy oneself," a novel "imperative to do nothing which might diminish the enjoyment of others." In both England and the

United States, he observed, the contemporary trend was "to treat mourning as morbid self-indulgence, and to give social admiration to the bereaved who hide their grief so fully that no one would guess anything had happened."

One way in which grief gets hidden is that death now occurs largely offstage. In the earlier tradition from which Mrs. Post wrote, the act of dying had not yet been professionalized. It did not typically involve hospitals. Women died in childbirth. Children died of fevers. Cancer was untreatable. At the time she undertook her book of etiquette, there would have been few American households untouched by the influenza pandemic of 1918. Death was up close, at home. The average adult was expected to deal competently, and also sensitively, with its aftermath. When someone dies, I was taught growing up in California, you bake a ham. You drop it by the house. You go to the funeral. If the family is Catholic you also go to the rosary but you do not wail or keen or in any other way demand the attention of the family. In the end Emily Post's 1922 etiquette book turned out to be as acute in its apprehension of this other way of death, and as prescriptive in its treatment of grief, as anything else I read. I will not forget the instinctive wisdom of the friend who, every day for those first few weeks, brought me a quart container of scallion-and-ginger congee from Chinatown. Congee I could eat. Congee was all I could eat.

5

There was something else I was taught growing up in California. When someone appears to have died you find out for sure by holding a hand mirror to the mouth and nose. If there is no exhaled moisture the person is dead. My mother taught me that. I forgot it the night John died. *Is he breathing*, the dispatcher had asked me. *Just come*, I had said.

December 30, 2003.

We had seen Quintana in the sixth-floor ICU at Beth Israel North.

We had noted the numbers on the respirator.

We had held her swollen hand.

We still don't know which way this is going, one of the ICU doctors had said.

We had come home. The ICU did not reopen after evening rounds until seven so it must have been past eight.

We had discussed whether to go out for dinner or eat in.

I said I would build a fire, we could eat in.

I have no memory of what we meant to eat. I do remember throwing out whatever was on the plates and in the kitchen when I came home from New York Hospital.

You sit down to dinner and life as you know it ends.

In a heartbeat.

Or the absence of one.

During the past months I have spent a great deal of time trying first to keep track of, and, when that failed, to reconstruct, the exact sequence of events that preceded and followed what happened that night. "At a point between Thursday, December 18, 2003, and Monday, December 22, 2003," one such reconstruction began, "Q complained of 'feeling terrible,' flu symptoms, thought she had strep throat." This reconstruction, which was preceded by the names and telephone numbers of doctors to whom I spoke not only at Beth Israel but at other hospitals in New York and other cities, continued. The heart of it was this: On Monday, December 22, she went with a fever of 103 to the emergency room at Beth Israel North, which had at the time a reputation for being the least-crowded emergency room on the Upper East Side of Manhattan, and was diagnosed with the flu. She was told to stay in bed and drink liquids. No chest X-ray was taken. On December 23 and 24 her fever fluctuated between 102 and 103. She was too ill to come to dinner on Christmas Eve. She and Gerry canceled plans to spend Christmas night and a few days after with his family in Massachusetts.

On Christmas Day, a Thursday, she called in the morning and said she was having trouble breathing. Her breathing sounded shallow, labored. Gerry took her back to the emergency room at Beth Israel North, where X-rays showed a dense infiltrate of pus and bacteria in the lower lobe of her right lung. Her pulse was elevated, 150-plus. She was extremely dehydrated. Her white count was almost zero. She was given Ativan, then Demerol. Her pneumonia, Gerry was told in the emergency room, was "a 5 on a scale of 10, what we used to call 'walking pneumonia.'" There was "nothing serious" (this may have been what I wanted to hear), but it was nonetheless decided to admit her to a sixth-floor ICU for monitoring.

By the time she reached the ICU that evening she was agitated. She was further sedated, then intubated. Her temperature was now 104-plus. One hundred percent of her oxygen was being supplied by the breathing tube; she was not at that point capable of breathing on her own. Late the next morning, Friday, December 26, it was learned that there was now pneumonia on both lungs, and that this pneumonia was, despite the massive IV administration of azithromycin, gentamicin, clindamycin, and vancomycin, growing. It was also learned—or assumed, since her blood pressure was dropping—that she was entering or had entered septic shock. Gerry was asked to allow two further invasive procedures, first the insertion of an arterial line and then the insertion of a second line that would go close to the heart to deal with the blood pressure problem. She was given neosynephrine to support her blood pressure at 90-plus over 60-plus.

On Saturday, December 27, we were told that she was being given what was then still a new Eli Lilly drug, Xigris, which would continue for ninety-six hours, four days. "This costs twenty thousand dollars," the nurse said as she changed the IV bag. I watched the fluid drip into one of the many tubes that were then keeping Quintana alive. I looked up Xigris on the Internet. One site said that the survival rate for sepsis patients treated with Xigris was 69 percent, as opposed to 56 percent for patients not treated with Xigris. Another site, a business newsletter, said that Eli Lilly's "sleeping giant," Xigris, was "struggling to overcome its problems in the sepsis market." This seemed in some ways a positive prism through which to view the situation: Quintana was not the child who had been a deliriously happy bride five months before and whose chance of surviving the next day or two could now be calibrated at a point between 56 and 69 percent, she was "the sepsis market," suggesting that there was still a consumer choice to be made. By Sunday, December 28, it had been possible to imagine that the sepsis market's "sleeping giant" was kicking in: the pneumonia had not decreased in size, but the neosynephrine supporting her blood pressure was stopped and the blood pressure was holding, at 95 over 40. On Monday, December 29, I was told by a physician's assistant that after his weekend absence he had come in that morning to find Quintana's condition "encouraging." I asked what exactly had encouraged him about her condition when he came in that morning. "She was still alive," the physician's assistant said.

On Tuesday, December 30, at 1:02 p.m. (according to the computer), I made these notes in anticipation of a conversation with one more specialist to whom I had placed a call:

Any effect on brain—from oxygen deficit? From high fever? From possible meningitis?

Several doctors have mentioned "not knowing if there is some underlying structure or blockage." Are they talking about a possible malignancy?

The assumption here is that this infection is bacterial—yet no bacteria has shown up in the cultures—is there any way of knowing it's not viral?

How does "flu" morph into whole-body infection?

The last question—*How does "flu" morph into whole-body infection?*—was added by John. By December 30 he had seemed fixed on this point. He had asked it many times in the preceding three or four days, of doctors and of physicians' assistants and of nurses and finally, most desperately, of me, and had never received an answer he found satisfactory. Something in this seemed to defy his understanding. Something in this defied my own understanding, but I was pretending that I could manage it. Here it was:

She had been admitted to the ICU on Christmas night.

She was in a hospital, we had kept telling each other on Christmas night. She was being taken care of. She would be safe where she was.

Everything else had seemed normal.

We had a fire. She would be safe.

Five days later everything outside the sixth-floor ICU at Beth Israel North still seemed normal: this was the part neither of us (although only John admitted it) could get past, one more case of maintaining a fixed focus on the clear blue sky from which the plane fell. There were still in the living room of the apartment the presents John and I had opened on Christmas night. There were still under and on a table in Quintana's old room the presents she had been unable to open on Christmas night because she was in the ICU. There were still on a table in the dining room the stacked plates and silver we had used on Christmas Eve. There were still on an American Express bill that came that day charges from the November trip we had made to Paris. When we left for Paris Quintana and Gerry had been planning their first Thanksgiving dinner. They had invited his mother and sister and brother-in-law. They were using their wedding china. Quintana had come by to get my mother's ruby crystal glasses. We had called them on Thanksgiving Day from Paris. They were roasting a turkey and pureeing turnips.

"And then—gone."

How does "flu" morph into whole-body infection?

I see the question now as the equivalent of a cry of helpless rage, another way of saying *How could this have happened when everything was normal*. In the cubicle where Quintana lay in the ICU, her fingers and face swollen with fluid, her lips cracked by fever around the breathing tube, her hair matted and soaked with sweat, the numbers on the respirator that night indicated that she was now receiving only 45 percent of her oxygen through the tube. John had kissed her swollen face. "More than one more day," he had whispered, another part of our family shorthand. The reference was to a line from a movie, Richard Lester's *Robin and Marian*. "I love you more than even one more day," Audrey Hepburn as Maid Marian says to Sean Connery as Robin Hood after she has given them both the fatal potion. John had whispered this every time he left the ICU. On our way out we managed to maneuver a doctor into talking to us. We asked if the decrease in delivered oxygen meant that she was getting better.

There was a pause.

This was when the ICU doctor said it: "We're still not sure which way this is going."

The way this is going is up, I remember thinking.

The ICU doctor was still talking. "She's really very sick," he was saying.

I recognized this as a coded way of saying that she was expected to die but I persisted: *The way this is going is up. It's going up because it has to go up.*

I believe in Cat.

I believe in God.

"I love you more than one more day," Quintana said three months later standing in the black dress at St. John the Divine. "As you used to say to me."

We were married on the afternoon of January 30, 1964, a Thursday, at the Catholic Mission of San Juan Bautista in San

Benito County, California. John wore a navy blue suit from Chipp. I wore a short white silk dress I had bought at Ransohoff's in San Francisco on the day John Kennedy was killed. Twelve-thirty p.m. in Dallas was still morning in California. My mother and I learned what happened only when we were leaving Ransohoff's for lunch and ran into someone from Sacramento. Since there were only thirty or forty people at San Juan Bautista on the afternoon of the wedding (John's mother, his younger brother Stephen, his brother Nick and Nick's wife Lenny and their four-year-old daughter, my mother and father and brother and sister-in-law and grandfather and aunt and a few cousins and family friends from Sacramento, John's roommate from Princeton, maybe one or two others), my intention for the ceremony had been to have no entrance, no "procession," to just stand up there and do it. "Principals emerge," I remember Nick saying helpfully: Nick got the plan, but the organist who had materialized did not, and suddenly I found myself on my father's arm, walking up the aisle and weeping behind my dark glasses. When the ceremony was over we drove to the lodge at Pebble Beach. There were little things to eat, champagne, a terrace that opened onto the Pacific, very simple. By way of a honeymoon we spent a few nights in a bungalow at the San Ysidro Ranch in Montecito and then, bored, fled to the Beverly Hills Hotel.

I had thought about that wedding on the day of Quintana's wedding.

Her wedding was simple too. She wore a long white dress and a veil and expensive shoes but her hair was in a thick braid down her back, as it had been when she was a child.

We sat in the choir at St. John the Divine. Her father walked her to the altar. There at the altar was Susan, her best friend in California since age three. There at the altar was her best friend in New York. There at the altar was her cousin Hannah. There was her cousin Kelley from California, reading a part of the service. There were the children of Gerry's stepdaughter, reading another part. There were the youngest children, small girls with leis, barefoot. There were watercress sandwiches, champagne, lemonade, peach-colored napkins to match the sorbet that came with the cake, peacocks on the lawn. She kicked off the expensive shoes and unpinned the veil. "Wasn't that just about perfect," she said when she called that evening. Her father and I allowed that it was. She and Gerry flew to St. Barth's. John and I flew to Honolulu.

July 26, 2003.

Four months and 29 days before she was admitted to the ICU at Beth Israel North.

Five months and four days before her father died.

During the first week or two after he died, at night, when the protective exhaustion would hit me and I would leave the relatives and friends talking in the living room and dining room and kitchen of the apartment and walk down the corridor to the bedroom and shut the door, I would avoid looking at the reminders of our early marriage that hung on the corridor walls. In fact I did not need to look, nor could I avoid them by not looking: I knew them by heart. There was a photograph of John and me taken on a location for *The Panic in Needle Park*. It was our first picture. We went with it to the Cannes festival. It was the first time I had ever been to Europe and we were traveling first-class on Twentieth Century–Fox and I boarded the plane barefoot, it was that period, 1971. There was a photograph of John and me and Quintana at Bethesda Fountain in Central Park in 1970, John and Quintana, age four, eating ice cream bars. We were in New York all that fall working on a picture with Otto Preminger. "She's in the office of Mr. Preminger who has no hair," Quintana advised a pediatrician who had asked where her mother was. There was a photograph of John and me and Quintana on the deck of the house we had in Malibu in the 1970s. The photograph appeared in *People*. When I saw it I realized that Quintana had taken advantage of a break in the day's shooting to apply, for the first time, eyeliner. There was a photograph Barry Farrell had taken of his wife, Marcia, sitting in a rattan chair in the house in Malibu and holding their then-baby daughter, Joan Didion Farrell.

Barry Farrell was now dead.

There was a photograph of Katharine Ross, taken by Conrad Hall during the Malibu period when she taught Quintana to swim by throwing a Tahitian shell in a neighbor's pool and telling Quintana the shell would be hers if she brought it up. This was a time, the early 1970s, when Katharine and Conrad and Jean and Brian Moore and John and I traded plants and dogs and favors and recipes and would have dinner at one or another of our houses a couple of times a week.

I remember that we all made soufflés. Conrad's sister Nancy in Papeete had shown Katharine how to make them work without effort and Katharine showed me and Jean. The trick was a less strict approach than generally advised. Katharine also brought back Tahitian vanilla beans for us, thick sheaves tied with raffia.

We did crème caramel with the vanilla for a while but nobody liked to caramelize the sugar.

We talked about renting Lee Grant's house above Zuma Beach and opening a restaurant, to be called "Lee Grant's House." Katharine and Jean and I would take turns cooking and John and Brian and Conrad would take turns running the front. This Malibu survivalist plan got abandoned because Katharine and Conrad separated and Brian was finishing a novel and John and I went to Honolulu to do a rewrite on a picture. We worked a lot in Honolulu. No one in New York could ever get the time difference straight so we could work all day without the phone ringing. There was a point in the 1970s when I wanted to buy a house there, and took John to look at many, but he seemed to interpret actually living in Honolulu as a less encouraging picture than staying at the Kahala.

Conrad Hall was now dead.

Brian Moore was now dead.

From an earlier house, a great wreck of a house on Franklin Avenue in Hollywood that we rented with its many bedrooms and its sun porches and its avocado trees and its overgrown clay tennis court for $450 a month, there was a framed verse that Earl McGrath had written on the occasion of our fifth anniversary:

> *This is the story of John Greg'ry Dunne*
> *Who, with his wife Mrs. Didion Do,*

*Was legally married with family of one
And lived on Franklin Avenue.
Lived with their beautiful child Quintana
Also known as Didion D
Didion Dunne
And Didion Do.
And Quintana or Didion D.
A beautiful family of one Dunne Dunne Dunne
(I mean a family of three)
Living in a style best called erstwhile
On Franklin Avenue.*

People who have recently lost someone have a certain look, recognizable maybe only to those who have seen that look on their own faces. I have noticed it on my face and I notice it now on others. The look is one of extreme vulnerability, nakedness, openness. It is the look of someone who walks from the ophthalmologist's office into the bright daylight with dilated eyes, or of someone who wears glasses and is suddenly made to take them off. These people who have lost someone look naked because they think themselves invisible. I myself felt invisible for a period of time, incorporeal. I seemed to have crossed one of those legendary rivers that divide the living from the dead, entered a place in which I could be seen only by those who were themselves recently bereaved. I understood for the first time the power in the image of the rivers, the Styx, the Lethe, the cloaked ferryman with his pole. I understood for the first time the meaning in the practice of suttee. Widows did not throw themselves on the burning raft out of grief. The burning raft was instead an accurate representation of the place to which their grief (not their families, not the community, not custom, *their grief*) had taken them. On the night John died we were thirty-one days short of our fortieth anniversary. You will have by now divined that the "hard sweet wisdom" in the last two lines of "Rose Aylmer" was lost on me.

I wanted more than a night of memories and sighs.

I wanted to scream.

I wanted him back.

6

Several years ago, walking east on Fifty-seventh Street between Sixth and Fifth Avenues on a bright fall day, I had what I believed at the time to be an apprehension of death. It was an effect of light: quick sunlight dappling, yellow leaves falling (but from what? were there even trees on West Fifty-seventh Street?), a shower of gold, spangled, very fast, a falling of the bright. Later I watched for this effect on similar bright days but never again experienced it. I wondered then if it had been a seizure, or stroke of some kind. A few years before that, in California, I had dreamed an image that, when I woke, I knew had been death: the image was that of an ice island, the jagged ridge seen from the air off one of the Channel Islands, except in this case all ice, translucent, a blued white, glittering in the sunlight. Unlike dreams in which the dreamer is anticipating death, inexorably sentenced to die but not yet there, there was in this dream no dread. Both the ice island and the fall of the bright on West Fifty-seventh Street seemed on the contrary transcendent, more beautiful than I could say, yet there was no doubt in my mind that what I had seen was death.

Why, if those were my images of death, did I remain so unable to accept the fact that he had died? Was it because I was failing to understand it as something that had happened to him? Was it because I was still understanding it as something that had happened to me?

Life changes fast.

Life changes in the instant.

You sit down to dinner and life as you know it ends.

The question of self-pity.

You see how early the question of self-pity entered the picture.

One morning during the spring after it happened I picked up

The New York Times and skipped directly from the front page to the crossword puzzle, a way of starting the day that had become during those months a pattern, the way I had come to read, or more to the point not to read, the paper. I had never before had the patience to work crossword puzzles, but now imagined that the practice would encourage a return to constructive cognitive engagement. The clue that first got my attention that morning was 6 Down, "Sometimes you feel like . . ." I instantly saw the obvious answer, a good long one that would fill many spaces and prove my competency for the day: "a motherless child."

Motherless children have a real hard time—
Motherless children have such a real hard time—
No.
6 Down had only four letters.

I abandoned the puzzle (impatience died hard), and the next day looked up the answer. The correct answer for 6 Down was "anut." "Anut?" A nut? Sometimes you feel like *a nut*? How far had I absented myself from the world of normal response?

Notice: the answer most instantly accessed ("a motherless child") was a wail of self-pity.

This was not going to be an easy failure of understanding to correct.

> *Avid its rush, that reeling blaze!*
> *Where is my father and Eleanor?*
> *Not where are they now, dead seven years,*
> *But what they were then?*
>   *No more? No more?*
> —DELMORE SCHWARTZ,
>   "Calmly We Walk Through This April's Day"

He believed he was dying. He told me so, repeatedly. I dismissed this. He was depressed. He had finished a novel, *Nothing Lost*, which was caught in the predictable limbo of a prolonged period between delivery and publication, and he was undergoing an equally predictable crisis of confidence about the book he was then beginning, a reflection on the meaning of patriotism that had not yet found its momentum. He had been dealing as well through most of the year with a series of enervating medical issues. His cardiac rhythm had been slipping with increasing frequency into atrial fibrillation. A normal sinus rhythm could be restored by cardioversion, an outpatient procedure in which he was given general anesthesia for a few minutes while his heart was electrically shocked, but a change in physical status as slight as catching a cold or taking a long plane flight could again disrupt the rhythm. His last such procedure, in April 2003, had required not one but two shocks. The steadily increasing frequency with which cardioversion had become necessary indicated that it was no longer a useful option. In June, after a series of consultations, he had undergone a more radical cardiac intervention, a radio-frequency ablation of the atrial-ventricular node and the subsequent implantation of the Medtronic Kappa 900 SR pacemaker.

During the course of the summer, buoyed by the pleasure of Quintana's wedding and by the apparent success of the pacemaker, his mood had seemed to lift. In the fall it dropped again. I recall a fight over the question of whether we should go to Paris in November. I did not want to go. I said we had too much to do and too little money. He said he had a sense that if he did not go to Paris in November he would never again go to Paris. I interpreted this as blackmail. That settles it then, I said, we're going. He left the table. We did not speak in any meaningful way for two days.

In the end we went to Paris in November.

I tell you that I shall not live two days, Gawain said.

A few weeks ago at the Council on Foreign Relations at Sixty-eighth and Park I noticed someone across from me reading the *International Herald Tribune*. One more example of slipping onto the incorrect track: I am no longer at the Council on Foreign Relations at Sixty-eighth and Park but sitting across from John at breakfast in the dining room of the Bristol in Paris in November 2003. We are each reading the *International Herald Tribune*, hotel copies, with little stapled cards showing the weather for the day. The cards for each of those November mornings in Paris showed an umbrella icon. We walked in the rain at the Jardin du Luxembourg. We escaped from the rain into St. Sulpice. There was a mass in progress. John took communion. We caught cold in the rain at the Jardin du Ranelagh. On the flight back to New York John's muffler and my jersey dress smelled of wet wool. On takeoff he held my hand until the plane began leveling.

He always did.

Where did that go?

In a magazine I see a Microsoft advertisement that shows the platform of the Porte des Lilas metro station in Paris.

I found yesterday in the pocket of an unworn jacket a used metro ticket from that November trip to Paris. "Only Episcopalians 'take' communion," he had corrected me one last time as we left St. Sulpice. He had been correcting me on this point for forty years. Episcopalians "took," Catholics "received." It was, he explained each time, a difference in attitude.

> *Not where are they now, dead seven years,*
> *But what they were then?*

That last cardioversion: April 2003. The one that had required two shocks. I remember a doctor explaining why it was done under anesthesia. "Because otherwise they jump off the table," he said. December 30, 2003: the sudden jump when the ambulance crew was using the defibrillating paddles on the living room floor. Was that ever a heartbeat or was it just electricity?

The night he died or the night before, in the taxi between Beth Israel North and our apartment, he said several things that for the first time made me unable to readily dismiss his mood as depression, a normal phase of any writer's life.

Everything he had done, he said, was worthless.

I still tried to dismiss it.

This might not be normal, I told myself, but neither was the condition in which we had just left Quintana.

He said that the novel was worthless.

This might not be normal, I told myself, but neither was it normal for a father to see a child beyond his help.

He said that his current piece in *The New York Review*, a review of Gavin Lambert's biography of Natalie Wood, was worthless.

This might not be normal, but what in the past several days had been?

He said he did not know what he was doing in New York. "Why did I waste time on a piece about Natalie Wood," he said.

It was not a question.

"You were right about Hawaii," he said then.

He may have meant that I had been right a day or so before when I said that when Quintana got better (this was our code for "if she lives") we could rent a house on the Kailua beach and she could recuperate there. Or he may have meant that I had been right in the 1970s when I wanted to buy a house in Honolulu. I preferred at the time to think the former but the past tense suggested the latter. He said these things in the taxi between Beth Israel North and our apartment either three hours before he died or twenty-seven hours before he died, I try to remember which and cannot.

7

Why did I keep stressing what was and was not normal, when nothing about it was?

Let me try a chronology here.

Quintana was admitted to the ICU at Beth Israel North on December 25, 2003.

John died on December 30, 2003.

I told Quintana that he was dead late on the morning of January 15, 2004, in the ICU at Beth Israel North, after the doctors had managed to remove the breathing tube and reduce sedation to a point at which she could gradually wake up. Telling her that day had not been the plan. The doctors had said that she would wake only intermittently, at first partially, and for a matter of days be able to absorb only limited information. If she woke and saw me she would wonder where her father was. Gerry and Tony and I had discussed this problem at length. We had decided that only Gerry should be with her when she first began to wake. She could focus on him, on their life together. The question of her father might not come up. I could see her later, maybe days later. I could tell her then. She would be stronger.

As planned, Gerry was with her when she first woke. As not planned, a nurse told her that her mother was outside in the corridor.

Then when is she coming in, she wanted to know.

I went in.

"Where's Dad," she whispered when she saw me.

Because three weeks of intubation had inflamed her vocal cords, even her whisper was barely audible. I told her what had happened. I stressed the history of cardiac problems, the long run of luck that had finally caught up with us, the apparent suddenness but actual inevitability of the event. She cried.

Gerry and I each held her. She dropped back into sleep.

"How's Dad," she whispered when I saw her that evening.

I began again. The heart attack. The history. The apparent suddenness of the event.

"But how is he *now*," she whispered, straining to be audible.

She had absorbed the sudden event part but not the outcome.

I told her again. In the end I would have to tell her a third time, in another ICU, this one at UCLA.

The chronology.

On January 19, 2004, she was moved from the sixth-floor ICU at Beth Israel North to a room on the twelfth floor. On January 22, 2004, still too weak to stand or sit unsupported and running a fever from a hospital infection acquired in the ICU, she was discharged from Beth Israel North. Gerry and I put her to bed in her old room in my apartment. Gerry went out to fill the prescriptions she had been given. She got out of bed to get another quilt from the closet and collapsed on the floor. I could not lift her and needed to get someone from the building to put her back to bed.

On the morning of January 25, 2004, she woke, still in my apartment, with severe chest pain and increasing fever. She was admitted that day to the Milstein Hospital at Columbia-Presbyterian after a diagnosis of pulmonary emboli was reached in the Presbyterian emergency room. Given her prolonged immobility at Beth Israel, I know now but did not know then, this was an entirely predictable development that could have been diagnosed before discharge from Beth Israel by the same imaging that was done three days later in the Presbyterian emergency room. After she was admitted to Milstein her legs were imaged to see if further clots had formed. She was placed on anticoagulants to prevent such further formation while the existing clots were allowed to dissolve.

On February 3, 2004, she was discharged from Presbyterian, still on anticoagulants. She began physical therapy to regain strength and mobility. Together, with Tony and Nick, she and I planned the service for John. The service took place at four o'clock on a Tuesday afternoon, March 23, 2004, at the Cathedral of St. John the Divine, where, at three o'clock in the presence of the family, John's ashes had been placed as planned in the chapel off the main altar. After the service Nick had arranged a reception at the Union Club. Eventually thirty or forty members of the family made their way back to John's and my apartment. I lit a fire. We had drinks. We had dinner. Quintana, although still fragile, had stood up in her black dress at the Cathedral and laughed with her cousins at dinner. On the morning of March 25, a day and a half later, she and Gerry were going to restart their life by flying to California and walking on the beach at Malibu for a few days. I had encouraged this. I wanted to see Malibu color on her face and hair again.

The next day, March 24, alone in the apartment, the obligation to bury my husband and see our daughter through her crisis formally fulfilled, I put away the plates and allowed myself to think for the first time about what would be required to restart my own life. I called Quintana to wish her a good trip. She was flying early the next morning. She sounded anxious. She was always anxious before a trip. Decisions about what to pack had seemed since childhood to trigger some fear of lost organization. Do you think I'll be okay in California, she said. I said yes. Definitely she would be okay in California. Going to California would in fact be the first day of the rest of her life. It occurred to me as I hung up that cleaning my office could be a step toward the first day of the rest of my own life. I began doing this. During most of the following day, Thursday, March 25, I continued doing this. At points during the quiet day I found myself thinking that possibly I had come through into a new season. In January I had watched ice floes form on the East River from a window at Beth Israel North. In February I had watched ice floes break up on the Hudson from a window at Columbia-Presbyterian. Now in March the ice was gone and I had done what I had to do for John and Quintana would come back from California restored. As the afternoon progressed (her plane would have landed, she would have picked up a car and driven up the Pacific Coast Highway) I imagined her already walking on the beach with Gerry in the thin March Malibu sunlight. I typed the Malibu zip code, 90265, into AccuWeather. There was sun, a high and low I do not remember but do remember thinking satisfactory, a good day in Malibu.

There would be wild mustard on the hills.

She could take him to see the orchids at Zuma Canyon.

She could take him to eat fried fish at the Ventura County line.

She had arranged to take him to lunch one day at Jean Moore's, she would be in the places in which she had spent her childhood. She could show him where we had gathered mussels for Easter lunch. She could show him where the butterflies were, where she had learned to play tennis, where she had learned from the Zuma Beach lifeguards how to swim out of a riptide. On the desk in my office there was a photograph taken when she was seven or eight, her hair long and blonde from the Malibu sun. Stuck in the back of the frame there was a crayoned note, left one day on the kitchen counter in Malibu: *Dear Mom, when you opened the door it was me who ran away XXXXXX—Q.*

At ten minutes past seven that evening I was changing to go downstairs, for dinner with friends who live in the building. I say "at ten minutes past seven" because that was when the phone rang. It was Tony. He said he was coming right over. I noted the time because I was due downstairs at seven-thirty but Tony's urgency was such that I did not say so. His wife, Rosemary Breslin, had spent the past fifteen years dealing with an undiagnosable blood disorder. Since shortly after John died she had been on an experimental protocol that had left her increasingly weak and required intermittent hospitalization at Memorial Sloan-Kettering. I knew that the long day at the Cathedral and later with the family had been strenuous for her. I stopped Tony as he was about to hang up. I asked if Rosemary was back in the hospital. He said it was not Rosemary. It was Quintana, who, even as we spoke, at ten minutes past seven in New York and ten minutes past four in California, was undergoing emergency neurosurgery at UCLA Medical Center in Los Angeles.

8

They had gotten off the plane.

They had picked up their shared bag.

Gerry was carrying the bag to the car rental shuttle, crossing the arrivals driveway ahead of Quintana. He looked back. Even today I have no idea what made him look back. I never thought to ask. I pictured it as one more case in which you heard someone talking and then you didn't, so you looked. *Life changes in the instant. The ordinary instant.* She was lying on her back on the asphalt. An ambulance was called. She was taken to UCLA. According to Gerry she was awake and lucid in the ambulance. It was only in the emergency room that she began convulsing and lost coherence. A surgical team was alerted. A CT scan was done. By the time they took her into surgery one of her pupils was fixed. The other became fixed as they wheeled her in. I would be told this more than once, in each case as evidence of the gravity of the condition and the critical nature of the intervention: "One pupil was fixed and the other went as we wheeled her in."

The first time I heard this I did not know the significance of what I was being told. By the second time I did. Sherwin B. Nuland, in *How We Die*, described having seen, as a third-year medical student, a cardiac patient whose "pupils were fixed in the position of wide black dilatation that signifies brain death, and obviously would never respond to light again." Again in *How We Die*, Dr. Nuland described the failing attempts of a CPR team to revive a patient who had suffered cardiac arrest in the hospital: "The tenacious young men and women see their patient's pupils become unresponsive to light and then widen until they are large fixed circles of impenetrable blackness. Reluctantly the team stops its efforts. . . . The room is strewn with the debris of the lost campaign." Was this what the New

York–Presbyterian ambulance crew saw in John's eyes on our living room floor on December 30, 2003? Was this what the UCLA neurosurgeons saw in Quintana's eyes on March 25, 2004? "Impenetrable blackness?" "Brain death?" Was that what they thought? I look at a printout of that day's CT report from UCLA and still go faint:

> The scan shows right hemispheric subdural hematoma, with evidence of acute bleeding. Active bleeding cannot be excluded. The hematoma causes marked mass effect upon the right cerebrum, subfalcial and early uncal herniation, with 19 mm of midline shift from right to left at the level of the third ventricle. The right lateral ventricle is subtotally effaced and the left lateral ventricle shows early entrapment. There is moderate to marked midbrain compression and the perimesencephalic cistern is effaced. A thin posterior falcine and left tentorial subdural hematomas are noted. A small parenchymal bleed, likely contusional, is noted in the right inferolateral frontal lobe. The cerebellar tonsils are at the level of the foramen magnum. There is no skull fracture. There is a large right parietal scalp hematoma.

March 25, 2004. Ten minutes past seven in the evening in New York.

She had come back from the place where doctors said "We still don't know which way this is going" and now she was there again.

For all I knew it had already gone the wrong way.

They could have told Gerry and Gerry could be trying to absorb it before calling me.

She could already be on her way to the hospital morgue.

Alone. On a gurney. With a transporter.

I had already imagined this scene, with John.

Tony arrived.

He repeated what he had told me on the telephone. He had gotten the call from Gerry at UCLA. Quintana was in surgery. Gerry could be reached by cell phone in the hospital lobby, which happened to double (UCLA was building a new hospital, this one was overcrowded and outdated) as the surgical waiting area.

We called Gerry.

One of the surgeons had just come out to give him an update. The surgical team was now "fairly confident" that Quintana would "leave the table," although they could not predict in what condition.

I remember realizing that this was meant as an improved assessment: the previous report from the operating room had been that the team was "not at all sure she would leave the table."

I remember trying and failing to understand the phrase "leave the table." Did they mean alive? Had they said "alive" and Gerry could not say it? *Whatever happens*, I remember thinking, *she will without question "leave the table."*

It was then maybe four-thirty in Los Angeles, seven-thirty in New York. I was not sure how long at that point the surgery had been in progress. I see now, since according to the CT report the scan had taken place at "15:06," six minutes past three in Los Angeles, that she had probably been in surgery only about half an hour. I got out an OAG guide to see who would still be flying that night to Los Angeles. Delta had a 9:40 p.m. out of Kennedy. I was about to call Delta when Tony said that he did not think that being in flight during the surgery was a good idea.

I remember a silence.

I remember setting aside the OAG.

I called Tim Rutten in Los Angeles, and asked him to go to the hospital to wait with Gerry. I called our accountant in Los Angeles, Gil Frank, whose own daughter had undergone emergency neurosurgery at UCLA a few months before, and he too said that he would go to the hospital.

That was as close as I could get to being there.

I set the table in the kitchen and Tony and I picked at coq au vin left from the dinner for the family after St. John the Divine. Rosemary arrived. We sat at the kitchen table and tried to develop what we referred to as a "plan." We used phrases like "the contingencies," delicately, as if one of the three of us might not know what "the contingencies" were. I remember calling Earl McGrath to see if I could use his house in Los Angeles. I remember using the words "if I need to," another delicate construction. I remember him cutting directly through this: he was flying to Los Angeles the next day on a friend's plane, I would go with them. Around midnight Gerry called and said that the surgery was finished. They would now do another CT scan to see if there was additional bleeding they had missed. If there was bleeding they would operate again. If there was not they would do a further procedure, the placement of a screen in the vena cava to prevent clots from entering the heart. About four a.m. New York time he called again, to say that the CT scan had shown no bleeding and they had placed the screen. He told me what the surgeons had told him about the operation itself. I made notes:

"Arterial bleed, artery gushing blood, like a geyser, blood all over the room, no clotting factor."

"Brain pushed to the left side."

When I got back to New York from Los Angeles late on the evening of April 30 I found these notes on a grocery list by the kitchen phone. I now know that the technical term for "brain pushed to the left side" is "midline shift," a significant predictive factor for poor outcome, but even then I knew that it was not good. What I had thought I needed on that March day five weeks before were Evian splits, molasses, chicken broth, and flaxseed meal.

Read, learn, work it up, go to the literature.
  Information is control.

On the morning after the surgery, before I went to Teterboro to get on the plane, I looked on the Internet for "fixed and dilated pupils." I found that they were called "FDPs." I read the abstract of a study done by researchers in the Department of Neurosurgery at the University Clinic in Bonn. The study followed ninety-nine patients who had either presented with or developed one or two FDPs. The overall mortality rate was

75 percent. Of the 25 percent who were still alive twenty-four months later, 15 percent had what the Glasgow Outcome Scale defined as an "unfavorable outcome" and 10 percent a "favorable outcome." I translated the percentages: of the ninety-nine patients, seventy-four died. Of the surviving twenty-five, at the end of two years, five were vegetative, ten were severely disabled, eight were independent, and two had made a full recovery. I also learned that fixed and dilated pupils indicated injury or compression of the third cranial nerve and the upper brainstem. "Third nerve" and "brainstem" were words that I would hear more often than I wanted to during the weeks to come.

9

You're safe, I remember whispering to Quintana when I first saw her in the ICU at UCLA. *I'm here. You're going to be all right.* Half of her skull had been shaved for the surgery. I could see the long cut and the metal staples that held it closed. She was again breathing only through an endotracheal tube. *I'm here. Everything's fine.*

"When do you have to leave," she asked me on the day when she could finally speak. She said the words with difficulty, her face tensed.

I said I would not leave until we could leave together.

Her face relaxed. She went back to sleep.

It occurred to me during those weeks that this had been, since the day we brought her home from St. John's Hospital in Santa Monica, my basic promise to her. I would not leave. I would take care of her. She would be all right. It also occurred to me that this was a promise I could not keep. I could not always take care of her. I could not never leave her. She was no longer a child. She was an adult. Things happened in life that mothers could not prevent or fix. Unless one of those things killed her prematurely, as one had almost done at Beth Israel and another could still do at UCLA, I would die before she did. I remembered discussions in lawyers' offices during which I had become distressed by the word "predecease." The word could not possibly apply. After each of these discussions I would see the words "mutual disaster" in a new and favorable light. Yet once on a rough flight between Honolulu and Los Angeles I had imagined such a mutual disaster and rejected it. The plane would go down. Miraculously, she and I would survive the crash, adrift in the Pacific, clinging to the debris. The dilemma was this: I would need, because I was menstruating and the blood would attract sharks, to abandon her, swim away, leave her alone.

Could I do this?

Did all parents feel this?

When my mother was near death at age ninety she told me that she was ready to die but could not. "You and Jim need me," she said. My brother and I were by then in our sixties.

You're safe.

I'm here.

One thing I noticed during the course of those weeks at UCLA was that many people I knew, whether in New York or in California or in other places, shared a habit of mind usually credited to the very successful. They believed absolutely in their own management skills. They believed absolutely in the power of the telephone numbers they had at their fingertips, the right doctor, the major donor, the person who could facilitate a favor at State or Justice. The management skills of these people were in fact prodigious. The power of their telephone numbers was in fact unmatched. I had myself for most of my life shared the same core belief in my ability to control events. If my mother was suddenly hospitalized in Tunis I could arrange for the American consul to bring her English-language newspapers and get her onto an Air France flight to meet my brother in Paris. If Quintana was suddenly stranded in the Nice airport I could arrange with someone at British Airways to get her onto a BA flight to meet her cousin in London. Yet I had always at some level apprehended, because I was born fearful, that some events in life would remain beyond my ability to control or manage them. Some events would just happen. This was one of those events. *You sit down to dinner and life as you know it ends.*

Many people to whom I spoke in those first days while Quintana lay unconscious at UCLA seemed free of this apprehension. Their initial instinct was that this event could be managed. In order to manage it they needed only information. They needed only to know how this had happened. They needed answers. They needed "the prognosis."

I had no answers.

I had no prognosis.

I did not know how this had happened.

There were two possibilities, both of them, I came to see, irrelevant. One possibility was that she had fallen and the trauma had caused a bleed into her brain, a danger of the anticoagulants she had been given to prevent emboli. The second possibility was that the bleed into her brain had occurred before the fall and in fact caused it. People on anticoagulants bleed. They bruise at a touch. The level of anticoagulant in the blood, which is measured by a number called the INR (International Normalized Ratio), is hard to control. The blood must be tested every few weeks and in some cases every few days. Minute and complicated changes must be made in dosage. The ideal INR for Quintana was, give or take a tenth of a point, 2.2. On the day she flew to Los Angeles it so happened that her INR was over 4, a level at which spontaneous bleeding can occur. When I got to Los Angeles and spoke to the chief surgeon, he said that he was "one hundred percent sure" the trauma had caused the bleed. Other doctors to whom I spoke were less certain. It was suggested by one that the flight alone could have caused sufficient changes in pressurization to precipitate a bleed.

I recall pressing the surgeon on this point, myself trying (one more time) to manage the situation, get answers. I was talking to him on a cell phone from the courtyard outside the UCLA Medical Center cafeteria. The cafeteria was named "Café Med." This was my first visit to Café Med and my introduction to its most noticeable regular, a small balding man (I assumed a Neuropsychiatric Institute patient with walkaround privileges) whose compulsion it was to trail one or another woman through the cafeteria, alternately spitting and mouthing enraged imprecations about how disgusting she was, how vile, what a piece of worthless trash. On this particular morning the small balding man had trailed me out to the courtyard and it was hard to make out what the surgeon was saying. "It was the trauma, there was a ruptured blood vessel, we saw it," I thought he said. This had not seemed to entirely address the question—a ruptured blood vessel did not categorically rule out the possibility that the ruptured blood vessel had preceded and caused the fall—but there in the Café Med courtyard with the small balding man spitting on my shoe I realized that the answer to the question made no difference. It had happened. It was the new fact on the ground.

During the course of this call from the surgeon, which took place on the first full day I spent in Los Angeles, I recall being told several other things.

I recall being told that her coma could continue for days or weeks.

I recall being told that it would be a minimum of three days before anyone could begin to know what shape her brain was in. The surgeon was "optimistic," but no prediction was possible. Many more urgent issues could come up in the next three or four or more days.

She could develop an infection.

She could develop pneumonia, she could develop an embolism.

She could develop further swelling, which would necessitate reoperating.

After I hung up I walked back into the cafeteria, where Gerry was having coffee with Susan Traylor and my brother's daughters, Kelley and Lori. I remember wondering whether to mention the more urgent issues the surgeon had mentioned. I saw when I looked at their faces that there was no reason not to: all four of them had been at the hospital before I got to Los Angeles. All four of them had already heard about the more urgent issues.

During the twenty-four December and January nights when Quintana was in the sixth-floor ICU at Beth Israel North I had kept on the table by my bed a paperback copy of *Intensive Care: A Doctor's Journal*, by John F. Murray, M.D., who had been from 1966 to 1989 chief of the Pulmonary and Critical Care Division at the University of California medical school in San Francisco. *Intensive Care* describes, day by day, a four-week period in a San Francisco General Hospital medical ICU for which Dr.

Murray was at the time the attending physician responsible for all patients, residents, interns, and medical students. I had read this account over and over. I had learned much that proved useful in the calibration of my daily dealings with the ICU doctors at Beth Israel North. I had learned for example that it was often difficult to gauge when the time was right for extubation, the removal of an endotracheal tube. I had learned that a common barrier to extubation was the edema so predictably seen in intensive care. I had learned that this edema was less often the result of an underlying pathology than of an excess in the administration of intravenous fluid, a failure to observe the distinction between hydration and overhydration, an error of caution. I had learned that many young residents made a similar error of caution when it came to extubation itself: their tendency, because the outcome was uncertain, was to delay the procedure longer than necessary.

I had registered these lessons. I had made use of them: the tentative question here, the expressed wish there. I had "wondered" if she might not be "waterlogged." ("Of course I don't know, I just know how she looks.") I had deliberately used the word "waterlogged." I had noticed a stiffening when I used the word "edema." I had further "wondered" if she might not be better able to breathe if she was less waterlogged. ("Of course I'm not a doctor, but it just seems logical.") I had again "wondered" if the monitored administration of a diuretic might not allow extubation. ("Of course this is a home remedy, but if I felt the way she looks I'd take a Lasix.") With *Intensive Care* as my guide it had seemed straightforward, intuitive. There was a way to know if you had made headway. You knew you had made headway when a doctor to whom you had made one or another suggestion presented, a day later, the plan as his own.

This was different. A certain derisive phrase had occurred to me during the edema contest of wills at Beth Israel North: *It's not brain surgery.* This was. When these doctors at UCLA said "parietal" and "temporal" to me I had no idea where in the brain they were talking about, let alone what they meant. "Right frontal" I thought I could understand. "Occipital"

I thought suggested "eye," but only on the misconceived reasoning that the word began with "oc," like "ocular." I went to the UCLA Medical Center bookstore. I bought a book described on its cover as a "concise overview of neuroanatomy and of its functional and clinical implications" as well as an "excellent review for the USMLE." This book was by Stephen G. Waxman, M.D., chief of neurology at Yale–New Haven, and was called *Clinical Neuroanatomy*. I skimmed successfully through some of the appendices, for example "Appendix A: The Neurologic Examination," but when I began to read the text itself I could think only of a trip to Indonesia during which I had become disoriented by my inability to locate the grammar in Bahasa Indonesia, the official language used on street signs and storefronts and billboards. I had asked someone at the American Embassy how to tell the verbs from the nouns. Bahasa was a language, he had said, in which the same word could be either a verb or a noun. *Clinical Neuroanatomy* seemed to be one more case in which I would be unable to locate the grammar. I put it on the table by my bed at the Beverly Wilshire Hotel, where it would remain for the next five weeks.

On further study of *Clinical Neuroanatomy*, say if I woke in the morning before *The New York Times* had arrived with its sedative crossword puzzle, even "Appendix A: The Neurologic Examination" seemed opaque. I had originally noticed the obvious familiar directives (ask the patient the name of the president, ask the patient to count backwards from one hundred by sevens), but as days passed I seemed focused on a mysterious narrative, identified in Appendix A as the "gilded-boy story," that could be used to test memory and comprehension. The patient could be told the story, Dr. Waxman suggested, then asked to retell it in his own words and explain its meaning. "At the coronation of one of the popes, about 300 years ago, a little boy was chosen to play the part of an angel."

So began the "gilded-boy story."

So far clear enough, although potentially troubling details

(three hundred years ago? play the part of an angel?) for someone emerging from coma.

It continued: "So that his appearance might be as magnificent as possible, he was covered from head to foot with a coating of gold foil. The little boy fell ill, and although everything possible was done for his recovery except the removal of the fatal golden covering, he died within a few hours."

What was the "meaning" of the "gilded-boy story"? Did it have to do with the fallibility of "the popes"? With the fallibility of authority in general? With the specific fallibility (note that "everything possible was done for his recovery") of medicine? What possible point could there be in telling this story to a patient immobilized in a neuro ICU at a major teaching hospital? What lesson could be drawn? Did they think that because it was a "story" it could be told without consequence? There was a morning on which the "gilded-boy story" seemed to represent, in its utter impenetrability and apparent disregard for the sensitivity of the patient, the entire situation with which I was faced. I went back to the UCLA Medical Center bookstore with the thought of checking other sources for an elucidation, but there was no mention of the gilded-boy story in the first several textbooks I picked up. In lieu of checking further, I bought, since the afternoon highs in Los Angeles were by then in the eighties and I had flown west with only the late-winter clothes I had been wearing in New York, several sets of blue cotton scrubs. So profound was the isolation in which I was then operating that it did not immediately occur to me that for the mother of a patient to show up at the hospital wearing blue cotton scrubs could only be viewed as a suspicious violation of boundaries.

10

I had first noticed what I came to know as "the vortex effect" in January, when I was watching the ice floes form on the East River from a window at Beth Israel North. At the join between the walls and the ceiling of the room from which I was watching the ice floes there happened to be a rose-patterned wallpaper border, a Dorothy Draper touch, left I supposed from the period when what was then Beth Israel North had been Doctors' Hospital. I myself had never been in Doctors' Hospital, but when I was in my twenties and working for *Vogue* it had figured in many conversations. It had been the hospital favored by *Vogue* editors for uncomplicated deliveries and for "resting," a kind of medical Maine Chance.

This had seemed a good line of thinking.

This had seemed better than thinking about why I was at Beth Israel North.

I had ventured further:

Doctors' Hospital was where X had the abortion that was bought and paid for by the district attorney's office. "X" was a woman with whom I had worked at *Vogue*. Seductive clouds of cigarette smoke and Chanel No. 5 and imminent disaster had trailed her through the Condé Nast offices, which were then in the Graybar Building. On a single morning, while I was attempting to put together a particularly trying *Vogue* feature called "People Are Talking About," she had found both that she needed an abortion and that her name had turned up in the files of a party girl operation under investigation by the district attorney's office. She had been cheerful about these two pieces of (what had seemed to me) devastating news. A deal had been struck. She had agreed to testify that she had been approached by the operation, and the district attorney's office had in turn arranged a D&C at Doctors' Hospital, no inconsiderable favor at a time when getting an abortion meant making a clandestine and potentially lethal appointment with someone whose first instinct in a crisis would be to vacate the premises.

The party girl operation and the arranged abortion and the years in which I had spent mornings putting together "People Are Talking About" still seemed a good line of thinking.

I remembered having used such an incident in my second novel, *Play It As It Lays*. The protagonist, a former model named Maria, had recently had an abortion, which was troubling her.

> Once a long time before Maria had worked a week in Ocho Rios with a girl who had just had an abortion. She could remember the girl telling her about it while they sat huddled next to a waterfall waiting for the photographer to decide the sun was high enough to shoot. It seemed that it was a hard time for abortions in New York, there had been arrests, no one wanted to do it. Finally the girl, her name was Ceci Delano, had asked a friend in the district attorney's office if he knew of anyone. "Quid pro quo," he had said, and, late the same day that Ceci Delano testified to a blue-ribbon jury that she had been approached by a party girl operation, she was admitted to Doctors' Hospital for a legal D&C, arranged and paid for by the district attorney's office.
>
> It had seemed a funny story as she told it, both that morning at the waterfall and later at dinner, when she repeated it to the photographer and the agency man and the fashion coordinator for the client. Maria tried now to put what had happened in Encino into the same spirited perspective, but Ceci Delano's situation seemed not to apply. In the end it was just a New York story.

This seemed to be working.

I had avoided thinking for at least two minutes about why I was at Beth Israel North.

I had moved on, into the period during which I was writing *Play It As It Lays*. The rented wreck of a house on Franklin Avenue in Hollywood. The votive candles on the sills of the big windows in the living room. The *té de limón* grass and aloe that grew by the kitchen door. The rats that ate the avocados. The sun porch on which I worked. Watching from the windows of the sun porch as Quintana ran through a sprinkler on the lawn.

I recall recognizing that I had hit more dangerous water but there had seemed no turning back.

I had been writing that book when Quintana was three.

When Quintana was three.

There it was, the vortex.

Quintana at three. The night she had put a seed pod from the garden up her nose and I had driven her to Children's Hospital. The pediatrician who specialized in seed pods had arrived in his dinner jacket. The next night she had put another seed pod up her nose, wanting to repeat the interesting adventure. John and I walking with her around the lake in MacArthur Park. The old man lurching from a bench. "That child is the picture of Ginger Rogers," the old man cried. I finished the novel, I was under contract to begin a column for *Life*, we took Quintana to Honolulu. *Life*'s idea for the first column was that I should introduce myself, "let the readers know who you are." I planned to write it from Honolulu, the Royal Hawaiian Hotel, we used to get a lanai suite on the press rate for twenty-seven dollars a night. While we were there the news of My Lai broke. I thought about the first column. It seemed to me that given this news I should write it from Saigon. By then it was a Sunday. *Life* had given me a printed card with the home numbers of its editors and also of lawyers in cities around the world. I took out the card and called my editor, Loudon Wainwright, to say I was going to Saigon. His wife answered the phone. She said he would have to call me back.

"He's watching the NFL game," John said when I hung up. "He'll call you at halftime."

He did. He said that I should stay where I was and introduce myself, that as far as Saigon went "some of the guys are going out." The topic did not seem open to further discussion. "There's a world in revolution out there and we can put you in it," George Hunt had said when he was still the managing editor of *Life* and offering me the job. By the time I finished

Play It As It Lays George Hunt had retired and some of the guys were going out.

"I warned you," John said. "I told you what working for *Life* would be like. Didn't I tell you? It would be like being nibbled to death by ducks?"

I was brushing Quintana's hair. The picture of Ginger Rogers.

I felt betrayed, humiliated. I should have listened to John.

I wrote the column letting the readers know who I was. It appeared. At the time it seemed an unexceptional enough eight hundred words in the assigned genre, but there was, at the end of the second paragraph, a line so out of synch with the entire *Life* mode of self-presentation that it might as well have suggested abduction by space aliens: "We are here on this island in the middle of the Pacific in lieu of filing for divorce." A week later we happened to be in New York. "Did you know she was writing it," many people asked John, sotto voce.

Did he know I was writing it?

He edited it.

He took Quintana to the Honolulu Zoo so I could rewrite it.

He drove me to the Western Union office in downtown Honolulu so I could file it.

At the Western Union office he wrote *REGARDS, DIDION* at the end of it. That was what you always put at the end of a cable, he said. Why, I said. Because you do, he said.

See where that particular vortex sucked me.

From the Dorothy Draper wallpaper border at Beth Israel North to Quintana at three and I should have listened to John.

I tell you that I shall not live two days, Gawain said.

The way you got sideswiped was by going back.

I saw immediately in Los Angeles that its potential for triggering this vortex effect could be controlled only by avoiding any venue I might associate with either Quintana or John. This would require ingenuity. John and I had lived in Los Angeles County from 1964 until 1988. Between 1988 and the time he died we had spent significant amounts of time there, usually at the very hotel in which I was now staying, the Beverly Wilshire. Quintana was born in Los Angeles County, at St. John's Hospital in Santa Monica. She went to school there, first in Malibu and later at what was then still the Westlake School for Girls (the year after she left it became coeducational, and was called Harvard-Westlake) in Holmby Hills.

For reasons that remain unclear to me the Beverly Wilshire itself only rarely triggered the vortex effect. In theory its every corridor was permeated with the associations I was trying to avoid. When we were living in Malibu and had meetings in town we would bring Quintana and stay at the Beverly Wilshire. After we moved to New York and needed to be in Los Angeles for a picture we would stay there, sometimes for a few days, sometimes for weeks at a time. We set up computers and printers there. We had meetings there. *What if*, someone was always saying in these meetings. We could work until eight or nine in the evening there and transmit the pages to whichever director or producer we were working with and then go to dinner at a Chinese restaurant on Melrose where we did not need a reservation. We always specified the old building. I knew the housekeepers. I knew the manicurists. I knew the doorman who would give John the bottled water when he came back from walking in the morning. I knew by reflex how to work the key and open the safe and adjust the shower head: I had stayed over the years in some dozens of rooms identical to the one in which I was now staying. I had last stayed in such a room in October 2003, alone, doing promotion, two months before John died. Yet the Beverly Wilshire seemed when Quintana was at UCLA the only safe place for me to be, the place where everything would be the same, the place where no one would know about or refer to the events of my recent life; the place where I would still be the person I had been before any of this happened.

What if.

Outside the exempt zone that was the Beverly Wilshire, I plotted my routes, I remained on guard.

Never once in five weeks did I drive into the part of

Brentwood in which we had lived from 1978 until 1988. When I saw a dermatologist in Santa Monica and street work forced me to pass within three blocks of our house in Brentwood, I did not look left or right. Never once in five weeks did I drive up the Pacific Coast Highway to Malibu. When Jean Moore offered me the use of her house on the Pacific Coast Highway, three-eighths of a mile past the house in which we had lived from 1971 until 1978, I invented reasons why it was essential for me to stay instead at the Beverly Wilshire. I could avoid driving to UCLA on Sunset. I could avoid passing the intersection at Sunset and Beverly Glen where for six years I had turned off to the Westlake School for Girls. I could avoid passing any intersection I could not anticipate, control. I could avoid keeping the car radio tuned to the stations I used to drive by, avoid locating KRLA, an AM station that had called itself "the heart and soul of rock and roll" and was still in the early 1990s programming the top hits of 1962. I could avoid punching in the Christian call-in station to which I had switched whenever the top hits of 1962 lost their resonance.

Instead I listened to NPR, a sedate morning show called *Morning Becomes Eclectic*. Every morning at the Beverly Wilshire I ordered the same breakfast, huevos rancheros with one scrambled egg. Every morning when I left the Beverly Wilshire I drove the same way to UCLA: out Wilshire, right on Glendon, slip left to Westwood, right on Le Conte and left at Tiverton. Every morning I noted the same banners fluttering from the light standards along Wilshire: *UCLA Medical Center—#1 in the West, #3 in the Nation*. Every morning I wondered whose ranking this was. I never asked. Each morning I inserted my ticket into the gate mechanism and each morning, if I inserted it right, the same woman's voice said "*Wel*-come to *U-C-L-A*." Each morning, if I timed it right, I got a parking place outside, on the Plaza 4 level, against the hedge. Late each afternoon I would drive back to the Beverly Wilshire, pick up my messages, and return a few of them. After the first week Gerry was flying back and forth between Los Angeles and New York, trying to work at least a few days a week, and if he was in New York I would call to give him the day's information or lack of it.

I would lie down. I would watch the local news. I would stand in the shower for twenty minutes and go out to dinner.

I went out to dinner every night I was in Los Angeles. I had dinner with my brother and his wife whenever they were in town. I went to Connie Wald's house in Beverly Hills. There were roses and nasturtiums and open fires in the big fireplaces, as there had been through all the years when John and I and Quintana would go there. Now Susan Traylor was there. I went to Susan's own house in the Hollywood hills. I had known Susan since she was three and I had known her husband Jesse since he and Susan and Quintana were in the fourth grade at the Point Dume School, and now they were looking after me. I ate in many restaurants with many friends. I had dinner quite often with Earl McGrath, whose intuitive kindness in this situation was to ask me every morning what I was doing that night and, if the answer was in any way vague, to arrange an untaxing dinner for two or three or four at Orso or at Morton's or at his house on Robertson Boulevard.

After dinner I would take a taxi back to the hotel and place my morning order for huevos rancheros. "One scrambled egg," the voice on the phone would prompt. "Exactly," I would say.

I plotted these evenings as carefully as I plotted the routes.

I left no time to dwell on promises I had no way of keeping.

You're safe. I'm here.

In the deep hush of *Morning Becomes Eclectic* the next day I would congratulate myself.

I could have been in Cleveland.

Yet.

I cannot count the days on which I found myself driving abruptly blinded by tears.

The Santa Ana was back.

The jacaranda was back.

One afternoon I needed to see Gil Frank, at his office on Wilshire, several blocks east of the Beverly Wilshire. In this previously untested territory (*terra cognita* for these purposes was west on Wilshire, not east) I caught sight, unprepared, of a movie theater in which John and I had in 1967 seen *The Graduate*. There had been no particular sense of moment about seeing *The Graduate* in 1967. I had been in Sacramento. John had picked me up at LAX. It had seemed too late to shop for dinner and too early to eat in a restaurant so we had gone to see *The Graduate* and then to dinner at Frascati's. Frascati's was gone but the theater was still there, if only to trap the unwary.

There were many such traps. One day I would notice a familiar stretch of coastal highway in a television commercial and realize it was outside the gate house, on the Palos Verdes Peninsula at Portuguese Bend, to which John and I had brought Quintana home from St. John's Hospital.

She was three days old.

We had placed her bassinet next to the wisteria in the box garden.

You're safe. I'm here.

Neither the house nor its gate could be seen in the commercial but I experienced a sudden rush of memories: getting out of the car on that highway to open the gate so that John could drive through; watching the tide come in and float a car that was sitting on our beach to be shot for a commercial; sterilizing bottles for Quintana's formula while the gamecock that lived on the property followed me companionably from window to window. This gamecock, named "Buck" by the owner of the house, had been abandoned on the highway, in the colorful opinion of the owner by "Mexicans on the run." Buck had a distinctive and surprisingly endearing personality, not unlike a Labrador. In addition to Buck this house also came equipped with peacocks, which were decorative but devoid of personality. Unlike Buck, the peacocks were fat and moved only as a last resort. At dusk they would scream and try to fly to their nests in the olive trees, a fraught moment because they would so often fall. Just before dawn they would scream again. One dawn I woke to the screaming and looked for John. I found him outside in the dark, tearing unripe peaches from a tree and hurling them at the peacocks, a characteristically straightforward if counterproductive approach to resolving an annoyance. When Quintana was a month old we were evicted. There was a clause in the lease that specified no children but the owner and his wife allowed that the baby was not the reason. The reason was that we had hired a pretty teenager named Jennifer to take care of her. The owner and his wife did not want strangers on the property, or as they said "behind the gate," particularly pretty teenagers named Jennifer, who would presumably have dates. We took a few months' lease on a house in town that belonged to Herman Mankiewicz's widow, Sara, who was going to be traveling. She left everything in the house as it was except one object, the Oscar awarded to Herman Mankiewicz for the screenplay of *Citizen Kane*. "You'll have parties, people will just get drunk and play with it," she said when she put it away. On the day we moved John was traveling with the San Francisco Giants, doing a piece on Willie Mays for *The Saturday Evening Post*. I borrowed my sister-in-law's station wagon, loaded it, put Quintana and Jennifer in the back seat, said goodbye to Buck, drove out, and let the totemic gate lock behind me for the last time.

All that and I had not even driven down there.

All I had done was catch sight of a commercial on television while I was dressing to go to the hospital.

Another day I would need to buy bottled water at the Rite Aid on Canon and remember that Canon was where The Bistro had been. In 1964 and 1965, when we were living in the gate house with the beach and the peacocks but could not afford even to tip the parking boys at restaurants, let alone eat in them, John and I used to park on the street on Canon and charge dinner at The Bistro. We took Quintana there on the day of her adoption, when she was not quite seven months old. They had given us Sidney Korshak's corner banquette and placed her carrier on the table, a centerpiece. At the courthouse that morning she had been the only baby, even the only child; all the other adoptions that day had seemed to involve adults adopting one another for tax reasons. "*Qué bonita, qué hermosa*," the busboys at The Bistro crooned when we brought her in at lunch. When she was six or seven we took her there for a birthday dinner. She was wearing a lime-green ruana I had bought for her in Bogotá. As we were about to leave the waiter had brought the ruana and she had flung it theatrically over her small shoulders.

Qué bonita, qué hermosa, the picture of Ginger Rogers.

John and I had been in Bogotá together. We had escaped from a film festival in Cartagena and gotten on an Avianca flight to Bogotá. An actor who had been at the film festival, George Montgomery, had also been on the flight to Bogotá. He had gone up to the cockpit. From where I was sitting I could see him chatting with the crew, then sliding into the pilot's seat.

I had nudged John, who was sleeping. "They're letting George Montgomery fly this plane over the Andes," I had whispered.

"It beats Cartagena," John said, and went back to sleep.

I did not that day on Canon get as far as the Rite Aid.

11

Sometime in June, after she had left UCLA and was in the sixth of what would be fifteen weeks as an inpatient at the Rusk Institute of Rehabilitation Medicine at New York University Medical Center in New York, Quintana told me that her memory not only of UCLA but of her arrival at Rusk was "all mudgy." She could remember some things about UCLA, yes, as she could not yet remember anything else since before Christmas (she did not for example remember speaking about her father at St. John the Divine, nor, when she first woke at UCLA, did she remember that he had died), but it was still "mudgy." Later she corrected this to "smudgy," but she did not need to: I knew exactly what she meant. On the neuro floors at UCLA they had called it "spotty," as in "her orientation is improving but still spotty." When I try to reconstruct those weeks at UCLA I recognize the mudginess in my own memory. There are parts of days that seem very clear and parts of days that do not. I clearly remember arguing with a doctor the day they decided to do the tracheostomy. She had by then been intubated for almost a week, the doctor said. UCLA did not leave tubes in for more than a week. I said that she had been intubated for three weeks at Beth Israel in New York. The doctor had looked away. "The rule at Duke was also a week," he said, as if under the impression that mention of Duke would settle the question. Instead it enraged me: *What is Duke to me*, I wanted to say but did not. *What is Duke to UCLA. Duke is North Carolina. UCLA is California. If I wanted the opinion of somebody in North Carolina I would call somebody in North Carolina.*

Her husband is right now on a flight to New York, I said instead. Surely this can wait until he lands.

Not really, the doctor said. Since it's already on the schedule.

The day they decided to do the tracheostomy was also the day they turned off the EEG.

"Everything's looking good," they kept saying. "She's going to get better sooner once we do the trach. She's already off the EEG, maybe you didn't notice that."

Maybe I didn't notice that?

My only child?

My unconscious child?

Maybe I didn't notice when I walked into the ICU that morning that her brain waves were gone? That the monitor above her bed was dark, dead?

This was now being presented as progress but it had not seemed so when I first saw it. I remembered reading in *Intensive Care* that the ICU nurses at San Francisco General turned off the monitors when a patient was near death, because their experience was that family members would focus on the screens rather than on the dying patient. I wondered if such a determination had been made in this case. Even after I was assured that this was not the case, I found myself averting my eyes from the blank EEG screen. I had grown used to watching her brain waves. It was a way of hearing her talk.

I did not see why, since the equipment was sitting there unused, they could not keep the EEG on.

Just in case.

I had asked.

I do not remember getting an answer. It was a period when I asked many questions that did not get answered. What answers I did get tended to the unsatisfactory, as in, "It's already on the schedule."

Everyone in the neuro units got a trach, they had kept saying to me that day. Everyone in the neuro units had muscular weaknesses that rendered the removal of the breathing tube problematic. A trach involved less risk of windpipe damage. A trach involved less risk of pneumonia. Look to your right, look to your left, both sides have trachs. A trach could be done with fentanyl and a muscle relaxant, she would be under anesthesia no more than an hour. A trach would leave no cosmetic effect to speak of, "only a little dimple scar," "as time goes by maybe no scar at all."

They kept mentioning this last point, as if the basis for my resistance to the trach was the scar. They were doctors, however freshly minted. I was not. Ergo, any concerns I had must be cosmetic, frivolous.

In fact I had no idea why I so resisted the trach.

I think now that my resistance came from the same fund of superstition from which I had been drawing since John died. If she did not have a trach she could be fine in the morning, ready to eat, talk, go home. If she did not have a trach we could be on a plane by the weekend. Even if they did not want her to fly, I could take her with me to the Beverly Wilshire, we could have our nails done, sit by the pool. If they still did not want her to fly we could drive out to Malibu, spend a few restorative days with Jean Moore.

If she did not have a trach.

This was demented, but so was I.

Through the printed blue cotton curtains that separated the beds I could hear people talking to their functionally absent husbands, fathers, uncles, co-workers. In the bed to Quintana's right was a man injured in a construction accident. The men who had been on the site at the time of the accident had come to see him. They stood around his bed and tried to explain what had happened. The rig, the cab, the crane, I heard a noise, I called out to Vinny. Each man gave his version. Each version differed slightly from the others. This was understandable, since each witness proceeded from a different point of view, but I recall wanting to intercede, help them coordinate their stories; it had seemed too much conflicting data to lay on someone with a traumatic brain injury.

"Everything's going along as usual and then all shit breaks loose," one said.

The injured man made no response, nor could he, since he had a trach.

To Quintana's left lay a man from Massachusetts who had been in the hospital for several months. He and his wife had been in Los Angeles visiting their children, there had been a fall from a ladder, he had seemed all right. One more perfectly ordinary day. Then he had trouble speaking. *Everything's going along as usual and then all shit breaks loose.* Now he had pneumonia. The children came and went. The wife was always there, pleading with him in a low mournful voice. The husband made no response: he too had a trach.

They did the trach for Quintana on the first of April, a Thursday afternoon.

By Friday morning enough of the sedation for the breathing tube had been metabolized out that she could open her eyes and squeeze my hand.

On Saturday I was told that the next day or Monday she would be moved from the ICU into a step-down neuro-observational unit on the seventh floor. The sixth and seventh floors at UCLA were all neuro.

I have no memory of when she was moved but I think it was some days after that.

One afternoon after she had been moved to the step-down unit I ran into the woman from Massachusetts in the Café Med courtyard.

Her husband too had left the ICU, and was moving now to what she called a "subacute rehab facility." We each knew that "subacute rehab facilities" were what medical insurance carriers and hospital discharge coordinators called nursing homes but this went unmentioned. She had wanted him moved to the eleven-bed acute rehab unit at UCLA Neuropsychiatric but he had not been accepted. That was the phrase she used, "not been accepted." She was concerned about how she would get to the subacute facility—one of the two with an available bed was near LAX, the other in Chinatown—because she did not drive. The children had jobs, important jobs, they could not always be driving her.

We sat in the sun.

I listened. She asked about my daughter.

I did not want to tell her that my daughter would be moving to the eleven-bed acute rehab unit at Neuropsychiatric.

At some point I noticed that I was trying like a sheepdog to herd the doctors, pointing out edema to one intern, reminding another to obtain a urine culture to check out the blood in the Foley catheter line, insisting on a Doppler ultrasound to see if the reason for the leg pain could be emboli, doggedly repeating—when the ultrasound indicated that she was in fact again throwing clots—that I wanted a specialist on coagulation called in to consult. I wrote down the name of the specialist I wanted. I offered to call him myself. These efforts did not endear me to the young men and women who made up the house staff ("If you want to manage this case I'm signing off," one finally said) but they made me feel less helpless.

I remember learning at UCLA the names of many tests and scales. The Kimura Box Test. The Two-Point Discrimination Test. The Glasgow Coma Scale, the Glasgow Outcome Scale. My comprehension of the meaning of these tests and scales remained obscure. I also remember learning, both at UCLA and before, at Beth Israel and Columbia-Presbyterian, the names of many resistant hospital bacteria. At Beth Israel there had been *Acinetobacter baumannii*, which was resistant to vancomycin. "That's how you know it's a hospital infection," I recall being told by a doctor I asked at Columbia-Presbyterian. "If it's resistant to vanc it's hospital. Because vanc only gets used in hospital settings." At UCLA there had been MRSA, methicillin-resistant *Staphylococcus aureus*, as opposed to MRSE, methicillin-resistant *Staphylococcus epidermidis*, which was what they first thought they had cultured and which had seemed to more visibly alarm the staff. "I can't say why but since you're pregnant you may want to transfer off," one therapist advised another during the MRSE scare, glancing at me as if I might not understand. There were many other names of hospital bacteria, but those were the big hitters. Whatever bacteria was shown to be the source of the new fever or urinary tract infection, it would mandate gowns, gloves, masks. It would provoke heavy sighing among the aides who were required to suit up before entering the room to empty a wastebasket. The methicillin-resistant *Staphylococcus aureus* at UCLA was an infection in the bloodstream, a bacteremia. When I heard this I expressed concern to the doctor who was examining Quintana that an infection in her bloodstream might again lead to sepsis.

"Well, you know, sepsis, it's a clinical term," the doctor said, then continued examining her.

I had pressed him.

"She's already in some degree of sepsis." He had seemed cheerful. "But we're continuing vanc. And so far her blood pressure is holding."

So. We were back to waiting to see if she lost blood pressure.

We were back to watching for septic shock.

Next we would be watching for ice floes on the East River.

In point of fact what I watched from the windows at UCLA was a swimming pool. I never once saw anyone swim in this swimming pool, although it was filled, filtered (I could see the little swirl where the water entered the filter and the bubbling where it reemerged), sparkling in the sun, and surrounded by patio tables, with parasols. One day when I was watching it I had a sharp memory of having gotten the idea to float candles and gardenias in the pool behind the house in Brentwood Park. We were having a party. It was an hour before the party but I was already dressed when the gardenia idea presented itself. I knelt on the coping and lit the candles and used the pool skimmer to guide the gardenias and candles into a random pattern. I stood up, pleased with the result. I put the pool skimmer away. When I glanced back at the pool, the gardenias had vanished and the candles were out, tiny drenched hulks bobbing furiously around the filter intake. They could not be sucked in because the filter was already clogged with gardenias. I spent the remaining forty-five minutes before the party cleaning the sodden gardenias from the filter and scooping out the candles and drying my dress with a hair dryer.

So far so good.

A memory of the house in Brentwood Park that involved neither John nor Quintana.

Unfortunately I thought of another. I had been alone in the kitchen of that house, late twilight, early evening, feeding the Bouvier we then had. Quintana was at Barnard. John was spending a few days at the apartment we had in New York. This would have been late 1987, the period during which he had begun talking about wanting us to spend more time in New York. I had discouraged this idea. Suddenly a red flashing light had filled the kitchen. I had gone to the window. There was an ambulance in front of a house across Marlboro Street, visible beyond the coral tree and two cords of stacked wood in our side yard. This was a neighborhood in which many houses, including the one across Marlboro Street, had side yards in which there were two cords of stacked wood. I had watched the house until the last light was gone and the ambulance left. The next morning when I was walking the Bouvier a neighbor told me what had happened. Two cords of stacked wood had not kept the woman in the house across Marlboro Street from becoming a widow at dinner.

I had called John in New York.

The red flashing light had by then seemed an urgent warning.

I said maybe he was right, we should spend more time in New York.

Watching the empty swimming pool from the window at UCLA I could see the vortex coming but could not deflect it. The vortex in this instance would be the memory's insistent appointment-in-Samarra aspect. Had I not made that call would Quintana have moved back to Los Angeles when she graduated from Barnard? Had she been living in Los Angeles would Beth Israel North have happened, would Presbyterian have happened, would she be in UCLA today? Had I not misread the meaning of the red flashing light in late 1987 would I be able to get in my car today and drive west on San Vicente and find John at the house in Brentwood Park? Standing in the pool? Re-reading *Sophie's Choice*?

Would I need to relive every mistake? If by accident I remembered the morning we drove down to St.-Tropez from Tony Richardson's house in the hills and had coffee on the street and bought the fish for dinner would I also need to remember the night I refused to swim in the moonlight because the

Mediterranean was polluted and I had a cut on my leg? If I remembered the gamecock at Portuguese Bend would I also need to remember the long drive home from dinner to that house, and how many nights as we passed the refineries on the San Diego Freeway one or the other of us had said the wrong thing? Or stopped speaking? Or imagined that the other had stopped speaking? "Each single one of the memories and expectations in which the libido is bound to the object is brought up and hypercathected, and detachment of the libido is accomplished in respect of it. . . . It is remarkable that this painful unpleasure is taken as a matter of course by us." So Freud explained what he saw as the "work" of grief, which as described sounded suspiciously like the vortex.

In point of fact the house in Brentwood Park from which I had seen the red flashing light and thought to evade it by moving to New York no longer existed. It was torn down to the ground and replaced (by a house marginally larger) a year after we sold it. The day we happened to be in Los Angeles and drove past the corner of Chadbourne and Marlboro and saw nothing left standing except the one chimney that allowed a tax advantage, I remembered the real estate agent telling me how meaningful it would be to the buyers were we to give them suitably inscribed copies of the books we had written in the house. We had done this. *Quintana and Friends*, *Dutch Shea, Jr.*, and *The Red White and Blue* for John, *Salvador*, *Democracy*, and *Miami* for me. When we saw the flattened lot from the car, Quintana, in the back seat, burst into tears. My first reaction was fury. I wanted the books back.

Did this corrective line of thinking stop the vortex?

Not hardly.

One morning when Quintana was still in the step-down unit because the persistence of her fever necessitated an echocardiogram to rule out endocarditis she lifted her right hand for the first time. This was significant because it was on the right side of her body that the effects of the trauma could be seen. Movement meant that the traumatized nerves remained alive.

Later that day she kept wanting to get out of bed, and fell into a sulk like a child when I said I would not help her. My memory of that day is not at all mudgy.

It was decided in late April that sufficient time had passed since the surgery to allow her to fly to New York. The issue until then had been pressurization and the potential it presented for swelling. She would need trained personnel to accompany her. A commercial flight was ruled out. Arrangements were made to medevac her: an ambulance from UCLA to an airport, an air ambulance to Teterboro, and an ambulance from Teterboro to New York University Hospital, where she would do neuro-rehab at the Rusk Institute. Many conversations were held between UCLA and Rusk. Many records were faxed. A CD-ROM of CT scans was prepared. A date was set for what even I was now calling "the transfer": Thursday, April 29. Early that Thursday morning as I was about to check out of the Beverly Wilshire I got a call from somewhere in Colorado. The flight had been delayed. The plane was in Tucson, where it had landed with "mechanical difficulties." The mechanics in Tucson would look at it when they came in, at ten mountain time. By early afternoon Pacific time it was clear that the plane would not be flying. Another plane would be available the next morning, but the next morning was a Friday, and UCLA did not like to transfer on Fridays. At the hospital I pressed the discharge coordinator to agree to the Friday transfer.

To delay the transfer into the following week could only dispirit and confuse Quintana, I said, sure of my ground.

Rusk had no problem with a Friday night admission, I said, less sure.

There was nowhere I could stay over the weekend, I lied.

By the time the discharge coordinator had agreed to the Friday transfer Quintana was asleep. I sat for a while in the sun on the plaza outside the hospital and watched a helicopter circling to land on the roof. Helicopters were always landing on the roof at UCLA, suggesting trauma all over Southern California, remote scenes of highway carnage, distant falling cranes, bad days ahead for the husband or wife or mother or father who had not yet (even as the helicopter landed and the trauma team rushed the stretcher into triage) gotten the call. I remembered a summer day in 1970 when John and I stopped for a red light on St. Charles Avenue in New Orleans and noticed the driver of the next car suddenly slump over his steering wheel. His horn sounded. Several pedestrians ran up. A police officer materialized. The light changed, we drove on. John had been unable to get this image out of his mind. There he was, he had kept saying later. He was alive and then he was dead and we were watching. We saw him at the instant it happened. We knew he was dead before his family did.

Just an ordinary day.

"And then—gone."

The day of the flight, when it came, had seemed to unfold with the nonsequential inexorability of a dream. When I turned on the news in the early morning there was a guerrilla action on the freeways, truckers protesting the price of gasoline. Huge semi trucks had been deliberately jackknifed and abandoned on Interstate 5. Witnesses reported that the first semis to stop had carried the TV crews. SUVs had been waiting to take the truckers themselves from the blocked freeway. The video as I watched it had seemed dislocatingly French, 1968. "Avoid the 5 if you can," the newscaster advised, then warned that according to "sources" (presumably the same TV crews who were traveling with the truckers) the truckers would also block other freeways, specifically the 710, the 60, and the 10. In the normal course of this kind of disruption it would have seemed unlikely that we could get from UCLA to the plane, but by the time the ambulance arrived at the hospital the entire French event seemed to have dematerialized, that phase of the dream forgotten.

There were other phases to come. I had been told the plane would be at Santa Monica Airport. The ambulance crew had been told Burbank. Someone made a call and was told Van Nuys. When we reached Van Nuys there were no planes in sight, only helicopters. That must be because you're going by helicopter, one of the ambulance attendants said, clearly ready to hand us off and get on with his day. I don't think so, I said, it's three thousand miles. The ambulance attendant shrugged and disappeared. The plane was located, a jet Cessna with room for the two pilots, the two paramedics, the stretcher to which Quintana was strapped, and, if I sat on a bench over the oxygen canisters, me. We took off. We flew for a while. One of the paramedics had a digital camera and was taking pictures of what he kept referring to as the Grand Canyon. I said I believed it was Lake Mead, Hoover Dam. I pointed out Las Vegas.

The paramedic continued taking pictures.

He also continued referring to it as the Grand Canyon.

Why do you always have to be right, I remembered John saying.

It was a complaint, a charge, part of a fight.

He never understood that in my own mind I was never right. Once in 1971, when we were moving from Franklin Avenue to Malibu, I found a message stuck behind a picture I was taking down. The message was from someone to whom I had been close before I married John. He had spent a few weeks with us in the house on Franklin Avenue. This was the message: "You were wrong." I did not know what I had been wrong about but the possibilities seemed infinite. I burned the message. I never mentioned it to John.

All right it's the Grand Canyon, I thought, shifting position on the bench over the oxygen canisters so that I could no longer see out the window.

Later we landed in a cornfield in Kansas to refuel. The pilots struck a deal with the two teenagers who managed the airstrip: during the refueling they would take their pickup to a McDonald's and bring back hamburgers. While we waited the paramedics suggested that we take turns getting some exercise. When my turn came I stood frozen on the tarmac for a moment, ashamed to be free and outside when Quintana could not be, then walked to where the runway ended and the corn started. There was a little rain and unstable air and I imagined a tornado coming. Quintana and I were Dorothy. We were both free. In fact we were out of here. John had written a tornado into *Nothing Lost*. I remembered reading the last-pass galleys in Quintana's room at Presbyterian and crying when I hit the passage with the tornado. The protagonists, J.J. McClure and Teresa Kean, see the tornado "in the far distance, black and then milky when the sun caught it, moving like a huge reticulated vertical snake." J.J. tells Teresa not to worry, this stretch had been hit before, twisters never hit the same place twice.

> The tornado finally set down without incident just across the Wyoming line. That night in the Step Right Inn, at the junction between Higginson and Higgins, Teresa asked if it was true that tornadoes never hit the same place twice. "I don't know," J.J. said. "It seemed logical. Like lightning. You were worried. I didn't want you worried." It was as close a declaration of love as J.J. was capable of making.

Back in the plane, alone with Quintana, I took one of the hamburgers the teenagers had brought and tore it into pieces so that she and I could share. After a few bites she shook her head. She had been allowed solid food for only a week or so and could not eat more. There was still a feeding tube in place in case she could not eat at all.

"Am I going to make it," she asked then.

I chose to believe that she was asking if she would make it to New York.

"Definitely," I told her.

I'm here. You're safe.

Definitely she would be okay in California, I remembered telling her five weeks before.

That night when we arrived at the Rusk Institute Gerry and Tony were waiting outside to meet the ambulance. Gerry asked how the flight had been. I said that we had shared a Big Mac in a cornfield in Kansas. "It wasn't a Big Mac," Quintana said. "It was a Quarter Pounder."

It had seemed to me on the day in Quintana's room at Presbyterian when I read the final proof for *Nothing Lost* that there might be a grammatical error in the last sentence of the passage about J.J. McClure and Teresa Kean and the tornado. I never actually learned the rules of grammar, relying instead only on what sounded right, but there was something here that I was not sure sounded right. The sentence in the last-pass galleys read: "It was as close a declaration of love as J.J. was capable of making." I would have added a preposition: "It was as close *to* a declaration of love as J.J. was capable of making."

I sat by the window and watched the ice floes on the Hudson and thought about the sentence. *It was as close a declaration of love as J.J. was capable of making.* It was not the kind of sentence, if you had written it, you would want wrong, but neither was it the kind of sentence, if that was the way you had written it, you would want changed. How had he written it? What did he have in mind? How would he want it? The decision was left to me. Any choice I made could carry the potential for abandonment, even betrayal. That was one reason I was crying in Quintana's hospital room. When I got home that night I checked the previous galleys and manuscripts. The error, if it was an error, had been there from the beginning. I left it as it was.

Why do you always have to be right.
Why do you always have to have the last word.
For once in your life just let it go.

12

The day on which Quintana and I flew east on the Cessna that refueled in the cornfield in Kansas was April 30, 2004. During May and June and the half of July that she spent at the Rusk Institute there was very little I could do for her. I could go down to East Thirty-fourth Street to see her in the late afternoons, and most afternoons I did, but she was in therapy from eight in the morning until four in the afternoon and exhausted by six-thirty or seven. She was medically stable. She could eat, the feeding tube was still in place but no longer necessary. She was beginning to regain movement in her right leg and arm. She was regaining the mobility in her right eye that she needed to read. On weekend days when she did not have therapy Gerry would take her to lunch and a movie in the neighborhood. He would eat dinner with her. Friends would join them for picnic lunches. For as long as she was at Rusk I could water the plants on her windowsill, I could find the marginally different sneakers her therapist had decreed, I could sit with her in the greenhouse off the Rusk lobby watching the koi in the pond, but once she left Rusk I would no longer be able to do even that. She was reaching a point at which she would need once again to be, if she was to recover, on her own.

I determined to spend the summer reaching the same point.

I did not yet have the concentration to work but I could straighten my house, I could get on top of things, I could deal with my unopened mail.

That I was only now beginning the process of mourning did not occur to me.

Until now I had been able only to grieve, not mourn. Grief was passive. Grief happened. Mourning, the act of dealing with grief, required attention. Until now there had been every urgent reason to obliterate any attention that might otherwise have been paid, banish the thought, bring fresh adrenaline to bear on the crisis of the day. I had passed an entire season during which the only words I allowed myself to truly hear were recorded: *Wel*-come to *U-C-L-A*.

I began.

Among the letters and books and magazines that had arrived while I was in Los Angeles was a thick volume called *Lives of '54*, prepared for what was by then the imminent fiftieth reunion of John's class at Princeton. I looked up John's entry. It read: "William Faulkner once said that a writer's obituary should read, 'He wrote books, then he died.' This is not an obit (at least as of 19 September 2002) and I am still writing books. So I'll stick with Faulkner."

I told myself: this was not an obit.

At least as of 19 September 2002.

I closed *Lives of '54*. A few weeks later I opened it again, and leafed through the other entries. One was from Donald H. ("Rummy") Rumsfeld, who noted: "After Princeton, the years seem like a blur, but the days seem more like rapid fire." I thought about this. Another, a three-page reflection by Lancelot L. ("Lon") Farrar, Jr., began: "Arguably our best-shared Princeton memory was Adlai Stevenson's address to the senior banquet."

I also thought about this.

I had been married to a member of the Class of '54 for forty years and he had never mentioned Adlai Stevenson's address to the senior banquet. I tried to think of anything at all he had mentioned about Princeton. He had many times mentioned the misguided entitlement he heard in the words "Princeton in the Nation's Service," the slogan Princeton had adopted from a speech by Woodrow Wilson. Other than that I could think of nothing except his saying a few days after our wedding (why did he say it? how had it come up?) that he had thought the Nassoons absurd. In fact, because he knew it amused me, he would sometimes impersonate the Nassoons in performance: the studied plunge of one hand into a pocket, the swirling of the ice cubes in the imaginary glass, the chin thrust into profile, the slight satisfied smile.

As I remember you—
We stood there together on a high windy slope—
Our faces to the weather and our hearts full of hope—

For forty years this song had figured in a private joke between us and I could not remember its name, let alone the rest of its lyrics. Finding the lyrics became a matter of some urgency. I could find only a single reference on the Internet, in an obituary from the *Princeton Alumni Weekly:*

> John MacFadyen '46 *49: John MacFadyen died February 18, 2000, in Damariscotta, Maine, near the village of Head Tide, where he and his wife, Mary-Esther, made their home. The cause of death was pneumonia, but his health failed for some years, particularly after his wife's death in 1977. John came to Princeton from Duluth in the "accelerated" summer of 1942. Gifted in music and arts, he contributed songs to Triangle, including, "As I Remember You," long a Nassoons favorite. John was the life of any party with a piano. Remembered was his rendition of "Shine, Little Glow Worm," played upside down from under the piano. After U.S. Army service in Japan, he returned to Princeton for a master's of fine arts in architecture. In the New York firm Harrison & Abramowitz, he designed a main United Nations building. John received the Rome Prize in architecture, and, newly wed to Mary-Esther Edge, spent 1952–53 at Rome's American Academy. His private architectural practice, noted especially for the design of the Wolf Trap Center for the Arts outside Washington, was interrupted by his service, during the 1960s, under Gov. Nelson Rockefeller, as executive director of the first state arts council. The class joins his children, Camilla, Luke, William, and John and three grandchildren in mourning the loss of one of our most unforgettable members.

"As I Remember You," long a Nassoons favorite.
But how about the death of Mary-Esther?

And how long ago was it when the life of any party last played "Shine, Little Glow Worm" upside down from under the piano?

What would I give to be able to discuss this with John?

What would I give to be able to discuss anything at all with John? What would I give to be able to say one small thing that made him happy? What would that one small thing be? If I had said it in time would it have worked?

A night or two before he died John asked me if I was aware how many characters died in the novel he had just sent to press, *Nothing Lost*. He had been sitting in his office making a list of them. I added one he had overlooked. Some months after he died I picked up a legal pad on his desk to make a note. On the legal pad, in very faint pencil, his handwriting, was the list. It read:

> *Teresa Kean*
> *Parlance*
> *Emmett McClure*
> *Jack Broderick*
> *Maurice Dodd*
> *Four people in car*
> *Charlie Buckles*
> *Percy—electric chair (Percy Darrow)*
> *Walden McClure*

Why was the pencil so faint, I wondered.
Why would he use a pencil that barely left a mark.
When did he begin seeing himself as dead?
"It's not black and white," a young doctor at Cedars-Sinai Medical Center in Los Angeles had told me, in 1982, about the divide between life and death. We had been standing in an ICU at Cedars watching Nick and Lenny's daughter Dominique, who had the night before been strangled to the point of death. Dominique was lying there in the ICU as if she were asleep but she would not recover. She was breathing only on life support.

Dominique had been the four-year-old at John's and my wedding.

Dominique had been the cousin who supervised Quintana's parties and took her shopping for prom dresses and stayed with her if we were out of town. *Roses are red, violets are blue*, read the card on a glass of flowers Quintana and Dominique left on the kitchen table for our return from one such trip. *I wish you weren't home and Dominique does too. Love, Happy Mother's Day, D & Q.*

I remember thinking that the doctor was wrong. For as long as Dominique lay in this ICU she was alive. She could not keep herself alive unaided but she was alive. That was white. When they turned off the life support there would be a matter of some minutes before her systems shut down and then she would be dead. That was black.

There were no faint traces about dead, no pencil marks.

Any faint traces, any pencil marks, were left "a night or two before he died," or "a week or two before," in any case decisively *before he died*.

There was a divide.

The abrupt finality of this divide was something about which I thought a great deal during the late spring and summer after I came home from UCLA. A close friend, Carolyn Lelyveld, died in May, at Memorial Sloan-Kettering. Tony Dunne's wife, Rosemary Breslin, died in June, at Columbia-Presbyterian. In each of those cases the phrase "after long illness" would have seemed to apply, trailing its misleading suggestion of release, relief, resolution. In each of those long illnesses the possibility of death had been in the picture, in Carolyn's case for some months, in Rosemary's since 1989, when she was thirty-two. Yet having seen the picture in no way deflected, when it came, the swift empty loss of the actual event. It was still black and white. Each of them had been in the last instant alive, and then dead. I realized that I had never believed in the words I had learned as a child in order to be confirmed as an Episcopalian: *I believe in the Holy Ghost, the Holy Catholic Church, the Communion of Saints, the forgiveness of sins, the resurrection of the body, and the life everlasting, amen.*

I did not believe in the resurrection of the body.

Nor had Teresa Kean, Parlance, Emmett McClure, Jack Broderick, Maurice Dodd, the four people in the car, Charlie Buckles, Percy Darrow, or Walden McClure.

Nor had my Catholic husband.

I imagined this way of thinking to be clarifying, but in point of fact it was so muddled as to contradict even itself.

I did not believe in the resurrection of the body but I still believed that given the right circumstances he would come back.

He who left the faint traces before he died, the Number Three pencil.

One day it seemed important that I reread *Alcestis*. I had last read it at sixteen or seventeen, for a paper on Euripides, but recalled it as somehow relevant to this question of the "divide." I remembered the Greeks in general but *Alcestis* in particular as good on the passage between life and death. They visualized it, they dramatized it, they made the dark water and the ferry into the mise-en-scène itself. I did reread *Alcestis*. What happens in the play is this: Admetus, the young king of Thessaly, has been condemned by Death to die. Apollo has interceded, gaining a promise from the Fates that Admetus, if he can find another mortal to die in his place, need not die immediately. Admetus approaches his friends and his parents, in vain. "I tell myself that we are a long time underground and that life is short, but sweet," his father tells him after declining to take his place.

Only the wife of Admetus, the young queen, Alcestis, volunteers. There is much wailing about her approaching death, but no one steps in to save her. She dies, at length: "I see the two-oared boat, / I see the boat on the lake! / And Charon, / Ferryman of the Dead, / Calls to me, his hand on the oar . . ." Admetus is overcome by guilt and shame and self-pity: "Alas! How bitter to me is that ferrying of which you speak! O my unhappy one, how we suffer!" He behaves in every way badly. He blames his parents. He insists that Alcestis is suffering less than he. After some pages (and quite enough) of this, Alcestis, by means of a remarkably (even for 430 B.C.) clumsy deus ex machina, is allowed to come back. She does not speak, but this is explained, again clumsily, as temporary, self-correcting: "You may not hear her voice until she is purified from her consecration to the Lower Gods, and until the third dawn is risen." If we rely on the text alone, the play ends happily.

This was not my memory of *Alcestis*, which suggests that I was already given, at sixteen or seventeen, to editing the text as I read it. The principal divergences between the text and my memory appear toward the end, when Alcestis returns from the dead. In my memory, the reason Alcestis does not speak is that she declines to speak. Admetus, as I remembered it, presses her, at which point, to his distress, since what she turns out to have on her mind are his revealed failings, she does speak. Admetus, alarmed, shuts off the prospect of hearing more by calling for celebration. Alcestis acquiesces, but remains remote, other. Alcestis is on the face of it back with her husband and children, again the young queen of Thessaly, but the ending ("my" ending) could not be construed as happy.

In some ways this is a better (more "worked out") story, one that at least acknowledges that death "changes" the one who has died, but it opens up further questions about the divide. If the dead were truly to come back, what would they come back knowing? Could we face them? We who allowed them to die? The clear light of day tells me that I did not allow John to die, that I did not have that power, but do I believe that? Does he?

Survivors look back and see omens, messages they missed.

They remember the tree that died, the gull that splattered onto the hood of the car.

They live by symbols. They read meaning into the barrage of spam on the unused computer, the delete key that stops working, the imagined abandonment in the decision to replace it. The voice on my answering machine is still John's. The fact that it was his in the first place was arbitrary, having to do with who was around on the day the answering machine last needed programming, but if I needed to retape it now I would do so with a sense of betrayal. One day when I was talking on the telephone in his office I mindlessly turned the pages of the dictionary that he had always left open on the table by the desk. When I realized what I had done I was stricken: what word had he last looked up, what had he been thinking? By turning the pages had I lost the message? Or had the message been lost before I touched the dictionary? Had I refused to hear the message?

I tell you that I shall not live two days, Gawain said.

Later in the summer I received another book from Princeton. It was a first edition copy of *True Confessions*, in, as the booksellers say, "good condition, original dust jacket slightly frayed." In fact it was John's own copy: he had apparently sent it to a classmate who was organizing, for the fiftieth reunion of the Class of 1954, an exhibition of books written by class members. "It occupied the position of honor," the classmate wrote to me, "since John was unquestionably the most distinguished writer in our class."

I studied the original dust jacket, slightly frayed, on the copy of *True Confessions*.

I remembered the first time I saw this jacket, or a mock-up of this jacket. It had sat around our house for days, as proposed designs and type samples and jackets for new books always did, the idea being to gauge whether or not it would wear well, continue to please the eye.

I opened the book. I looked at the dedication. "For Dorothy Burns Dunne, Joan Didion, Quintana Roo Dunne," the dedication read. "Generations."

I had forgotten this dedication. I had *not sufficiently appreciated it*, a persistent theme by that stage of whatever I was going through.

I re-read *True Confessions*. I found it darker than I had remembered it. I re-read *Harp*. I found a different, less sunny, version of the summer we watched *Tenko* and went to dinner at Morton's.

Something else had happened toward the end of that summer.

In August there had been a memorial service for an acquaintance (this was not in itself the "something else" that happened), a French tennis player in his sixties who had been killed in an accident. The memorial service had been on someone's court in Beverly Hills. "I met my wife at the service," John had written in *Harp*, "coming directly from a doctor's appointment in Santa Monica, and as I sat there under the hot August sun, death was very much on my mind. I thought Anton had actually died under the best possible circumstances for him, a moment of terror as he realized the inevitable outcome of the accident, then an instant later the eternal dark."

> The service ended and the parking attendant brought my car. As we drove away, my wife said, "What did the doctor say?"
>
> There had not been an appropriate moment to mention my visit to the doctor in Santa Monica. "He scared the shit out of me, babe."
>
> "What did he say?"
>
> "He said I was a candidate for a catastrophic cardiac event."

A few pages further in *Harp*, the writer, John, examines the veracity of this (his own) account. He notes a name changed, a certain dramatic restructuring, a minor time collapse. He asks himself: "Anything else?" This was the answer he gave: "When I told my wife he scared the shit out of me, I started to cry."

Either I had not remembered this or I had determinedly chosen not to remember this.

I had *not sufficiently appreciated it*.

Was that what he experienced as he himself died? "A moment of terror as he realized the inevitable outcome of the accident, then an instant later the eternal dark"? In the sense that it happens one night and not another, the mechanism of a typical cardiac arrest could be construed as essentially accidental: a sudden spasm ruptures a deposit of plaque in a coronary artery, ischemia follows, and the heart, deprived of oxygen, enters ventricular fibrillation.

But how did he experience it?

The "moment of terror," the "eternal dark"? Did he accurately intuit this when he was writing *Harp*? Did he, as we would say to each other to the point of whether something was accurately reported or perceived, "get it right"? What about the "eternal dark" part? Didn't the survivors of near-death experiences always mention "the white light"? It occurs to me as I write that this "white light," usually presented dippily (evidence of afterlife, higher power), is in fact precisely consistent with the oxygen deficit that occurs as blood flow to the brain decreases. "Everything went white," those whose blood pressure has dropped say of the instant before they faint. "All the color drained out," those bleeding internally report of the moment when blood loss goes critical.

The "something else" that happened toward the end of that summer, which must have been 1987, was the series of events that followed the appointment with the doctor in Santa Monica and the memorial service on the tennis court in Beverly Hills. A week or so later an angiogram was done. The angiogram showed a 90 percent occlusion of the left anterior descending artery, or LAD. It also showed a long 90 percent narrowing in the circumflex marginal artery, which was considered significant mainly because the circumflex marginal artery fed the same area of the heart as the occluded LAD. "We call it the widow-maker, pal," John's cardiologist in New York later said of the LAD. A week or two after the angiogram (it was by then September of that year, still summer in Los Angeles) an angioplasty was done. The results after two weeks, as demonstrated by an exercise echocardiogram, were said to be "spectacular." Another exercise echo after six months confirmed this success. Thallium scans over the next few years and a subsequent angiogram in 1991 gave the same confirmation. I recall that John and I took different views of what had happened in 1987. As he saw it, he now had a death sentence, temporarily suspended. He often said, after the 1987 angioplasty, that he now knew how he was going to die. As I saw it, the timing had been providential, the intervention successful, the problem solved, the mechanism fixed. You no more know how you're going to die than I do or anyone else does, I remember saying. I realize now that his was the more realistic view.

13

I used to tell John my dreams, not to understand them but to get rid of them, clear my mind for the day. "Don't tell me your dream," he would say when I woke in the morning, but in the end he would listen.

When he died I stopped having dreams.

In the early summer I began to dream again, for the first time since it happened. Since I can no longer pass them off to John I find myself thinking about them. I remember a passage from a novel I wrote in the mid-1990s, *The Last Thing He Wanted:*

> Of course we would not need those last six notes to know what Elena's dreams were about.
>
> Elena's dreams were about dying.
>
> Elena's dreams were about getting old.
>
> Nobody here has not had (will not have) Elena's dreams.
>
> We all know that.
>
> The point is that Elena didn't.
>
> The point is that Elena remained remote most of all to herself, a clandestine agent who had so successfully compartmentalized her operation as to have lost access to her own cutouts.

I realize that Elena's situation is my own.

In one dream I am hanging a braided belt in a closet when it breaks. About a third of the belt just drops off in my hands. I show the two pieces to John. I say (or he says, who knows in dreams) that this was his favorite belt. I determine (again, I think I determine, I should have determined, my half-waking mind tells me to do the right thing) to find him an identical braided belt.

In other words to fix what I broke, *bring him back*.

The similarity of this broken braided belt to the one I found in the plastic bag I was given at New York Hospital does not escape my attention. Nor does the fact that I am still thinking *I broke it, I did it, I am responsible.*

In another dream John and I are flying to Honolulu. Many other people are going, we have assembled at Santa Monica Airport. Paramount has arranged planes. Production assistants are distributing boarding passes. I board. There is confusion. Others are boarding but there is no sign of John. I worry that there is a problem with his boarding pass. I decide that I should leave the plane, wait for him in the car. While I am waiting in the car I realize that the planes are taking off, one by one. Finally there is no one but me on the tarmac. My first thought in the dream is anger: John has boarded a plane without me. My second thought transfers the anger: Paramount has not cared enough about us to put us on the same plane.

What "Paramount" was doing in this dream would require another discussion, not relevant.

As I think about the dream I remember *Tenko*. *Tenko*, as the series progresses, takes its imprisoned Englishwomen through their liberation from the Japanese camp and their reunions in Singapore with their husbands, which do not go uniformly well. There seemed for some a level at which the husband was held responsible for the ordeal of imprisonment. There seemed a sense, however irrational, of having been abandoned. Did I feel abandoned, left behind on the tarmac, did I feel anger at John for leaving me? Was it possible to feel anger and simultaneously to feel responsible?

I know the answer a psychiatrist would give to that question.

The answer would have to do with the well-known way in which anger creates guilt and vice versa.

I do not disbelieve this answer but it remains less suggestive to me than the unexamined image, the mystery of being left alone on the tarmac at Santa Monica Airport watching the planes take off one by one.

We all know that.
The point is that Elena didn't.

I wake at what seems to be three-thirty in the morning and find a television set on, MSNBC. Either Joe Scarborough or Keith Olbermann is talking to a husband and wife, passengers on a flight from Detroit to Los Angeles, "Northwest 327" (I actually write this down, to tell to John), on which "a terrorist tryout" is said to have occurred. The incident seems to have involved fourteen men said to be "Arabs" who, at some point after takeoff from Detroit, began gathering outside the coach lavatory, entering one by one.

The couple now being interviewed on-screen reports having exchanged signals with the crew.

The plane landed in Los Angeles. The "Arabs," all fourteen of whom had "expired visas" (this seemed to strike MSNBC as more unusual than it struck me), were detained, then released. Everyone, including the couple on-screen, had gone about their day. It was not, then, "a terrorist attack," which seemed to be what made it "a terrorist tryout."

I need in the dream to discuss this with John.

Or was it even a dream?

Who is the director of dreams, would he care?

Was it only by dreaming or writing that I could find out what I thought?

When the twilights got long in June I forced myself to eat dinner in the living room, where the light was. After John died I had begun eating by myself in the kitchen (the dining room was too big and the table in the living room was where he had died), but when the long twilights came I had a strong sense that he would want me to see the light. As the twilights began to shorten I retreated again to the kitchen. I began spending more evenings alone at home. I was working, I would say. By the time August came I was in fact working, or trying to work, but I also wanted not to be out, exposed. One night I found myself taking from the cupboard not one of the plates I normally used but a crackled and worn Spode plate, from a set mostly broken or chipped, in a pattern no longer made, "Wickerdale." This had been a set of dishes, cream with a garland of small rose and blue flowers and ecru leaves, that John's mother had given him for the apartment he rented on East Seventy-third Street before we were married. John's mother was dead. John was dead. And I still had, of the "Wickerdale" Spode, four dinner plates, five salad plates, three butter plates, a single coffee cup, and nine saucers. I came to prefer these dishes to all others. By the end of the summer I was running the dishwasher a quarter full just to make sure that at least one of the four "Wickerdale" dinner plates would be clean when I needed it.

At a point during the summer it occurred to me that I had no letters from John, not one. We had only rarely been far or long apart. There had been the week or two or three here and there when one of us was doing a piece. There had been a month in 1975 when I taught at Berkeley during the week and flew home to Los Angeles on PSA every weekend. There had been a few weeks in 1988 when John was in Ireland doing research for *Harp* and I was in California covering the presidential primary. On all such occasions we had spoken on the telephone several times a day. We counted high telephone bills as part of our deal with each other, the same way we counted high bills for the hotels that enabled us to take Quintana out of school and fly somewhere and both work at the same time in the same suite. What I had instead of letters was a souvenir of one such hotel suite: a small black wafer-thin alarm clock he gave me one Christmas in Honolulu when we were doing a crash rewrite on a picture that never got made. It was one of those many Christmases on which we exchanged not "presents" but small practical things to make a tree. This alarm clock had stopped working during the year before he died, could not be repaired, and, after he died, could not be thrown out. It could not even be removed from the table by my bed. I also had a set of colored Buffalo pens, given to me the same Christmas, in the same spirit. I did many sketches of palm trees that Christmas, palm trees moving in the wind, palm trees dropping fronds, palm trees bent by the December *kona* storms. The colored Buffalo pens had long since gone dry, but, again, could not be thrown out.

I remember having had on that particular New Year's Eve in Honolulu a sense of well-being so profound that I did not want to go to sleep. We had ordered mahimahi and Manoa lettuce vinaigrette for the three of us from room service. We had tried for a festive effect by arranging leis over the printers and computers we were using for the rewrite. We had found candles and lit them and played the tapes Quintana had wrapped up to put under the tree. John had been reading on the bed and had fallen asleep about eleven-thirty. Quintana had gone downstairs to see what was happening. I could see John sleeping. I knew Quintana was safe, she had been going downstairs to see what was happening in this hotel (sometimes alone, sometimes with Susan Traylor, who often came along with Quintana when we were working in Honolulu) since she was six or seven years old. I sat on a balcony overlooking the Waialae Country Club golf course and finished the bottle of wine we had drunk with dinner and watched the neighborhood fireworks all over Honolulu.

I remember one last present from John. It was my birthday, December 5, 2003. Snow had begun falling in New York around ten that morning and by evening seven inches had accumulated, with another six due. I remember snow avalanching off the slate roof at St. James' Church across the street. A plan to meet Quintana and Gerry at a restaurant was canceled. Before dinner John sat by the fire in the living room and read to me out loud. The book from which he read was a novel of my own, *A Book of Common Prayer*, which he happened to have in the living room because he was re-reading it to see how something worked technically. The sequence he read out loud was one in which Charlotte Douglas's husband Leonard pays a visit to the narrator, Grace Strasser-Mendana, and lets her know that what is happening in the country her family runs will not end well. The sequence is complicated (this was in fact the sequence John had meant to re-read to see how it worked technically), broken by other action and requiring the reader to pick up the undertext in what Leonard Douglas and Grace Strasser-Mendana say to each other. "Goddamn," John said to me when he closed the book. "Don't ever tell me again you can't write. That's my birthday present to you."

I remember tears coming to my eyes.

I feel them now.

In retrospect this had been my omen, my message, the early snowfall, the birthday present no one else could give me.

He had twenty-five nights left to live.

14

There came a time in the summer when I began feeling fragile, unstable. A sandal would catch on a sidewalk and I would need to run a few steps to avoid the fall. What if I didn't? What if I fell? What would break, who would see the blood streaming down my leg, who would get the taxi, who would be with me in the emergency room? Who would be with me once I came home?

I stopped wearing sandals. I bought two pairs of Puma sneakers and wore them exclusively.

I started leaving lights on through the night. If the house was dark I could not get up to make a note or look for a book or check to make sure I had turned off the stove. If the house was dark I would lie there immobilized, entertaining visions of household peril, the books that could slide from the shelf and knock me down, the rug that could slip in the hallway, the washing machine hose that could have flooded the kitchen unseen in the dark, the better to electrocute whoever turned on a light to check the stove. That this was something more than prudent caution first came to my attention one afternoon when an acquaintance, a young writer, came by to ask if he could write a profile about me. I heard myself say, too urgent, that I could not possibly be written about. I was in no shape to be written about. I heard myself overstressing this, fighting to regain balance, avert the fall.

I thought about this later.

I realized that for the time being I could not trust myself to present a coherent face to the world.

Some days later I was stacking some copies of *Daedalus* that were lying around the house. Stacking magazines seemed at that point the limit of what I could do by way of organizing my life. Careful not to push this limit too far, I opened one of the copies of *Daedalus*. There was a story by Roxana Robinson, called "Blind Man." In this story, a man is driving in the rain at night to deliver a lecture. The reader picks up danger signals: the man cannot immediately recall the subject of his lecture, he takes his small rented car into the fast lane oblivious to an approaching SUV; there are references to someone, "Juliet," to whom something troubling has happened. Gradually we learn that Juliet was the man's daughter, who, on her first night alone after a college suspension and rehab and a restorative few weeks in the country with her mother and father and sister, had done enough cocaine to burst an artery in her brain and die.

One of the several levels on which the story disturbed me (the most obvious being the burst artery in the child's brain) was this: the father has been rendered fragile, unstable. The father is me.

In fact I know Roxana Robinson slightly. I think of calling her. She knows something I am just beginning to learn. But it would be unusual, intrusive, to call her: I have met her only once, at a cocktail party on a roof. Instead I think about people I know who have lost a husband or wife or child. I think particularly about how these people looked when I saw them unexpectedly—on the street, say, or entering a room—during the year or so after the death. What struck me in each instance was how exposed they seemed, how raw.

How fragile, I understand now.

How unstable.

I open another issue of *Daedalus*, this one devoted to the concept of "happiness." One piece on happiness, the joint work of Robert Biswas-Diener of the University of Oregon and Ed Diener and Maya Tamir of the University of Illinois, Champaign-Urbana, noted that although "research has shown that people can adapt to a wide range of good and bad life events in less than two months," there remained "some events to which people are slow or unable to adapt completely." Unemployment was one such event. "We also find," the authors added, "that it takes the average widow many years after her spouse's death to regain her former level of life satisfaction."

Was I "the average widow"? What in fact would have been my "former level of life satisfaction"?

I see a doctor, a routine follow-up. He asks how I am. This should not be, in a doctor's office, an unforeseeable question. Yet I find myself in sudden tears. This doctor is a friend. John and I went to his wedding. He married the daughter of friends who lived across the street from us in Brentwood Park. The ceremony took place under their jacaranda tree. In the first days after John died this doctor had come by the house. When Quintana was at Beth Israel North he had gone up with me on a Sunday afternoon and talked to the doctors on the unit. When Quintana was at Columbia-Presbyterian, his own hospital although she was not his patient, he had stopped in to see her every evening. When Quintana was at UCLA and he happened to be in California he had taken an afternoon to come by the neuroscience unit and talk to the doctors there. He had talked to them and then he had talked to the neuro people at Columbia and then he had explained it all to me. He had been kind, helpful, encouraging, a true friend. In return I was crying in his office because he asked how I was.

"I just can't see the upside in this," I heard myself say by way of explanation.

Later he said that if John had been sitting in the office he would have found this funny, as he himself had found it. "Of course I knew what you meant to say, and John would have known too, you meant to say you couldn't see the light at the end of the tunnel."

I agreed, but this was not in fact the case.

I had meant pretty much exactly what I said: I couldn't see the upside in this.

As I thought about the difference between the two sentences I realized that my impression of myself had been of someone who could look for, and find, the upside in any situation. I had believed in the logic of popular songs. I had looked for the silver lining. I had walked on through the storm. It occurs to me now that these were not even the songs of my generation. They were the songs, and the logic, of the generation or two that preceded my own. The score for my generation was Les Paul and Mary

Ford, "How High the Moon," a different logic altogether. It also occurs to me, not an original thought but novel to me, that the logic of those earlier songs was based on self-pity. The singer of the song about looking for the silver lining believes that clouds have come her way. The singer of the song about walking on through the storm assumes that the storm could otherwise take her down.

I kept saying to myself that I had been lucky all my life. The point, as I saw it, was that this gave me no right to think of myself as unlucky now.

This was what passed for staying on top of the self-pity question.

I even believed it.

Only at a later point did I begin to wonder: what exactly did "luck" have to do with it? I could not on examination locate any actual instances of "luck" in my history. ("That was lucky," I once said to a doctor after a test revealed a soluble problem that would have been, untreated, less soluble. "I wouldn't call it lucky," she said, "I'd call it the game plan.") Nor did I believe that "bad luck" had killed John and struck Quintana. Once when she was still at the Westlake School for Girls, Quintana mentioned what she seemed to consider the inequable distribution of bad news. In the ninth grade she had come home from a retreat at Yosemite to learn that her uncle Stephen had committed suicide. In the eleventh grade she had been woken at Susan's at six-thirty in the morning to learn that Dominique had been murdered. "Most people I know at Westlake don't even know anyone who died," she said, "and just since I've been there I've had a murder and a suicide in my family."

"It all evens out in the end," John said, an answer that bewildered me (what did it mean, couldn't he do better than that?) but one that seemed to satisfy her.

Several years later, after Susan's mother and father died within a year or two of each other, Susan asked if I remembered John telling Quintana that it all evened out in the end. I said I remembered.

"He was right," Susan said. "It did."

I recall being shocked. It had never occurred to me that John meant that bad news will come to each of us. Either Susan or Quintana had surely misunderstood. I explained to Susan that John had meant something entirely different: he had meant that people who get bad news will eventually get their share of good news.

"That's not what I meant at all," John said.

"I knew what he meant," Susan said.

Had I understood nothing?

Consider this matter of "luck."

Not only did I not believe that "bad luck" had killed John and struck Quintana but in fact I believed precisely the opposite: I believed that I should have been able to prevent whatever happened. Only after the dream about being left on the tarmac at the Santa Monica Airport did it occur to me that there was a level on which I was not actually holding myself responsible. I was holding John and Quintana responsible, a significant difference but not one that took me anywhere I needed to be. *For once in your life just let it go.*

15

A few months after John died, in the late winter of 2004, after Beth Israel and Presbyterian but before UCLA, I was asked by Robert Silvers at *The New York Review of Books* if I wanted him to submit my name for credentials to cover the Democratic and Republican summer conventions. I had looked at the dates: late July in Boston for the Democratic convention, the week before Labor Day in New York for the Republican convention. I had said yes. At the time it had seemed a way of committing to a normal life without needing actually to live it for another season or two, until spring had come and summer had come and fall was near.

Spring had come and gone, largely at UCLA.

In the middle of July Quintana was discharged from the Rusk Institute.

Ten days later I went to Boston for the Democratic convention. I had not anticipated that my new fragility would travel to Boston, a city devoid, I thought, of potentially tricky associations. I had been with Quintana in Boston only once, on a book tour. We had stayed at the Ritz. Her favorite stop on this tour had been Dallas. She had found Boston "all white." "You mean you didn't see many black people in Boston," Susan Traylor's mother had said when Quintana got back to Malibu and reported on her trip. "No," Quintana had said. "I mean it's not in color." The last several times I had needed to be in Boston I had gone alone, and in each case arranged the day so as to get the last shuttle back; the single time I could remember being there with John was for a preview of *True Confessions*, and all I remembered of that was having lunch at the Ritz and walking with John to Brooks Brothers to pick up a shirt and hearing, after the picture was shown and the response evaluated, this disheartening assessment of its commercial prospects:

True Confessions could do very well, the market researcher said, among adults with sixteen-plus years of education.

I would not be staying at the Ritz.

There would be no need to go to Brooks Brothers.

There would be market researchers, but what bad news they delivered would not be mine.

I did not realize that there was still room for error until I was walking to the Fleet Center for the opening of the convention and found myself in tears. The first day of the Democratic convention was July 26, 2004. The day of Quintana's wedding had been July 26, 2003. Even as I waited in the security line, even as I picked up releases in the press center, even as I located my seat and stood for the national anthem, even as I bought a hamburger at the McDonald's in the Fleet Center and sat on the lowest step of a barricaded stairway to eat it, the details sprang back. "In another world" was the phrase that would not leave my mind. Quintana sitting in the sunlight in the living room having her hair braided. John asking me which of two ties I preferred. Opening the boxes of flowers on the grass outside the cathedral and shaking the water off the leis. John giving a toast before Quintana cut the cake. The pleasure he took in the day and the party and her transparent happiness. "More than one more day," he had whispered to her before he walked her to the altar.

"More than one more day," he had whispered to her on the five days and nights he saw her in the Beth Israel North ICU.

"More than one more day," I had whispered to her in his absence on the days and nights that followed.

As you used to say to me, she had said when she stood in her black dress at St. John the Divine on the day we committed his ashes.

I recall being seized by the overwhelming conviction that I needed to get out of the Fleet Center, now. I have only rarely experienced panic but what set in next was recognizably panic. I remember trying to calm myself by seeing it as a Hitchcock movie, every shot planned to terrify but ultimately artifice, a game. There was the proximity of my assigned section to the netting that held the balloons for the balloon drop. There were the shadowy silhouettes moving on the high catwalks. There was the steam or smoke leaking from a vent over the sky boxes. There were, once I fled my seat, the corridors that seemed to go nowhere, mysteriously emptied, the walls slanted and distorted (the Hitchcock movie I was seeing would have to be *Spellbound*) ahead of me. There were the immobilized escalators. There were the elevators that did not respond to the push of the button. There were, once I managed to get downstairs, the empty commuter trains frozen in place beyond the locked glass wall (again, slanted and distorted as I approached it) that opened to the North Station tracks.

I got out of the Fleet Center.

I watched the end of that night's session on television in my room at the Parker House. There had seemed about this room at the Parker House when I first walked into it the day before something déjà vu, which I had put from my mind. Only now, as I was watching C-SPAN and listening to the air conditioner cycle on and off on its own schedule, did I remember: I had stayed in just such a room at the Parker House for a few nights between my junior and senior years at Berkeley. I had been in New York for a college promotion *Mademoiselle* then ran (the "Guest Editor" program, memorialized by Sylvia Plath in *The Bell Jar*) and was returning to California via Boston and Quebec, an "educational" itinerary arranged, in retrospect dreamily, by my mother. The air conditioner had been cycling on and off on its own schedule even in 1955. I could remember sleeping until afternoon, miserable, then taking a subway to Cambridge, where I must have walked around aimlessly and taken the subway back.

These shards from 1955 were coming to me in such shredded (or "spotty," or even "mudgy") form (what did I do in Cambridge, what possibly could I have done in Cambridge?) that I had trouble holding them, but I tried, because for so long as I was thinking about the summer of 1955 I would not be thinking about John or Quintana.

In the summer of 1955 I had taken a train from New York to Boston.

In the summer of 1955 I had taken another train from Boston to Quebec. I stayed in a room at the Château Frontenac that did not have its own bathtub.

Did mothers always try to press on their daughters the itineraries of which they themselves had dreamed?

Did I?

This was not working.

I tried going further back, earlier than 1955, to Sacramento, high school dances at Christmastime. This felt safe. I thought about the way we danced, close. I thought about the places on the river we went after the dances. I thought about the fog on the levee driving home.

I fell asleep maintaining focus on the fog on the levee.

I woke at four a.m. The point about the fog on the levee was that you couldn't see the white line, someone had to walk ahead to guide the driver. Unfortunately there had been another place in my life where the fog got so thick that I had to walk ahead of the car.

The house on the Palos Verdes Peninsula.

The one to which we brought Quintana when she was three days old.

When you came off the Harbor Freeway and through San Pedro and onto the drive above the sea you hit the fog.

You (I) got out of the car to walk the white line.

The driver of the car was John.

I did not risk waiting for the panic to follow. I got a taxi to Logan. I avoided looking, as I bought a coffee at the Starbucks franchise outside the Delta shuttle, at its decorative garland of red-white-and-blue foil strips, presumably conceived as a festive "convention" touch but instead glittering forlornly, Christmas in the tropics. *Mele Kalikimaka.* Merry Christmas in Hawaiian. The little black alarm clock I could not throw away. The dried-out Buffalo pens I could not throw away. On the flight to LaGuardia I remember thinking that the most beautiful things I had ever seen had all been seen from airplanes. The way the American west opens up. The way in which, on a polar flight across the Arctic, the islands in the sea give way imperceptibly to lakes on the land. The sea between Greece and Cyprus in the morning. The Alps on the way to Milan. I saw all those things with John.

How could I go back to Paris without him, how could I go back to Milan, Honolulu, Bogotá?

I couldn't even go to Boston.

A week or so before the Democratic convention, Dennis Overbye of *The New York Times* had reported a story involving Stephen W. Hawking. At a conference in Dublin, according to the *Times*, Dr. Hawking said that he had been wrong thirty years before when he asserted that information swallowed by a black hole could never be retrieved from it. This change of mind was "of great consequence to science," according to the *Times*, "because if Dr. Hawking had been right, it would have violated a basic tenet of modern physics: that it is always possible to reverse time, run the proverbial film backward and reconstruct what happened in, say, the collision of two cars or the collapse of a dead star into a black hole."

I had clipped this story, and carried it with me to Boston.

Something in the story seemed urgent to me, but I did not know what it was until a month later, the first afternoon of the Republican convention in Madison Square Garden. I was on the Tower C escalator. The last time I had been on such an escalator in the Garden was with John, in November, the night before we flew to Paris. We had gone with David and Jean Halberstam to see the Lakers play the Knicks. David had gotten seats through the commissioner of the NBA, David Stern. The Lakers won. Rain had been sluicing down the glass beyond the escalator. "It's good luck, an omen, a great way to start this trip," I remembered John saying. He did not mean the good seats and he did not mean the Laker win and he did not mean the rain, he meant we were doing something we did not ordinarily do, which had become an issue with him. We were not having any fun, he had recently begun pointing out. I would take exception (didn't we do this, didn't we do that) but I had also known what he meant. He meant doing things not because we were expected to do them or had always done them or should do them but because we wanted to do them. He meant wanting. He meant living.

This trip to Paris was the one over which we had fought.

This trip to Paris was the one he said he needed to take because otherwise he would never see Paris again.

I was still on the Tower C escalator.

Another vortex revealed itself.

The last time I covered a convention at Madison Square Garden had been 1992, the Democratic convention.

John would wait until I came uptown at eleven or so to have dinner with me. We would walk to Coco Pazzo on those hot July nights and split an order of pasta and a salad at one of the little unreserved tables in the bar. I do not think we ever discussed the convention during these late dinners. On the Sunday afternoon before it began I had talked him into going uptown with me to a Louis Farrakhan event that never materialized, and between the improvisational nature of the scheduling and the walk back downtown from 125th Street his tolerance for the 1992 Democratic convention was pretty much exhausted.

Still.

He waited every night to eat with me.

I thought about all this on the Tower C escalator and suddenly it occurred to me: I had spent a minute or two on this escalator thinking about the November night in 2003 before we flew to Paris and about those July nights in 1992 when we would eat late at Coco Pazzo and about the afternoon we had stood around 125th Street waiting for the Louis Farrakhan event that never happened. I had stood on this escalator thinking about those days and nights without once thinking I could change their outcome. I realized that since the last morning of 2003, the morning after he died, I had been trying to reverse time, run the film backward.

It was now eight months later, August 30, 2004, and I still was.

The difference was that all through those eight months I had been trying to substitute an alternate reel. Now I was trying only to reconstruct the collision, the collapse of the dead star.

16

I said I knew what John meant when he said we were not having any fun.

What he meant was something that had to do with Joe and Gertrude Black, a couple we had met in Indonesia in December 1980. We were there on a USIA trip, giving lectures and meeting Indonesian writers and academics. The Blacks had shown up in a classroom one morning at Gadjah Mada University in Jogjakarta, an American couple apparently at home in the remote and in many ways alien tropic of central Java, their faces open and strikingly luminous. "The critical theories of Mr. I. A. Richards," I remember a student asking me that morning. "What think?" Joe Black was then in his fifties, Gertrude a year or two younger but again, I suppose in her fifties. He had retired from the Rockefeller Foundation and come to Jogjakarta to teach political science at Gadjah Mada. He had grown up in Utah. As a young man he had been an extra in John Ford's *Fort Apache*. He and Gertrude had four children, one of whom had been, he said, hit hard by the 1960s. We talked to the Blacks only twice, once at Gadjah Mada and a day later at the airport, when they came to see us off, but each of these conversations was curiously open, as if we had found ourselves stranded together on an island. Over the years John mentioned Joe and Gertrude Black frequently, in each case as exemplary, what he thought of as the best kind of American. They represented something personal to him. They were models for the life he wanted us eventually to live. Because he had mentioned them again a few days before he died I searched his computer for their names. I found the names in a file called "AAA Random Thoughts," one of the files in which he kept notes for the book he was trying to get off the ground. The note after their names was cryptic: "Joe and Gertrude Black: The concept of service."

I knew what he meant by that too.

He had wanted to be Joe and Gertrude Black. So had I. We hadn't made it. "Fritter away" was a definition in the crossword that morning. The word it defined was five letters, "waste." Was that what we had done? Was that what he thought we had done?

Why didn't I listen when he said we weren't having any fun?

Why didn't I move to change our life?

According to the computer dating the file called "AAA Random Thoughts" was last amended at 1:08 p.m. on December 30, 2003, the day of his death, six minutes after I saved the file that ended *how does "flu" morph into whole-body infection*. He would have been in his office and I would have been in mine. I cannot stop where this leads me. We should have been together. Not necessarily in a classroom in central Java (I do not have a sufficiently deluded view of either of us to see that scenario intact, nor was a classroom in central Java what he meant) but together. The file called "AAA Random Thoughts" was eighty pages long. What it was he added or amended and saved at 1:08 p.m. that afternoon I have no way of knowing.

17

Grief turns out to be a place none of us know until we reach it. We anticipate (we know) that someone close to us could die, but we do not look beyond the few days or weeks that immediately follow such an imagined death. We misconstrue the nature of even those few days or weeks. We might expect if the death is sudden to feel shock. We do not expect this shock to be obliterative, dislocating to both body and mind. We might expect that we will be prostrate, inconsolable, crazy with loss. We do not expect to be literally crazy, cool customers who believe that their husband is about to return and need his shoes. In the version of grief we imagine, the model will be "healing." A certain forward movement will prevail. The worst days will be the earliest days. We imagine that the moment to most severely test us will be the funeral, after which this hypothetical healing will take place. When we anticipate the funeral we wonder about failing to "get through it," rise to the occasion, exhibit the "strength" that invariably gets mentioned as the correct response to death. We anticipate needing to steel ourselves for the moment: will I be able to greet people, will I be able to leave the scene, will I be able even to get dressed that day? We have no way of knowing that this will not be the issue. We have no way of knowing that the funeral itself will be anodyne, a kind of narcotic regression in which we are wrapped in the care of others and the gravity and meaning of the occasion. Nor can we know ahead of the fact (and here lies the heart of the difference between grief as we imagine it and grief as it is) the unending absence that follows, the void, the very opposite of meaning, the relentless succession of moments during which we will confront the experience of meaninglessness itself.

*

As a child I thought a great deal about meaninglessness, which seemed at the time the most prominent negative feature on the horizon. After a few years of failing to find meaning in the more commonly recommended venues I learned that I could find it in geology, so I did. This in turn enabled me to find meaning in the Episcopal litany, most acutely in the words *as it was in the beginning, is now and ever shall be, world without end*, which I interpreted as a literal description of the constant changing of the earth, the unending erosion of the shores and mountains, the inexorable shifting of the geological structures that could throw up mountains and islands and could just as reliably take them away. I found earthquakes, even when I was in them, deeply satisfying, abruptly revealed evidence of the scheme in action. That the scheme could destroy the works of man might be a personal regret but remained, in the larger picture I had come to recognize, a matter of abiding indifference. No eye was on the sparrow. No one was watching me. *As it was in the beginning, is now and ever shall be, world without end.* On the day it was announced that the atomic bomb had been dropped on Hiroshima those were the words that came immediately to my ten-year-old mind. When I heard a few years later about mushroom clouds over the Nevada test site those were again the words that came to mind. I began waking before dawn, imagining that the fireballs from the Nevada test shots would light up the sky in Sacramento.

Later, after I married and had a child, I learned to find equal meaning in the repeated rituals of domestic life. Setting the table. Lighting the candles. Building the fire. Cooking. All those soufflés, all that crème caramel, all those daubes and albóndigas and gumbos. Clean sheets, stacks of clean towels, hurricane lamps for storms, enough water and food to see us through whatever geological event came our way. *These fragments I have shored against my ruins*, were the words that came to mind then. These fragments mattered to me. I believed in them. That I could find meaning in the intensely personal nature of my life as a wife and mother did not seem inconsistent with finding meaning in the vast indifference of geology and the test shots; the two systems existed for me on parallel tracks that occasionally converged, notably during earthquakes. In my unexamined mind there was always a point, John's and my death, at which the tracks would converge for a final time. On the Internet I recently found aerial photographs of the house on the Palos Verdes Peninsula in which we had lived when we were first married, the house to which we had brought Quintana home from St. John's Hospital in Santa Monica and put her in her bassinet by the wisteria in the box garden. The photographs, part of the California Coastal Records Project, the point of which was to document the entire California coastline, were hard to read conclusively, but the house as it had been when we lived in it appeared to be gone. The tower where the gate had been seemed intact but the rest of the structure looked unfamiliar. There seemed to be a swimming pool where the wisteria and box garden had been. The area itself was identified as "Portuguese Bend landslide." You could see the slumping of the hill where the slide had occurred. You could also see, at the base of the cliff on the point, the cave into which we used to swim when the tide was at exactly the right flow.

The swell of clear water.

That was one way my two systems could have converged.

We could have been swimming into the cave with the swell of clear water and the entire point could have slumped, slipped into the sea around us. The entire point slipping into the sea around us was the kind of conclusion I anticipated. I did not anticipate cardiac arrest at the dinner table.

You sit down to dinner and life as you know it ends.

The question of self-pity.

People in grief think a great deal about self-pity. We worry it, dread it, scourge our thinking for signs of it. We fear that our actions will reveal the condition tellingly described as "dwelling on it." We understand the aversion most of us have to "dwelling on it." Visible mourning reminds us of death, which is construed as unnatural, a failure to manage the situation. "A single person is missing for you, and the whole world is empty," Philippe Ariès wrote to the point of this aversion in

Western Attitudes toward Death. "But one no longer has the right to say so aloud." We remind ourselves repeatedly that our own loss is nothing compared to the loss experienced (or, the even worse thought, not experienced) by he or she who died; this attempt at corrective thinking serves only to plunge us deeper into the self-regarding deep. (*Why didn't I see that, why am I so selfish.*) The very language we use when we think about self-pity betrays the deep abhorrence in which we hold it: self-pity is *feeling sorry for yourself*, self-pity is *thumb-sucking*, self-pity is *boo hoo poor me*, self-pity is the condition in which those feeling sorry for themselves *indulge*, or even *wallow*. Self-pity remains both the most common and the most universally reviled of our character defects, its pestilential destructiveness accepted as given. "Our worst enemy," Helen Keller called it. *I never saw a wild thing / sorry for itself*, D. H. Lawrence wrote, in a much-quoted four-line homily that turns out on examination to be free of any but tendentious meaning. *A small bird will drop frozen dead from a bough / without ever having felt sorry for itself.*

This may be what Lawrence (or we) would prefer to believe about wild things, but consider those dolphins who refuse to eat after the death of a mate. Consider those geese who search for the lost mate until they themselves become disoriented and die. In fact the grieving have urgent reasons, even an urgent need, to feel sorry for themselves. Husbands walk out, wives walk out, divorces happen, but these husbands and wives leave behind them webs of intact associations, however acrimonious. Only the survivors of a death are truly left alone. The connections that made up their life—both the deep connections and the apparently (until they are broken) insignificant connections—have all vanished. John and I were married for forty years. During all but the first five months of our marriage, when John was still working at *Time*, we both worked at home. We were together twenty-four hours a day, a fact that remained a source of both merriment and foreboding to my mother and aunts. "For richer for poorer but never for lunch," one or another of them frequently said in the early years of our marriage. I could not count the times during the average day when something would come up that I needed to tell him. This impulse did not end with his death. What ended was the possibility of response. I read something in the paper that I would normally have read to him. I notice some change in the neighborhood that would interest him: Ralph Lauren has expanded into more space between Seventy-first and Seventy-second Streets, say, or the empty space where the Madison Avenue Bookshop used to be has finally been leased. I recall coming in from Central Park one morning in mid-August with urgent news to report: the deep summer green has faded overnight from the trees, the season is already changing. *We need to make a plan for the fall*, I remember thinking. *We need to decide where we want to be at Thanksgiving, Christmas, the end of the year.*

I am dropping my keys on the table inside the door before I fully remember. There is no one to hear this news, nowhere to go with the unmade plan, the uncompleted thought. There is no one to agree, disagree, talk back. "I think I am beginning to understand why grief feels like suspense," C. S. Lewis wrote after the death of his wife. "It comes from the frustration of so many impulses that had become habitual. Thought after thought, feeling after feeling, action after action, had H. for their object. Now their target is gone. I keep on through habit fitting an arrow to the string, then I remember and have to lay the bow down. So many roads lead thought to H. I set out on one of them. But now there's an impassable frontierpost across it. So many roads once; now so many cul de sacs."

We are repeatedly left, in other words, with no further focus than ourselves, a source from which self-pity naturally flows. Each time this happens (it happens still) I am struck again by the permanent impassibility of the divide. Some people who have lost a husband or wife report feeling that person's presence, receiving that person's advice. Some report actual sightings, what Freud described in "Mourning and Melancholia" as "a clinging to the object through the medium of a hallucinatory wishful psychosis." Others describe not a visible apparition but just a "very strongly felt presence." I experienced neither. There have been a few occasions (the day they wanted to do the trach at UCLA, for example) on which I asked John point blank what to do. I said I needed his help. I said I could not do this alone. I said these things out loud, actually vocalized the words.

I am a writer. Imagining what someone would say or do comes to me as naturally as breathing.

Yet on each occasion these pleas for his presence served only to reinforce my awareness of the final silence that separated us. Any answer he gave could exist only in my imagination, my edit. For me to imagine what he could say only in my edit would seem obscene, a violation. I could no more know what he would say about UCLA and the trach than I could know whether he meant to leave the "to" out of the sentence about J.J. McClure and Teresa Kean and the tornado. We imagined we knew everything the other thought, even when we did not necessarily want to know it, but in fact, I have come to see, we knew not the smallest fraction of what there was to know.

When something happens to me, he would frequently say.

Nothing will happen to you, I would say.

But if it does.

If it does, he would continue. If it did, for example, I was not to move to a smaller apartment. If it did I would be surrounded by people. If it did I would need to make plans to feed these people. If it did I would marry again within the year.

You don't understand, I would say.

And in fact he did not. Nor did I: we were equally incapable of imagining the reality of life without the other. This will not be a story in which the death of the husband or wife becomes what amounts to the credit sequence for a new life, a catalyst for the discovery that (a point typically introduced in such accounts by the precocious child of the bereaved) "you can love more than one person." Of course you can, but marriage is something different. Marriage is memory, marriage is time. "She didn't know the songs," I recall being told that a friend of a friend had said after an attempt to repeat the experience. Marriage is not only time: it is also, parodoxically, the denial of time. For forty years I saw myself through John's eyes. I did not age. This year for the first time since I was twenty-nine I saw myself through the eyes of others. This year for the first time since I was twenty-nine I realized that my image of myself was of someone significantly younger. This year I realized that one reason I was so often sideswiped by memories of Quintana at three was this: when Quintana was three I was thirty-four. I remember Gerard Manley Hopkins: *Margaret, are you grieving / Over Goldengrove unleaving?* and *It is the blight man was born for, / It is Margaret you mourn for.*

It is the blight *man* was born for.

We are not idealized wild things.

We are imperfect mortal beings, aware of that mortality even as we push it away, failed by our very complication, so wired that when we mourn our losses we also mourn, for better or for worse, ourselves. As we were. As we are no longer. As we will one day not be at all.

Elena's dreams were about dying.

Elena's dreams were about getting old.

Nobody here has not had (will not have) Elena's dreams.

Time is the school in which we learn, / Time is the fire in which we burn: Delmore Schwartz again.

I remember despising the book Dylan Thomas's widow Caitlin wrote after her husband's death, *Leftover Life to Kill*. I remember being dismissive of, even censorious about, her "self-pity," her "whining," her "dwelling on it." *Leftover Life to Kill* was published in 1957. I was twenty-two years old. Time is the school in which we learn.

18

At the time I began writing these pages, in October 2004, I still did not understand how or why or when John died. I had been there. I had watched while the EMS team tried to bring him back. I still did not know how or why or when. In early December 2004, almost a year after he died, I finally received the autopsy report and emergency room records I had first requested from New York Hospital on the fourteenth of January, two weeks after it happened and one day before I told Quintana that it had happened. One reason it took eleven months to receive these records, I realized when I looked at them, was that I myself had written the wrong address on the hospital's request form. I had at that time lived at the same address on the same street on the Upper East Side of Manhattan for sixteen years. Yet the address I had given the hospital was on another street altogether, where John and I had lived for the five months immediately following our wedding in 1964.

A doctor to whom I mentioned this shrugged, as if I had told him a familiar story.

Either he said that such "cognitive deficits" could be associated with stress or he said that such cognitive deficits could be associated with grief.

It was a mark of those cognitive deficits that within seconds after he said it I had no idea which he had said.

According to the hospital's Emergency Department Nursing Documentation Sheet, the Emergency Medical Services call was received at 9:15 p.m. on the evening of December 30, 2003.

According to the log kept by the doormen the ambulance arrived five minutes later, at 9:20 p.m. During the next forty-five minutes, according to the Nursing Documentation Sheet, the following medications were given, by either direct injection or IV infusion: atropine (times three), epinephrine (times three), vasopressin (40 units), amiodarone (300 mg), high-dose epinephrine (3 mg), and high-dose epinephrine again (5 mg). According to the same documentation the patient was intubated at the scene. I have no memory of an intubation. This may be an error on the part of whoever did the documentation, or it may be another cognitive deficit.

According to the log kept by the doormen the ambulance left for the hospital at 10:05 p.m.

According to the Emergency Department Nursing Documentation Sheet the patient was received for triage at 10:10 p.m. He was described as asystolic and apneic. There was no palpable pulse. There was no pulse via sonography. The mental status was unresponsive. The skin color was pale. The Glasgow Coma Scale rating was 3, the lowest rating possible, indicating that eye, verbal, and motor responses were all absent. Lacerations were seen on the right forehead and the bridge of the nose. Both pupils were fixed and dilated. "Lividity" was noted.

According to the Emergency Department Physician's Record the patient was seen at 10:15 p.m. The physician's notation ended: "Cardiac arrest. DOA—likely massive M.I. Pronounced 10:18 p.m."

According to the Nursing Flow Chart the IV was removed and the patient extubated at 10:20 p.m. At 10:30 p.m. the notation was "wife at bedside—George, soc. worker, at bedside with wife."

According to the autopsy report, examination showed a greater than 95 percent stenosis of both the left main and the left anterior descending arteries. Examination also showed "slight myocardial pallor on TCC staining, indicative of acute infarct in distribution of left anterior descending artery."

I read this paperwork several times. The elapsed time indicated that the time spent at New York Hospital had been, as I had thought, just bookkeeping, hospital procedure, the regularization of a death. Yet each time I read the official sheets I noticed a new detail. On my first reading of the Emergency Department Physician's Record I had not for example registered the letters "DOA." On my first reading of the Emergency Department Physician's Record I was presumably still assimilating the Emergency Department Nursing Documentation Sheet.

"Fixed and dilated" pupils. FDPs.

Sherwin Nuland: "The tenacious young men and women see their patient's pupils become unresponsive to light and then widen until they are large fixed circles of impenetrable blackness. Reluctantly the team stops its efforts. . . . The room is strewn with the debris of the lost campaign . . ."

Fixed circles of impenetrable blackness.

Yes. That was what the ambulance crew saw in John's eyes on our living room floor.

"Lividity." Post-mortem lividity.

I knew what "lividity" meant because it is an issue in morgues. Detectives point it out. It can be a way of determining time of death. After circulation stops, blood follows the course of gravity, pooling wherever the body is resting. There is a certain amount of time before this pooled blood becomes visible to the eye. What I could not remember was what that amount of time was. I looked up "lividity" in the handbook on forensic pathology that John kept on the shelf above his desk. "Although lividity is variable, it normally begins to form immediately after death and is usually clearly perceptible within an hour or two." If lividity was clearly perceptible to the triage nurses by 10:10 p.m., then, it would have started forming an hour before.

An hour before was when I was calling the ambulance.

Which meant he was dead then.

After that instant at the dinner table he was never not dead.

I now know how I'm going to die, he had said in 1987 after the left anterior descending artery had been opened by angioplasty.

You no more know how you're going to die than I do or anyone else does, I had said in 1987.

We call it the widowmaker, pal, his cardiologist in New York had said about the left anterior descending artery.

*

Through the summer and fall I had been increasingly fixed on locating the anomaly that could have allowed this to happen.

In my rational mind I knew how it happened. In my rational mind I had spoken to many doctors who told me how it happened. In my rational mind I had read David J. Callans in *The New England Journal of Medicine:* "Although the majority of cases of sudden death from cardiac causes involve patients with preexisting coronary artery disease, cardiac arrest is the first manifestation of this underlying problem in 50 percent of patients. . . . Sudden cardiac arrest is primarily a problem in patients outside of the hospital; in fact, approximately 80 percent of cases of sudden death from cardiac causes occur at home. The rate of success of resuscitation in patients with out-of-hospital cardiac arrest has been poor, averaging 2 to 5 percent in major urban centers. . . . Resuscitation efforts initiated after eight minutes are almost always doomed to fail." In my rational mind I had read Sherwin Nuland in *How We Die:* "When an arrest occurs elsewhere than the hospital, only 20 to 30 percent survive, and these are almost always those who respond quickly to the CPR. If there has been no response by the time of arrival in the emergency room, the likelihood of survival is virtually zero."

In my rational mind I knew that.

I was not however operating from my rational mind.

Had I been operating from my rational mind I would not have been entertaining fantasies that would not have been out of place at an Irish wake. I would not for example have experienced, when I heard that Julia Child had died, so distinct a relief, so marked a sense that *this was finally working out:* John and Julia Child could have dinner together (this had been my immediate thought), she could cook, he could ask her about the OSS, they would amuse each other, like each other. They had once done a breakfast together, in a season when each was promoting a book. She had inscribed a copy of *The Way to Cook* and given it to him.

I found the copy of *The Way to Cook* in the kitchen and looked at the inscription.

"*Bon appetit* to John Gregory Dunne," it read.

Bon appetit to John Gregory Dunne and Julia Child and the OSS.

Nor, had I been operating from my rational mind, would I have given such close attention to "health" stories on the Internet and pharmaceutical advertising on television. I fretted for example over a Bayer commercial for a low-dose aspirin that was said to "significantly reduce" the risk of a heart attack. I knew perfectly well how aspirin reduces the risk of heart attack: it keeps the blood from clotting. I also knew that John was taking Coumadin, a far more powerful anticoagulant. Yet I was seized nonetheless by the possible folly of having overlooked low-dose aspirin. I fretted similarly over a study done by UC–San Diego and Tufts showing a 4.65 percent increase in cardiac death over the fourteen-day period of Christmas and New Year's. I fretted over a study from Vanderbilt demonstrating that erythromycin quintupled the risk of cardiac arrest if taken in conjunction with common heart medications. I fretted over a study on statins, and the 30 to 40 percent jump in the risk of heart attack for patients who stopped taking them.

As I recall this I realize how open we are to the persistent message that we can avert death.

And to its punitive correlative, the message that if death catches us we have only ourselves to blame.

Only after I read the autopsy report did I begin to believe what I had been repeatedly told: nothing he or I had done or not done had either caused or could have prevented his death. He had inherited a bad heart. It would eventually kill him. The date on which it would kill him had already been, by many medical interventions, postponed. When that date did come, no action I could have taken in our living room—no home defibrillator, no CPR, nothing short of a fully equipped crash cart and the technical facility to follow cardioversion within seconds with IV medication—could have given him even one more day.

The one more day *I love you more than.*

As you used to say to me.

Only after I read the autopsy report did I stop trying to

reconstruct the collision, the collapse of the dead star. The collapse had been there all along, invisible, unsuspected.

Greater than 95 percent stenosis of both the left main and the left anterior descending arteries.

Acute infarct in distribution of left anterior descending artery, the LAD.

That was the scenario. The LAD got fixed in 1987 and it stayed fixed until everybody forgot about it and then it got unfixed. *We call it the widowmaker, pal,* the cardiologist had said in 1987.

I tell you that I shall not live two days, Gawain said.

When something happens to me, John had said.

19

I have trouble thinking of myself as a widow. I remember hesitating the first time I had to check that box on the "marital status" part of a form. I also had trouble thinking of myself as a wife. Given the value I placed on the rituals of domestic life, the concept of "wife" should not have seemed difficult, but it did. For a long time after we were married I had trouble with the ring. It was loose enough to slip off my left ring finger, so for a year or two I wore it on my right. After I burned the right finger taking a pan from the oven, I put the ring on a gold chain around my neck. When Quintana was born and someone gave her a baby ring I added her ring to the chain.

This seemed to work.

I still wear the rings that way.

"You want a different kind of wife," I frequently said to John in the first years of our marriage. I usually said this on the way back to Portuguese Bend after dinner in town. It was typically the initial volley in those fights that started as we passed the refineries off the San Diego Freeway. "You should have married someone more like Lenny." Lenny was my sister-in-law, Nick's wife. Lenny entertained and had lunch with friends and ran her house effortlessly and wore beautiful French dresses and suits and was always available to look at a house or give a baby shower or take visitors from out of town to Disneyland. "If I wanted to marry someone more like Lenny I would have married someone more like Lenny," John would say, at first patiently, then less so.

In fact I had no idea how to be a wife.

In those first years I would pin daisies in my hair, trying for a "bride" effect.

Later I had matching gingham skirts made for me and Quintana, trying for "young mother."

My memory of those years is that both John and I were improvising, flying blind. When I was clearing out a file drawer recently I came across a thick file labeled "Planning." The very fact that we made files labeled "Planning" suggests how little of it we did. We also had "planning meetings," which consisted of sitting down with legal pads, stating the day's problem out loud, and then, with no further attempt to solve it, going out to lunch. Such lunches were festive, as if to celebrate a job well done. Michael's, in Santa Monica, was a typical venue. In this particular "Planning" file I found several Christmas lists from the 1970s, a few notes on telephone calls, and, the bulk of the file, many notes, again dating from the 1970s, having to do with projected expenses and income. A mood of desperation permeates these notes. There was a note made for a meeting with Gil Frank on April 19, 1978, when we were trying to sell the house in Malibu to pay for the house in Brentwood Park on which we had already put down a $50,000 deposit. We could not sell the house in Malibu because it rained all that spring. Slopes fell. The Pacific Coast Highway was closed. No one could even look at the house unless they already lived on the Malibu side of the washout. Over a period of some weeks we had only one viewer, a psychiatrist who lived in the Malibu Colony. He left his shoes outside in the driving rain to "get the feel of the house," walked around barefoot on the tile floor, and reported to his son, who reported to Quintana, that the house was "cold." This was the note made on April 19 of that year: *We must assume we will not sell Malibu until end of year. We have to assume the worst so that any improvement will seem better.*

A note made a week later, I can only think for a "planning meeting": *Discuss: Abandon Brentwood Park? Eat the $50,000?*

Two weeks later we flew to Honolulu, thinking to escape the rain and sort out our dwindling options. The next morning when we came in from swimming there was a message: the sun had come out in Malibu and we had an offer within range of the asking.

What had encouraged us to think that a resort hotel in Honolulu was the place to solve a cash shortfall?

What lesson did we take from the fact that it worked?

Twenty-five years later, confronted with a similar shortfall and similarly deciding to sort it out in Paris, how could we have seen it as economizing because we got one ticket free on the Concorde?

In the same file drawer I found a few paragraphs John had written in 1990, on our twenty-sixth anniversary. "She wore sunglasses throughout the service the day we got married, at the little mission church in San Juan Bautista, California; she also wept through the entire ceremony. As we walked down the aisle, we promised each other that we could get out of this next week and not wait until death did us part."

That worked too. Somehow it had all worked.

Why did I think that this improvisation could never end?

If I had seen that it could, what would I have done differently?

What would he?

20

I am writing now as the end of the first year approaches. The sky in New York is dark when I wake at seven and darkening again by four in the afternoon. There are colored Christmas lights on the quince branches in the living room. There were also colored Christmas lights on quince branches in the living room a year ago, on the night it happened, but in the spring, not long after I brought Quintana home from UCLA, those strings burned out, went dead. This served as a symbol. I bought new strings of colored lights. This served as a profession of faith in the future. I take the opportunity for such professions where and when I can invent them, since I do not yet actually feel this faith in the future.

I notice that I have lost the skills for ordinary social encounters, however undeveloped those skills may have been, that I had a year ago. During the Republican convention I was invited to a small party at a friend's apartment. I was happy to see the friend and I was happy to see her father, who was the reason for the party, but I found conversation with others difficult. I noticed as I was leaving that the Secret Service was there but lacked even the patience to stay long enough to learn what important person was coming. On another evening during the Republican convention I went to a party given by *The New York Times* in the Time Warner building. There were candles and gardenias floating in glass cubes. I could not focus on whoever I was talking to. I was focused only on the gardenias getting sucked into the filter at the house in Brentwood Park.

On such occasions I hear myself trying to make an effort and failing.

I notice that I get up from dinner too abruptly.

I also notice that I do not have the resilience I had a year ago. A certain number of crises occur and the mechanism that floods the situation with adrenaline burns out. Mobilization becomes unreliable, slow or absent. In August and September, after the Democratic and Republican conventions but before the election, I wrote, for the first time since John died, a piece. It was about the campaign. It was the first piece I had written since 1963 that he did not read in draft form and tell me what was wrong, what was needed, how to bring it up here, take it down there. I have never written pieces fluently but this one seemed to be taking even longer than usual: I realized at some point that I was unwilling to finish it, because there was no one to read it. I kept telling myself that I had a deadline, that John and I never missed deadlines. Whatever I finally did to finish this piece was as close as I have ever come to imagining a message from him. The message was simple: *You're a professional. Finish the piece.*

It occurs to me that we allow ourselves to imagine only such messages as we need to survive.

The trach at UCLA, I recognize now, was going to happen with or without me.

Quintana resuming her life, I recognize now, was going to happen with or without me.

Finishing this piece, which was to say resuming my own life, was not.

When I checked the piece for publication I was startled and unsettled by how many mistakes I had made: simple errors of transcription, names and dates wrong. I told myself that this was temporary, part of the mobilization problem, further evidence of those cognitive deficits that came with either stress or grief, but I remained unsettled. Would I ever be right again? Could I ever again trust myself not to be wrong?

Do you always have to be right? He had said that.

Is it impossible for you to consider the possibility that you might be wrong?

Increasingly I find myself focusing on the similarities between these December days and the same December days a year ago. In certain ways those similar days a year ago have more clarity for me, a sharper focus. I do many of the same things. I make the same lists of things undone. I wrap Christmas presents in the same colored tissue, write the same messages on the same postcards from the Whitney gift shop, affix the postcards to the colored tissue with the same gold notary seals. I write the same checks for the building staff, except the checks are now imprinted with only my name. I would not have changed the checks (any more than I would change the voice on the answering machine) but it was said to be essential that John's name now appear only on trust accounts. I order the same kind of ham from Citarella. I fret the same way over the number of plates I will need on Christmas Eve, count and recount. I keep an annual December dentist's appointment and realize as I am putting the sample toothbrushes into my bag that no one will be waiting for me in the reception room, reading the papers until we can go to breakfast at 3 Guys on Madison Avenue. The morning goes empty. When I pass 3 Guys I look the other way. A friend asks me to go with her to hear the Christmas music at St. Ignatius Loyola, and we walk home in the dark in the rain. That night the first snow falls, although only a dusting, no avalanching off the roof of St. James', nothing like my birthday a year ago.

My birthday a year ago when he gave me the last present he would ever give me.

My birthday a year ago when he had twenty-five nights left to live.

On the table in front of the fireplace I notice something out of place in the stack of books nearest the chair in which John sat to read when he woke in the middle of the night. I have deliberately left this stack untouched, not from any shrine-building impulse but because I did not believe that I could afford to think about what he read in the middle of the night. Now someone has placed on top of the stack, balanced precariously, a large illustrated coffee-table book, *The Agnelli Gardens at Villar Perosa*. I move *The Agnelli Gardens at Villar Perosa*. Beneath it is a heavily marked copy of John Lukacs's *Five Days in London: May 1940*, in which there is a laminated bookmark that reads, in a child's handwriting, *John—happy reading to you—from John, age 7*. I am at first puzzled by the bookmark, which under the lamination is dusted with festive pink glitter, then remember: the Creative Artists Agency, as a Christmas project every year, "adopts" a group of Los Angeles schoolchildren, each of whom in turn makes a keepsake for a designated CAA client.

He would have opened the box from CAA on Christmas night.

He would have stuck the bookmark in whatever book was on top of that stack.

He would have had one hundred and twenty hours left to live.

How would he have chosen to live those one hundred and twenty hours?

Beneath the copy of *Five Days in London* is a copy of *The New Yorker* dated January 5, 2004. A copy of *The New Yorker* with that issue date would have been delivered to our apartment on Sunday, December 28, 2003. On Sunday, December 28, 2003, according to John's calendar, we had dinner at home with Sharon DeLano, who had been his editor at Random House and was at that time his editor at *The New Yorker*. We would have had dinner at the table in the living room. According to my kitchen notebook we ate linguine Bolognese and a salad and cheese and a baguette. At that point he would have had forty-eight hours left to live.

Some premonition of this timetable was why I had not touched the stack of books in the first place.

I don't think I'm up for this, he had said in the taxi on our way down from Beth Israel North that night or the next night. He was talking about the condition in which we had once again left Quintana.

You don't get a choice, I had said in the taxi.

I have wondered since if he did.

21

"She's still beautiful," Gerry had said as he and John and I left Quintana in the ICU at Beth Israel North.

"He said she's still beautiful," John said in the taxi. "Did you hear him say that? She's still beautiful? She's lying there swollen up with tubes coming out of her and he said—"

He could not continue.

That happened on one of those late December nights a few days before he died. Whether it happened on the 26th or the 27th or the 28th or the 29th I have no idea. It did not happen on the 30th because Gerry had already left the hospital by the time we got there on the 30th. I realize that much of my energy during the past months has been given to counting back the days, the hours. At the moment he was saying in the taxi on the way down from Beth Israel North that everything he had done was worthless did he have three hours left to live or did he have twenty-seven? Did he know how few hours there were, did he feel himself going, was he saying that he did not want to leave? *Don't let the Broken Man catch me*, Quintana would say when she woke from bad dreams, one of the "sayings" John put in the box and borrowed for Cat in *Dutch Shea, Jr.* I had promised her that we would not let the Broken Man catch her.

You're safe.

I'm here.

I had believed that we had that power.

Now the Broken Man was in the ICU at Beth Israel North waiting for her and now the Broken Man was in this taxi waiting for her father. Even at three or four she had recognized that when it came to the Broken Man she could rely only on her own efforts: *If the Broken Man comes I'll hang onto the fence and won't let him take me.*

She hung onto the fence. Her father did not.

I tell you I shall not live two days.

What gives those December days a year ago their sharper focus is their ending.

22

As the grandchild of a geologist I learned early to anticipate the absolute mutability of hills and waterfalls and even islands. When a hill slumps into the ocean I see the order in it. When a 5.2 on the Richter Scale wrenches the writing table in my own room in my own house in my own particular Welbeck Street I keep on typing. A hill is a transitional accommodation to stress, and ego may be a similar accommodation. A waterfall is a self-correcting maladjustment of stream to structure, and so, for all I know, is technique. The very island to which Inez Victor returned in the spring of 1975—Oahu, an emergent post-erosional land mass along the Hawaiian Ridge—is a temporary feature, and every rainfall or tremor along the Pacific plates alters its shape and shortens its tenure as Crossroads of the Pacific. In this light it is difficult to maintain definite convictions about what happened down there in the spring of 1975, or before.

This passage is from the beginning of a novel I wrote during the early 1980s, *Democracy*. John named it. I had begun it as a comedy of family manners with the title *Angel Visits*, a phrase defined by *Brewer's Dictionary of Phrase and Fable* as "delightful intercourse of short duration and rare occurrence," but when it became clear that it was going in a different direction I had kept writing without a title. When I finished John read it and said I should call it *Democracy*. I looked up the passage after the 9.0 Richter earthquake along a six-hundred-mile section of the Sumatran subduction zone had triggered the tsunami that wiped out large parts of coastline bordering the Indian Ocean.

I am unable to stop trying to imagine this event.

There is no video of what I try to imagine. There are no beaches, no flooded swimming pools, no hotel lobbies breaking up like rotted pilings in a storm. What I want to see happened under the surface. The India Plate buckling as it thrust under the Burma Plate. The current sweeping unseen through the deep water. I do not have a depth chart for the Indian Ocean but can pick up the broad outline even from my Rand McNally cardboard globe. Seven hundred and eighty meters off Banda Aceh. Twenty-three hundred between Sumatra and Sri Lanka. Twenty-one hundred between the Andamans and Thailand and then a long shallowing toward Phuket. The instant when the leading edge of the unseen current got slowed by the continental shelf. The buildup of water as the bottom of the shelf began to shallow out.

As it was in the beginning, is now and ever shall be, world without end.

It is now December 31, 2004, a year and a day.

On December 24, Christmas Eve, I had people for dinner, just as John and I had done on Christmas Eve a year before. I told myself that I was doing this for Quintana but I was also doing it for myself, a pledge that I would not lead the rest of my life as a special case, a guest, someone who could not function on her own. I built a fire, I lit candles, I laid out plates and silver on a buffet table in the dining room. I put out some CDs, Mabel Mercer singing Cole Porter and Israel Kamakawiwo'ole singing "Over the Rainbow" and an Israeli jazz pianist named Liz Magnes playing "Someone to Watch Over Me." John had been seated next to Liz Magnes once at a dinner at the Israeli mission and she had sent him the CD, a Gershwin concert she had given in Marrakech. In its ability to suggest drinks at the King David Hotel in Jerusalem during the British period this CD had seemed to John spectrally interesting, recovered evidence of a vanished world, one more reverberation from World War One. He referred to it as "the Mandate music." He had put it on while he was reading before dinner the night he died.

About five in the afternoon on the 24th I thought I could

not do the evening but when the time came the evening did itself.

Susanna Moore sent leis from Honolulu for her daughter Lulu and Quintana and me. We wore the leis. Another friend brought a gingerbread house. There were many children. I played the Mandate music, although the noise level was such that no one heard it.

On Christmas morning I put away the plates and silver and in the afternoon I went up to St. John the Divine, where there were mainly Japanese tourists. There were always Japanese tourists at St. John the Divine. On the afternoon Quintana got married at St. John the Divine there had been Japanese tourists snapping pictures as she and Gerry left the altar. On the afternoon we placed John's ashes in the chapel off the main altar at St. John the Divine an empty Japanese tour bus had caught fire and burned outside, a pillar of flame on Amsterdam Avenue. On Christmas Day the chapel off the main altar was blocked off, part of the cathedral reconstruction. A security guard took me in. The chapel was emptied, filled only with scaffolding. I ducked under the scaffolding and found the marble plate with John's name and my mother's name. I hung the lei from one of the brass rods that held the marble plate to the vault and then I walked from the chapel back into the nave and out the main aisle, straight toward the big rose window.

As I walked I kept my eyes on the window, half blinded by its brilliance but determined to keep my gaze fixed until I caught the moment in which the window as approached seems to explode with light, fill the entire field of vision with blue. The Christmas of the Buffalo pens and the black wafer alarm clock and the neighborhood fireworks all over Honolulu, the Christmas of 1990, the Christmas during which John and I had been doing the crash rewrite on the picture that never got made, had involved that window. We had staged the denouement of the picture at St. John the Divine, placed a plutonium device in the bell tower (only the protagonist realizes that the device is at St. John the Divine and not the World Trade towers), blown the unwitting carrier of the device straight out through the big rose window. We had filled the screen with blue that Christmas.

*

I realize as I write this that I do not want to finish this account.

Nor did I want to finish the year.

The craziness is receding but no clarity is taking its place.

I look for resolution and find none.

I did not want to finish the year because I know that as the days pass, as January becomes February and February becomes summer, certain things will happen. My image of John at the instant of his death will become less immediate, less raw. It will become something that happened in another year. My sense of John himself, John alive, will become more remote, even "mudgy," softened, transmuted into whatever best serves my life without him. In fact this is already beginning to happen. All year I have been keeping time by last year's calendar: what were we doing on this day last year, where did we have dinner, is it the day a year ago we flew to Honolulu after Quintana's wedding, is it the day a year ago we flew back from Paris, *is it the day*. I realized today for the first time that my memory of this day a year ago is a memory that does not involve John. This day a year ago was December 31, 2003. John did not see this day a year ago. John was dead.

I was crossing Lexington Avenue when this occurred to me.

I know why we try to keep the dead alive: we try to keep them alive in order to keep them with us.

I also know that if we are to live ourselves there comes a point at which we must relinquish the dead, let them go, keep them dead.

Let them become the photograph on the table.

Let them become the name on the trust accounts.

Let go of them in the water.

Knowing this does not make it any easier to let go of him in the water.

In fact the apprehension that our life together will decreasingly be the center of my every day seemed today on Lexington Avenue so distinct a betrayal that I lost all sense of oncoming traffic.

I think about leaving the lei at St. John the Divine.

A souvenir of the Christmas in Honolulu when we filled the screen with blue.

During the years when people still left Honolulu on the Matson Lines the custom at the moment of departure was to throw leis on the water, a promise that the traveler would return. The leis would get caught in the wake and go bruised and brown, the way the gardenias in the pool filter at the house in Brentwood Park had gone bruised and brown.

The other morning when I woke I tried to remember the arrangement of the rooms in the house in Brentwood Park. I imagined myself walking through the rooms, first on the ground floor and then on the second. Later in the day I realized that I had forgotten one.

The lei I left at St. John the Divine would have gone brown by now.

Leis go brown, tectonic plates shift, deep currents move, islands vanish, rooms get forgotten.

I flew into Indonesia and Malaysia and Singapore with John, in 1979 and 1980.

Some of the islands that were there then would now be gone, just shallows.

I think about swimming with him into the cave at Portuguese Bend, about the swell of clear water, the way it changed, the swiftness and power it gained as it narrowed through the rocks at the base of the point. The tide had to be just right. We had to be in the water at the very moment the tide was right. We could only have done this a half dozen times at most during the two years we lived there but it is what I remember. Each time we did it I was afraid of missing the swell, hanging back, timing it wrong. John never was. You had to feel the swell change. You had to go with the change. He told me that. No eye is on the sparrow but he did tell me that.

BLUE NIGHTS

This book is for Quintana

I

In certain latitudes there comes a span of time approaching and following the summer solstice, some weeks in all, when the twilights turn long and blue. This period of the blue nights does not occur in subtropical California, where I lived for much of the time I will be talking about here and where the end of daylight is fast and lost in the blaze of the dropping sun, but it does occur in New York, where I now live. You notice it first as April ends and May begins, a change in the season, not exactly a warming—in fact not at all a warming—yet suddenly summer seems near, a possibility, even a promise. You pass a window, you walk to Central Park, you find yourself swimming in the color blue: the actual light is blue, and over the course of an hour or so this blue deepens, becomes more intense even as it darkens and fades, approximates finally the blue of the glass on a clear day at Chartres, or that of the Cerenkov radiation thrown off by the fuel rods in the pools of nuclear reactors. The French called this time of day "l'heure bleue." To the English it was "the gloaming." The very word "gloaming" reverberates, echoes—the gloaming, the glimmer, the glitter, the glisten, the glamour—carrying in its consonants the images of houses shuttering, gardens darkening, grass-lined rivers slipping through the shadows. During the blue nights you think the end of day will never come. As the blue nights draw to a close (and they will, and they do) you experience an actual chill, an apprehension of illness, at the moment you first notice: the blue light is going, the days are already shortening, the summer is gone. This book is called "Blue Nights" because at the time I began it I found my mind turning increasingly to illness, to the end of promise, the dwindling of the days, the inevitability of the fading, the dying of the brightness. Blue nights are the opposite of the dying of the brightness, but they are also its warning.

2

July 26 2010.

Today would be her wedding anniversary.

Seven years ago today we took the leis from the florist's boxes and shook the water in which they were packed onto the grass outside the Cathedral of St. John the Divine on Amsterdam Avenue. The white peacock spread his fan. The organ sounded. She wove white stephanotis into the thick braid that hung down her back. She dropped a tulle veil over her head and the stephanotis loosened and fell. The plumeria blossom tattooed just below her shoulder showed through the tulle. "Let's do it," she whispered. The little girls in leis and pale dresses skipped down the aisle and walked behind her up to the high altar. After all the words had been said the little girls followed her out the front doors of the cathedral and around past the peacocks (the two iridescent blue-and-green peacocks, the one white peacock) to the Cathedral house. There were cucumber and watercress sandwiches, a peach-colored cake from Payard, pink champagne.

Her choices, all.

Sentimental choices, things she remembered.

I remembered them too.

When she said she wanted cucumber and watercress sandwiches at her wedding I remembered her laying out plates of cucumber and watercress sandwiches on the tables we had set up around the pool for her sixteenth-birthday lunch. When she said she wanted leis in place of bouquets at her wedding I remembered her at three or four or five getting off a plane at Bradley Field in Hartford wearing the leis she had been given when she left Honolulu the night before. The temperature in Connecticut that morning was six degrees below zero and she had no coat (she had been wearing no coat when we left Los

Angeles for Honolulu, we had not expected to go on to Hartford) but she had seen no problem. Children with leis don't wear coats, she advised me.

Sentimental choices.

On the day of that wedding she got all her sentimental choices except one: she had wanted the little girls to go barefoot in the cathedral (memory of Malibu, she was always barefoot in Malibu, she always had splinters from the redwood deck, splinters from the deck and tar from the beach and iodine for the scratches from the nails in the stairs in between) but the little girls had new shoes for the occasion and wanted to wear them.

> MR. AND MRS. JOHN GREGORY DUNNE
> REQUEST THE HONOR OF YOUR PRESENCE
> AT THE MARRIAGE OF THEIR DAUGHTER,
> QUINTANA ROO
> TO
> MR. GERALD BRIAN MICHAEL
> ON SATURDAY THE TWENTY-SIXTH OF JULY
> AT TWO O'CLOCK

The stephanotis.

Was that another sentimental choice?

Did she remember the stephanotis?

Is that why she wanted it, is that why she wove it into her braid?

At the house in Brentwood Park in which we lived from 1978 until 1988, a house so determinedly conventional (two stories, center-hall plan, shuttered windows, and a sitting room off every bedroom) as to seem in situ idiosyncratic ("their suburbia house in Brentwood" was how she referred to the house when we bought it, a twelve-year-old establishing that it was not her decision, not her taste, a child claiming the distance all children imagine themselves to need), there was stephanotis growing outside the terrace doors. I would brush the waxy flowers when I went out to the garden. Outside the same doors there were beds of lavender and also mint, a tangle of mint, made lush by a dripping faucet. We moved into that house the summer she was about to start the seventh grade at what was then still the Westlake School for Girls in Holmby Hills. This was like yesterday. We moved out of that house the year she was about to graduate from Barnard. This too was like yesterday. The stephanotis and mint were dead by then, killed when the man who was buying the house insisted that we rid it of termites by tenting it and pumping in Vikane and chloropicrin. At the time this buyer bid on the house he sent us word via the brokers, apparently by way of closing the deal, that he wanted the house because he could picture his daughter marrying in the garden. This was a few weeks before he required us to pump in the Vikane that killed the stephanotis, killed the mint, and also killed the pink magnolia into which the twelve-year-old who took so assiduously removed a view of our suburbia house in Brentwood had until then been able to look from her second-floor sitting-room windows. The termites, I was quite sure, would come back. The pink magnolia, I was also quite sure, would not.

We closed the deal and moved to New York.

Where in fact I had lived before, from the time I was twenty-one and just out of the English Department at Berkeley and starting work at *Vogue* (a segue so profoundly unnatural that when I was asked by the Condé Nast personnel department to name the languages in which I was fluent I could think only of Middle English) until I was twenty-nine and just married.

Where I have lived again since 1988.

Why then do I say I lived much of this time in California?

Why then did I feel so sharp a sense of betrayal when I exchanged my California driver's license for one issued by New York? Wasn't that actually a straightforward enough transaction? Your birthday comes around, your license needs renewing, what difference does it make where you renew it? What difference does it make that you have had this single number on your license since it was assigned to you at age fifteen-and-a-half by the state of California? Wasn't there always an error on that driver's license anyway? An error you knew about? Didn't that license say you were five-foot-two? When you knew perfectly well you were at best—(max height, top height ever, height before you lost a half inch to age)—when you knew perfectly well you were at best five-foot-one-and-three-quarters?

Why did I make so much of the driver's license?

What was that about?

Did giving up the California license say that I would never again be fifteen-and-a-half?

Would I want to be?

Or was the business with the license just one more case of "the apparent inadequacy of the precipitating event"?

I put "the apparent inadequacy of the precipitating event" in quotes because it is not my phrase.

Karl Menninger used it, in *Man Against Himself*, by way of describing the tendency to overreact to what might seem ordinary, even predictable, circumstances: a propensity, Dr. Menninger tells us, common among suicides. He cites the young woman who becomes depressed and kills herself after cutting her hair. He mentions the man who kills himself because he has been advised to stop playing golf, the child who commits suicide because his canary died, the woman who kills herself after missing two trains.

Notice: not one train, *two* trains.

Think that over.

Consider what special circumstances are required before this woman throws it all in.

"In these instances," Dr. Menninger tells us, "the hair, the golf, and the canary had an exaggerated value, so that when they were lost or when there was even a threat that they might be lost, the recoil of severed emotional bonds was fatal."

Yes, clearly, no argument.

"The hair, the golf, and the canary" had each been assigned an exaggerated value (as presumably had the second of those two missed trains), but why? Dr. Menninger himself asks this question, although only rhetorically: "But why should such extravagantly exaggerated over-estimations and incorrect evaluations exist?" Did he imagine that he had answered the question simply by raising it? Did he think that all he had to do was formulate the question and then retreat into a cloud of theoretical psychoanalytic references? Could I seriously have construed changing my driver's license from California to New York as an experience involving "severed emotional bonds"?

Did I seriously see it as loss?

Did I truly see it as separation?

And before we leave this subject of "severed emotional bonds":

The last time I saw the house in Brentwood Park before its title changed hands we stood outside watching the three-level Allied van pull away and turn onto Marlboro Street, everything we then owned, including a Volvo station wagon, already inside and on its way to New York. After the van moved out of sight we walked through the empty house and out across the terrace, a good-bye moment rendered less tender by the lingering reek of Vikane in the house and the stiff dead leaves where the pink magnolia and stephanotis had been. I smelled Vikane even in New York, every time I unpacked a carton. The next time I was in Los Angeles and drove past the house it was gone, a teardown, to be replaced a year or two later by a house marginally bigger (a new room over the garage, an additional foot or two in a kitchen already large enough to accommodate a square Chickering grand piano that remained mostly unnoticed) but lacking (for me) the resolute conventionality of the original. Some years later in a Washington bookstore I met the daughter, the one the buyer had said he could picture marrying in the garden. She was at school somewhere in Washington (Georgetown? George Washington?), I was there to give a reading at Politics and Prose. She introduced herself. I grew up in your house, she said. Not exactly, I refrained from saying.

John always said we moved "back" to New York.

I never did.

Brentwood Park was then, New York was now.

Brentwood Park before the Vikane had been a time, a period, a decade, during which everything had seemed to connect.

Our suburbia house in Brentwood.

It was exactly that. She called it.

There had been cars, a swimming pool, a garden.

There had been agapanthus, lilies of the Nile, intensely blue starbursts that floated on long stalks. There had been gaura, clouds of tiny white blossoms that became visible at eye level only as the daylight faded.

There had been English chintzes, chinoiserie toile.

There had been a Bouvier des Flandres motionless on the stair landing, one eye open, on guard.

Time passes.

Memory fades, memory adjusts, memory conforms to what we think we remember.

Even memory of the stephanotis in her braid, even memory of the plumeria tattoo showing through the tulle.

It is horrible to see oneself die without children. Napoléon Bonaparte said that.

What greater grief can there be for mortals than to see their children dead. Euripides said that.

When we talk about mortality we are talking about our children.

I said that.

I think now of that July day at St. John the Divine in 2003 and am struck by how young John and I appeared to be, how well. In actual fact neither of us was in the least well: John had that spring and summer undergone a series of cardiac procedures, most recently the implantation of a pacemaker, the efficacy of which remained in question; I had three weeks before the wedding collapsed on the street and spent the several nights following in a Columbia Presbyterian ICU being transfused for an unexplained gastrointestinal bleed. "You're just going to swallow a little camera," they said in the ICU when they were trying to demonstrate to themselves what was causing the bleed. I recall resisting: since I had never in my life been able to swallow an aspirin it seemed unlikely that I could swallow a camera.

"Of course you can, it's only a *little* camera."

A pause. The attempt at briskness declined into wheedling:

"It's really a *very* little camera."

In the end I did swallow the very little camera, and the very little camera transmitted the desired images, which did not demonstrate what was causing the bleed but did demonstrate that with sufficient sedation anyone could swallow a very little camera. Similarly, in another less than entirely efficient use of high-tech medicine, John could hold a telephone to his heart, dial a number, and get a reading on the pacemaker, which proved, I was told, that at the given instant he dialed the number (although not necessarily before or after) the device was operating.

Medicine, I have had reason since to notice more than once, remains an imperfect art.

Yet all had seemed well when we were shaking the water off the leis onto the grass outside St. John the Divine on July 26 2003. Could you have seen, had you been walking on Amsterdam Avenue and caught sight of the bridal party that day, how utterly unprepared the mother of the bride was to accept what would happen before the year 2003 had even ended? The father of the bride dead at his own dinner table? The bride herself in an induced coma, breathing only on a respirator, not expected by the doctors in the intensive care unit to live the night? The first in a cascade of medical crises that would end twenty months later with her death?

Twenty months during which she would be strong enough to walk unsupported for possibly a month in all?

Twenty months during which she would spend weeks at a time in the intensive care units of four different hospitals?

In all of those intensive care units there were the same blue-and-white printed curtains. In all of those intensive care units there were the same sounds, the same gurgling through plastic tubing, the same dripping from the IV line, the same rales, the same alarms. In all of those intensive care units there were the same requirements to guard against further infections, the donning of the double gowns, the paper slippers, the surgical cap, the mask, the gloves that pulled on only with difficulty and left a rash that reddened and bled. In all of those intensive care units there was the same racing through the unit when a code was called, the feet hitting the floor, the rattle of the crash cart.

This was never supposed to happen to her, I remember thinking—outraged, as if she and I had been promised a special exemption—in the third of those intensive care units.

By the time she reached the fourth I was no longer invoking this special exemption.

When we talk about mortality we are talking about our children.

I just said that, but what does it mean?

All right, of course I can track it, of course you can track it, another way of acknowledging that our children are hostages to fortune, but when we talk about our children what are we saying? Are we saying what it meant to us to have them? What it meant to us not to have them? What it meant to let them go? Are we talking about the enigma of pledging ourselves to protect the unprotectable? About the whole puzzle of being a parent?

Time passes.

Yes, agreed, a banality, of course time passes.

Then why do I say it, why have I already said it more than once?

Have I been saying it the same way I say I have lived most of my life in California?

Have I been saying it without hearing what I say?

Could it be that I heard it more this way: *Time passes, but not so aggressively that anyone notices*? Or even: *Time passes, but not for me*? Could it be that I did not figure in either the general nature or the permanence of the slowing, the irreversible changes in mind and body, the way in which you wake one summer morning less resilient than you were and by Christmas find your ability to mobilize gone, atrophied, no longer extant? The way in which you live most of your life in California, and then you don't? The way in which your awareness of this passing time—this permanent slowing, this vanishing resilience—multiplies, metastasizes, becomes your very life?

Time passes.

Could it be that I never believed it?

Did I believe the blue nights could last forever?

3

Last spring, 2009, I had some warnings, flags on the track, definite notices of darkening even before the blue nights came.

L'heure bleue. The gloaming.

Not even yet evident when that year's darkening gave its first notices.

The initial such notice was sudden, the ringing telephone you wish you had never answered, the news no one wants to get: someone to whom I had been close since her childhood, Natasha Richardson, had fallen on a ski slope outside Quebec (spring break, a family vacation, a bunny slope, *this was never supposed to happen to her*) and by the time she noticed that she did not feel entirely well she was dying, the victim of an epidural hematoma, a traumatic brain injury. She was the daughter of Vanessa Redgrave and Tony Richardson, who was one of our closest friends in Los Angeles. The first time I ever saw her she had been maybe thirteen or fourteen, not yet entirely comfortable in her own skin, an uncertain but determined adolescent with a little too much makeup and startlingly white stockings. She had come from London to visit her father at his house on Kings Road in Hollywood, an eccentrically leveled structure that had belonged to Linda Lovelace, the star of *Deep Throat*. Tony had bought the house and proceeded to fill it with light and parrots and whippets. When Tasha arrived from London he had brought her to dinner with us at La Scala. The dinner had not been planned as a party for her arrival but there had happened to be many people her father and we knew at La Scala that night and her father had made it feel like one. She had been pleased. A few years later Quintana had been at the same uncertain age and Tasha, by then seventeen, was spending the summer at Le Nid du Duc, the village her father had invented, an entertainment of his own, a director's conceit, in the hills of the Var above Saint-Tropez.

To say that Tasha was spending the summer at Le Nid du Duc fails to adequately suggest the situation. In fact, by the time John and I arrived in France that summer, Tasha was running Le Nid du Duc, the seventeen-year-old chatelaine of what amounted to a summer-long house party for a floating thirty people. Tasha was managing the provisioning of the several houses that made up the compound. Tasha was cooking and serving, entirely unaided, three meals a day for the basic thirty as well as for anyone else who happened up the hill and had a drink and waited for the long tables under the lime trees to be set—not only cooking and serving but, as Tony noted in his memoir *The Long-Distance Runner*, "completely unfazed when told that there'd be an extra twenty for lunch."

Most astonishingly, at seventeen, Tasha was undertaking the induction into adult life not only of her sisters Joely and Katharine but of two Los Angeles eighth-graders, one of them Quintana, the other Kenneth and Kathleen Tynan's daughter Roxana, both avid to grow up, each determined to misbehave. Tasha made certain that Quintana and Roxana got to the correct spot on the beach at Saint-Tropez every afternoon, that summer's correct spot of choice being the Aqua Club. Tasha made certain that Quintana and Roxana got a proper introduction to the Italian boys who trailed them on the beach, a "proper introduction" for Tasha entailing a meal at the long tables under the lime trees at Le Nid du Duc. Tasha came up from the Aqua Club and Tasha did a perfect beurre blanc for the fish Tony had bought that morning and Tasha watched Quintana and Roxana mesmerize the Italian boys into believing that they were dealing not with fourteen-year-olds last seen in the pastel cotton uniforms of the Westlake and Marlborough Schools for Girls in Los Angeles but with preternaturally sophisticated undergraduates from UCLA.

And never ever, not once, not ever, did I hear Tasha blow the whistle on that or on any other of the summer's romantic fables.

Au contraire.

Tasha devised the fables, Tasha wrote the romance.

The last time I ever saw her was a few nights after she fell on the bunny slope outside Quebec, in a room at Lenox Hill Hospital in New York, lying as if about to wake.

She was not about to wake.

She had been flown down from Montreal while her family met in New York.

When I left the hospital after seeing her there were photographers outside, waiting for clear camera lines on the family.

I circled around them onto Park Avenue and walked on home.

Her first marriage, to the producer Robert Fox, had taken place in my apartment. She had filled the rooms with quince blossoms for the ceremony. The blossoms had eventually fallen but the branches had remained, brittle and dusty, twigs breaking off, nonetheless still passing as decorative elements in the living room. When I walked in from Lenox Hill that night the apartment seemed full of photographs of Tasha and of her father and mother. Her father on location for *The Border*, riding a Panavision camera. Her father on location in Spain, wearing a red windbreaker, directing Melanie Griffith and James Woods on an HBO project he and John and I did together. Her mother backstage at the Booth Theater on West Forty-fifth Street, the year she and I did a play together. Tasha herself, talking to John at one of the long tables she had arranged outside for the wedding dinner on her farm in Millbrook when she was married a second time, this time to Liam Neeson.

She had managed that wedding on the farm as before and after she managed summers at Le Nid du Duc.

She had managed even a priest, a wedding mass. She had kept referring to the priest as "Father Dan." It was only when he stood to actually do the ceremony that I realized that "Father Dan" was Daniel Berrigan, one of the activist Berrigan brothers. It seemed that Daniel Berrigan had been an advisor on Roland Joffé's *The Mission*. It seemed that Liam had played a role in *The Mission*. Tasha had designed the entire event, in other words, as a piece of theater, the very kind of moment Tony liked best in the world. He particularly would have liked Tasha forgetting the wafers for the mass, tearing up long baguettes to pass in their place, but Tony was dead by the day of that wedding.

Tasha died in March 2009.

This was never supposed to happen to her.

On her twenty-first birthday her father had made a film of the lunch he gave in her honor at Linda Lovelace's former house on Kings Road. John had wished her happy birthday, on film. Quintana and Fiona Lewis and Tamara Asseyev had sung "Girls Just Want to Have Fun," on film. After lunch we had untied rafts of white balloons and watched them drift over the Hollywood hills, on film. These are the lines from W. H. Auden that Tony quoted that afternoon as "the best twenty-first birthday wish you can make for anyone":

> *So I wish you first a*
> *Sense of theatre; only*
> *Those who love illusion*
> *And know it will go far—*

Tasha and her father and John and Quintana and the whippets and the parrots and the white balloons, all still there, on film.

I have a copy of the film.

So I wish you first a sense of theatre—

So her father would have said at the wedding in Millbrook.

The second such warning, this one not at all sudden, came in April 2009.

Because I had been showing symptoms of neuritis, or neuropathy, or neurological inflammation (there seemed no general agreement on what to call it), an MRI was done, then an MRA. Neither suggested a definitive reason for the symptoms at hand but images of the Circle of Willis showed evidence of a 4.2 mm by 3.4 mm aneurysm deep in that circle of arteries—the anterior cerebral, the anterior communicating, the internal carotid, the posterior cerebral, and the posterior communicating—at the base of my brain. This finding, the several neurologists who examined the images stressed, was "entirely incidental," had "nothing to do with what we're looking for," and was not even necessarily significant. One of the neurologists ventured that this particular aneurysm "doesn't look ready to blow"; another suggested that "if it does blow, you won't live through it."

This seemed to be offered as encouraging news, and I accepted it as such. At that instant in April 2009 I realized that I was no longer, if I had ever been, afraid to die: I was now afraid not to die, afraid that I might damage my brain (or my heart or my kidneys or my nervous system) and survive, continue living.

Had there been an instant when Tasha was afraid not to die?

Had there been an instant when Quintana was afraid not to die?

Toward the very end, say, for example on the August morning when I walked into the ICU overlooking the river at New York-Cornell and one of what must have been twenty doctors in the unit happened to mention (a point of interest, a teachable moment, Grand Rounds for two students, the husband and the mother of the patient) that they were doing hand compression because the patient could no longer get enough oxygen through the ventilator? Only he did not say "the ventilator," he said "the vent"? And I asked dutifully (the attentive student, up on the vernacular) how long it had been since the patient could get enough oxygen through the vent? And the doctor said it had been at least an hour?

Did I get this all wrong?

Did I misunderstand a key point?

Could they have actually let an hour go by without mentioning to me that her brain had already been damaged by insufficient oxygen?

Put the question another way: what if the attentive student had never asked?

Would they have mentioned it at all?

One further turn of the screw: if I had never asked would she still be alive?

Warehoused somewhere?

No longer sentient but alive, not dead?

What greater grief can there be for mortals than to see their children dead?

Was there an instant when she knew what was in store for her that August morning in the ICU overlooking the river at New York–Cornell?

Did the instant occur that August morning when she was in fact dying?

Or had it occurred years before, when she thought she was?

4

"When Quintana was a little girl, we moved to Malibu, to a house overlooking the Pacific." So began the toast John delivered in the Cathedral house at St. John the Divine on the afternoon she wove the stephanotis into her braid and cut the peach-colored cake from Payard. There were aspects of living in that house overlooking the Pacific that he failed to mention—he failed to mention for example the way the wind would blow down through the canyons and whine under the eaves and lift the roof and coat the white walls with ash from the fireplace, he failed to mention for example the king snakes that dropped from the rafters of the garage into the open Corvette I parked below, he failed to mention for example that king snakes were locally considered a valuable asset because the presence of a king snake in your Corvette was understood to mean (I was never convinced that it did) that you didn't have a rattlesnake in your Corvette—but the following is what he did mention. I can quote what he mentioned exactly because after he mentioned it he wrote it down. He wanted her to have it in his words, his exact memory, in his exact words, of her childhood:

> The house didn't have any heat—it had old baseboard heaters, but we were always afraid they'd burn the place up—and so we heated it from this huge walk-in fireplace in the living room. In the morning I'd get up and bring in wood for the day—we used about a cord of wood a week—and then I'd get Q up and make her breakfast and get her ready for school. Joan was trying to finish a book that year, and she would work until two or three in the morning, then have a drink and read some poetry before she came to bed. She always made Q's lunch the night

before, and put it in this little blue lunchbox. You should have seen those lunches: they weren't your basic peanut butter and jelly schoolbox lunch. Thin little sandwiches with their crusts cut off, cut into four triangular pieces, kept fresh in Saran Wrap. Or else there would be homemade fried chicken, with little salt and pepper shakers. And for dessert, stemmed strawberries, with sour cream and brown sugar.

So I'd take Q to school, and she'd walk down this steep hill. All the kids wore uniforms—Quintana wore a plaid jumper and a white sweater, and her hair—she was a towhead in that Malibu sun—her hair was in a ponytail. I would watch her disappear down that hill, the Pacific a great big blue background, and I thought it was as beautiful as anything I'd ever seen. So I said to Joan, "You got to see this, babe." The next morning Joan came with us, and when she saw Q disappear down that hill she began to cry.

Today Quintana is walking back up that hill. She's not the towhead with the plaid jumper and the blue lunchbox and the ponytail. She's the Princess Bride—and at the top of that hill stands her Prince. Will you join me please in toasting Gerry and Quintana.

We did.
We joined him in toasting Gerry and Quintana.
We toasted Gerry and Quintana at St. John the Divine and a few hours later, in their absence, at a Chinese restaurant on West Sixty-fifth Street with my brother and his family, we toasted Gerry and Quintana again. We wished them happiness, we wished them health, we wished them love and luck and beautiful children. On that wedding day, July 26, 2003, we could see no reason to think that such ordinary blessings would not come their way.
Do notice:
We still counted happiness and health and love and luck and beautiful children as "ordinary blessings."

5

Seven years later.
   July 26 2010.
Laid out on a table in front of me today is a group of photographs sent to me only recently but all taken in 1971, summer or fall, in or around the unheated house in Malibu mentioned in the wedding toast. We had moved into that house in January 1971, on a perfectly clear day which turned so foggy that by the time I drove back to the house from a late-day run to the Trancas Market, three-and-a-half miles down the Pacific Coast Highway, I could no longer find the driveway. Since sundown fogs in January and February and March turned out to be as much a given of that stretch of coast as wildfires would be in September and October and November, this disappearance of the driveway was by no means an unusual turn of events: the preferred method for finding it was to hold your breath, avert your mind from the unseeable cliff below, rising two-hundred-some feet from open ocean, and turn left.

Neither the fogs nor the wildfires figure in the photographs.

There are eighteen images.

Each is of the same child at the same age, Quintana at five, her hair, as noted in the wedding toast, bleached by the beach sun. In some she is wearing her plaid uniform jumper, also noted in the toast. In a few she is wearing a cashmere turtleneck sweater I brought her from London when we went that May to do promotion for the European release of *The Panic in Needle Park*. In a few she is wearing a checked gingham dress trimmed in eyelet, a little faded and a little too big for her, the look of a hand-me-down. In others she has on cutoff jeans and a denim Levi jacket with metal studs, a bamboo fishing pole against her shoulder, artfully arranged there (by her) in a spirit less of fishing than of styling, a prop to accessorize the outfit.

The photographs were taken by one of her West Hartford cousins, Tony Dunne, who had arrived on leave from Williams to spend a few months in Malibu. He had been in Malibu only a day or two when she began to lose her first baby tooth. She had noticed the tooth loosening, she had wiggled the tooth, the tooth loosened further. I tried to remember how this situation had been handled in my own childhood. My most coherent memory involved my mother tying a piece of thread around the loose tooth, attaching the thread to a doorknob, and slamming the door. I tried this. The tooth stayed fixed in place. She cried. I grabbed the car keys and screamed for Tony: tying the thread to the doorknob had so exhausted my aptitude for improvisational caretaking that my sole remaining thought was to get her to the emergency room at UCLA Medical Center, thirty-some miles into town. Tony, who grew up with three siblings and many cousins, tried without success to convince me that UCLA Medical Center might be overkill. "Just let me try just this one thing first," he said finally, and pulled the tooth.

The next time a tooth got loose she pulled it herself. I had lost my authority.

Was I the problem? Was I always the problem?

In the note Tony included when he sent the photographs a few months ago he said that each image represented something he had seen in her. In some she is melancholy, large eyes staring directly into the lens. In others she is bold, daring the camera. She covers her mouth with her hand. She obscures her eyes with a polka-dotted cotton sun hat. She marches through the wash at the edge of the sea. She bites her lip as she swings from an oleander branch.

A few of these photographs are familiar to me.

A copy of one of them, one in which she is wearing the cashmere turtleneck sweater I bought her in London, is framed on my desk in New York.

There is also on my desk in New York a framed photograph she herself took one Christmas on Barbados: the rocks outside the rented house, the shallow sea, the wash of surf. I remember the Christmas she took that picture. We had arrived on Barbados at night. She had gone immediately to bed and I had sat outside listening to a radio and trying to locate a line I believed to be from Claude Lévi-Strauss's *Tristes Tropiques* but was never able to find: "The tropics are not exotic, they are merely out of date." At some point after she went to sleep news had come on the radio: since our arrival on Barbados the United States had invaded Panama. When the first light came I had woken her with this necessary, or so it seemed to me, information. She had covered her face with the sheet, clearly indicating no interest in pursuing the topic. I had nonetheless pressed it. I knew "exactly yesterday" we were going to invade Panama last night, she had said. I asked how she had known "exactly yesterday" we were going to invade Panama last night. Because all the SIPA photographers were stopping by the office yesterday, she said, picking up credentials for the Panama invasion. SIPA was the photo agency for which she then worked. She had again burrowed beneath the sheet. I did not ask why she had not thought the invasion of Panama worth a mention on the five-hour flight down. "*For Mom and Dad*," the inscription on the photograph reads. "*Try to imagine the seductive sea if you can, love XX, Q.*"

She had known exactly yesterday we were going to invade Panama last night.

The tropics were not exotic, they were merely out of date.

Try to imagine the seductive sea if you can.

Even in those Malibu photographs which are unfamiliar, I recognize certain elements: the improvised end table by a chair in the living room, one of my mother's "Craftsman" dinner knives on the table we identified as "Aunt Kate's," the straightbacked wooden Hitchcock chairs my mother-in-law had painted black-and-gold to send to us from Connecticut.

The oleander branch on which she swings is familiar, the curve of the beach on which she kicks through the wash is familiar.

The clothes of course are familiar.

I had for a while seen them every day, washed them, hung them to blow in the wind on the clotheslines outside my office window.

I wrote two books watching her clothes blow on those lines.
Brush your teeth, brush your hair, shush I'm working.

So read the list of "Mom's Sayings" that she posted one day in the garage, an artifact of the "club" she had started with a child who lived down the beach.

What remained until now unfamiliar, what I recognize in the photographs but failed to see at the time they were taken, are the startling depths and shallows of her expressions, the quicksilver changes of mood.

How could I have missed what was so clearly there to be seen?

Did I not read the poem she brought home that year from the school on the steep hill? The school to which she wore the plaid uniform jumper and carried the blue lunchbox? The school to which John watched her walk every morning and thought it was as beautiful as anything he had ever seen?

"The World," this poem is called, and I recognize her careful printing, quixotically executed on a narrow strip of construction paper fourteen inches long but only two inches wide. I see that careful printing every day: the strip of construction paper is now framed on a wall behind my kitchen in New York, along with a few other mementos of the period: a copy of Karl Shapiro's "California Winter," torn from *The New Yorker*; a copy of Pablo Neruda's "A Certain Weariness," typed by me on one of the several dozen Royal manuals my father had bought (along with a few mess halls, a fire tower, and the regulation khaki Ford jeep on which I learned to drive) at a government auction; a postcard from Bogotá, sent by John and me to Quintana in Malibu; a photograph showing the coffee table in the beach house living room after dinner, the candles burning down and the silver baby cups filled with santolina; a mimeographed notice from the Topanga–Las Virgenes Fire District instructing residents of the district what to do "when the fire comes."

Do note: not "*if* the fire comes."

When the fire comes.

No one at the Topanga–Las Virgenes Fire District was talking about what most people see when they hear the words "brush fire," a few traces of smoke and an occasional lick of flame: at the Topanga–Las Virgenes Fire District they were talking about fires that burned on twenty-mile fronts and spotted ahead twelve-foot flames as they moved.

This was not forgiving territory: consider finding the driveway.

Also consider "The World" itself, its eccentric strip of construction paper and careful printing obscuring one side of the mimeographed notice from the Topanga–Las Virgenes Fire District. Since the choices made by the careful printer may or may not have meaning, I give you the text of "The World" with her spacing, her single misspelling:

THE
WORLD

The world
Has nothing
But morning
And night
It has no
Day or lunch
So this world
Is poor and desertid.
This is some
Kind of an
Island with
Only three
Houses on it
In these
Families are
2,1,2, people
In each house
So 2,1,2 make
Only 5 people
On this
Island.

In point of fact the beach on which we lived, our personal "some Kind of an Island," did have "Only three Houses on it," or, more correctly, it had only three houses that were occupied year-round. One of these three houses was owned by Dick Moore, a cinematographer who, when he was not on a location, lived there with his two daughters, Marina and Tita. It was Tita Moore who started the club with Quintana that entailed posting "Mom's Sayings" in our garage. Tita and Quintana also had an entrepreneurial enterprise, "the soap factory," the business mission of which was to melt down and reshape all remaining bars of the gardenia-scented I. Magnin soap I used to order by the box and sell the result to passers-by on the beach. Since both ends of this beach were submerged by the tide, no more than two or three passers-by would actually materialize during the soap factory's operating hours, enabling me to buy back my own I. Magnin soap, reconfigured from pristine ivory ovals into gray blobs. I have no memory of the other "Families" in these houses, but in our own I would have said that there were not "2, 1, 2, people" but "3 people."

Possibly Quintana saw our personal "some Kind of an Island" differently.

Possibly she had reason to.

Brush your teeth, brush your hair, shush I'm working.

Once when we were living in the beach house we came home to find that she had placed a call to what was known familiarly on our stretch of the coast as "Camarillo." Camarillo was at that time a state psychiatric facility twenty-some miles north of us in Ventura County, the hospital in which Charlie Parker once detoxed and then memorialized in "Relaxin' at Camarillo," the institution sometimes said to have provided inspiration to the Eagles for "Hotel California."

She had called Camarillo, she advised us, to find out what she needed to do if she was going crazy.

She was five years old.

On another occasion we came home to the beach house and found that she had placed a call to Twentieth Century–Fox.

She had called Twentieth Century–Fox, she explained, to find out what she needed to do to be a star.

Again, she was five years old, maybe six.

Tita Moore is dead now, she died before Quintana did.

Dick Moore is dead now too, he died last year.

Marina called me recently.

I do not remember what Marina and I talked about but I know we did not talk about the club with "Mom's Sayings" in the garage and I know we did not talk about the soap factory and I know we did not talk about how the ends of the beach got submerged by the tide.

I say this because I do not believe that either Marina or I could have managed such a conversation.

> *Relax, said the night man—*
> *We are programmed to receive—*
> *You can check out any time you like—*
> *But you can never leave—*

So goes the lyric to "Hotel California."

Depths and shallows, quicksilver changes.

She was already a person. I could never afford to see that.

6

What about the "Craftsman" dinner knife of my mother's? The "Craftsman" dinner knife on Aunt Kate's table, the one I recognize in the photographs? Was it the same "Craftsman" dinner knife that dropped through the redwood slats of the deck into the iceplant on the slope? The same "Craftsman" dinner knife that stayed lost in the iceplant until the blade was pitted and the handle scratched? The knife we found only when we were correcting the drainage on the slope in order to pass the geological inspection required to sell the house and move to Brentwood Park? The knife I saved to pass on to her, a memento of the beach, of her grandmother, of her childhood?

I still have the knife.

Still pitted, still scratched.

I also still have the baby tooth her cousin Tony pulled, saved in a satin-lined jeweler's box, along with the baby teeth she herself eventually pulled and three loose pearls.

The baby teeth were to have been hers as well.

7

In fact I no longer value this kind of memento.

I no longer want reminders of what was, what got broken, what got lost, what got wasted.

There was a period, a long period, dating from my childhood until quite recently, when I thought I did.

A period during which I believed that I could keep people fully present, keep them with me, by preserving their mementos, their "things," their totems.

The detritus of this misplaced belief now fills the drawers and closets of my apartment in New York. There is no drawer I can open without seeing something I do not want, on reflection, to see. There is no closet I can open with room left for the clothes I might actually want to wear. In one closet that might otherwise be put to such use I see, instead, three old Burberry raincoats of John's, a suede jacket given to Quintana by the mother of her first boyfriend, and an angora cape, long since moth-eaten, given to my mother by my father not long after World War Two. In another closet I find a chest of drawers and perilously stacked assortment of boxes. I open one of the boxes. I find photographs taken by my grandfather when he was a mining engineer in the Sierra Nevada in the early years of the twentieth century. In another of the boxes I find the scraps of lace and embroidery that my mother had salvaged from her own mother's boxes of mementos.

The jet beads.

The ivory rosaries.

The objects for which there is no satisfactory resolution.

In the third of the boxes I find skein after skein of needlepoint yarn, saved in the eventuality that remedial stitches might ever be required on a canvas completed and given away in 2001. In the chest of drawers I find papers written by Quintana when she was still at the Westlake School for Girls: the research study on stress, the analysis of Angel Clare's role in *Tess of the d'Urbervilles*. I find her Westlake summer uniforms, I find her navy-blue gym shorts. I find the blue-and-white pinafore she wore for volunteering at St. John's Hospital in Santa Monica. I find the black wool challis dress I bought her when she was four at Bendel's on West Fifty-seventh Street. When I bought that black wool challis dress Bendel's was still on West Fifty-seventh Street. It was that long ago. Bendel's became after Geraldine Stutz stopped running it just another store but when it was still on West Fifty-seventh Street and I bought that dress it was special, it was everything I wanted either one of us to wear, it was all Holly's Harp chiffon and lettuce edges and sizes zero and two.

Other objects for which there is no satisfactory resolution.

I continue opening boxes.

I find more faded and cracked photographs than I want ever again to see.

I find many engraved invitations to the weddings of people who are no longer married.

I find many mass cards from the funerals of people whose faces I no longer remember.

In theory these mementos serve to bring back the moment.

In fact they serve only to make clear how inadequately I appreciated the moment when it was here.

How inadequately I appreciated the moment when it was here is something else I could never afford to see.

8

Her depths and shallows, her quicksilver changes.
Of course they were not allowed to remain just that, depths, shallows, quicksilver changes.

Of course they were eventually assigned names, a "diagnosis." The names kept changing. Manic depression for example became OCD and OCD was short for obsessive-compulsive disorder and obsessive-compulsive disorder became something else, I could never remember just what but in any case it made no difference because by the time I did remember there would be a new name, a new "diagnosis." I put the word "diagnosis" in quotes because I have not yet seen that case in which a "diagnosis" led to a "cure," or in fact to any outcome other than a confirmed, and therefore an enforced, debility.

Yet another demonstration of medicine as an imperfect art.

She was depressed. She was anxious. Because she was depressed and because she was anxious she drank too much. This was called medicating herself. Alcohol has its own well-known defects as a medication for depression but no one has ever suggested—ask any doctor—that it is not the most effective anti-anxiety agent yet known. This would seem a fairly straightforward dynamic, yet, once medicalized—once the depths and shallows and quicksilver changes had been assigned names—it appeared not to be. We went through many diagnoses, many conditions that got called by many names, before the least programmatic among her doctors settled on one that seemed to apply. The name of the condition that seemed to apply was this: "borderline personality disorder." "Patients with this diagnosis are a complex mixture of strengths and weaknesses that confuse the diagnostician and frustrate the psychotherapist." So notes a 2001 *New England Journal of Medicine* review of John G. Gunderson's *Borderline Personality Disorder: A*

Clinical Guide. "Such patients may seem charming, composed, and psychologically intact one day and collapse into suicidal despair the next." The review continues: "Impulsivity, affective lability, frantic efforts to avoid abandonment, and identity diffusion are all hallmarks."

I had seen most of these hallmarks.

I had seen the charm, I had seen the composure, I had seen the suicidal despair.

I had seen her wishing for death as she lay on the floor of her sitting room in Brentwood Park, the sitting room from which she had been able to look into the pink magnolia. *Let me just be in the ground*, she had kept sobbing. *Let me just be in the ground and go to sleep.*

I had seen the impulsivity.

I had seen the "affective lability," the "identity diffusion."

What I had not seen, or what I had in fact seen but had failed to recognize, were the "frantic efforts to avoid abandonment."

How could she have ever imagined that we could abandon her?

Had she no idea how much we needed her?

I recently read for the first time several fragments of what she had referred to at the time she wrote them as "the novel I'm writing just to show you." She must have been thirteen or fourteen when this project occurred to her. "Some of the events are based on the truth and the others are fictitious," she advises the reader at the outset. "The names have not yet been definitively changed." The protagonist in these fragments, also fourteen and also named Quintana (although sometimes referred to by other names, presumably trials for the definitive changes to come), believes she may be pregnant. She consults, in a plot point that seems specifically crafted to "confuse the diagnostician and frustrate the psychotherapist," her pediatrician. The pediatrician advises her that she must tell her parents. She does so. Her idea of how her parents would respond seems, like the entire rest of the plot point involving the pregnancy, confused, a fantasy, a manifestation of what might be extreme emotional distress or might be no more than narrative inventiveness: "They said that they would provide the abortion but after that they did not even care about her any more. She could live in their suburbia house in Brentwood, but they didn't even care what she did any more. That was fine in her book. Her father had a bad temper, but it showed that they cared very much about their only child. Now, they didn't even care any more. Quintana would lead her life any way she wanted."

At this point the fragment skids to an abrupt close: "On the next pages you will find out why and how Quintana died and her friends became complete burnouts at the age of eighteen."

So ended the novel she was writing just to show us.

Show us what?

Show us that she could write a novel?

Show us why and how she would die?

Show us what she believed our reaction would be?

Now, they didn't even care any more.

No.

She had no idea how much we needed her.

How could we have so misunderstood one another?

Had she chosen to write a novel because we wrote novels? Had it been one more obligation pressed on her? Had she felt it as a fear? Had we?

What follows are notes I made about a figure who at an earlier point had populated her nightmares, a fantast she called The Broken Man and described so often and with such troubling specificity that I was frequently moved to check for him on the terrace outside her second-floor windows. "He has on a blue work shirt, like a repair man," she repeatedly told me. "Short sleeves. He has his name always on his shirt. On the right-hand side. His name is David, Bill, Steve, one of those common names. I would guess this man is maybe age fifty to fifty-nine. Cap like a Dodger cap, navy blue, *GULF* on it. Brown belt, navy-blue pants, black really shiny shoes. And he talks to me in a really deep voice: *Hello, Quintana. I'm going to lock you here in the garage.* After I became five I never ever dreamed about him."

David, Bill, Steve, one of those common names?

Name always on his shirt? On the right-hand side?

Cap like a Dodger cap, navy blue, *GULF* on it?

After she became five she never ever dreamed about him?

It was when she said "I would guess this man is maybe age fifty to fifty-nine" that I realized my fear of The Broken Man to be as unquestioning as her own.

9

On this question of fear.

When I began writing these pages I believed their subject to be children, the ones we have and the ones we wish we had, the ways in which we depend on our children to depend on us, the ways in which we encourage them to remain children, the ways in which they remain more unknown to us than they do to their most casual acquaintances; the ways in which we remain equally opaque to them.

The ways in which for example we write novels "just to show" each other.

The ways in which our investments in each other remain too freighted ever to see the other clear.

The ways in which neither we nor they can bear to contemplate the death or the illness or even the aging of the other.

As the pages progressed it occurred to me that their actual subject was not children after all, at least not children *per se*, at least not children *qua* children: their actual subject was this refusal even to engage in such contemplation, this failure to confront the certainties of aging, illness, death.

This fear.

Only as the pages progressed further did I understand that the two subjects were the same.

When we talk about mortality we are talking about our children.

Hello, Quintana. I'm going to lock you here in the garage.

After I became five I never ever dreamed about him.

Once she was born I was never not afraid.

I was afraid of swimming pools, high-tension wires, lye under the sink, aspirin in the medicine cabinet, The Broken Man himself. I was afraid of rattlesnakes, riptides, landslides, strangers who appeared at the door, unexplained fevers, elevators without operators and empty hotel corridors. The source of the fear was obvious: it was the harm that could come to her. A question: if we and our children could in fact see the other clear would the fear go away? Would the fear go away for both of us, or would the fear go away only for me?

10

She was born in the first hour of the third day of March, 1966, at St. John's Hospital in Santa Monica. We were told that we could adopt her late the afternoon of the same day, March third, when Blake Watson, the obstetrician who delivered her, called the house at Portuguese Bend in which we then lived, forty-some miles down the coast from Santa Monica. I was taking a shower and burst into tears when John came into the bathroom to report what Blake Watson had said. "I have a beautiful baby girl at St. John's," is what he had said. "I need to know if you want her." The baby's mother, he had said, was from Tucson. She had been staying with relatives in California for the birth of the baby. An hour later we stood outside the window of the nursery at St. John's looking at an infant with fierce dark hair and rosebud features. The beads on her wrist spelled out not her name but "N.I.," for "No Information," which was the hospital's response to any questions that might be asked about a baby being placed for adoption. One of the nurses had tied a pink ribbon in the fierce dark hair. "Not *that* baby," John would repeat to her again and again in the years that followed, reenacting the nursery scene, the recommended "choice" narrative, the moment when, of all the babies in the nursery, we picked her. "Not *that* baby . . . *that* baby. The baby with the ribbon."

"Do *that baby*," she would repeat in return, a gift to us, an endorsement of our wisdom in opting to follow the recommended choice narrative. The choice narrative is no longer universally favored by professionals of child care, but it was in 1966. "Do it again. Do the baby with the ribbon."

And later: "Do the part about Dr. Watson calling." Blake Watson was already a folk figure in this recital.

And then: "Tell the part about the shower."

Even the shower had become part of the recommended choice narrative.

March 3, 1966.

After we left St. John's that night we stopped in Beverly Hills to tell John's brother Nick and his wife, Lenny. Lenny offered to meet me at Saks in the morning to buy a layette. She was taking ice from a crystal bucket, making celebratory drinks. Making celebratory drinks was what we did in our family to mark any unusual, or for that matter any usual, occasion. In retrospect we all drank more than we needed to drink but this did not occur to any of us in 1966. Only when I read my early fiction, in which someone was always downstairs making a drink and singing "Big Noise blew in from Winnetka," did I realize how much we all drank and how little thought we gave to it. Lenny added more ice to my glass and took the crystal bucket to the kitchen for a refill. "Saks because if you spend eighty dollars they throw in the bassinette," she added as she went.

I took the glass and put it down.

I had not considered the need for a bassinette.

I had not considered the need for a layette.

The baby with the fierce dark hair stayed that night and the next two in the nursery at St. John's and at some point during each of those nights I woke in the house at Portuguese Bend to the same chill, hearing the surf break on the rocks below, dreaming that I had forgotten her, left her asleep in a drawer, gone into town for dinner or a movie and made no provision for the infant who could even then be waking alone and hungry in the drawer in Portuguese Bend.

Dreaming in other words that I had failed.

Been given a baby and failed to keep her safe.

When we think about adopting a child, or for that matter about having a child at all, we stress the "blessing" aspect.

We omit the instant of the sudden chill, the "what-if," the free fall into certain failure.

What if I fail to take care of this baby?

What if this baby fails to thrive, what if this baby fails to love me?

And worse yet, worse by far, so much worse as to be

unthinkable, except I did think it, everyone who has ever waited to bring a baby home thinks it: *what if I fail to love this baby?*

March 3, 1966.

Until that instant when Lenny mentioned the bassinette it had all happened very fast. Until the bassinette it had all seemed casual, even blithe, not different in spirit from the Jax jerseys and printed cotton Lilly Pulitzer shifts we were all wearing that year: on New Year's weekend 1966 John and I had gone to Cat Harbor, on the far side of Catalina Island, on Morty Hall's boat. Morty Hall was married to Diana Lynn. Diana was a close friend of Lenny's. At some point on the boat that weekend (presumably at a point, given the drift of the excursion, when we were having or thinking about having or making or thinking about making a drink) I had mentioned to Diana that I was trying to have a baby. Diana had said I should talk to Blake Watson. Blake Watson had delivered her and Morty's four children. Blake Watson had also delivered the adopted daughter of Howard and Lou Erskine, old friends of Nick and Lenny's (Howard had gone to Williams with Nick) who happened to be on the boat that weekend. Maybe because the Erskines were there or maybe because I had mentioned wanting a baby or maybe because we had all had the drink we were thinking about having, the topic of adoption had entered the ether. Diana herself, it seemed, had been adopted, but this information had been withheld from her until she was twenty-one and it had become necessary for some financial reason that she know. Her adoptive parents had handled the situation by revealing the secret to (this had not seemed unusual at the time) Diana's agent. Diana's agent had handled the situation by taking Diana to lunch at (nor at the time had this) the Beverly Hills Hotel. Diana got the news in the Polo Lounge. She could remember fleeing into the bougainvillea around the bungalows, screaming.

That was all.

Yet the next week I was meeting Blake Watson.

When he called us from the hospital and asked if we wanted the beautiful baby girl there had been no hesitation: we wanted her. When they asked us at the hospital what we would call the beautiful baby girl there had been no hesitation: we would call her Quintana Roo. We had seen the name on a map when we were in Mexico a few months before and promised each other that if ever we had a daughter (dreamy speculation, no daughter had been in the offing) Quintana Roo would be her name. The place on the map called Quintana Roo was still not yet a state but a territory.

The place on the map called Quintana Roo was still frequented mainly by archaeologists, herpetologists, and bandits. The institution that became spring break in Cancún did not yet exist. There were no bargain flights. There was no Club Med.

The place on the map called Quintana Roo was still terra incognita.

As was the infant in the nursery at St. John's.

L'adoptada, she came to be called in the household. The adopted one.

M'ija she was also called. My daughter.

Adoption, I was to learn although not immediately, is hard to get right.

As a concept, even what was then its most widely approved narrative carried bad news: if someone "chose" you, what does that tell you?

Doesn't it tell you that you were available to be "chosen"?

Doesn't it tell you, in the end, that there are only two people in the world?

The one who "chose" you?

And the other who didn't?

Are we beginning to see how the word "abandonment" might enter the picture? Might we not make efforts to avoid such abandonment? Might not such efforts be characterized as "frantic"? Do we want to ask ourselves what follows? Do we need to ask ourselves what words come next to mind? Isn't one of those words "fear"? Isn't another of those words "anxiety"?

Terra incognita, as I had seen it until then, meant free of complications.

That terra incognita could present its own complications had never occurred to me.

11

On the day her adoption became legal, a hot September afternoon in 1966, we took her from the courthouse in downtown Los Angeles to lunch at The Bistro in Beverly Hills. At the courthouse she had been the only baby up for adoption; the other prospective adoptees that day were all adults, petitioning to adopt one another for one or another tax advantage. At The Bistro, too, more predictably, she was the only baby. *Qué hermosa*, the waiters crooned. *Qué chula*. They gave us the corner banquette usually saved for Sidney Korshak, a gesture the import of which would be clear only to someone who had lived in that particular community at that particular time. "Let's just say a nod from Korshak, and the Teamsters change management," the producer Robert Evans would later write by way of explaining who Sidney Korshak was. "A nod from Korshak, and Vegas shuts down. A nod from Korshak, and the Dodgers suddenly can play night baseball." The waiters placed her carrier on the table between us. She was wearing a blue-and-white dotted organdy dress. She was not quite seven months old. As far as I was concerned this lunch at Sidney Korshak's banquette at The Bistro was the happy ending to the choice narrative. We had chosen, the beautiful baby girl had accepted our choice, no natural parent had stood up at the courthouse and exercised his or her absolute legal right under the California law covering private adoptions to simply say no, she's mine, I want her back.

The issue, as I preferred to see it, was now closed.

The fear was now gone.

She was ours.

What I would not realize for another few years was that I had never been the only person in the house to feel the fear.

What if you hadn't answered the phone when Dr. Watson called, she would suddenly say. *What if you hadn't been home, what if you couldn't meet him at the hospital, what if there'd been an accident on the freeway, what would happen to me then?*

Since I had no adequate answer to these questions, I refused to consider them.

She considered them.

She lived with them.

And then she didn't.

"You have your wonderful memories," people said later, as if memories were solace. Memories are not. Memories are by definition of times past, things gone. Memories are the Westlake uniforms in the closet, the faded and cracked photographs, the invitations to the weddings of the people who are no longer married, the mass cards from the funerals of the people whose faces you no longer remember. Memories are what you no longer want to remember.

12

Sidney Korshak, 88, Dies; Fabled Fixer for the Chicago Mob:
So read the headline on Sidney Korshak's obituary, when he died in 1996, in *The New York Times*. "It was a tribute to Sidney Korshak's success that he was never indicted, despite repeated Federal and state investigations," the obituary continued. "And the widespread belief that he had in fact committed the very crimes the authorities could never prove made him an indispensable ally of leading Hollywood producers, corporate executives and politicians."

Thirty years before Morty Hall had declared on principle that he and Diana would refuse to go to any party given by Sidney Korshak.

I remember Morty and Diana arguing heatedly at dinner one night over this entirely hypothetical point.

Morty and Diana and the heated argument at dinner about whether or not to refuse to go to a party given by Sidney Korshak are, I have to conclude, what people mean when they mention my wonderful memories.

I recently saw Diana in an old commercial, one of those curiosities that turn up on YouTube. She is wearing a pale mink stole, draping herself over the hood of an Olds 88. In her smoky voice, she introduces the Olds 88 as "the hottest number I know." The Olds 88 at this point begins to talk to Diana, mentioning its own "rocket engine" and "hydra-matic drive." Diana wraps herself in the pale mink stole. "This is *great*," she replies to the Olds 88, again in the smoky voice.

It occurs to me that Diana does not sound in this Olds 88 commercial as if she would necessarily refuse to go to a party given by Sidney Korshak.

It also occurs to me that no one who now comes across this Olds 88 commercial on YouTube would know who Sidney

Korshak was, or for that matter who Diana was, or even what an Olds 88 was.

Time passes.

Diana is dead now. She died in 1971, at age forty-five, of a cerebral bleed.

She had collapsed after a wardrobe fitting for a picture she was due to start in a few days, the third lead, after Tuesday Weld and Anthony Perkins, in *Play It As It Lays*, for which John and I had written the screenplay and in which she was replaced by Tammy Grimes. The last time I saw her was in an ICU at Cedars-Sinai in Los Angeles. Lenny and I had gone together to Cedars to see her. The next time Lenny and I were in an ICU at Cedars together it was to see her and Nick's daughter Dominique, who had been strangled outside her house in Hollywood. "She looks even worse than Diana did," Lenny whispered when she saw Dominique, her intake of breath so sudden that I could barely hear her. I knew what Lenny was saying. Lenny was saying that Diana had not lived. Lenny was saying that Dominique was not going to live. I knew this—I suppose I had known it from the time the police officer who called identified himself as "Homicide"—but did not want to hear anyone say it. I ran into one of Diana's daughters a few months ago, in New York. We had lunch in the neighborhood. Diana's daughter remembered that we had last seen each other when Diana was still alive and living in New York and I had brought Quintana to play with her daughters. We promised to keep in touch. It occurred to me as I walked home that I had seen too many people for the last time in one or another ICU.

13

For everything there is a season.
   Ecclesiastes, yes, but I think first of The Byrds, "Turn Turn Turn."

I think first of Quintana Roo sitting on the bare hardwood floors of the house on Franklin Avenue and the waxed terra-cotta tiles of the house in Malibu listening to The Byrds on eight-track.

The Byrds and The Mamas and the Papas, "Do You Wanna Dance?"

"I wanna dance," she would croon back to the eight-track.

For everything there is a season. *I'd miss having the seasons*, people from New York like to say by way of indicating the extraordinary pride they take in not living in Southern California. In fact Southern California does have seasons: it has for example "fire season" or "the season when the fire comes," and it also has "the season when the rain comes," but such Southern California seasons, arriving as they do so theatrically as to seem strokes of random fate, do not inexorably suggest the passage of time. Those other seasons, the ones so prized on the East Coast, do. Seasons in Southern California suggest violence, but not necessarily death. Seasons in New York—the relentless dropping of the leaves, the steady darkening of the days, the blue nights themselves—suggest only death. For my having a child there was a season. That season passed. I have not yet located the season in which I do not hear her crooning back to the eight-track.

I still hear her crooning back to the eight-track.
I wanna dance.
The same way I still see the stephanotis in her braid, the plumeria tattoo through her veil.

Something else I still see from that wedding day at St. John the Divine: the bright red soles on her shoes.

She was wearing Christian Louboutin shoes, pale satin with bright red soles.

You saw the red soles when she kneeled at the altar.

14

Before she was born we had been planning a trip to Saigon. We had assignments from magazines, we had credentials, we had everything we needed.

Including, suddenly, a baby.

That year, 1966, during which the American military presence in Vietnam would reach four hundred thousand and American B-52s had begun bombing the North, was not widely considered an ideal year to take an infant to Southeast Asia, yet it never occurred to me to abandon or even adjust the plan. I even went so far as to shop for what I imagined we would need: Donald Brooks pastel linen dresses for myself, a flowered Porthault parasol to shade the baby, as if she and I were about to board a Pan Am flight and disembark at *Le Cercle Sportif*.

In the end this trip to Saigon did not take place, although its cancellation was by no means based on what might have seemed the obvious reason—we canceled, it turned out, because John had to finish the book he had contracted to write about César Chávez and his National Farm Workers Association and the DiGiorgio grape strike in Delano—and I mention Saigon at all only by way of suggesting the extent of my misconceptions about what having a child, let alone adopting one, might actually entail.

How could I not have had misconceptions?

I had been handed this perfect baby, out of the blue, at St. John's Hospital in Santa Monica. She could not have been more exactly the baby I wanted. In the first place she was beautiful. *Hermosa, chula*. Strangers stopped me on the street to tell me so. "I have a beautiful baby girl at St. John's," Blake Watson had said, and he did. Everyone sent dresses, an homage to the beautiful baby girl. There the dresses were in her closet, sixty of them (I counted them, again and again), immaculate little wisps of batiste and Liberty lawn on miniature wooden hangers. The miniature wooden hangers, too, were a gift to the beautiful baby girl, another homage from her instantly acquired relatives, besotted aunts and uncles and cousins in West Hartford (John's family) and Sacramento (mine). I recall changing her dress four times on the afternoon the State of California social worker made her mandated visit to observe the candidate for adoption in the home environment.

We sat on the lawn.

The candidate for adoption played at our feet.

I did not mention to the social worker that Saigon had until recently figured in the candidate's future.

Nor did I mention that current itineraries called for her to sojourn instead at the Starlight Motel in Delano.

Arcelia, who cleaned the house and laundered the wisps of batiste, busied herself watering, as anticipated.

"As anticipated" because I had prepped Arcelia for the visit.

The thought of an unstructured encounter between Arcelia and a State of California social worker had presented spectral concerns from the outset, imagined scenarios that kept me awake at four in the morning and only multiplied as the date of the visit approached: what if the social worker were to notice that Arcelia spoke only Spanish? What if the social worker were to happen into the question of Arcelia's papers? What would the social worker put in her report if she divined that I was entrusting the perfect baby to an undocumented alien?

The social worker remarked, in English, on the fine weather.

I tensed, fearing a trap.

Arcelia smiled, beatific, and continued watering.

I relaxed.

At which point Arcelia, no longer beatific but dramatic, flung the hose across the lawn and snatched up Quintana, screaming *"Víbora!"*

The social worker lived in Los Angeles, she had to know what *víbora* meant, *víbora* in Los Angeles meant snake and snake in Los Angeles meant rattlesnake. I was relatively certain that the rattlesnake was a fantasy but I nonetheless guided Arcelia and Quintana inside, then turned to the social worker. It's a game, I lied. Arcelia pretends she sees a snake. We all laugh. Because you can see. There is no snake.

There could be no snake in Quintana Roo's garden.

Only later did I see that I had been raising her as a doll.

She would never have faulted me for that.

She would have seen it as a logical response to my having been handed, out of the blue at St. John's Hospital in Santa Monica, the beautiful baby girl, herself. At the house after her christening at St. Martin of Tours Catholic Church in Brentwood we had watercress sandwiches and champagne and later, for anyone still around at dinner time, fried chicken. The house we were renting that spring belonged to Sara Mankiewicz, Herman Mankiewicz's widow, who was traveling for six months, and although she had packed away the china she did not want used along with Herman Mankiewicz's Academy Award for *Citizen Kane* (you'll have friends over, she had said, they'll get drunk, they'll want to play with it) she had left out her Minton dinner plates, the same pattern as the Minton tiles that line the arcade south of Bethesda Fountain in Central Park, for me to use. I had not used the Minton dinner plates before the christening but I put them on a buffet table that night for the fried chicken. I remember Diana eating a chicken wing off one of them, a fleck of rosemary from the chicken the only blemish on her otherwise immaculate manicure. The perfect baby slept in one of her two long white christening dresses (she had two long white christening dresses because she had been given two long white christening dresses, one batiste, the other linen, another homage) in the Saks bassinette. John's brother Nick took photographs. I look at those photographs now and am struck by how many of the women present were wearing Chanel suits and David Webb bracelets, and smoking cigarettes. It was a time of my life during which I actually believed that somewhere between frying the chicken to serve on Sara Mankiewicz's Minton dinner plates and buying the Porthault parasol to shade the beautiful baby girl in Saigon I had covered the main "motherhood" points.

15

There was a reason why I told you about Arcelia and the sixty dresses.

I was not unaware as I did so that a certain number of readers (more than some of you might think, fewer than the less charitable among you will think) would interpret this apparently casual information (she dressed her baby in clothes that needed washing and ironing, she had help in the house to do this washing and ironing) as evidence that Quintana did not have an "ordinary" childhood, that she was "privileged."

I wanted to lay this on the table.

"Ordinary" childhoods in Los Angeles very often involve someone speaking Spanish, but I will not make that argument.

Nor will I even argue that she had an "ordinary" childhood, although I remain unsure about exactly who does.

"Privilege" is something else.

"Privilege" is a judgment.

"Privilege" is an opinion.

"Privilege" is an accusation.

"Privilege" remains an area to which—when I think of what she endured, when I consider what came later—I will not easily cop.

I look again at the photographs Nick took at the christening.

In fact the afternoon these photographs were taken, the afternoon at St. Martin of Tours and Sara Mankiewicz's house, the afternoon when Quintana wore the two christening dresses and I wore one of the pastel linen Donald Brooks dresses I had bought under the misunderstanding that they would be needed in Saigon, was never what I considered her "real" christening. (One question: would you have called buying pastel linen dresses for Saigon a mark of "privilege"? Or would you have called it more a mark of bone stupidity?) Her "real" christening had taken place in a tiled sink at the house in Portuguese Bend, a few days after we brought her home from the nursery at St. John's Hospital in Santa Monica. John had christened her himself, and told me only after the fact.

I recall a certain defensiveness on this issue.

What he said when he told me was not exactly along the lines of "I thought we might christen the baby, what do you think."

What he said when he told me was more along the lines of "I just christened the baby, take it or leave it."

It seemed that he had worried because the date I had arranged at St. Martin of Tours was two months away.

It seemed that he had not wanted to risk consigning our not yet christened baby to limbo.

I knew why he had not told me this before the fact.

He had not told me this before the fact because I was not a Catholic, and he had imagined objection.

Of the two of us, however, it was I who thought of that day in the tiled sink as the "real" christening.

The other christening, the christening at which the photographs were taken, was the "dress-up" christening.

Certain faces spring out at me from the photographs.

Connie Wald, wearing one of the several Chanel suits in evidence that afternoon, in her case one of blue-and-cream tweed lined in cyclamen-pink silk. It was Connie who gave Quintana one of the two long white dresses she wore at the church and after. Until Connie was in her nineties, when she developed a neuropathy, she still swam every day of her life. She cut back on the regimen of daily laps and stopped driving herself around Beverly Hills in an aged Rolls-Royce but otherwise continued exactly as before. She still wore the Claire McCardell dresses she had been given when she was a McCardell model in the 1940s. She still gave two or three dinner parties a week, cooked herself, mixed young and old in a way that flattered everyone present, lit huge fires in her library and filled the tables with salted almonds and fat pitchers of nasturtiums and the roses she still grew herself. Connie had been married to the producer Jerry Wald, who was said to have been Budd Schulberg's model for Sammy Glick in *What Makes Sammy Run* and who had died a few years before I met her. She once told me about the six weeks she spent in Nevada establishing the residency she needed to divorce her previous husband and marry Jerry Wald. She did not spend the six weeks in Las Vegas, because Las Vegas as we later knew it did not yet exactly exist. She spent the six weeks twenty miles from Las Vegas, in Boulder City, which had been built by the Bureau of Reclamation as the construction camp for Hoover Dam and in which both gambling and union membership were prohibited by law. I asked her what she had found to do for six weeks in Boulder City. She said that Jerry had given her a dog, which she walked, every day, through the identical streets lined with matching government bungalows that constituted Boulder City and on across the dam. I recall this striking me as the most intrepid story I ever heard about how someone did or did not stay in Las Vegas, a topic not entirely deficient in intrepid stories.

Diana.

Diana Lynn, Diana Hall.

Hers is another face that springs out from the photographs taken that day.

In this photograph she is holding a champagne flute and smoking a cigarette. It occurs to me as I look at her photograph that it was Diana who had made that day possible. It was Diana who had drawn me into the conversation about adoption over the New Year's weekend on Morty's boat. It was Diana who had talked to Blake Watson, it was Diana who had intuited how deeply I needed Quintana. It was Diana who had changed my life.

16

Some of us feel this overpowering need for a child and some of us don't. It had come over me quite suddenly, in my mid-twenties, when I was working for *Vogue*, a tidal surge. Once this surge hit I saw babies wherever I went. I followed their carriages on the street. I cut their pictures from magazines and tacked them on the wall next to my bed. I put myself to sleep by imagining them: imagining holding them, imagining the down on their heads, imagining the soft spots at their temples, imagining the way their eyes dilated when you looked at them.

Until then pregnancy had been only a fear, an accident to be avoided at any cost.

Until then I had felt nothing but relief at the moment each month when I started to bleed. If that moment was delayed by even a day I would leave my office at *Vogue* and, looking for instant reassurance that I was not pregnant, go see my doctor, a Columbia Presbyterian internist who had come to be known, because his mother-in-law had been editor in chief of *Vogue* and his office was always open to fretful staff members, as "the *Vogue* doctor." I recall sitting in his examining room on East Sixty-seventh Street one morning waiting for the results of the most recent rabbit test I had implored him to do. He came into the room whistling, and began misting the plants on the window sill.

The test, I prompted.

He continued misting the plants.

I needed to know the results, I said, because I was leaving to spend Christmas in California. I had the ticket in my bag. I opened the bag. I showed him.

"You might not need a ticket to California," he said. "You might need a ticket to Havana."

I correctly understood this to be intended as reassuring, his baroque way of saying that I might need an abortion and that he could help me get one, yet my immediate response was to vehemently reject the proposed solution: it was delusional, it was out of the question, it was beyond discussion.

I couldn't possibly go to Havana.

There was a revolution in Havana.

In fact there was: it was December 1958, Fidel Castro would enter Havana within days.

I mentioned this.

"There's always a revolution in Havana," the *Vogue* doctor said.

A day later I started to bleed, and cried all night.

I thought I was regretting having missed this interesting moment in Havana but it turned out the surge had hit and what I was regretting was not having the baby, the still unmet baby, the baby I would eventually bring home from St. John's Hospital in Santa Monica. *What if you hadn't been home, what if you couldn't meet Dr. Watson at the hospital, what if there'd been an accident on the freeway, what would happen to me then.* Not long ago, when I read the fragment of the novel written just to show us, the scrap in which the protagonist thinks she might be pregnant and elects to address the situation by consulting her pediatrician, I remembered that morning on East Sixty-seventh Street. *Now, they didn't even care any more.*

17

There are certain moments in those first years with her that I remember very clearly.

These very clear moments stand out, recur, speak directly to me, on some levels flood me with pleasure and on others still break my heart.

I remember very clearly for example that her earliest transactions involved what she called "sundries." She invested this word, which she used as a synonym for "possessions" but seemed to derive from the "sundries shops" in the many hotels to which she had already been taken, with considerable importance, dizzying alternations of infancy and sophistication. One day after she had asked me for a Magic Marker I found her marking off an empty box into "drawers," or areas meant for specific of these "sundries." The "drawers" she designated were these: "Cash," "Passport," "My IRA," "Jewelry," and, finally—I find myself hardly able to tell you this—"Little Toys."

Again, the careful printing.

The printing alone I cannot forget.

The printing alone breaks my heart.

Another moment, not, on examination, dissimilar: I remember very clearly the Christmas night at her grandmother's house in West Hartford when John and I came in from a movie to find her huddled alone on the stairs to the second floor. The Christmas lights were off, her grandmother was asleep, everyone in the house was asleep, and she was patiently waiting for us to come home and address what she called "the new problem." We asked what the new problem was. "I just noticed I have cancer," she said, and pulled back her hair to show us what she had construed to be a growth on her scalp. In fact it was chicken pox, obviously contracted before she left nursery school in

Malibu and just now surfacing, but had it been cancer, she had prepared her mind to be ready for cancer.

A question occurs to me:

Did she emphasize "new" when she mentioned "the new problem"?

Was she suggesting that there were also "old" problems, undetailed, problems with which she was for the moment opting not to burden us?

A third example: I remember very clearly the doll's house she constructed on the bookshelves of her bedroom at the beach. She had worked on it for several days, after studying a similar improvisation in an old copy of *House & Garden* ("Muffet Hemingway's doll's house" was how she identified the prototype, taking her cue from the *House & Garden* headline), but this was its first unveiling. Here was the living room, she explained, and here was the dining room, and here was the kitchen, and here was the bedroom.

I asked about an undecorated and apparently unallocated shelf.

That, she said, would be the projection room.

The projection room.

I tried to assimilate this.

Some people we knew in Los Angeles did in fact live in houses with projection rooms but to the best of my knowledge she had never seen one. These people who lived in houses with projection rooms belonged to our "working" life. She, I had imagined, belonged to our "private" life. Our "private" life, I had also imagined, was separate, sweet, inviolate.

I set this distinction to one side and asked how she planned to furnish the projection room.

There would need to be a table for the telephone to the projectionist, she said, then stopped to consider the empty shelf.

"And whatever I'll need for Dolby Sound," she added then.

As I describe these very clear memories I am struck by what they have in common: each involves her trying to handle adult life, trying to be a convincing grown-up person at an age when she was still entitled to be a small child. She could talk about "My IRA" and she could talk about "Dolby Sound" and she could talk about "just noticing" she had cancer, she could call Camarillo to find out what she needed to do if she was going crazy and she could call Twentieth Century–Fox to find out what she needed to do to be a star, but she was not actually prepared to act on whatever answers she got. "Little Toys" could still assume equal importance. She could still consult her pediatrician.

Was this confusion about where she stood in the chronological scheme of things our doing?

Did we demand that she be an adult?

Did we ask her to assume responsibility before she had any way of doing so?

Did our expectations prevent her from responding as a child?

I recall taking her, when she was four or five, up the coast to Oxnard to see *Nicholas and Alexandra*. On the drive home from Oxnard she referred to the czar and czarina as "Nicky and Sunny," and said, when asked how she had liked the picture, "I think it's going to be a big hit."

In other words, despite having just been told what had seemed to me as I watched it a truly harrowing story, a story that placed both parents and children in unthinkable peril—a peril to children more unthinkable still because its very source lay in the bad luck of having been born to these particular parents—she had resorted without hesitation to the local default response, which was an instant assessment of audience potential. Similarly, a few years later, taken to Oxnard to see *Jaws*, she had watched in horror, then, while I was still unloading the car in Malibu, skipped down to the beach and dove into the surf. About certain threats I considered real she remained in fact fearless. When she was eight or nine and enrolled in Junior Lifeguard, a program run by the Los Angeles County lifeguards that entailed being repeatedly taken out beyond the Zuma Beach breakers on a lifeguard boat and swimming back in, John and I arrived to pick her up and found the beach empty. Finally we saw her, alone, huddled in a towel behind a dune. The lifeguards, it seemed, were insisting, "for absolutely no reason," on taking everyone home. I said there must be a reason. "Only the sharks," she said. I looked at her. She was clearly disappointed, even a little disgusted, impatient with the turn the morning had taken. She shrugged. "They were just blues," she said then.

When I remember the "sundries" I am forced to remember the hotels in which she had stayed before she was five or six or seven. I say "forced to remember" because my images of her in these hotels are tricky. On the one hand those images survive as my truest memories of the paradox she was—of the child trying not to appear as a child, of the strenuousness with which she tried to present the face of a convincing adult. On the other hand it is just such images—the same images—that encourage a view of her as "privileged," somehow deprived of a "normal" childhood.

On the face of it she had no business in these hotels.

The Lancaster and the Ritz and the Plaza Athénée in Paris.

The Dorchester in London.

The St. Regis and the Regency in New York, and also the Chelsea. The Chelsea was for those trips to New York when we were not on expenses. At the Chelsea they would find her a crib downstairs and John would bring her breakfast from the White Tower across the street.

The Fairmont and the Mark Hopkins in San Francisco.

The Kahala and the Royal Hawaiian in Honolulu. "Where did the morning went," she would ask at the Royal Hawaiian when she woke, still on mainland time, and found the horizon dark. "Imagine a five-year-old walking to the reef," she would say at the Royal Hawaiian, near a swoon, when we held her hands and swung her through the shallow sea.

The Ambassador and the Drake in Chicago.

It was at the Ambassador, in the Pump Room at midnight, that she ate caviar for the first time, a mixed success since she wanted it again at every meal thereafter and did not yet entirely understand the difference between "on expenses" and "not on expenses." She had happened to be in the Pump Room at midnight because we had taken her that night to Chicago Stadium to see a band we were following, Chicago, research for *A Star Is Born*. She had sat through the concert onstage, on one of the amps. The band had played "Does Anybody Really Know What Time It Is," and "25 or 6 to 4." She had referred to the band as "the boys."

When we left Chicago Stadium with the boys that night the crowd had rocked the car, delighting her.

She did not want to go to her grandmother's in West Hartford the next day, she had advised me when we got back to the Ambassador, she wanted to go to Detroit with the boys.

So much for keeping our "private" life separate from our "working" life.

In fact she was inseparable from our working life. Our working life was the very reason she happened to be in these hotels. When she was five or six, for example, we took her with us to Tucson, where *The Life and Times of Judge Roy Bean* was shooting. The Hilton Inn, where the production was based during its Tucson location, sent a babysitter to stay with her while we watched the dailies. The babysitter asked her to get Paul Newman's autograph. A crippled son was mentioned. Quintana got the autograph, delivered it to the babysitter, then burst into tears. It was never clear to me whether she was crying about the crippled son or about feeling played by the babysitter. Dick Moore was the cinematographer on *The Life and Times of Judge Roy Bean* but she seemed to make no connection between this Dick Moore she encountered at the Hilton Inn in Tucson and the Dick Moore she encountered on our beach. On our beach everyone was home, and so was she. At the Hilton Inn in Tucson everyone was working, and so was she. "Working" was a way of being she understood at her core. When she was nine I took her with me on an eight-city book tour: New York, Boston, Washington, Dallas, Houston, Los Angeles, San Francisco, Chicago. "How do you like our monuments," Katharine Graham had asked her in Washington. She had seemed mystified but game. "What monuments," she had asked with interest, entirely unaware that most children who visited Washington were shown the Lincoln Memorial instead of National Public Radio and *The Washington Post*. Her favorite city on this tour had been Dallas. Her least favorite had been Boston. Boston, she had complained, was "all white."

"You mean you didn't see many black people in Boston," Susan Traylor's mother had suggested when Quintana got back to Malibu and reported on her trip.

"No," Quintana said, definite on this point. "I mean it's not in color."

She had learned to order triple lamb chops from room service on this trip.

She had learned to sign her room number for Shirley Temples on this trip.

If a car or an interviewer failed to show up at the appointed time on this trip she had known what to do: check the schedule and "call Wendy," Wendy being the publicity director at Simon & Schuster. She knew which bookstores reported to which best-seller lists and she knew the names of their major buyers and she knew what a green room was and she knew what agents did. She knew what agents did because before she was four, on a day when my schedule for household help had fallen apart, I had taken her with me to a meeting at the William Morris office in Beverly Hills. I had prepared her, explained that the meeting was about earning the money that paid for the triple lamb chops from room service, impressed on her the need for not interrupting or asking when we could leave. This preparation, it turned out, was entirely unnecessary. She was far too interested to interrupt. She accepted a glass of water when one was offered to her, managed the heavy Baccarat glass without dropping it, listened attentively but did not speak. Only at the end of the meeting did she ask the William Morris agent the question apparently absorbing her: "But when do you give her the money?"

When we noticed her confusions did we consider our own?

I still have the "Sundries" box in my closet, marked as she marked it.

18

I do not know many people who think they have succeeded as parents. Those who do tend to cite the markers that indicate (their own) status in the world: the Stanford degree, the Harvard MBA, the summer with the white-shoe law firm. Those of us less inclined to compliment ourselves on our parenting skills, in other words most of us, recite rosaries of our failures, our neglects, our derelictions and delinquencies. The very definition of success as a parent has undergone a telling transformation: we used to define success as the ability to encourage the child to grow into independent (which is to say into adult) life, to "raise" the child, to let the child go. If a child wanted to try out his or her new bicycle on the steepest hill in the neighborhood, there may have been a pro forma reminder that the steepest hill in the neighborhood descended into a four-way intersection, but such a reminder, because independence was still seen as the desired end of the day, stopped short of nagging. If a child elected to indulge in activity that could end badly, such negative possibilities may have gotten mentioned once, but not twice.

It so happened that I was a child during World War Two, which meant that I grew up in circumstances in which even more stress than usual was placed on independence. My father was a finance officer in the Army Air Corps, and during the early years of the war my mother and brother and I followed him from Fort Lewis in Tacoma to Duke University in Durham to Peterson Field in Colorado Springs. This was not hardship but neither was it, given the overcrowding and dislocation that characterized life near American military facilities in 1942 and 1943, a sheltered childhood. In Tacoma we were lucky enough to rent what was called a guest house but was actually one large room with its own entrance. In Durham we again lived in one room, this one not large and not with its own entrance, in a house that belonged to a Baptist preacher and his family. This room in Durham came with "kitchen privileges," which amounted in practice to occasional use of the family's apple butter. In Colorado Springs we lived, for the first time, in an actual house, a four-room bungalow near a psychiatric hospital, but did not unpack: there was no point in unpacking, my mother pointed out, since "orders"—a mysterious concept that I took on faith—could arrive any day.

My brother and I were expected in each of these venues to adapt, make do, both invent a life and simultaneously accept that any life we invented would be summarily upended by the arrival of "orders." Who gave the orders was never clear to me. In Colorado Springs, where my father was stationed for longer than he had been in either Tacoma or Durham, my brother scouted the neighborhood, and made friends. I trolled the grounds of the psychiatric hospital, recorded the dialogue I overheard, and wrote "stories." I did not at the time think this an unreasonable alternative to staying in Sacramento and going to school (later it occurred to me that if I had stayed in Sacramento and gone to school I might have learned to subtract, a skill that remains unmastered), but it would have made no difference if I had. There was a war in progress. That war did not revolve around or in any way hinge upon the wishes of children. In return for tolerating these home truths, children were allowed to invent their own lives. The notion that they could be left to their own devices—were in fact best left so— went unquestioned.

Once the war was over, and we were again home in Sacramento, this laissez-faire approach continued. I remember getting my learner's driving permit at age fifteen-and-a-half and interpreting it as a logical mandate to drive from Sacramento to Lake Tahoe after dinner, two or three hours up one of the switchbacked highways into the mountains and, if you just turned around and kept driving, which was all we did, since we already had whatever we wanted to drink in the car with us, two or three hours back. This disappearance into the heart of the Sierra Nevada on what amounted to an overnight

DUI went without comment from my mother and father. I remember, above Sacramento at about the same age, getting sluiced into a diversion dam while rafting on the American River, then dragging the raft upstream and doing it again. This too went without comment.

All gone.

Virtually unimaginable now.

No time left on the schedule of "parenting" for tolerating such doubtful pastimes.

Instead, ourselves the beneficiaries of this kind of benign neglect, we now measure success as the extent to which we manage to keep our children monitored, tethered, tied to us. Judith Shapiro, when she was president of Barnard, was prompted to write an op-ed piece in *The New York Times* advising parents to show a little more trust in their children, stop trying to manage every aspect of their college life. She mentioned the father who had taken a year off from his job to supervise the preparation of his daughter's college applications. She mentioned the mother who had accompanied her daughter to a meeting with her dean to discuss a research project. She mentioned the mother who had demanded, on the grounds that it was she who paid the tuition bills, that her daughter's academic transcript be sent to her directly.

"You pay $35,000 a year, you want services," Tamar Lewin of *The New York Times* was told by the director of "the parents' office" at Northeastern in Boston, an office devoted to the tending of parents having become a virtually ubiquitous feature of campus administration. For a *Times* piece a few years ago on the narrowing of the generation gap on campus, Ms. Lewin spoke not only to the tenders of the parents but also to the students themselves, one of whom, at George Washington University, allowed that she used well over three thousand cellphone minutes a month talking to her family. She seemed to view this family as an employable academic resource. "I might call my dad and say, 'What's going on with the Kurds?' It's a lot easier than looking it up. He knows a lot. I would trust almost anything my dad says." Asked if she ever thought she might be too close to her parents, another George Washington student had seemed only puzzled: "They're our parents," she had said. "They're supposed to help us. That's almost their job."

We increasingly justify such heightened involvement with our children as essential to their survival. We keep them on speed dial. We watch them on Skype. We track their movements. We expect every call to be answered, every changed plan reported. We fantasize unprecedented new dangers in their every unsupervised encounter. We mention terrorism, we share anxious admonitions: "It's different now." "It's not the way it was." "You can't let them do what we did."

Yet there were always dangers to children.

Ask anyone who was a child during the supposedly idyllic decade advertised to us at the time as the reward for World War Two. New cars. New appliances. Women in high-heeled pumps and ruffled aprons removing cookie sheets from ovens enameled in postwar "harvest" colors: avocado, gold, mustard, brown, burnt orange. This was as safe as it got, except it wasn't: ask any child who was exposed during this postwar harvest fantasy to the photographs from Hiroshima and Nagasaki, ask any child who saw the photographs from the death camps.

"I *have to know* about this."

So Quintana said when I found her hiding under the covers of her bed in Malibu, stunned, disbelieving, flashlight in hand, studying a book of old *Life* photographs that she had come across somewhere.

There were blue-and-white checked gingham curtains in the windows of her room in Malibu.

I remember them blowing as she showed me the book.

She was showing me the photographs Margaret Bourke-White did for *Life* of the ovens at Buchenwald.

That was what she *had to know*.

Or ask the child who would not allow herself to fall asleep during most of 1946 because she feared the fate of six-year-old Suzanne Degnan, who on January seventh of that year had been kidnapped from her bed in Chicago, dissected in a sink, and disposed of in pieces in the sewers of the far north side.

Six months after Suzanne Degnan's disappearance a seventeen-year-old University of Chicago sophomore named William Heirens was arrested and sentenced to life imprisonment.

Or ask the child who nine years later followed the California search for fourteen-year-old Stephanie Bryan, who vanished while walking home from her Berkeley junior high school through the parking lot of the Claremont Hotel, her customary shortcut, and was next seen several hundred miles from Berkeley, buried in a shallow grave in California's most northern mountains. Five months after Stephanie Bryan's disappearance a twenty-seven-year-old University of California accounting student was arrested, charged with her death, and within two years convicted and executed in the gas chamber at San Quentin.

Since the events surrounding the disappearances and deaths of both Suzanne Degnan and Stephanie Bryan occurred in circulation areas served by aggressive Hearst papers, both cases were extensively and luridly covered. The lesson taught by the coverage was clear: childhood is by definition perilous. To be a child is to be small, weak, inexperienced, the dead bottom of the food chain. Every child knows this, or did.

Knowing this is why children call Camarillo.

Knowing this is why children call Twentieth Century–Fox.

"This case has been a haunting one all my life as I was a grown-up eight-year-old when it happened and followed it every day in the *Oakland Tribune* from day one till the end." So wrote an internet correspondent in response to a recent look back at the Stephanie Bryan case. "I had to read it when my parents weren't around as they didn't think it was fitting to be reading about a homicide at my age."

As adults we lose memory of the gravity and terrors of childhood.

Hello, Quintana. I'm going to lock you here in the garage.

After I became five I never ever dreamed about him.

I have to know about this.

One of her abiding fears, I learned much later, was that John would die and there would be no one but her to take care of me.

How could she have even imagined that I would not take care of her?

I used to ask that.

Now I ask the reverse:

How could she have even imagined that I *could* take care of her?

She saw me as needing care myself.

She saw me as frail.

Was that her anxiety or mine?

I learned about this fear when she was temporarily off the ventilator in one or another ICU, I have no memory which.

I told you, they were all the same.

The blue-and-white printed curtains. The gurgling through plastic tubing. The dripping from the IV line, the rales, the alarms.

The codes. The crash cart.

This was never supposed to happen to her.

It must have been the ICU at UCLA.

Only at UCLA was she off the ventilator long enough to have had this conversation.

You have your wonderful memories.

I do, but they blur.

They fade into one another.

They become, as Quintana a month or two later described the only memory she could summon of the five weeks she spent in the ICU at UCLA, "all mudgy."

I tried to tell her: I too have trouble remembering.

Languages mingle: do I need an *abogado* or do I need an *avocat*?

Names vanish. The names for example of California counties, once so familiar that I recited them in alphabetized order (Alameda and Alpine and Amador, Calaveras and Colusa and Contra Costa, Madera and Marin and Mariposa) now elude me.

The name of one county I do remember.

The name of this single county I always remember.

I had my own Broken Man.

I had my own stories about which I had to know.

Trinity.

The name of the county in which Stephanie Bryan had been found buried in the shallow grave was Trinity.

The name of the test site at Alamogordo that had led to the photographs from Hiroshima and Nagasaki was also Trinity.

19

"What we need here is a montage, music over.
How she: talked to her father and xxxx and xxxxx—
"xx," he said.
"xxx," she said.
"*How she:*
"*How* she did this and *why* she did that and *what the music was* when they did x and x and xxx—
"*How he, and also she*—"

The above are notes I made in 1995 for a novel I published in 1996, *The Last Thing He Wanted*. I offer them as a representation of how comfortable I used to be when I wrote, how easily I did it, how little thought I gave to what I was saying until I had already said it. In fact, in any real sense, what I was doing then was never writing at all: I was doing no more than sketching in a rhythm and letting that rhythm tell me what it was I was saying. Many of the marks I set down on the page were no more than "xxx," or "xxxx," symbols that meant "copy tk," or "copy to come," but do notice: such symbols were arranged in specific groupings. A single "x" differed from a double "xx," "xxx" from "xxxx." The number of such symbols had a meaning. The arrangement was the meaning.

The same passage, rewritten, which is to say "written" in any real sense at all, became more detailed: "What we want here is a montage, music over. *Angle on Elena.* Alone on the dock where her father berthed the *Kitty Rex*. Working loose a splinter on the planking with the toe of her sandal. Taking off her scarf and shaking out her hair, damp from the sweet heavy air of South Florida. *Cut to Barry Sedlow.* Standing in the door of the frame shack, under the sign that read RENTALS

GAS BAIT BEER AMMO. Leaning against the counter. Watching Elena through the screen door as he waited for change. *Angle on the manager.* Sliding a thousand-dollar bill beneath the tray in the cash register, replacing the tray, counting out the hundreds. No place you could not pass a hundred. There in the sweet heavy air of South Florida. Havana so close you could see the two-tone Impalas on the Malecón. Goddamn but we had some fun there."

More detailed, yes.

"She" now has a name: Elena.

"He" now has a name: Barry Sedlow.

But again, do notice: it had all been there in the original notes. It had all been there in the symbols, the marks on the page. It had all been there in the "xxx" and the "xxxx."

I supposed this process to be like writing music.

I have no idea whether or not this was an accurate assessment, since I neither wrote nor read music. All I know now is that I no longer write this way. All I know now is that writing, or whatever it was I was doing when I could proceed on no more than "xxx" and "xxxx," whatever it was I was doing when I imagined myself hearing the music, no longer comes easily to me. For a while I laid this to a certain weariness with my own style, an impatience, a wish to be more direct. I encouraged the very difficulty I was having laying words on the page. I saw it as evidence of a new directness. I see it differently now. I see it now as frailty. I see it now as the very frailty Quintana feared.

We are moving into another summer.

I find myself increasingly focused on this issue of frailty.

I fear falling on the street, I imagine bicycle messengers knocking me to the ground. The approach of a child on a motorized scooter causes me to freeze mid-intersection, play dead. I no longer go for breakfast to Three Guys on Madison Avenue: what if I were to fall on the way?

I feel unsteady, unbalanced, as if my nerves are misfiring, which may or may not be an exact description of what my nerves are in fact doing.

I hear a new tone when acquaintances ask how I am, a tone I have not before noticed and find increasingly distressing, even humiliating: these acquaintances seem as they ask impatient, half concerned, half querulous, as if no longer interested in the answer.

As if all too aware that the answer will be a complaint.

I determine to speak, if asked how I am, only positively.

I frame the cheerful response.

What I believe to be the cheerful response as I frame it emerges, as I hear it, more in the nature of a whine.

Do not whine, I write on an index card. *Do not complain. Work harder. Spend more time alone.*

I push-pin the index card to the corkboard on which I collect notes.

"*Struck by a train nine days before our wedding*," one note on the corkboard reads. "*Left the house that morning and was killed that afternoon in the crash of a small plane*," another reads. "*It was the second of January, 1931*," a third reads. "*I ran a little coup. My brother became president. He was more mature. I went to Europe.*"

These notes I push-pin to the corkboard are intended at the time I make them to restore my ability to function, but have so far not done so. I study the notes again. *Who* was struck by the train nine days before her wedding? Or was it nine days before *his* wedding? *Who* left the house that morning and was killed that afternoon in the crash of the small plane? *Who*, above all, ran the little coup on the second of January, 1931? And in what country?

I abandon the attempt to answer these questions.

The telephone rings.

Grateful for the interruption, I pick it up. I hear the voice of my nephew Griffin. He feels the need to report that he has been getting calls from "concerned friends." The focus of their concern is my health, specifically my weight. I am no longer grateful. I point out that I have weighed the same amount since the early 1970s, when I picked up paratyphoid during a film festival on the Caribbean coast of Colombia and by the time I got home had dropped so much weight that my mother had to fly to Malibu to feed me. Griffin says that he recognizes this. He is aware that my weight has not fluctuated since he was old enough to notice it. He is reporting only what these "concerned friends" have mentioned to him.

Griffin and I understand each other, which means in this case that we are able to change the subject. I consider asking him if he knows who it was who ran the little coup on the second of January, 1931, and in what country, but do not. In the absence of another subject I tell him about a taxi driver I recently encountered on my way from the Four Seasons Hotel in San Francisco to SFO. This taxi driver told me that he had been analyzing drill sites around Houston until the oil boom went belly up. His father had been a construction supervisor, he said, which meant that he had grown up on the construction sites of the big postwar high dams and power reactors. He mentioned Glen Canyon on the Colorado. He mentioned Rancho Seco outside Sacramento. He mentioned, when he learned that I was a writer, wanting himself to write a book about "intercourse between the United States and Japan." He had proposed such a book to Simon & Schuster but Simon & Schuster, he now believed, had passed the proposal on to another writer.

"Fellow by the name of Michael Crichton," he said. "I'm not saying he stole it, I'm just saying they used my ideas. But hey. Ideas are free."

Around San Bruno he began mentioning Scientology.

I tell you this true story just to prove that I can.

That my frailty has not yet reached a point at which I can no longer tell a true story.

Weeks pass, then months.

I go to a rehearsal room on West Forty-second Street to watch a run-through of a play, a new production of a Broadway musical for which two close friends wrote the lyrics in the 1970s.

I sit on a folding metal chair. Behind me I hear voices I recognize (the two close friends and their collaborator, who wrote the book) but I feel too uncertain to turn around. The songs, some familiar and some new, continue. The reprises roll around. As I sit on the folding metal chair I begin to fear getting up. As the finale approaches, I experience outright panic. What if my feet no longer move? What if my muscles lock? What if this neuritis or neuropathy or neurological inflammation has evolved into a condition more malign? I once in my late twenties had an exclusionary diagnosis of multiple sclerosis, believed later by the neurologist who made the diagnosis to be in remission, but what if it is no longer in remission? What if it never was? What if it has returned? What if I stand up from this folding chair in this rehearsal room on West Forty-second Street and collapse, fall to the floor, the folding metal chair collapsing with me?

Or what if—

(Another series of dire possibilities occurs to me, this series even more alarming than the last—)

What if the damage extends beyond the physical?

What if the problem is now cognitive?

What if the absence of style that I welcomed at one point—the directness that I encouraged, even cultivated—what if this absence of style has now taken on a pernicious life of its own?

What if my new inability to summon the right word, the apt thought, the connection that enables the words to make sense, the rhythm, the music itself—

What if this new inability is systemic?

What if I can never again locate the words that work?

20

I see a new neurologist, at Columbia Presbyterian.

The new neurologist has answers: all new neurologists have answers, usually wishful. New neurologists remain the last true believers in the power of wishful thinking. The answers offered by this particular new neurologist are for me to gain weight and devote a minimum of three hours a week to physical therapy.

I have been through this catechism before.

I happen to have been a remarkably small child. I say remarkably for a reason: something about my size was such that perfect strangers could always be relied upon to remark on it. "You're not very thick," I recall a French doctor saying when I went to see him in Paris for an antibiotic prescription. This was true enough, but I grew tired of hearing it. I grew particularly tired of hearing it when it was presented as something I might otherwise have missed. I was short, I was thin, I could circle my wrists with my thumb and index finger. My earliest memories involve being urged by my mother to gain weight, as if my failure to do so were willful, an act of rebellion. I was not allowed to get up from the table until I had eaten everything on my plate, a rule that led mainly to new and inventive ways of eating nothing on my plate. The "clean-plate club" was frequently mentioned. "Good eaters" were commended. "She's not a human garbage can," I recall my father exploding in my defense. As an adult I came to see this approach to food as more or less guaranteeing an eating disorder, but I never mentioned this theory to my mother.

Nor do I mention it to the new neurologist.

Actually the new neurologist offers, in addition to gaining weight and doing physical therapy, a third, although equally wishful, answer: the exclusionary diagnosis I received in my late twenties notwithstanding, I do not have multiple sclerosis. He is vehement on this point. There is no reason to believe that I have multiple sclerosis. Magnetic Resonance Imaging, a technique not yet available when I was in my late twenties, conclusively demonstrates that I do not have multiple sclerosis.

In that case, I ask, trying to summon an appearance of faith in whatever he chooses to answer, what is it that I do have?

I have neuritis, a neuropathy, a neurological inflammation.

I overlook the shrug.

I ask what caused this neuritis, this neuropathy, this neurological inflammation.

Not weighing enough, he answers.

It does not escape me that the consensus on what is wrong with me has once again insinuated the ball into my court.

I am referred to a dietitian on this matter of gaining weight.

The dietitian makes (the inevitable) protein shakes, brings me freshly laid eggs (better) from a farm in New Jersey and perfect vanilla ice cream (better still) from Maison du Chocolat on Madison Avenue.

I drink the protein shakes.

I eat the freshly laid eggs from the farm in New Jersey and the perfect vanilla ice cream from Maison du Chocolat on Madison Avenue.

Nonetheless.

I do not gain weight.

I have an uneasy sense that the consensus solution has already failed.

I find, on the other hand, somewhat to my surprise, that I actively like physical therapy. I keep regular appointments at a Columbia Presbyterian sports medicine facility at Sixtieth and Madison. I am impressed by the strength and general tone of the other patients who turn up during the same hour. I study their balance, their proficiency with the various devices recommended by the therapist. The more I watch, the more encouraged I am: *this stuff really works*, I tell myself. The thought makes me cheerful, optimistic. I wonder how many appointments it will take to reach the apparently effortless control already achieved by my fellow patients. Only during my third week of physical therapy do I learn that these particular fellow patients are in fact the New York Yankees, loosening up between game days.

21

Today as I walk home from the Columbia Presbyterian sports medicine facility at Sixtieth and Madison I find the optimism engendered by proximity to the New York Yankees fading. In fact my physical confidence seems to be reaching a new ebb. My cognitive confidence seems to have vanished altogether. Even the correct stance for telling you this, the ways to describe what is happening to me, the attitude, the tone, the very words, now elude my grasp.

The tone needs to be direct.

I need to talk to you directly, I need to *address the subject as it were*, but something stops me.

Is this another kind of neuropathy, a new frailty, am I no longer able to talk directly?

Was I ever?

Did I lose it?

Or is the subject in this case a matter I wish not to address?

When I tell you that I am afraid to get up from a folding chair in a rehearsal room on West Forty-second Street, of what am I really afraid?

22

What if you hadn't been home when Dr. Watson called—
  What if you couldn't meet him at the hospital—
What if there'd been an accident on the freeway—
What would happen to me then?

All adopted children, I am told, fear that they will be abandoned by their adoptive parents as they believe themselves to have been abandoned by their natural. They are programmed, by the unique circumstances of their introduction into the family structure, to see abandonment as their role, their fate, the destiny that will overtake them unless they outrun it.

Quintana.

All adoptive parents, I do not need to be told, fear that they do not deserve the child they were given, that the child will be taken from them.

Quintana.

Quintana is one of the areas about which I have difficulty being direct.

I said early on that adoption is hard to get right but I did not tell you why.

"Of course you won't tell her she's adopted," many people said at the time she was born, most of these people the age of my parents, a generation, like that of Diana's parents, for which adoption remained obscurely shameful, a secret to be kept at any cost. "You couldn't possibly tell her."

Of course we could possibly tell her.

In fact we had already told her. *L'adoptada, m'ija.* There was never any question of not telling her. What were the alternatives? Lie to her? Leave it to her agent to take her to lunch at the Beverly Hills Hotel? Before too many years passed I would write about her adoption, John would write about her adoption, Quintana herself would agree to be one of the children interviewed for a book by the photographer Jill Krementz called *How It Feels to Be Adopted*. Over those years we had received periodic communications from women who had seen these mentions of her adoption and believed her to be their own lost daughter, women who had themselves given up infants for adoption and were now haunted by the possibility that this child about whom they had read could be that missing child.

This beautiful child, this perfect child.

Qué hermosa, qué chula.

We responded to each of these communications, we followed up, we explained how the facts did not coincide, the dates did not tally, why the perfect child could not be theirs.

We considered our role fulfilled, the case closed.

Still.

The recommended choice narrative did not end, as I had imagined it would (hoped it would, dreamed it would), with the perfect child placed on the table between us for lunch at The Bistro (Sidney Korshak's corner banquette, the blue-and-white dotted organdy dress) on the hot day in September 1966 when the adoption became final.

Thirty-two years later, in 1998, on a Saturday morning when she was alone in her apartment and vulnerable to whatever bad or good news arrived at her door, the perfect child received a Federal Express letter from a young woman who convincingly identified herself as her sister, her full sister, one of two younger children later born, although we had not before known this, to Quintana's natural mother and father. At the time of Quintana's birth the natural mother and father had not yet been married. At a point after her birth they married, had the two further children, Quintana's full sister and brother, and then divorced. According to the letter from the young woman who identified herself as Quintana's sister, the mother and sister lived now in Dallas. The brother, from whom the mother was estranged, lived in another city in Texas. The father, who had remarried and fathered another child, lived in Florida. The sister, who had learned from her mother only a few weeks before that

Quintana existed, had determined immediately, against the initial instincts of her mother, to locate her.

She had resorted to the internet.

On the internet she had found a private detective who said that he could locate Quintana for two hundred dollars.

Quintana had an unlisted telephone number.

The two hundred dollars was for accessing her Con Ed account.

The sister had agreed to the deal.

It had taken the detective only ten further minutes to call the sister back with a street address and apartment number in New York.

14 Sutton Place South. Apartment 11D.

The sister had written the letter.

She had sent it to Apartment 11D at 14 Sutton Place South via Federal Express.

"Saturday delivery," Quintana said when she showed us the letter, still in its Federal Express envelope. "The FedEx came *Saturday delivery.*" I remember her repeating these words, emphasizing them, *Saturday delivery, the FedEx came Saturday delivery*, as if maintaining focus on this one point could put her world back together.

23

I cannot easily express what I thought about this.

On the one hand, I told myself, it could hardly be a surprise. We had spent thirty-two years considering just such a possibility. We had for many of those years seen such a possibility even as a probability. Quintana's mother, through a bureaucratic error on the part of the social worker, had been told not only our names and Quintana's name but the name under which I wrote. We did not lead an entirely private life. We gave lectures, we attended events, we got photographed. We could be easily found. We had discussed how it would happen. There would be a letter. There would be a phone call. The caller would say such and such. Whichever one of us took the call would say such and such and such. We would meet.

It would be logical.

It would all, when it happened, make sense.

In an alternate scenario, Quintana herself would choose to undertake the search, initiate the contact. Should she wish to do so, the process would be simple. Through another bureaucratic error, a bill from St. John's Hospital in Santa Monica had reached us without the mother's name redacted. I had seen the name only once but it had remained imprinted on my memory. I had thought it a beautiful name.

We had discussed this with our lawyer. We had authorized him, should Quintana ask, to give her whatever help she wanted or needed.

This too would be logical.

This too would all, when it happened, make sense.

On the other hand, I told myself, it now seemed too late, not the right time.

There comes a point, I told myself, at which a family is, for better or for worse, finished.

Yes. I just told you. *Of course* I had considered this possibility. Accepting it would be something else.

A while back, to another point, I mentioned that we had taken her with us to Tucson while *The Life and Times of Judge Roy Bean* was shooting there.

I mentioned the Hilton Inn and I mentioned the babysitter and I mentioned Dick Moore and I mentioned Paul Newman but there was a part of that trip that I did not mention.

It happened on our first night in Tucson.

We had left her with the babysitter. We had watched the dailies. We had met in the Hilton Inn dining room for dinner. Halfway through dinner—a few too many people at the table, a little too much noise, just another working dinner on a motion picture on just another location—it had struck me: this was not, for me, just another location.

This was Tucson.

We had not been told much about her natural family but we had been told one thing: her mother was from Tucson. Her mother was from Tucson and I knew her mother's name.

I never considered not doing what I did next.

I got up from dinner and found a pay phone with a Tucson telephone book.

I looked up the name.

I showed the name to John.

Without discussion we went back to the crowded table in the dining room and told the producer of *The Life and Times of Judge Roy Bean* that we needed to speak to him. He followed us into the lobby. There in a corner of the lobby of the Hilton Inn we talked to him for three or four minutes. It was imperative, we said, that no one should know we were in Tucson. It was especially imperative, we said, that no one should know Quintana was in Tucson. I did not want to pick up the Tucson paper, I said, and see any cute items about children on the *Judge Roy Bean* location. I asked him to alert the unit publicity people. I stressed that under no condition should Quintana's name appear in connection with the picture.

There was no reason to think that it would but I had to be sure.

I had to cover that base.

I had to make that effort.

I believed as I did so that I was protecting both Quintana and her mother.

I tell you this now by way of suggesting the muddled impulses that can go hand in hand with adoption.

A few months after the arrival of the FedEx Saturday delivery, Quintana and her sister met, first in New York and then in Dallas. In New York Quintana showed her visiting sister Chinatown. She took her shopping at Pearl River. She brought her to dinner with John and me at Da Silvano. She invited her friends and cousins to her apartment for drinks so that they and her sister could all meet. The two sisters looked like twins. When Griffin walked into Quintana's apartment and saw the sister he inadvertently greeted her as "Q." Margaritas were mixed. Guacamole was made. There was about this initial weekend meeting a spirit of willed excitement, determined camaraderie, resolute discovery.

It would be a month or so later, in Dallas, before the will and the determination and the resolution all failed her.

When she called after twenty-four hours in Dallas she had seemed distraught, on the edge of tears.

In Dallas she had been introduced for the first time not only to her mother but to many other members of what she was now calling her "biological family," strangers who welcomed her as their long-missing child.

In Dallas these strangers had shown her snapshots, remarked on her resemblance to one or another cousin or aunt or grandparent, seemingly taken for granted that she had chosen by her presence to be one of them.

On her return to New York she had begun getting regular calls from her mother, whose initial resistance to the idea of a reunion (in the first place it wasn't a reunion, her mother had punctiliously pointed out, since they had never met in the first place) seemed to have given way to a need to discuss the events that had led to the adoption. These calls came in the morning, typically at a time when Quintana was just about to leave for work. She did not want to cut her mother short but neither did she want to be late for work, particularly because *Elle Décor*, the magazine for which she was at that time the photography editor, was undergoing a staff realignment and she felt her job to be in jeopardy. She discussed this conflict with a psychiatrist. After the discussion with the psychiatrist she wrote to her mother and sister saying that "being found" ("I was found" had evolved into her arrestingly equivocal way of referring to what had happened) was proving "too much to handle," "too much and too soon," that she needed to "step back," "catch up for a while" with what she still considered her real life.

In reply she received a letter from her mother saying that she did not want to be a burden and so had disconnected her telephone.

This was the point at which it seemed clear that not one of us would escape those muddled impulses.

Not Quintana's mother, not Quintana's sister, certainly not me.

Not even Quintana.

Quintana who referred to the shattering of her known world as "being found."

Quintana who had called Nicholas and Alexandra "Nicky and Sunny" and seen their story as "a big hit."

Quintana who had imagined The Broken Man in such convincing detail.

Quintana who told me that after she became five she never ever dreamed about The Broken Man.

A few weeks after her mother disconnected her telephone another message arrived, although not from her mother and not from her sister.

She received a letter from her natural father in Florida.

Over the time that passed between the time she knew herself to have been adopted and the time she was "found," a period of some thirty years, she had many times mentioned her other mother. "My other mommy," and later "my other mother," had been from the time she first spoke the way she referred to her. She had wondered who and where this other mother was. She had wondered what she looked like. She had considered and ultimately rejected the possibility of finding out. John had once asked her, when she was small, what she would do if she met her "other mommy." "I'd put one arm around Mom," she had said, "and one arm around my other mommy, and I'd say 'Hello, Mommies.'"

She had never, not once, mentioned her other father.

I have no idea why but the picture in her mind seemed not to include a father.

"What a long strange journey this has been," the letter from Florida read.

She burst into tears as she read it to me.

"On top of everything else," she said through the tears, "my father has to be a Deadhead."

Three years later the final message arrived, this one from her sister.

Her sister wanted her to know that their brother had died. The cause of death was unclear. His heart was mentioned.

Quintana had never met him.

I am not sure of the dates but I think he would have been born the year she was five.

After I became five I never ever dreamed about him.

This call to say that he had died may have been the last time the sisters spoke.

When Quintana herself died, her sister sent flowers.

24

I find myself leafing today for the first time through a journal she kept in the spring of 1984, a daily assignment for an English class during her senior year at the Westlake School for Girls. "I had an exciting revelation while studying a poem by John Keats," this volume of the journal begins, on a page dated March 7, 1984, the one-hundred-and-seventeenth entry since she had begun keeping the journal in September of 1983. "In the poem, 'Endymion,' there is a line that seems to tell my present fear of life: *Pass into nothingness*."

This March 7, 1984, entry continues, moves into a discussion of Jean-Paul Sartre and Martin Heidegger and their respective understandings of the abyss, but I am no longer following the argument: automatically, without thinking, appallingly, as if she were still at the Westlake School and had asked me to take a look at her paper, I am editing it.

For example:

Delete commas setting off title "Endymion."

"Tell," as in "a line that seems to tell my present fear of life," is of course wrong.

"Describe" would be better.

"Suggest" would be better still.

On the other hand: "tell" might work: try "tell" as she uses it.

I try it: *She "tells" her present fear of life in relation to Sartre.*

I try it again: *She "tells" her present fear of life in relation to Heidegger. She "tells" her understanding of the abyss. She qualifies her understanding of the abyss: "This is merely how I interpret the abyss; I could be wrong."*

Considerable time passes before I realize that my preoccupation with the words she used has screened off any possible apprehension of what she was actually saying when she wrote her journal entry on that March day in 1984.

Was that deliberate?

Was I screening off what she said about her fear of life the same way I had screened off what she said about her fear of The Broken Man?

Hello, Quintana? I'm going to lock you here in the garage?

After I became five I never ever dreamed about him?

Did I all her life keep a baffle between us?

Did I prefer not to hear what she was actually saying?

Did it frighten me?

I try the passage again, this time reading for meaning.

What she said: *My present fear of life.*

What she said: *Pass into nothingness.*

What she was actually saying: *The World has nothing but Morning and Night. It has no Day or Lunch. Let me just be in the ground. Let me just be in the ground and go to sleep.* When I tell you that I am afraid to get up from a folding chair in a rehearsal room on West Forty-second Street, is this what I am actually saying?

Does it frighten me?

25

Let me again try to talk to you directly.

On my last birthday, December 5, 2009, I became seventy-five years old.

Notice the odd construction there—*I became seventy-five years old*—do you hear the echo?

I *became* seventy-five? I *became* five?

After I became five I never ever dreamed about him?

Also notice—in notes that talk about aging in their first few pages, notes called *Blue Nights* for a reason, notes called *Blue Nights* because at the time I began them I could think of little other than the inevitable approach of darker days—how long it took me to tell you that one salient fact, how long it took me to *address the subject as it were*. Aging and its evidence remain life's most predictable events, yet they also remain matters we prefer to leave unmentioned, unexplored: I have watched tears flood the eyes of grown women, loved women, women of talent and accomplishment, for no reason other than that a small child in the room, more often than not an adored niece or nephew, has just described them as "wrinkly," or asked how old they are. When we are asked this question we are always undone by its innocence, somehow shamed by the clear bell-like tones in which it is asked. What shames us is this: the answer we give is never innocent. The answer we give is unclear, evasive, even guilty. Right now when I answer this question I find myself doubting my own accuracy, rechecking the increasingly undoable arithmetic (born December 5 1934, subtract 1934 from 2009, do this in your head and watch yourself get muddled by the interruption of the entirely irrelevant millennium), insisting to myself (no one else particularly cares) that there must be a mistake: only yesterday I was in my fifties, my forties, only yesterday I was thirty-one.

Quintana was born when I was thirty-one.

Only yesterday Quintana was born.

Only yesterday I was taking Quintana home from the nursery at St. John's Hospital in Santa Monica.

Enveloped in a silk-lined cashmere wrapper.

Daddy's gone to get a rabbit skin to wrap his baby bunny in.

What if you hadn't been home when Dr. Watson called?

What would happen to me then?

Only yesterday I was holding her in my arms on the 405.

Only yesterday I was promising her that she would be safe with us.

We then called the 405 the San Diego Freeway.

It was only yesterday when we still called the 405 the San Diego, it was only yesterday when we still called the 10 the Santa Monica, it was only the day before yesterday when the Santa Monica did not yet exist.

Only yesterday I could still do arithmetic, remember telephone numbers, rent a car at the airport and drive it out of the lot without freezing, stopping at the key moment, feet already on the pedals but immobilized by the question of which is the accelerator and which the brake.

Only yesterday Quintana was alive.

I disengage my feet from the pedals, first one, then the other.

I invent a reason for the Hertz attendant to start the rental car.

I am seventy-five years old: this is not the reason I give.

26

A doctor to whom I occasionally talk suggests that I have made an inadequate adjustment to aging.

Wrong, I want to say.

In fact I have made no adjustment whatsoever to aging.

In fact I had lived my entire life to date without seriously believing that I would age.

I had no doubt that I would continue to wear the red suede sandals with four-inch heels that I had always preferred.

I had no doubt that I would continue to wear the gold hoop earrings on which I had always relied, the black cashmere leggings, the enameled beads.

My skin would develop flaws, fine lines, even brown spots (this, at seventy-five, was what passed for a realistic cosmetic assessment), but it would continue to look as it had always looked, basically healthy. My hair would lose its original color but color could continue to be replaced by leaving the gray around the face and twice a year letting Johanna at Bumble and Bumble highlight the rest. I would recognize that the models I encountered on these semiannual visits to the color room at Bumble and Bumble were significantly younger than I was, but since these models I encountered on my semiannual visits to the color room at Bumble and Bumble were at most sixteen or seventeen there could be no reason to interpret the difference as a personal failure. My memory would slip but whose memory does not slip. My eyesight would be more problematic than it might have been before I began seeing the world through sudden clouds of what looked like black lace and was actually blood, the residue of a series of retinal tears and detachments, but there would still be no question that I could see, read, write, navigate intersections without fear.

No question that it could not be fixed.

Whatever "it" was.

I believed absolutely in my own power to surmount the situation.

Whatever "the situation" was.

When my grandmother was seventy-five she experienced a cerebral hemorrhage, fell unconscious to the sidewalk not far from her house in Sacramento, was taken to Sutter Hospital, and died there that night. This was "the situation" for my grandmother. When my mother was seventy-five she was diagnosed with breast cancer, did two cycles of chemotherapy, could not tolerate the third or fourth, nonetheless lived until she was two weeks short of her ninety-first birthday (when she did die it was of congestive heart failure, not cancer) but was never again exactly as she had been. Things went wrong. She lost confidence. She became apprehensive in crowds. She was no longer entirely comfortable at the weddings of her grandchildren or even, in truth, at family dinners. She made mystifying, even hostile, judgments. When she came to visit me in New York for example she pronounced St. James' Episcopal Church, the steeple and slate roof of which constitute the entire view from my living room windows, "the single ugliest church I have ever seen." When, on her own coast and at her own suggestion, I took her to see the jellyfish at the Monterey Bay Aquarium, she fled to the car, pleading vertigo from the movement of the water.

I recognize now that she was feeling frail.

I recognize now that she was feeling then as I feel now.

Invisible on the street.

The target of any wheeled vehicle on the scene.

Unbalanced at the instant of stepping off a curb, sitting down or standing up, opening or closing a taxi door.

Cognitively challenged not only by simple arithmetic but by straightforward news stories, announced changes in traffic flow, the memorization of a telephone number, the seating of a dinner party.

"Estrogen actually made me feel better," she said to me not long before she died, after several decades without it.

Well, yes. Estrogen had made her feel better.

This turns out to have been "the situation" for most of us.

And yet:

And still:

Despite all evidence:

Despite recognizing that my skin and my hair and even my cognition are all reliant on the estrogen I no longer have:

Despite recognizing that I will not again wear the red suede sandals with the four-inch heels and despite recognizing that the gold hoop earrings and the black cashmere leggings and the enameled beads no longer exactly apply:

Despite recognizing that for a woman my age even to note such details of appearance will be construed by many as a manifestation of misplaced vanity:

Despite all that:

Nonetheless:

That being seventy-five could present as a significantly altered situation, an altogether different "it," did not until recently occur to me.

27

Something happened to me early in the summer.

Something that altered my view of my own possibilities, shortened, as it were, the horizon.

I still have no idea what time it was when it happened, or why it was that it happened, or even in any exact way what it was that happened. All I know is that midway through June, after walking home with a friend after an early dinner on Third Avenue in the eighties, I found myself waking on the floor of my bedroom, left arm and forehead and both legs bleeding, unable to get up. It seemed clear that I had fallen, but I had no memory of falling, no memory whatsoever of losing balance, trying to regain it, the usual preludes to a fall. Certainly I had no memory of losing consciousness. The diagnostic term for what had happened (I was to learn before the night ended) was "syncope," fainting, but discussions of syncope, centering as they did on "pre-syncope symptoms" (palpitations, lightheadedness, dizziness, blurred or tunnel vision), none of which I could identify, seemed not to apply.

I had been alone in the apartment.

There were thirteen telephones in the apartment, not one of which was at that moment within reach.

I remember lying on the floor and trying to visualize the unreachable telephones, count them off room by room.

I remember forgetting one room and counting off the telephones a second and then a third time.

This was dangerously soothing.

I remember deciding in the absence of any prospect of help to go back to sleep for a while, on the floor, the blood pooling around me.

I remember pulling a quilt down from a wicker chest, the only object I could reach, and folding it under my head.

I remember nothing else until I woke a second time and managed on this attempt to summon enough traction to pull myself up.

At which point I called a friend.

At which point he came over.

At which point, since I was still bleeding, we took a taxi to the emergency room at Lenox Hill Hospital.

It was I who said Lenox Hill.

Let me repeat: it was I who said Lenox Hill.

Weeks later, this one fact was still troubling me as much as anything else about the entire sequence of events that night: *it was I who said Lenox Hill*. I got into a taxi in front of my apartment, which happens to be equidistant from two hospitals, Lenox Hill and New York Cornell, *and I said Lenox Hill*. Saying Lenox Hill instead of New York Cornell did not demonstrate a developed instinct for self-preservation. Saying Lenox Hill instead of New York Cornell demonstrated only that I was at that moment incapable of taking care of myself. Saying Lenox Hill instead of New York Cornell proved the point humiliatingly made by every nurse and aide and doctor to whom I spoke in the two nights I would eventually spend at Lenox Hill, the first night in the emergency room and the second in a cardiac unit, where a bed happened to be available and where it was erroneously assumed that because I had been given a bed in the cardiac unit I must have a cardiac problem: I was old. I was too old to live alone. I was too old to be allowed out of bed. I was too old even to recognize that if I had been given a bed in the cardiac unit I must have a cardiac problem.

"Your cardiac problem isn't showing up on the monitors," one nurse kept reporting, accusingly.

I tried to process what she was saying.

Processing what people were saying was not at that moment my long suit, but this nurse seemed to be suggesting that my "cardiac problem" was not showing up on the monitors because I had deliberately detached the electrodes.

I countered.

I said that to the best of my knowledge I did not have a cardiac problem.

She countered.

"Of course you have a cardiac problem," she said. And then, closing the issue: "Because otherwise you wouldn't be in the cardiac unit."

I had no answer for that.

I tried to pretend I was home.

I tried to figure out whether it was day or night: if it was day I had a shot at going home, but in the hospital there was no day or night.

Only shifts.

Only waiting.

Waiting for the IV nurse, waiting for the nurse with the narcotics key, waiting for the transporter.

Will someone please take the catheter out.

That transfusion was ordered at eleven this evening.

"How do you normally get around your apartment," someone in scrubs kept asking, marveling at what he seemed to consider my entirely unearned mobility, finally providing his own answer: "Walker?"

Demoralization occurs in the instant: I have trouble expressing the extent to which two nights of relatively undemanding hospitalization negatively affected me. There had been no surgery. There had been no uncomfortable procedures. There had been no real discomfort at all, other than emotional. Yet I felt myself to be the victim of a gross misunderstanding: I wanted only to go home, get the blood washed out of my hair, stop being treated as an invalid. Instead the very opposite was happening. My own doctor, who was based at Columbia Presbyterian, happened to be in St. Petersburg with his family: he called me at Lenox Hill during an intermission at the Kirov Ballet. He wanted to know what I was doing at Lenox Hill. So, at that point, did I. The doctors on the scene, determined to track down my phantom "cardiac problem," seemed willing to permanently infantilize me. Even my own friends, dropping by after work, very much in charge, no blood in their hair, sentient adults placing and receiving calls, making arrangements for dinner, bringing me perfect chilled soups that I could not eat because the hospital bed was so angled as to prevent sitting upright, were now talking about the need to get me "someone in the house": it was increasingly as if I had taken a taxi to Lenox Hill and woken up in *Driving Miss Daisy*.

With effort, I managed to convey this point.

I got released from Lenox Hill.

My own doctor got back from St. Petersburg.

After further days of unproductive cardiac monitoring the cardiac hypothesis was abandoned.

An appointment was made with yet another new neurologist, this one at New York Cornell.

Many tests were scheduled and done.

A new MRI, to establish whether or not there had been significant changes.

There had not been.

A new MRA, to see whether or not there had been any enlargement of the aneurysm visualized on the previous MRAs.

There had not been.

A new ultrasound, to establish whether or not there had been increased calcification of the carotid artery.

There had not been.

And, finally, a full-body PET scan, meant to show any abnormalities in the heart, the lungs, the liver, the kidneys, the bones, the brain: in fact anywhere in the body.

I repeatedly slid in and out of the PET scanner.

Forty minutes passed, then a change of position and another fifteen.

I lay motionless on the scanner.

It seemed impossible to imagine this coming up clean.

It would be one more version of the bed in the cardiac unit: a full-body PET scan had been ordered, *ergo*, as night follows day, there would need to be abnormalities for the full-body PET scan to show.

A day later I was given the results.

There were, surprisingly, no abnormalities seen in the scan.

Everyone agreed on this point. Everyone used the word "surprisingly."

Surprisingly, there were no abnormalities to explain why I felt as frail as I did.

Surprisingly, there were no abnormalities to tell me why I was afraid to get up from a folding chair in a rehearsal room on West Forty-second Street.

Only then did I realize that during the three weeks that had passed between taking the taxi to Lenox Hill, on the fourteenth of June, and receiving the results of the full-body PET scan, on the eighth of July, I had allowed this year's most deeply blue nights to come and go without my notice.

What does it cost to lose those weeks, that light, the very nights in the year preferred over all others?

Can you evade the dying of the brightness?

Or do you evade only its warning?

Where are you left if you miss the message the blue nights bring?

"Have you ever had a moment where everything in your life just stopped?" This was the way that this question was raised by Kris Jenkins, a three-hundred-and-sixty-pound Jets defensive tackle, after he tore, six plays into his tenth NFL season, both his meniscus and his anterior cruciate ligament. "So fast, but in slow motion? Like all your senses shut down? Like you're watching yourself?"

I offer you a second way of approaching the moment where everything in your life just stops, this one from the actor Robert Duvall: "I exist very nicely between the words 'action' and 'cut.'"

And even a third way: "It doesn't present as pain," I once heard an oncological surgeon say of cancer.

28

I find myself thinking exclusively about Quintana.
I need her with me.

Behind the house on Franklin Avenue in Hollywood in which we lived from the day we left Sara Mankiewicz's Minton plates until the day we moved into the beach house, a period of some four years, there was a clay tennis court, weeds growing through the cracked clay. I remember watching her weed it, kneeling on fat baby knees, the ragged stuffed animal she addressed as "Bunny Rabbit" at her side.

Daddy's gone to get a rabbit skin to wrap his baby bunny in.

In a few weeks she will have been dead five years.

Five years since the doctor said that the patient had been unable to get enough oxygen through the vent for at least an hour now.

Five years since Gerry and I left her in the ICU overlooking the river at New York Cornell.

I can now afford to think about her.

I no longer cry when I hear her name.

I no longer imagine the transporter being called to take her to the morgue after we left the ICU.

Yet I still need her with me.

In lieu of her presence I leaf through the books on a table in my office, each one a book she gave me.

One is called *Baby Animals and Their Mothers*, and is just that, black-and-white photographs of baby animals and their mothers: mostly comforting favorites (not unlike Bunny Rabbit), lambs and ewes, foals and mares, but also less common baby animals and their mothers: hedgehogs, koala bears, llamas. Stuck in the pages of *Baby Animals and Their Mothers* I find a French postcard showing a baby polar bear and its mother. "*Câlin sur la banquise*," the caption reads in French, and then, in English: "Cuddling on the ice floe."

"Just a few things I found on my travels that reminded me of you," the note on the card reads, in printing less careful than it once was but still recognizable.

Still hers.

Beneath *Baby Animals and Their Mothers* is Jean-Dominique Bauby's *The Diving Bell and the Butterfly*, an account, by a former editor in chief of French *Elle*, of what it had felt like to have a cerebrovascular accident on a date he knew to have been the eighth of December and next wake at the end of January, unable to speak, able to move only by blinking one eyelid: the condition known as "locked-in syndrome." (Did anyone use the word "syncope"? Did anyone use the words "pre-syncope symptoms"? Can we find any clues here? Any clue to Jean-Dominique Bauby's situation? Any clue to my own?) For reasons that I did not at the time entirely understand and have not since wanted to explore, *The Diving Bell and the Butterfly* had been when it was published extremely meaningful to Quintana, so markedly so that I never told her that I did not much like it, or for that matter even entirely believe it.

Only later, when she was for most purposes locked into her own condition, confined to a wheelchair and afflicted by the detritus of a bleed into her brain and the subsequent neurosurgery, did I begin to see its point.

Beginning to see its point was when I stopped wanting to explore the reasons why it might have been so markedly meaningful to Quintana.

Just let me be in the ground.

Just let me be in the ground and go to sleep.

I return *The Diving Bell and the Butterfly* to the table in my office.

I align it with *Baby Animals and Their Mothers*.

Câlin sur la banquise.

This business of the ice floes is familiar to me. I did not need *Baby Animals and Their Mothers* to bring the image of the ice floes alive. In the first year of Quintana's hospitalizations I had watched ice floes from her hospital windows: ice floes on the East River from her windows at Beth Israel North, ice floes on the Hudson from her windows at Columbia Presbyterian. I think now of those ice floes and imagine having seen, floating past on one or another slab of breaking ice, a baby polar bear and its mother, heading for the Hell Gate Bridge.

I imagine having shown the baby polar bear and its mother to Quintana.

Câlin sur la banquise.

Just let me be in the ground.

I resolve to forget the ice floes.

I have thought enough about the ice floes.

Thinking about the ice floes is like thinking about the transporter being called to take her to the morgue.

I walk into Central Park and sit for a while on a bench to which is attached a brass plaque indicating that a memorial contribution has been made to the Central Park Conservancy. There are now in the park many such brass plaques, many such benches. "*Quintana Roo Dunne Michael 1966–2005*," the plaque on this bench reads. "*In summertime and wintertime.*" A friend had made the contribution, and asked me to write out what I wanted the plaque to read. The same friend had come to visit Quintana when she was doing therapy in the neuro-rehab unit at UCLA, and after she saw Quintana had a cafeteria lunch with me in the hospital patio. It did not occur to either of us on the day we had the cafeteria lunch in the hospital patio at UCLA that Quintana's recovery would end at this bench.

So we still thought of that year.

Quintana's "recovery."

We had no idea then how rare recovery can be.

No idea that "recovery," like "adoption," remains one of those concepts that sounds more plausible than it turns out to be.

Câlin sur la banquise.

The wheelchair.

The detritus of the bleed, the neurosurgery.

In summertime and wintertime.

I wonder if in those revised circumstances she remembered *The Diving Bell and the Butterfly*, what it meant to her then.

She did not want to talk about those revised circumstances.

She wanted to believe that if she did not "dwell" on them she would wake one morning and find them corrected.

"Like when someone dies," she once said by way of explaining her approach, "don't dwell on it."

29

Stop all the clocks, cut off the telephone,
Prevent the dog from barking with a juicy bone,
Silence the pianos and with muffled drum
Bring out the coffin, let the mourners come.

Let aeroplanes circle moaning overhead
Scribbling on the sky the message He Is Dead,
Put crêpe bows round the white necks of the public doves,
Let the traffic policemen wear black cotton gloves.

He was my North, my South, my East and West,
My working week and my Sunday rest,
My noon, my midnight, my talk, my song;
I thought that love would last for ever: I was wrong.

The stars are not wanted now; put out every one,
Pack up the moon and dismantle the sun,
Pour away the ocean and sweep up the wood;
For nothing now can ever come to any good.

So go W. H. Auden's "Funeral Blues," sixteen lines that, during the days and weeks immediately after John died, spoke directly to the anger—the unreasoning fury, the blind rage—that I found myself feeling. I later showed "Funeral Blues" to Quintana. I told her that I was thinking of reading it at the memorial service she and I were then planning for John. She implored me not to do so. She said she liked nothing about the poem. She said it was "wrong." She was vehement on this point. At the time I thought she was upset by the tone of the poem, its raw rhythms, the harshness with which it rejects the world, the sense it gives off of a speaker about to explode.

I now think of her vehemence differently. I now think she saw "Funeral Blues" as dwelling on it.

On the afternoon she herself died, August 26, 2005, her husband and I left the ICU overlooking the river at New York Cornell and walked through Central Park. The leaves on the trees were already losing their intensity, still weeks from dropping but ready to drop, not exactly faded but fading. At the time she entered the hospital, late in May or early in June, the blue nights had been just making their appearance. I had first noticed them not long after she was admitted to the ICU, which happened to be in the Greenberg Pavilion. In the lobby of the Greenberg Pavilion there hung portraits of its major benefactors, the most prominent of whom had played founding roles in the insurance conglomerate AIG and so had figured in news stories about the AIG bailout. During the first weeks I had reason to visit the ICU in the Greenberg Pavilion I was startled by the familiarity of these faces in the portraits, and, in the early evening, when I came downstairs from the ICU, would pause to study them. Then I would walk out into the increasingly intense blue of that time of day in that early summer season.

This routine seemed for a while to bring luck.

It was a period when the doctors in the ICU did not seem uniformly discouraging.

It was a period when improvement seemed possible.

There was even mention of a step-down unit, although the step-down unit never exactly materialized.

Then one night, leaving the ICU and pausing as usual by the AIG portraits, I realized: there would be no step-down unit.

The light outside had already changed.

The light outside was no longer blue.

She had so far since entering this ICU undergone five surgical interventions. She had remained ventilated and sedated throughout. The original surgical incision had never been closed. I had asked her surgeon how long he could continue doing this. He had mentioned a surgeon at Cornell who had done eighteen such interventions on a single patient.

"And that patient lived," the surgeon had said.

In what condition, I had asked.

"Your daughter wasn't in great condition when she arrived here," the surgeon had said.

So that was where we were. The light outside was already darkening. The summer was already ending and she was still upstairs in the ICU overlooking the river and the surgeon was saying she wasn't in great condition when they put her there.

In other words she was dying.

I now knew she was dying.

There was now no way to avoid knowing it. There would now be no way to believe the doctors when they tried not to seem discouraging. There would now be no way to pretend to myself that the spirit of the AIG founders would pull this one out. She would die. She would not necessarily die that night, she would not necessarily die the next day, but we were now on track to the day she would die.

August 26 was the day she would die.

August 26 was the day Gerry and I would leave the ICU overlooking the river and walk into Central Park.

I see as I write this that there is no uniformity in the way I refer to Gerry. Sometimes I call him "Gerry," sometimes I call him "her husband." She liked the sound of that. *Her husband. My husband.*

She would say it again and again.

When she could still speak.

Which, as the days continued to shorten and the track to narrow, was by no means every day.

You notice we're doing hand compression.

Because the patient could no longer get enough oxygen through the vent.

For at least an hour now.

In an underpass beneath one of the bridges in Central Park that day someone was playing a saxophone. I do not remember what song he was playing but I remember that it was torchy and I remember stopping under the bridge, turning aside, eyes on the fading leaves, unable to hold back tears.

"The power of cheap music," Gerry said, or maybe I only thought it.

Gerry. Her husband.

The day she cut the peach-colored cake from Payard.

The day she wore the shoes with the bright-red soles.

The day the plumeria tattoo showed through her veil.

In fact I was not even crying for the saxophone.

I was crying for the tiles, the Minton tiles in the arcade south of Bethesda Fountain, Sara Mankiewicz's pattern, Quintana's christening. I was crying for Connie Wald walking her dog through Boulder City and across Hoover Dam. I was crying for Diana holding the champagne flute and smoking the cigarette in Sara Mankiewicz's living room. I was crying for Diana who had talked to Blake Watson so that I could bring the beautiful baby girl he had delivered home from the nursery at St. John's Hospital in Santa Monica.

Diana who would die in the ICU at Cedars in Los Angeles.

Dominique who would die in the ICU at Cedars in Los Angeles.

The beautiful baby girl who would die in the ICU in the Greenberg Pavilion at New York Cornell.

You notice we're doing hand compression.

Because the patient can no longer get enough oxygen through the vent.

For at least an hour now.

Like when someone dies, don't dwell on it.

30

Six weeks after she died we had a service for her, at the Dominican Church of St. Vincent Ferrer on Lexington Avenue. Gregorian chant was sung. A movement from Schubert's Piano Sonata in B-flat was played. Her cousin Griffin read a few paragraphs John had written about her in *Quintana & Friends:* "Quintana will be eleven this week. She approaches adolescence with what I can only describe as panache, but then watching her journey from infancy has always been like watching Sandy Koufax pitch or Bill Russell play basketball." Her cousin Kelley read a poem she had written as a child in Malibu about the Santa Ana winds:

> *Gardens are dead*
> *Animals not fed*
> *Flowers don't smell*
> *Dry is the well*
> *People's careers slide right down*
> *Brain in the pan turns around*
> *People mumble as leaves crumble*
> *Fire ashes tumble.*

Susan Traylor, her best friend since they met at nursery school in Malibu, read a letter from her. Calvin Trillin spoke about her. Gerry read a Galway Kinnell poem that she had liked, Patti Smith sang her a lullaby that she had written for her own son. I read the poems by Wallace Stevens and T. S. Eliot, "Domination of Black" and "New Hampshire," with which I had put her to sleep when she was a baby. "Do the peacocks," she would say once she could talk. "Do the peacocks," or "do the apple trees."

"Domination of Black" had peacocks in it.

"New Hampshire" had apple trees in it.

I think of "Domination of Black" every time I see the peacocks at St. John the Divine.

I did the peacocks that day at St. Vincent Ferrer.

I did the apple trees.

The following day her husband and my brother and his family and Griffin and his father and I went up to St. John the Divine and placed her ashes in a marble wall in St. Ansgar's Chapel along with those of my mother and John.

My mother's name was already on the marble wall at St. John the Divine.

EDUENE JERRETT DIDION
MAY 30 1910–MAY 15 2001

John's name was already on it.

JOHN GREGORY DUNNE
MAY 25 1932–DECEMBER 30 2003

There had been two spaces remaining, the names not yet engraved.

Now there was one.

During the month or so after placing first my mother's and then John's ashes in the wall at St. John the Divine I had the same dream, repeated again and again. In the dream it was always six in the afternoon, the hour at which the evensong bells are rung and the cathedral doors are closed and locked.

In the dream I hear the six o'clock bells.

In the dream I see the cathedral darkening, the doors locking.

You can imagine the dream from there.

When I left the cathedral after placing her ashes in the marble wall I avoided thinking about the dream.

I promised myself that I would maintain momentum.

"Maintain momentum" was the imperative that echoed all the way downtown.

In fact I had no idea what would happen if I lost it.

In fact I had no idea what it was.

I assumed, incorrectly, that it had something to do with movement, traveling, checking in and out of hotels, going to and from the airport.

I tried this.

A week after placing the ashes in the wall at St. John the Divine, I flew to Boston and back to New York and then to Dallas and back to New York and then to Minneapolis and back to New York, doing promotion for *The Year of Magical Thinking*. The following week, again doing promotion and still under the misapprehension that momentum was about traveling, I flew to Washington and back and then to San Francisco and Los Angeles and Denver and Seattle and Chicago and Toronto and finally to Palm Springs, where I was to spend Thanksgiving with my brother and his family. From various points on this itinerary, over the course of which I began to grasp that just going to and from the airport might be insufficient, that some further effort might be required, I spoke by telephone to Scott Rudin, and agreed that I should write and he should produce and David Hare should direct a one-character play, intended for Broadway, based on *The Year of Magical Thinking*.

The three of us, Scott, David, and I, met for the first time on this project a month after Christmas.

A week before Easter, in a tiny theater on West Forty-second Street, we watched the first readings of the play.

A year later it opened, starring Vanessa Redgrave in its single role, at the Booth Theater on West Forty-fifth Street.

As ways of maintaining momentum go this one turned out to be better than most: I remember liking the entire process a good deal. I liked the quiet afternoons backstage with the stage managers and electricians, I liked the way the ushers gathered for instructions downstairs just before the half-hour call. I liked the presence of Shubert security outside, I liked the weight of the stage door as I opened it against the wind through Shubert Alley, I liked the secret passages to and from the stage. I liked that Amanda, who ran the stage door at night, kept on her desk a tin of the cookies she baked. I liked that Lauri, who managed the Booth for the Shubert Organization and was doing graduate work in medieval literature, became our ultimate authority on a few lines in the play that involved Gawain. I liked the fried chicken and cornbread and potato salad and greens we brought in from Piece o' Chicken, a kitchen storefront near Ninth Avenue. I liked the matzo-ball soup we brought in from the Hotel Edison coffee shop. I liked the place to sit we set up backstage, the little improvised table with the checked tablecloth and the electrified candle and the menu that read "Café Didion."

I liked watching the performance from a balcony above the lights.

I liked being up there alone with the lights and the play.

I liked it all, but most of all I liked the fact that although the play was entirely focused on Quintana there were, five evenings and two afternoons a week, these ninety full minutes, the run time of the play, during which she did not need to be dead.

During which the question remained open.

During which the denouement had yet to play out.

During which the last scene played did not necessarily need to be played in the ICU overlooking the East River.

During which the bells would not necessarily sound and the doors would not necessarily be locked at six.

During which the last dialogue heard did not necessarily need to concern the vent.

Like when someone dies, don't dwell on it.

31

On the evening late in August when the play closed Vanessa took the yellow roses provided for her curtain calls and laid them on the stage, beneath the photograph of John and Quintana on the deck in Malibu that was the closing drop of the set Bob Crowley had designed for the production.

The theater cleared.

I was gratified to see how slowly it cleared, as if the audience shared my wish not to leave John and Quintana alone.

We stood in the wings and drank champagne.

Before I left that evening someone pointed out the yellow roses Vanessa had laid on the stage floor and asked if I wanted to take them.

I did not want to take the yellow roses.

I did not want the yellow roses touched.

I wanted the yellow roses right there, where Vanessa had left them, with John and Quintana on the stage of the Booth, lying there on the stage all night, lit only by the ghost light, still there on the stage right down to the inevitable instant of the morning's eight-a.m. load-out. "*Performance 144 + 23 Previews + 1 Actors Fund,*" the stage manager's performance notes read for that night. "*Magical evening. Lovely final show. Call from the director pre-show. Roses at the call. Champagne toast. Guests included Griffin Dunne and daughter Hannah and Marian Seldes. Café Didion served up its final Piece o' Chicken and sides.*" By that evening when the play closed it seemed clear that I had in fact maintained momentum, but it also seemed clear that maintaining momentum had been at a certain cost. This cost had always been predictable but I only that night began to put it into words. One phrase that came to mind that night was "pushing yourself." Another was "beyond endurance."

32

"I fell prey to water intoxication or low sodium, which is characterized by hallucination, memory loss, and corporeal ineptness; a veritable cornucopia of psychoses. I could hear voices, see four different images on the television at one time, read a book in which each word cd separate to fill the page. I'd ask people on the phone who they thought they were talking to cause i certainly didn't know. & I fell constantly. On top of this phantasmagoric experience, I had a stroke." So wrote the playwright Ntozake Shange, in *In the Fullness of Time: 32 Women on Life After 50*, about the maladies that struck her from the blue in her fifties. "The stroke put an end to nanoseconds of images & left a body with diminished vision, no strength, immobile legs, slurred speech, and no recollection of how to read."

She learned to remember how to read.

She learned to remember how to write.

She learned to remember how to walk, how to talk.

She became the person Quintana dreamed of becoming, the person who, by *not dwelling on it*, wakes one morning and finds her revised circumstances corrected. "I am not dead, I am older," she tells us from this improved perspective. "But I can still memorize a stanza or two. What I have memorized is my child's face at different points in her life."

33

Ill health, which is another way of describing what it can cost to maintain momentum, overtakes us when we can imagine no reason to expect it. I can tell you to the hour when it overtook me—a Thursday morning, August 2, 2007—when I woke with what seemed to be an earache and a reddened area on my face that I mistook for a staph infection.

I remember thinking of this as trying, time-consuming, the waste of a morning I could not afford.

Because I had what I mistook for an earache I would need that morning to see an otolaryngologist.

Because I had what I mistook for a staph infection I would need that morning to see a dermatologist.

Before noon I had been diagnosed: not an earache, not a staph infection, but herpes zoster, shingles, an inflammation of the nervous system, an adult recurrence, generally thought to have been triggered or heightened by stress, of the virus responsible for childhood chickenpox.

"Shingles": it sounded minor, even mildly comical, something about which a great-aunt might complain, or an elderly neighbor; an amusing story tomorrow.

Tomorrow. When I will be fine. Restored. Well.

Telling the amusing story.

You'll never guess what it turned out to be. "Shingles," imagine.

Nothing to worry about then, I remember saying to the doctor who made the diagnosis.

Zoster can be a pretty nasty virus, the doctor said, guarded.

Still in the mode for maintaining momentum, and still oblivious to the extent to which maintaining momentum was precisely what had led me to the doctor's office, I did not ask in what ways zoster could be a pretty nasty virus.

Instead I went home, smoothed some translucent foundation over what had now been established as not a staph infection, took one of the antiviral tablets the doctor had given me, and left for West Forty-fifth Street. I left for West Forty-fifth Street not because I felt any better (in fact I felt worse) but because going to the theater had been my plan for the day, going to the theater was that day's momentum: get to the Booth in time for the 3:30 understudy rehearsal, walk across West Forty-fifth Street during the break and pick up fried chicken and greens to eat backstage, stay for the performance and have a drink afterwards with Vanessa and whoever else was around. "*Direct, engaging, well-tempered,*" the stage manager's performance notes for the evening read. "*Ms. Redgrave nervous pre-show. Vortex very clear. Rapt audience. Cell phone at very top of show. In attendance: Joan Didion (piece o' chicken at the café, show, and ladies' cocktail hour). Hot humid day; stage temp: comfortable.*"

I have no memory of Ms. Redgrave nervous pre-show.

I have no memory of the ladies' cocktail hour. I am told that it featured daiquiris, blended backstage by Vanessa's dresser, and that I had one.

I remember only that the hot humid day with the comfortable stage temperature was followed, for me, by a week of 103-degree fever, three weeks of acute pain in the nerves on the left side of my head and face (including, inconveniently, those nerves that trigger headaches, earaches, and toothaches), and after that by a condition the neurologist described as "postviral ataxia" but I could describe only as "not knowing where my body starts and stops."

I can only think that this may have been what Ntozake Shange meant by "corporeal ineptness."

I no longer had any balance.

I dropped whatever I tried to pick up.

I could not tie my shoes, I could not button a sweater or clip my hair off my face, the simplest acts of fastening and unfastening were now beyond me.

I could no longer catch a ball.

I mention the ball only because (I do not in fact normally catch balls during the course of the day) the single accurate description I would hear or read of these symptoms I was just then beginning to experience was that provided by a professional tennis player, James Blake, who, after a season of considerable stress—he had fractured a vertebra in his neck before the French Open and by the time he was healing his father was dying—woke one morning in his early twenties with similar symptoms. "Instantly, I realized just how many things were wrong," he later wrote, in *Breaking Back: How I Lost Everything and Won Back My Life*, about his initial attempt to return to what had been his life. "Not only was my balance off, but my vision was messed up as well—I had a hard time tracking the ball from Brian's and Evan's rackets to my own. I could see them hit it, I'd sort of lose it for a moment, then suddenly it would register much closer to me. This was especially disconcerting because neither Brian nor Evan hit anywhere near as hard as the average tour player."

He tries to run right for a shot, and finds that his coordination has gone wherever his vision went.

He tries to volley, just hit a few balls, and finds that the balls now hit him.

He asks the neurotologist to whom he has been referred at Yale–New Haven how long he should expect these symptoms to last.

"At least three months," the neurotologist says. "Or it could take four years."

This is not what the professional tennis player wants to hear, nor is it what I want to hear.

Still.

I maintain faith (another word for momentum) that my own symptoms, which have continued to recur in slightly altered incarnations and have so far lasted closer to four years than to three months, will improve, lessen, even resolve.

I do what I can to encourage this resolution, I follow instructions.

I regularly report to Sixtieth and Madison for physical therapy.

I keep the freezer stocked with Maison du Chocolat vanilla ice cream.

I collect encouraging news, even focus on it.

For example:

James Blake has since returned to the tour. I fix on this fact.

Meanwhile, like Ntozake Shange, I memorize my child's face.

34

I find myself studying, in a copy of *The New York Review of Books*, a Magnum photograph of Sophia Loren taken during a Christian Dior fashion show in Paris in 1968. In this photograph Sophia Loren is sitting on a gilt chair, wearing a silk turban and smoking a cigarette, achingly polished, forever soignée as she watches "the bride," the traditional end of the show. It occurs to me that this Magnum photograph would have been taken not long after Sophia Loren herself had been "the bride," in fact twice the bride, married in France to Carlo Ponti for the second time after the annulment of their original Mexican marriage, the marriage for which he had been charged with bigamy and threatened with excommunication in Italy.

A "scandal" of the time.

It has become hard to remember how reliably "scandal" once came our way.

Elizabeth Taylor and Richard Burton, a scandal.

Ingrid Bergman and Roberto Rossellini, a scandal.

Sophia Loren and Carlo Ponti, a scandal.

I continue studying the photograph.

I imagine the object of this particular scandal leaving Dior and going to lunch in the courtyard of the Plaza Athénée.

I imagine her sitting with Carlo Ponti in the courtyard, eating an éclair with a fork, the vines that line the courtyard blowing slightly, ivy, *lierre*, sunlight glowing pink through the red canvas canopies over the windows. I imagine the sound of the little birds that flock in the *lierre*, a twittering, a constant presence and an occasional—when, say, a metal shutter is opened, or when, say, Sophia Loren rises from her table to cross the courtyard—swelling of birdsong.

I imagine her leaving the Plaza Athénée, photographers

flashing around her as she slides into a waiting car on the Avenue Montaigne.

The cigarette, the silk turban.

It strikes me that she looks in this photograph not unlike the women in the photographs Nick took at Quintana's christening.

Quintana's christening was in 1966, this Christian Dior show was two years later, 1968: 1966 and 1968 were a world removed from each other in the political and cultural life of the United States but they were for women who presented themselves a certain way the same time. It was a way of looking, it was a way of being. It was a period. What became of that way of looking, that way of being, that time, that period? What became of the women smoking cigarettes in their Chanel suits and their David Webb bracelets, what became of Diana holding the champagne flute and one of Sara Mankiewicz's Minton plates? What became of Sara Mankiewicz's Minton plates? What became of the clay tennis court at the house on Franklin Avenue in Hollywood, the court I watched Quintana weed on her fat baby knees? What gave Quintana the idea that weeding a court on which no one ever played—even the net was down, punched through during years of neglect, dragging in the weeds and the dust that got scuffed off the clay—was a necessary task, her assignment, her duty? Was weeding the unused tennis court at the house on Franklin Avenue something like equipping the projection room in the doll's house in Malibu? Was weeding the unused tennis court something like writing a novel? Was it one more way of assuming an adult role? Why did she so need to assume an adult role? Whatever became of those fat baby knees, whatever became of Bunny Rabbit?

As it happens I know what became of Bunny Rabbit.

She left Bunny Rabbit in a suite at the Royal Hawaiian Hotel in Honolulu.

I learned this halfway across the Pacific, when she was sitting next to me in the darkened upstairs cabin on the evening Pan Am flight back to Los Angeles.

There was still a Pan Am then.

There was still a TWA then.

There was still a Pan Am and there was still a TWA and

Bendel's was still on West Fifty-seventh Street and it still had Holly's Harp chiffons and lettuce edges and sizes zero and two.

Sitting next to me on that evening flight back to Los Angeles my child mourned Bunny Rabbit's cruel fate: Bunny Rabbit was lost, Bunny Rabbit was left behind, Bunny Rabbit had been abandoned. Yet by the time we taxied into the gate at LAX she had successfully translated Bunny Rabbit's cruel fate into Bunny Rabbit's good luck: the Royal Hawaiian, the suite, the room-service breakfasts. Where did the morning went. The white sand, the swimming pool. Walking to the reef. Swimming off the raft. Bunny Rabbit was even now, we could be certain, swimming off the raft.

Swim off the raft, walk to the reef.
Imagine a five-year-old walking to the reef.
Like when someone dies, don't dwell on it.
How could I not still need that child with me?

I feel impelled to locate, by way of establishing at least one survivor of the period, a recent photograph of Sophia Loren.

I type her name into Google Images.

I find such a photograph: Sophia Loren arriving at some kind of publicity event, one of those red-carpet arrivals during which the PR people hover close, alerting the photographers to the approach of the celebrity. As I check the caption on the photograph I notice in passing that Sophia Loren was born in 1934, the same year in which I myself was born. I am spellbound: Sophia Loren, too, is seventy-five years old. Sophia Loren is seventy-five years old and no one on that red carpet, to my knowledge, is yet suggesting that she is making an inadequate adjustment to aging. This entirely meaningless discovery floods me with restored hope, a revived sense of the possible.

35

When we lose that sense of the possible we lose it fast.

One day we are absorbed by dressing well, following the news, keeping up, coping, what we might call *staying alive*; the next day we are not. One day we are turning the pages of whatever has arrived in the day's mail with real enthusiasm—maybe it is *Vogue*, maybe it is *Foreign Affairs*, whatever it is we are intensely interested, pleased to have this handbook to *keeping up*, this key to *staying alive*—yet the next day we are walking uptown on Madison past Barney's and Armani or on Park past the Council on Foreign Relations and we are not even glancing at their windows. One day we are looking at the Magnum photograph of Sophia Loren at the Christian Dior show in Paris in 1968 and thinking yes, it could be me, I could wear that dress, I was in Paris that year; a blink of the eye later we are in one or another doctor's office being told what has already gone wrong, why we will never again wear the red suede sandals with the four-inch heels, never again wear the gold hoop earrings, the enameled beads, never now wear the dress Sophia Loren is wearing. The sun damage inflicted when we swam off the raft in our twenties against all advice is only now surfacing (we were told not to burn, we were told what would happen, we were told to wear sunscreen, we ignored all warnings): melanoma, squamous cell, long hours now spent watching the dermatologist carve out the carcinomas with the names we do not want to hear.

Long hours now spent getting the intravenous infusions of the medication that promises to replace the bone lost to aging.

Long hours now spent getting the intravenous infusions and wondering why the Vitamin D we thought we were accumulating by not wearing sunscreen failed to realize its bone-building potential.

Long hours now spent waiting for the scans, waiting for the EEGs, sitting in frigid waiting rooms turning the pages of *The Wall Street Journal* and *AARP The Magazine* and *Neurology Today* and the alumnae magazines of the Columbia and Cornell medical schools.

Sitting in frigid waiting rooms once again producing the insurance cards, once again explaining why, the provider's preference notwithstanding, the Writers Guild–Industry Health Plan needs to be the primary and Medicare the secondary, not, despite my age—my age is now an issue in every waiting room—vice versa.

Sitting in frigid waiting rooms once again filling out the New York–Presbyterian questionnaires.

Sitting in frigid waiting rooms once again listing the medications and the symptoms and the descriptions and dates of previous hospitalizations: just make up the dates, just take a guess and stand by it, for some reason "1982" always comes to mind, *well, fine, "1982" it is, "1982" will have to do*, there can be no way to get the answer to this question right.

Sitting in frigid waiting rooms trying to think of the name and telephone number of the person I want notified in case of emergency.

Whole days now spent on this one question, this question with no possible answer: *who do I want notified in case of emergency?*

I think it over. I do not want even to consider "in case of emergency."

Emergency, I continue to believe, is what happens to someone else.

I say that I continue to believe this even as I know that I do not.

I mean, think back: what about that business with the folding metal chair in the rehearsal room on West Forty-second Street? What exactly was I afraid of there? What did I fear in that rehearsal room if not an "emergency"? Or what about walking home after an early dinner on Third Avenue and waking up in a pool of blood on my own bedroom floor? Might not waking up in a pool of blood on my own bedroom floor qualify as an "emergency"?

All right. Accepted. "In case of emergency" could apply.
Who to notify. I try harder.
Still, no name comes to mind.

I could give the name of my brother, but my brother lives three thousand miles from what might be defined in New York as an emergency. I could give Griffin's name, but Griffin is shooting a picture. Griffin is on location. Griffin is sitting in the dining room of one or another Hilton Inn—a few too many people at the table, a little too much noise—and Griffin is not picking up his cell. I could give the name of whichever close friend in New York comes first to mind, but the close friend in New York who comes first to mind is actually, on reflection, not even in New York, out of town, out of the country, away, certainly unreachable in the best case, possibly unwilling in the worst.

As I consider the word "unwilling" my lagging cognition kicks in.

The familiar phrase "need to know" surfaces.
The phrase "need to know" has been the problem all along.
Only one person needs to know.
She is of course the one person who needs to know.
Let me just be in the ground.
Let me just be in the ground and go to sleep.
I imagine telling her.
I am able to imagine telling her because I still see her.
Hello, Mommies.
The same way I still see her weeding the clay court on Franklin Avenue.

The same way I still see her sitting on the bare floor crooning back to the eight-track.

Do you wanna dance. I wanna dance.

The same way I still see the stephanotis in her braid, the same way I still see the plumeria tattoo through her veil. The same way I still see the bright-red soles on her shoes as she kneels at the altar. The same way I still see her, in the darkened upstairs cabin on the evening Pan Am from Honolulu to LAX, inventing the unforeseen uptick in Bunny Rabbit's fortunes.

I know that I can no longer reach her.

I know that, should I try to reach her—should I take her hand as if she were again sitting next to me in the upstairs cabin on the evening Pan Am from Honolulu to LAX, should I lull her to sleep against my shoulder, should I sing her the song about Daddy gone to get the rabbit skin to wrap his baby bunny in—she will fade from my touch.

Vanish.

Pass into nothingness: the Keats line that frightened her.

Fade as the blue nights fade, go as the brightness goes.

Go back into the blue.

I myself placed her ashes in the wall.

I myself saw the cathedral doors locked at six.

I know what it is I am now experiencing.

I know what the frailty is, I know what the fear is.

The fear is not for what is lost.

What is lost is already in the wall.

What is lost is already behind the locked doors.

The fear is for what is still to be lost.

You may see nothing still to be lost.

Yet there is no day in her life on which I do not see her.

SOUTH AND WEST

From a Notebook

*For John and Quintana
and for Earl*

Contents

285
Notes on the South

341
California Notes

NOTES ON THE SOUTH

John and I were living on Franklin Avenue in Los Angeles. I had wanted to revisit the South, so we flew there for a month in 1970. The idea was to start in New Orleans and from there we had no plan. We went wherever the day took us. I seem to remember that John drove. I had not been back since 1942–43, when my father was stationed in Durham, North Carolina, but it did not seem to have changed that much. At the time, I had thought it might be a piece.

New Orleans

> . . . the purple dream
> Of the America we have not been,
> The tropic empire, seeking the warm sea,
> The last foray of aristocracy . . .
> STEPHEN VINCENT BENÉT, *John Brown's Body*

> Would that I could represent to you the dangerous
> nature of the ground, its oozing, spongy,
> and miry disposition . . .
> JOHN JAMES AUDUBON, *The Birds of America*, 1830

In New Orleans in June the air is heavy with sex and death, not violent death but death by decay, overripeness, rotting, death by drowning, suffocation, fever of unknown etiology. The place is physically dark, dark like the negative of a photograph, dark like an X-ray: the atmosphere absorbs its own light, never reflects light but sucks it in until random objects glow with a morbid luminescence. The crypts above ground dominate certain vistas. In the hypnotic liquidity of the atmosphere all motion slows into choreography, all people on the street move as if suspended in a precarious emulsion, and there seems only a technical distinction between the quick and the dead.

One afternoon on St. Charles Avenue I saw a woman die, fall forward over the wheel of her car. "Dead," pronounced an old woman who stood with me on the sidewalk a few inches from where the car had veered into a tree. After the police ambulance came I followed the old woman through the aqueous light of the Pontchartrain Hotel garage and into the coffee shop. The death had seemed serious but casual, as if it had taken place in a pre-Columbian city where death was expected, and did not in the long run count for much.

"Whose fault is it," the old woman was saying to the waitress in the coffee shop, her voice trailing off.

"It's nobody's fault, Miss Clarice."

"They can't help it, no."

"They can't help at all." I had thought they were talking about the death but they were talking about the weather. "Richard used to work at the Bureau and he told me, they can't help what comes in on the radar." The waitress paused, as if for emphasis. "They simply cannot be held to account."

"They just can't," the old woman said.

"It comes in on the radar."

The words hung in the air. I swallowed a piece of ice.

"And we get it," the old woman said after a while.

It was a fatalism I would come to recognize as endemic to the particular tone of New Orleans life. Bananas would rot, and harbor tarantulas. Weather would come in on the radar, and be bad. Children would take fever and die, domestic arguments would end in knifings, the construction of highways would lead to graft and cracked pavement where the vines would shoot back. Affairs of state would turn on sexual jealousy, in New Orleans as if in Port-au-Prince, and all the king's men would turn on the king. The temporality of the place is operatic, childlike, the fatalism that of a culture dominated by wilderness. "All we know," said the mother of Carl Austin Weiss of the son who had just shot and killed Huey Long in a corridor of the Louisiana State Capitol Building in Baton Rouge, "is that he took living seriously."

As it happens I was taught to cook by someone from Louisiana, where an avid preoccupation with recipes and food among men was not unfamiliar to me. We lived together for some years, and I think we most fully understood each other when once I tried to kill him with a kitchen knife. I remember spending whole days cooking with N., perhaps the most pleasant days we spent together. He taught me to fry chicken and to make a brown rice stuffing for fowl and to chop endive with garlic and lemon juice and to lace everything I did with

Tabasco and Worcestershire and black pepper. The first present he ever gave me was a garlic press, and also the second, because I broke the first. One day on the Eastern Shore we spent hours making shrimp bisque and then had an argument about how much salt it needed, and because he had been drinking Sazeracs for several hours he poured salt in to make his point. It was like brine, but we pretended it was fine. Throwing the chicken on the floor, or the artichoke. Buying crab boil. Discussing endlessly the possibilities of an artichoke-and-oyster casserole. After I married he still called me up occasionally for recipes.

> I guess you think this is a better machine than that Wop affair. I guess you think you have redwood flagstones in your backyard. I guess you think your mother used to be County Cookie Chairman. I guess you think I take up a lot of room in a small bed. I guess you think Schrafft's has chocolate leaves. I guess you think Mr. Earl "Elbow" Reum has more personality than I. I guess you think there are no lesbians in Nevada. I guess you think you know how to wash sweaters by hand. I guess you think you get picked on by Mary Jane and that people serve you bad whiskey. I guess you think you haven't got pernicious anemia. Take those vitamins. I guess you think southerners are somewhat anachronistic.

—is a message that man left me when I was twenty-two.

The first time I was ever in the South was in late 1942, early 1943. My father was stationed in Durham, North Carolina, and my mother and brother and I took a series of slow and overcrowded trains to meet him there. At home in California I had cried at night, I had lost weight, I had wanted my father. I had imagined the Second World War as a punishment specifically designed to deprive me of my father, had counted up my errors and, with an egocentricity which then approached autism and which afflicts me still in dreams and fevers and marriage, found myself guilty.

Of the trip I recall mainly that a sailor who had just been

torpedoed on the *Wasp* in the Pacific gave me a silver-and-turquoise ring, and that we missed our connection in New Orleans and could get no room and sat up one night on a covered verandah of the St. Charles Hotel, my brother and I in matching seersucker sunsuits and my mother in a navy-blue-and-white-checked silk dress dusty from the train. She covered us with the mink coat she had bought before her marriage and wore until 1956. We were taking trains instead of driving because a few weeks before in California she had lent the car to an acquaintance who drove it into a lettuce truck outside Salinas, a fact of which I am certain because it remains a source of rancor, in my father's dialogue, to this day. I last heard it mentioned a week ago. My mother made no response, only laid out another hand of solitaire.

In Durham we had one room with kitchen privileges in the house of a lay minister whose children ate apple butter on thick slabs of bread all day long and referred to their father in front of us as "Reverend Caudill." In the evenings Reverend Caudill would bring home five or six quarts of peach ice cream, and he and his wife and children would sit on the front porch spooning peach ice cream from the cartons while we lay in our room watching our mother read and waiting for Thursday.

Thursday was the day we could take the bus to Duke University, which had been taken over by the military, and spend the afternoon with my father. He would buy us a Coca-Cola in the student union and walk us around the campus and take snapshots of us, which I now have, and look at from time to time: two small children and a woman who resembles me, sitting by the lagoon, standing by the wishing well, the snapshots always lightstruck or badly focused and, in any case, now faded. Thirty years later I am certain that my father must also have been with us on weekends, but I can only suggest that his presence in the small house, his tension and his aggressive privacy and his preference for shooting craps over eating peach ice cream, must have seemed to me so potentially disruptive as to efface all memory of weekends.

On the days of the week which were not Thursday I played with a set of paper dolls lent me by Mrs. Caudill, the dolls bearing the faces of Vivien Leigh, Olivia de Havilland, Ann Rutherford, and Butterfly McQueen as they appeared in *Gone With the Wind*, and I also learned from the neighborhood children to eat raw potatoes dipped in the soft dust from beneath the house. I know now that eating pica is common in the undernourished South, just as I know now why the driver of the bus on the first Thursday we went out to Duke refused to leave the curb until we had moved from the back seat to the front, but I did not know it then. I did not even know then that my mother found our sojourn of some months in Durham less than ideal.

I could never precisely name what impelled me to spend time in the South during the summer of 1970. There was no reportorial imperative to any of the places I went at the time I went: nothing "happened" anywhere I was, no celebrated murders, trials, integration orders, confrontations, not even any celebrated acts of God.

I had only some dim and unformed sense, a sense which struck me now and then, and which I could not explain coherently, that for some years the South and particularly the Gulf Coast had been for America what people were still saying California was, and what California seemed to me not to be: the future, the secret source of malevolent and benevolent energy, the psychic center. I did not much want to talk about this.

I had only the most ephemeral "picture" in my mind. If I talked about it I could mention only Clay Shaw, and Garrison, and a pilot I had once met who flew between the Gulf and unnamed Caribbean and Central American airstrips for several years on small planes with manifests that showed only "tropical flowers," could mention only some apprehension of paranoia and febrile conspiracy and baroque manipulation and peach ice cream and an unpleasant evening I had spent in 1962 on the Eastern Shore of Maryland. In short I could only sound deranged. And so instead of talking about it I flew south one day in the summer of 1970, rented a car, and drove for a month or so around Louisiana and Mississippi and Alabama, saw no spokesmen, covered no events, did nothing at all but try to find out, as usual, what was making the picture in my mind.

In New Orleans, the old people sitting in front of houses and hotels on St. Charles Avenue, barely rocking. In the Quarter I saw them again (along with desolate long-haired children), sitting on balconies, an ironing board behind them, gently rocking, sometimes not rocking at all but only staring. In New Orleans they have mastered the art of the motionless.

In the evening I visited in the Garden District. "Olly olly oxen free" echoing in the soft twilight, around the magnolias and the trees with fluffy pods of pink. What I saw that night was a world so rich and complex and I was almost disoriented, a world complete unto itself, a world of smooth surfaces broken occasionally by a flash of eccentricity so deep that it numbed any attempt at interpretation.

"I guess nobody knows more about the South than the people in this room right now," my host allowed several times before dinner. We were at his house in the Garden District with the requisite bound volumes of the *Sewanee* and the *Southern Review* and the requisite Degas portrait of his great-great-grandmother, and he was talking about his wife and their friend, an architect of good Mobile family who specialized in the restoration and building of New Orleans Greek Revival houses.

And of course he was talking about himself. "Ben C.," the others called him, their voices fondly inflected. "You just *stop* that, Ben C.," as he bullied the two women, his sister and his wife working together on a Junior League project, a guidebook to New Orleans. Already Ben C. had demanded to know what "athletics" my husband played, and why I had been allowed, in the course of doing some reporting a few years before, to "spend time consorting with a lot of marijuana-smoking hippie trash."

"Who allowed you?" he repeated.

I said that I did not know quite what he meant.

Ben C. only stared at me.

"I mean, who wouldn't have allowed me?"

"You *do* have a husband?" he said finally. "This man I've thought was your husband for several years, he *is* your husband?"

The evening, it developed, had started off wrong for Ben C. It seemed that he had called some of his cousins to come for dinner, and they had made excuses, and he had found that "inexcusable." It further seemed that the excuse made by one cousin, who it would turn out was a well-known southern writer, was a previous engagement with the director of a Head Start program, and Ben C. had found that particularly inexcusable.

"What am I meant to conclude?" he demanded rhetorically of his wife. "Am I meant to conclude he's certifiable?"

"Maybe you're meant to conclude he didn't care to come to dinner," she said, and then, as if to cover her irreverence, she sighed. "I only hope he doesn't get too mixed up with the Negroes. You know what happened to George Washington Cable."

I tried to remember what had happened to George Washington Cable.

"He ended up having to go *north*, is what happened."

I said that I wanted only to know what people in the South were thinking and doing.

He continued to gaze at me. He had the smooth, rounded face of well-off New Orleans, that absence of angularity which characterizes the local genetic pool. I tried to think who had incurred his wrath by going up north and whining.

"I would just guess that we know a little more about the subject," Ben C. said finally, his voice rising, "than one Mr. Willie Morris."

We ate trout with shallots and mushrooms. We drank some white wine, we drank some more bourbon. We passed the evening. I never learned why the spectre of one Mr. Willie Morris had materialized in that living room in the Garden District, nor did I ask.

Ben C.'s wife and sister, Mrs. Benjamin C. Toledano and Mrs. Beauregard Redmond, soon to be Mrs. Toledano Redmond, had many suggestions for understanding the South. I must walk Bourbon or Royal to Chartres, I must walk Chartres to Esplanade. I must have coffee and doughnuts at the French Market. I should not miss St. Louis Cathedral, the Presbytère, the Cabildo. We should have lunch at Galatoire's: trout amandine or trout Marguery. We should obtain a copy of *The Great Days of the Garden District*. We should visit Asphodel, Rosedown, Oakley Plantation. Stanton Hall in Natchez. The Grand Hotel in Point Clear. We should have dinner at Manale's, tour Coliseum Square Park. I should appreciate the grace, the beauty of their way of life. These graceful preoccupations seemed to be regarded by the women in a spirit at once dedicated and merely tolerant, as if they lived their lives on several quite contradictory levels.

One afternoon we took the ferry to Algiers and drove an hour or so down the river, in Plaquemines Parish. This is peculiar country. Algiers is a doubtful emulsion of white frame bungalows and jerry-built apartment complexes, the Parc Fontaine Apts. and so forth, and the drive on down the river takes you through a landscape more metaphorical than any I have seen outside the Sonoran Desert.

Here and there one is conscious of the levee, off to the left. Corn and tomatoes grow aimlessly, as if naturalized. I am too accustomed to agriculture as agribusiness, the rich vistas of the California valleys where all the resources of Standard Oil and the University of California have been brought to bear on glossy constant productivity. No Hunting of Quadrupeds, a sign read in Belle Chasse. What could that mean? Can you hunt reptiles? Bipeds? There are dead dogs by the road, and a sinking graveyard in a grove of live oak.

Getting close to Port Sulphur we began to see sulphur works, the tanks glowing oddly in the peculiar light. We ran over three snakes in the hour's drive, one of them a thick black moccasin already dead, twisted across the one lane. There were run-down antiques places, and tomato stands, and a beauty shop called Feminine Fluff. The snakes, the rotting undergrowth, sulphurous light: the images are so specifically those of the nightmare world that when we stopped for gas, or directions,

I had to steel myself, deaden every nerve, in order to step from the car onto the crushed oyster shells in front of the gas station. When we got back to the hotel I stood in the shower for almost half an hour trying to wash myself clean of the afternoon, but then I started thinking about where the water came from, what dark places it had pooled in.

When I think now about New Orleans I remember mainly its dense obsessiveness, its vertiginous preoccupation with race, class, heritage, style, and the absence of style. As it happens, these particular preoccupations all involve distinctions which the frontier ethic teaches western children to deny and to leave deliberately unmentioned, but in New Orleans such distinctions are the basis of much conversation, and lend that conversation its peculiar childlike cruelty and innocence. In New Orleans they also talk about parties, and about food, their voices rising and falling, never still, as if talking about anything at all could keep the wilderness at bay. In New Orleans the wilderness is sensed as very near, not the redemptive wilderness of the western imagination but something rank and old and malevolent, the idea of wilderness not as an escape from civilization and its discontents but as a mortal threat to a community precarious and colonial in its deepest aspect. The effect is lively and avaricious and intensely self-absorbed, a tone not uncommon in colonial cities, and the principal reason I find such cities invigorating.

New Orleans to Biloxi, Mississippi

On the Chef Menteur Highway out of New Orleans there is the sense of swamp reclaimed to no point. Dismal subdivisions evoke the romance of Evangeline on their billboards. Shacks along the road sell plaster statues of the Virgin Mary. The gas stations advertise Free Flag Decals. Lake Pontchartrain can be seen now and then on the left, and the rusted hulks of boats at marine repair places.

The rest of it is swamp. Crude signs point down dirt roads, and along the road are shacks, or "camps," for fishing. Postboxes are supported on twisted rigid chains, as if the inhabitants are as conscious as the traveler of the presence of snakes. The light is odd, more peculiar still than the light in New Orleans, light entirely absorbed by what it strikes.

We stopped at a trinket shack called the Beachcomber. A boy was filling the Pepsi machine outside. Towels hung limply on a display clothesline: "Put Your (picture of a HEART) in Dixie or Get Your (picture of an ASS) OUT!" Inside were boxes of shells and dried devilfish. "They get 'em from Mexico," the boy said.

Across the Mississippi line we took a side road through the pine forest toward what the sign said would be E. Ansley Estates. Rain was beginning to fall, and as we passed a pond a dozen or so boys were climbing out of the water and into two cars. One felt the rain had spoiled their day, and they would be at loose ends, restless. The cliché of the lonely road in the South took on a certain meaning here. The road was scattered occasionally with armadillo shells. The rain continued. The boys and their cars disappeared. We did not find E. Ansley Estates, or any settlement at all.

Signs for fireworks, signs for a reptile farm ahead. The rain let up and we stopped at the reptile farm. The Reptile House was a small shack out in back of the main roadside building, across a dirt yard where chickens ran loose. The place was dirty, littered with peanut shells and empty six-pack cartons marked Dad's Root Beer and Suncrest Orange Drink. There were a few capuchin monkeys, and a couple of big lethargic boas in packing cases, and a Holbrook's king snake and a couple of rattlers. A cage marked COPPERHEAD appeared to be empty. There was a family in the Reptile House when we were there, a boy about nine and a father and a woman in slacks with her hair piled high and lacquered.

We stood, the five of us, and looked restlessly out into the driving rain, trapped together in the Reptile House. The dust outside was turning to deep mud. Alligators thrashed in a muddy pool a few yards away. A little farther a sign said Snake Pit.

"I never would've stopped if I'd known it was outside," the woman said.

"Known what was outside?" her husband said.

"The Snake Pit, of course. What do you *think* is outside?"

The man drummed his fingers on top of a packing case. The boa inside slid deeper into its coil. To make conversation I asked the man if they had visited a far building marked Reptile House.

"There aren't no reptiles upstairs there," he said, and then, as if I might doubt it: "She told us, there aren't no reptiles upstairs. She said not to go in."

"Maybe there are some reptiles downstairs?" I suggested.

"I don't know about that," he said. "I just wouldn't go in."

"Of course *you* wouldn't," the woman said mildly. She was still staring at the Snake Pit.

I was leaning on the empty copperhead box listening to the rain hiss when an uneasy feeling came over me that the hissing came from inside the box. I looked again and there it was, a copperhead, almost hidden by its shed skins.

We gave up on one another, and on the possibility of the rain's stopping, and ran through the mud back to the main house. I slipped and fell in the mud and had an instant of irrational panic that there were snakes in the mud and all around me.

In the trinket shop the woman and I each paid a dime to use the restroom. With another dime I got a cup of cold coffee from a machine and tried to stop being chilled. The woman bought her son a china potty with a little child disappearing down the drain and the inscription "Goodbye Sweet World." I bought a cheap beach towel printed with a Confederate flag. It is ragged and gray now and sits in my linen closet in California amid thick and delicately colored Fieldcrest beach towels, and my child prefers it to the good ones.

Pass Christian to Gulfport

At Pass Christian in the summer of 1970 the debris of the 1969 hurricane had become the natural look of the landscape. The big houses along the water were abandoned, the schools and churches were wiped out, the windows of places hung askew. The devastation along the Gulf had an inevitability about it: the coast was reverting to its natural state. There were For Sale signs all over, but one could not imagine buyers. I remembered people talking about Pass Christian as a summer place, and indeed the houses had once been pretty and white and the American flags unfaded, but even in the good years there must have been an uneasiness there. They sat on those screened porches and waited for something to happen. The place must have always failed at being a resort, if the special quality of a resort is defined as security: there is here that ominous white/dark light so characteristic of the entire Gulf.

The city hall in Pass Christian faces away from the Gulf, and when you happen upon it from the front it looks like a façade from a studio back lot, abandoned a long time ago. Through the shattered windows one sees the dark glare of the Gulf. You want to close your eyes.

Long Beach seemed poorer, or harder hit, or both. There were none of those big white houses with the screened porches here. There were trailers, and a twisted pool ladder that marked the place where a swimming pool had been before the hurricane. Mass was being held in the school gym. On the beach there was an occasional woman with children. The women wore two-piece bathing suits, shorts and halters, not bikinis. All along the coast there were cars parked and tables set up to sell colored discs that whir in the air, apparently indefinitely. On the cars are hand-lettered signs that read SPACE STATION. You can see discs shimmering in the light from a long way off.

At Gulfport, the county seat of Harrison County, a tanker, broken clean in half during the hurricane, lay rusting offshore. The heat was relentless, the streets downtown broad and devoid of trees. *The Losers* was playing at the Sand Theatre in Gulfport, and would be playing at The Avenue in Biloxi. We went into a café downtown to get something to eat. CAFÉ is all the sign said. The menu had red beans and rice, and the only sounds in the place in the afternoon stillness were the whirring of the air conditioner and the click of a pinball machine. Everyone in the place seemed to have been there a long time, and to know everyone else. After a while a man got up from his beer and walked to the door. "Off to the infirmary," he said over his shoulder.

Between Gulfport and Biloxi, the shingles were ripped from the houses facing the Gulf. Live oak trees were twisted and broken. A long way in the distance one could see the Biloxi Lighthouse, a white tower glowing peculiarly in the strange afternoon light.

I had never expected to come to the Gulf Coast married.

Biloxi

Everything seems to go to seed along the Gulf: walls stain, windows rust. Curtains mildew. Wood warps. Air conditioners cease to function. In our room at the Edgewater Gulf Hotel, where the Mississippi Broadcasters' Convention was taking place, the air conditioner in the window violently shook and rattled every time it was turned on. The Edgewater Gulf is an enormous white hotel which looks like a giant laundry, and has the appearance of being on the verge of condemnation. The swimming pool is large and unkempt, and the water smells of fish. Behind the hotel is a new shopping center built around an air-conditioned mall, and I kept escaping there, back into mid-stream America.

In the elevator at the Edgewater Gulf:

"Walter, I believe you've grown the most of any town in the state of Mississippi."

"Well, the figures are in question."

"Didn't quite total as high as the chamber of commerce thought they would?"

"No well—"

"Same in Tupelo. In Tupelo they demanded a recount."

"Well, frankly, I don't think we've got all those people . . . they see the cars, they think they live here, but they come in from around, spend a dollar a day—"

"Dollar, top."

The two men faced the front of the elevator as they spoke, not each other. The dialogue was grave. The possibility of "growth" in small Mississippi towns is ever yearned for, and ever denied. The Mississippi Broadcasters' was, everyone assured me, "the best damn convention in the state of Mississippi."

One evening after dinner we drove around Biloxi, and stopped to watch a Pony League game being played under bright lights. A handful of men in short-sleeved shirts and women in faded cotton blouses and Capri pants sat in the bleachers, watching the children play, Holiday Inn versus Burger Chef. Below the bleachers some children played barefoot in the dust, and a police car was parked, its motor idling, its doors open. There was no one in the car. The game broke up finally, to no one's satisfaction.

There are railroad tracks running through all the towns in Mississippi, or so it seems, and at every crossing is a sign that reads MISSISSIPPI LAW/STOP. The tracks are raised and the wild carrot grows around them.

After the Pony League game broke up we went to get a beer in a bar a few blocks away, and there were some of the other people from the bleachers, and no children in evidence. It was apparently just a way to pass a few hours on a summer evening. They had already seen *The Losers*, say, and it was hot in the house, and supper was finished at sundown.

Another way to pass the time that evening (but I believe it was an almost imperceptibly more middle-class pastime) was at the Kiwanis Fishing Rodeo, where the biggest fish caught that day were displayed in trays of ice. In the sawdust under the awning a small girl sat, stringing the pop tops from beer cans into a necklace.

One morning at 10:30 a.m. during the Mississippi Broadcasters' Convention there was, in the ballroom of the Edgewater Gulf, an event designated on the program as the Ladies' Brunch. The Billy Fane Trio played, and Bob McRaney, Sr., of WROB West Point, presided. "The Billy Fane Trio is becoming something of an institution as regards our convention," he said, and then he introduced another act: "We have an act this morning that . . . I think . . . unless you've been an Indian on a reservation and not many of us have . . . you'll find rather novel and unusual to say the least. Out in Colorado . . . or out somewhere in the West there . . . there's a very quaint little village named Taos. And we have a young man this morning who has perfected a Taos Hoop Dance . . . It's Allen Thomas, from Franklinton, Louisiana, . . . with Martin Belcher on the Indian drums."

"You'll love this act," someone at my table said. "We saw it at the high school up on 49."

"I wish I could play organ like that," someone else said when the Billy Fane Trio was playing.

"Don't you, though?"

"You-all ought to come visit with us," a third woman said. They were all young women, the oldest among them perhaps thirty. "I'd play organ for you."

"We'll never get up there," the first woman said. "I never been anyplace I wanted to go."

A drawing was held for door prizes, the first prize being a room paneled in Masonite. The women genuinely wanted the Masonite room, and they also wanted the carving set, the playing cards, the pair of Miss America shoes, the lighted cosmetic mirror, and the woodcut of Christ. They recalled among them who had won door prizes in years past, and their wistful envy of each winner suffused the room. Little girls in sandals and sundresses played at the edge of the ballroom, waiting for their mothers, who were now, during the drawing, as children themselves.

The isolation of these people from the currents of American life in 1970 was startling and bewildering to behold. All their information was fifth-hand, and mythicized in the handing down. Does it matter where Taos is, after all, if Taos is not in Mississippi?

At the Mississippi Broadcasters' awards banquet, there were many jokes and parables. Here is a joke: "Can you tell me what you'd get if you crossed a violin with a rooster? The answer is, if you looked out in your chicken yard you might see someone fiddling around with your rooster." This seemed to me an interesting joke, in that no element of it was amusing, yet everyone roared, and at tables all around me it was repeated for those who had missed the punch line.

And here is a parable I heard that night: "There was a bee buzzing in a clover field, and a cow came along and swallowed the bee, and the bee buzzed around and it was warm and sleepy and the bee went to sleep, and when the bee woke up, the cow was gone." As I recall, this parable illustrated some point about broadcasting good tidings rather than bad, and it seemed to make the point very clearly to the audience, but it continued to elude me.

Someone at the rostrum mentioned repeatedly that we were "entering the space age in the new decade," but we seemed very far from that, and in any case had we not already entered the space age? I had the feeling that I had been too long on the Gulf Coast, that my own sources of information were distant and removed, that like the women at the Ladies' Brunch I might never get anywhere I wanted to go. One of the awards that night was for the Best Program Series by a Female.

The luncheon was honoring Congressman William Colmer (D-Miss.), who had been thirty-eight years in the House and was chairman of the House Rules Committee. He was receiving the Broadcasters' Man of the Year award, and had come with his AA, his mother, and his secretary. In accepting his award Rep. Colmer murmured something about "bad apples in every lot," and, about the interest of the rest of the nation in the state of Mississippi, "like havin' an obstetrician in New Jersey when the baby's bein' born in Mississippi."

"We get a lot of bad publicity down here," said someone accepting a Distinguished Public Service award. The solidarity engendered by outside disapproval, a note struck constantly. It seemed to have reached a point where all Mississippians were bonded together in a way simply not true of the residents of any other state. They could be comfortable only with each other. Any differences they might have, class or economic or even in a real way racial, seemed outweighed by what they shared.

Charles L. Sullivan, introduced as "lieutenant governor of the state of Mississippi and a member of the Clarksdale Baptist Church," rose to speak. "I have come to think we are living in the era of the demonstrators—unruly, unwashed, uninformed, and sometimes un-American people—disrupting private and public life in this country." He complained of the press, "for whom two loud 'Ah Hate Mississippis' would be sufficient. This adult generation accomplished more than any generation in the history of civilization—it started the exploration of God's limitless space. I simply will not hear them cry Pig for a situation they themselves began. Ah don't believe the right to disagree is the right to destroy the University at Jackson or Kent State or [the "even" was implicit] Berkeley. If it is true, as they say, that they have despaired of the democratic process, then I and my fellow demonstrators shall absolutely insist that if our system is to be changed it shall be changed in the ballot box and not in the streets." He finally ended on the rote ending to southern speeches: "We can live together in the dignity and freedom which their Creator surely intended."

With many of the Highway Patrol as honored guests there was an undertone to this lunch and throughout his speech, since it was the Highway Patrol who had done the shooting at Jackson.

Random notes from the weekend: The black station manager from Gulfport standing in line talking to Stan Torgerson from Meridian about black programming, Torgerson saying he programs Top 40, no deep blues or soul, and he owns a record store too "so I know goddamn well what they buy." Bob Evans from WNAG Grenada, trying to explain the class structure of Mississippi towns in terms of five families, with the banker always number one because he makes the loans. A black girl, a student at Jackson State, presented a list of demands at an afternoon meeting and everyone explained to me that she did it "very courteously." A tribute to coverage during Hurricane Camille, "Broadcasting working in symphonic harmony with the weather bureau and the civil defense authorities." After that crisis "celebrities from all over the U.S. came down, Bob Hope, the Golddiggers, Bobby Goldsboro. Bob Hope coming down, that really made people see that the country cared." Mrs. McGrath from Jackson leaning close to tell me Jackson State was a setup.

The Gulf Coast resorts live to a certain extent on illegal

gambling, places back up in the pinewoods known to all visitors. The Mafia is strong on the Coast.

The Ladies at the Brunch, on the subject of TV:

"I keep it on for my stories."

"Need to have it for the stories."

"I hear the radio only in the kitchen."

How about driving, I asked. The pretty young woman looked at me as if truly bewildered.

"Drive where?" she asked.

I did not know why we were going to Meridian instead of Mobile as planned, but it seemed, after a few days, imperative to leave the Gulf and the steaming air.

On the Road from Biloxi to Meridian

There was occasional rain and an overcast sky and the raw piney woods. On an AM station out of Biloxi, 1400 on the dial, I listened to Richard Brannan tell a parable about "a sailing trip to the Bahama Islands." The radio was out, but finally they got a fix and headed for port. "Everybody gets happy when the right direction is found," he said. "I mention this because there is another ship in danger of losing its way . . . the old ship of state." Then they played "America the Beautiful" with an angel choir. It was a Sunday. Here and all over were the trailer-sales lots with the signs that said REPOSSESSIONS, the trailers bearing plates from all over the South.

In McHenry, Mississippi, a gas station and a few shacks and a dirt road leading back into the pines, three barefoot children played in the dust by the gas station. A little girl with long unkempt blond hair and a dirty periwinkle-blue dress that hung below her knees carried around an empty Sprite bottle. The older of the two boys got the Coke machine open and they all squabbled gently over their choices. A pickup pulled in with the back piled high with broken furniture and dirty mattresses: it sometimes seemed to me that mattresses were on the move all over the South. A middle-aged blond woman was pumping gas. "One of the boys is off today, so they got me working," she said. We drove on, past cattle, a Church of God, a Jax (Fabacher) beer sign, and the Wiggin Lumber Co. Mfrs. Southern Yellow Pine Lumber.

A somnolence so dense it seemed to inhibit breathing hung over Hattiesburg, Mississippi, at two or three o'clock of that Sunday afternoon. There was no place to get lunch, no place to get gas. On the wide leafy streets the white houses were set back. Sometimes I would see a face at a window. I saw no one on the streets.

Outside Hattiesburg we stopped at a CAFÉ–GAS–TRUCK STOP to get a sandwich. A blond girl with a pellagra face stood sullenly behind the cash register, and a couple of men sat in a booth. Behind the counter was a woman in a pink Dacron housedress. No flicker of expression crossed her classic mountain face, and her movements were so slow as to be hypnotic. She made a kind of ballet of scooping ice into a glass. Behind her a soft-ice-cream machine oozed and plopped, and every now and then ice cubes would fall in the ice machine. Neither she nor the girl nor the two men spoke during the time we were there. The jukebox played "Sweet Caroline." They all watched me eat a grilled-cheese sandwich. When we went back out into the blazing heat one of the men followed us and watched as we drove away.

In Laurel, pop. 29,000: FREE FLAG DECALS, as everywhere. PUMP YOUR OWN GAS SAVE 5¢. It's Fun. Shacks on the backstreets. A black woman sitting on her front porch on the backseat from a car.

Cannibalized rusting automobiles everywhere, in ditches, the kudzu taking over. White wild flowers, red dirt. The pines here are getting lower, bushier. Polled Herefords. In a time when we have come to associate untouched land with parkland, a luxury, Mississippi seemed rich in appearance. One forgets that this is pre-industrial, not parkland purchased at great cost in an industrial society. There is very little of this hill land under the least cultivation. A patch of corn here, but nothing else.

A few signs in Enterprise, Mississippi: SEVEN HAMBURGERS FOR $1. FOOTLONG BARBECUE 30¢. People sitting on the porches.

Basic City, Mississippi, a town not on the map. You go in on a road and there, at the confluence of two railroad tracks, is a quite beautiful white frame house with a green lawn and gazebo. Lacy white flowers. The eccentricity of its location renders the viewer speechless. Across one set of tracks is a sign: PRIVATE DOGWOOD SPRINGS M.E. SKELTON'S FAMILY, OWNER. BASIC CITY MISS. Back on the road, the road into Meridian, 11, is the BASIC COURT CAFÉ AIR COND. When I left Basic City a train was moaning, the Meridian & Bigbee line. One is conscious of trains in the South. It is a true earlier time.

Swimming at the Howard Johnson's in Meridian

The Howard Johnson's in Meridian is just off Interstate 20, the intersection of Interstate 20—running east and west—and Interstate 59—running north and south from New Orleans to New York. Population 58,000, and beyond the grass and the cyclone fence the big rigs hurtle between Birmingham and Jackson and New Orleans. Sitting by the pool at six o'clock I felt the euphoria of Interstate America: I could be in San Bernardino, or Phoenix, or outside Indianapolis. Children splash in the pool. A three-year-old veers perilously toward the deep end, and her mother calls her back. The mother and her three children are from Georgia, and are staying at the Howard Johnson's while they try to find a new house in Meridian.

"I don't never want to go back to Georgia," the little boy says. "I want this to be my home." "This *will* be your home," the mother says. "Soon as Daddy and I find a house." "I mean this," the little boy says. "This motel."

Another woman appeared and called an older child, a boy twelve or thirteen, in for supper. "We're going to get supper now," she said. "Hell," the boy muttered, and stalked after her wrapped in a Confederate-flag beach towel. The sky darkened, thunder clapped, the three-year-old cried, and we all went inside to the air-conditioned chill. In a half hour or so the rain stopped, and at midnight I could hear the older children splashing in the lighted pool.

Meridian Notes

On the far side of the parking lot at the Howard Johnson's in Meridian is a raw field with a mudhole and a tiny duck house, with ducks. The ducks shake the muddy water from their white feathers.

In Weidmann's Restaurant, paintings are hung for sale: we sat beneath one with a calling card taped beneath it. "Mrs. Walter Albert Green," the card was engraved, and then, in a neat hand, "Dalewood Lake 'Oil' York, Ala. Price $35.00." There was also a painting appalling in its apprehension of human silences, called "In Between," by James A. Harris, $150. During the few days that I was in Meridian the painting and James A. Harris and his life in Meridian began to haunt me, and I tried to call him, but never reached him. He was at the air force base.

Gibson's Discount, ubiquitous. Mercedes-Benz Agency and "Citroën Service," certainly not so. Coca-Cola signs and the Mid-South Business College and Townsend's College of Cosmetology and the Hotel Lamar shut down. I tried to make an appointment with the director of Townsend's Academy of Cosmetology but he said he wasn't interested in any magazines at the present time. We had misunderstood each other, or we had not. I had an appointment with the director, Mrs. Lewis, of the Mid-South Business College, but when I arrived the doors were locked. I stood a while in the cool corridors of the Lamar Building and went downstairs and drank a Coca-Cola and came back, but the doors were still locked. We had misunderstood one another, or we had not.

An Afternoon in Meridian with Stan Torgerson

When I called Stan Torgerson for lunch at his radio station, WQIC, and asked him the best place to lunch, he said Weidmann's, "but it wouldn't win any Holiday Magazine awards." In fact it had, and was not a bad restaurant, but everyone in Mississippi begins on the defensive. "I'll be the biggest man in a green shirt to come through the door," he advised me. He was, at lunch, wary at first. He said he didn't think I knew what I was doing. I agreed. He refused a drink, saying he wasn't in New York City. Stan Torgerson came out of the cold North (Minnesota, I think) and headed to Memphis, where he went into broadcasting. He worked in Miami, and then, for a year, in San Diego, living in La Jolla. He felt ill at ease in La Jolla—his neighbors kept to themselves, had their own interests—and he wanted to get back south. His son had won a football scholarship to Ole Miss. He was worried about his children and drugs in California. "Excuse me," he said, "but I just haven't reached the point where I think pot is a way of life."

When the black radio station in Meridian came up for sale he bought it. He also broadcasts the Ole Miss games, something he began doing when he was in Memphis. "That's right," he said, "I own the ethnic station, WQIC. In its thirteenth year of serving the black community here." He programs gospel and soul, and reaches 180,000 blacks in several Mississippi and Alabama counties, "the thirty-second-largest black market in the country, sixty miles in all directions and forty-three percent of that area is black. We serve a major black market, program soul music and gospel music, but what does that mean? A month ago in *Billboard* there was a survey pointing out that the Top 40–format stations are playing basically soul. Jackson 5 with 'ABC,' 'Turn Back the Hands of Time,' that's Top 40 but it's soul. Once in a while we throw in some blue-eyed soul, like Dusty Springfield with 'Son of a Preacher Man.' We don't play rock because our people don't dig it. We don't play your underground groups like the Jefferson Airplane . . . We have goodly reason to believe that ten to fifteen percent of our audience is white; some of the phone calls we get in the afternoon for dedications, they're definitely white voices. We get thirty-six percent of the audience."

He said I was probably wondering why he came back to Mississippi. "I came because I dearly love this state. I had a son—he'll be a senior this fall—playing football at the University of Mississippi."

He pointed out that Meridian was timber country, hill country. Pulpwood is the backbone of the agricultural product. He pointed out how progressive Meridian was: its three new hospitals. "In most southern cities there is a much stronger tendency to old-line money . . . Southern retailers stayed in business privately, home-owned, until very recently. In most cases the retailer has just begun to feel the competition from the chains. There's the greatest business opportunity in the country right here in the South . . . We don't have a McDonald's in a city of almost fifty thousand people, don't have any of these franchises here yet. You give me one corner of one intersection in Jackson, Mississippi, or you give me the whole ball of wax right here in Meridian, I'd take the whole ball of wax and I'd put a McDonald's on one corner, a Burger Chef on the other, a Shoney's Po' Boy 'cross the street . . ."

His voice kept on, weaving ever higher flights of economic possibility. "There is and *must* be," he said, a "continued turning to the South by industry. The climate is certainly one reason. Another is that the South *wants* industry, and is willing to give a tax advantage to get it. Another, of course, is that there is a relatively low level of unionism in the South. Lockheed assembles tail sections here and ships them to California for assembly . . .

"Atlanta is the magic city for the young around here, across the whole social spectrum . . . The great migration out in the past ten years has been black, they get these glowing letters, and of course they've got relatively liberal welfare programs in some of the northern states . . . No doubt, too, there appears to be greater opportunity in the North."

More on the progressive nature of Meridian: "Our radio station has probably got as fine a list of blue-chip clients as any in town, black or not. We've got all four banks, and anyone in retailing who's interested in doing business with the black—the black's dollar is very important. The minimum wage was probably the most important thing to happen along these lines, and then food stamps were a good deal, I would say they added millions of dollars to our economy.

"We are in a transitional phase. There's a tremendous push to education on the part of young blacks. The schools here are completely integrated. Of course neither you nor I can change the older black, the forty-year-old, his life patterns are settled.

"Ole Miss has its standards to keep up. As more and more blacks get an educational advantage, you'll see blacks at Ole Miss. There's a feeling among some black leaders that because these kids have not had advantages they should get some kind of educational break, but basically what has to happen is the standards have to stay up and the people come up to meet them."

We were driving through town at night, and Stan Torgerson interrupted himself to point out the post office. "There's the post office, the courthouse where the famous Philadelphia trials were held, the trials for the so-called Philadelphia deaths."

"If there were elm trees hanging over the street it would be very midwestern," Stan observed as we drove through the residential district. He pointed out his $29,500 house, a two-story frame, "twenty-eight hundred square feet, with magnolia, dogwood, and pecan trees." He pointed out Poplar Drive, the "Park Avenue of Meridian, Mississippi, all the houses built by the old-line families."

Fervently, he kept reverting to the wholesomeness of life in Meridian. His daughter, who would be a high school senior in the fall, had "her sports, her outdoor activities, her swimming. It's a quiet, pacific type of living, which is one of the reasons I wanted to come back down here. The kids are taught to say 'sir' and 'ma'am.' I know it's very fashionable to poke fun at the South, but I'll pit our slum area any day against the slum areas where the Cubans and Puerto Ricans live in Miami, Florida, and Miami'll lose."

Meridian is the largest city between Jackson and Birmingham, and there is a naval base there which means a great deal to the community. At apartment buildings largely inhabited by the navy there are cars with plates from all over the country.

Some random social observations from Stan Torgerson included: most of the local children go to college within the state, at Ole Miss or Mississippi or Southern Mississippi; the other country club, built with federal money, has a membership which includes "assistant managers of stores and some navy people"; most of the subdivisions in Meridian feature "custom houses." Torgerson paused dramatically, to emphasize the versatility of the new blood in town: "A fabric store."

I asked if some children did not leave, and he allowed that some did. "Nothing here for the kid with an engineering degree. And of course the girls go where they marry. Southern girls are notoriously husband hunting, but I guess that's the same anywhere." It occurred to me almost constantly in the South that had I lived there I would have been an eccentric and full of anger, and I wondered what form the anger would have taken. Would I have taken up causes, or would I have simply knifed somebody?

Torgerson was wound up now, and I could not stop his peroration. "There's been a great metamorphosis in recent years in the South, the Volkswagen dealership for example comparable in size to anything you'll find anywhere.

"The KKK which used to be a major factor in this community isn't a factor anymore, both the membership and the influence have diminished, and I cannot think of any place where the black is denied entrance, with the possible exception of private clubs. We don't have any antagonistic-type black leaders working against racial harmony. Since the advent of black pride, black power, there is a little tendency to be self-segregating. On our station, we have a program we call *Adventures in Black History*, to point out the contributions black people have made—a black minister does it. I have blacks working in the WQIC Soul Shop, and there's a black druggist here, a man eminently qualified, who is a local boy who went north and came back, received his training at the University of Illinois. We have a certain degree of black business, including this gas station here, which is owned by a black. The key is racial harmony, and education, and we'll try to provide our people with both, 'cause we're gonna live together a long time. Every major retailer hires black clerks, Sears has a couple of black department heads, there's a black business college here, and a black and white Career Training Institute.

"Of course we have transplants, too, new ideas, like any other hybrid we're generally stronger. We're not nearly as inbred as we used to be. We've been withdrawn in this part of the South for many, many years, but we've become more aggressive, and as people come in they've helped us become more aggressive—we don't wear crinolines anymore, no we don't.

"And about our politics, well, George Wallace got a lot of votes in Indiana, let's face it. I'm not saying I'm going to have a black minister come home to dinner tonight, 'cause I'm not. But things are changing. I had a man the other day, owns an appliance store, he never believed you could send a black repairman into somebody's house. Now he can't find a white . . . He asks me if I know a black man who makes a good appearance. That's progress . . .

"Of course, there's a tremendous lack of skilled blacks, and the problem is training and education. It's no longer a matter of lack of opportunity, it's a matter of lack of skills. We're still two generations from full equality, but so are they in Chicago, in Detroit, and have you ever been in Harlem?"

Glazed by the two hours in which this man in the green shirt had laid Meridian out before us as an entrepreneur's dream, a Shoney's Po' Boy on every corner and progress everywhere, even at the country club, I dropped him off and drove through the still-deserted streets of the downtown. A few black women were on the streets, and they carried umbrellas against the sun. It was almost five o'clock. In the middle of 22nd Avenue, the main street of Meridian, there was a man holding a shotgun. He had on a pink shirt and a golfing cap, and in one ear there was a hearing aid. He raised the shotgun and shot toward the roof of a building several times.

I stopped the car and watched him a while, then approached him. "What are you shooting at?" I asked.

"*Pi-ea*gins," he said cheerfully.

In this one demented afternoon Mississippi lost much of its power to astonish me.

Because I had fallen and hurt a rib in New Orleans, and the rib pained me in the steaming heat and when I swam or turned in bed, I decided to see a doctor in Meridian. I was unsure how long it would be before I was again in a town big enough to have an emergency clinic, and here there were, Stan Torgerson had told me repeatedly, four hospitals, and I even knew the name of one, the Rush Foundation Hospital, and so I went there. One of the younger Rush doctors looked at my rib and sent me for an X-ray. I do not know if it was Dr. Vaughn Rush or Dr. Lowry Rush, who are brothers, or Dr. Gus Rush, who is a cousin. Before the doctor came in a nurse took my history, and she seemed not to believe a word I said. While I waited in my white smock I began to see it through her eyes: A woman walks into a clinic, a stranger to Meridian. She has long straight hair, which is not seen in the South among respectable women past the age of fourteen, and she complains of an injured rib. She gives her address as Los Angeles, but says the rib was injured in a hotel room in New Orleans. She says she is just "traveling through" Meridian. This is not a story to inspire confidence, and I knew it as I told it, which made meeting her eyes difficult.

Dr. Rush himself was willing to let this story go at face value, more or less.

"Just traveling on vacation," he said.

"Actually I'm a writer," I said. "I like going places I've never been."

"Traveling alone?" He pressed at my rib.

"With my husband."

This did not sound exactly right, either, because I was not wearing my wedding ring. There was a long pause.

"I went to school up north," he said. "I liked it a lot up there. I thought once I wouldn't mind living up there."

"But you came back here."

"But . . ." he said, "I came back here."

*

One evening in Meridian we went to the movies: *Loving* was playing with George Segal and Eva Marie Saint. The audience, what there was of it, gazed at the screen as if the movie were Czech. As it happened I had seen Eva Marie Saint a few weeks before, at dinner at someone's house in Malibu, and the distance between Malibu and this movie house in Meridian seemed limitless. How had I gotten from there to here: there, as always, was the question.

NOTE: Thinking about southern girls I had known in New York, the astonishing way their life in the South remained more vivid to them than anything that was happening to them in the city. Esther Nicol, when told I had been a Tri Delt at Berkeley, sniffed and said that at Ole Miss the Tri Delt house was "mostly Mississippi girls." To Esther, who was from Memphis, this meant something real. Again, remembering having lunch with a girl from Nashville who was working at Condé Nast. She would have to leave in a month, she told me, because home in Nashville the season was beginning and her grandmother was giving a party.

NOTE: On being asked for identification when I ordered a drink in the rural South. Before I came south I had not been taken for seventeen in considerable years, but several times in that month I had to prove I was eighteen. It is assumed that grown women will have their hair done, is all I could think.

NOTE: Remembering that in Durham in 1942 there was something, or was said to be something, called Push Day, when blacks would push whites on the streets. People avoided going downtown shopping on Push Day, which was either Tuesday or Wednesday. And there was that time in Durham, when Mother and my brother, Jimmy, and I got on a bus to go out to Duke and the driver would not start because we were sitting in the back of the bus.

On the Road from Meridian to Tuscaloosa, Alabama

Signs: WELCOME TO ALABAMA! TAKE A FUN BREAK! 782,000 ALABAMA BAPTISTS WELCOME YOU!

Dixie Gas stations, all over, with Confederate flags and grillwork.

Boys working on the road between Cuba and Demopolis. Making measurements with fishing poles. Sumter County, Alabama, around in here, is 80 percent black. We crossed the Demopolis Rooster Bridge over the Tombigbee River, another still, brown river. I think I never saw water that appeared to be running in any part of the South. A sense of water moccasins.

In Demopolis around lunchtime the temperature was 96 degrees and all movement seemed liquid. An Alabama state trooper drove slowly around town. I put a penny in a weighing machine on the main street. My weight was ninety-six, and my fortune was "You are inclined to let your heart rule your head."

In the drugstore a young girl was talking to the woman at the counter. "I'm gonna run off and get married," the girl said. "Who to?" the woman asked. The girl crumpled her straw paper. "I'm gonna get married," she said stubbornly, "I don't care who."

To get out of the sun I sat a while in the Demopolis library and contemplated a newspaper photograph of the Demopolis police force (nine of them) pouring out 214 gallons of confiscated moonshine. The moonshine had been confiscated after a four-hour chase and tracking with a bloodhound. The driver of the moonshine car, Clarence Bunyan Barrett of Cedartown, Georgia, was fined $435 and released.

At the desk a small birdlike woman about seventy was chatting with the librarian.

"*The Nashville Sound* in yet?"

"Still on order," the librarian said.

"How 'bout *The World of Fashion*?"

"Still out."

"Put me down on the waiting list for *The World of Fashion*."

The French Lieutenant's Woman was moving briskly that summer in the Demopolis library. The temperature at two was 98 degrees.

Greene County rolls gently, trees and grass, a light clear green. Pasture. The land looks rich, and many people from Birmingham, etc. (rich people) maintain places here to hunt.

The southern myth: a small bungalow named Grayfield, lots and lots of small one-story houses with two-by-four pillars.

Eutaw, Alabama, is a town the train goes through. Children were bicycling in town, barely moving in the leafy still air. There were tiger lilies everywhere, wild or naturalized. We listened to country music on the radio. There was a funeral taking place at the Eutaw Baptist Church at 4 p.m. on June 16, and the mourners made a frieze outside the church with a group of children on a penny hike. The coin spinning on the sidewalk and the children kneeling to see, with the adults in black around them. In Eutaw there was a white swimming pool and a black swimming pool, and an apartment house, the Colonial Apts., where the sign read APPLY JIMMY'S GRILL.

In the Eutaw City Hall I asked a clerk where the Chamber of Commerce was, but she could not, or would not, tell me. On a corner was a locked-up Teen Center, with posters inside that read GO TIDE and FREAK-OUT. There was one poster of a peace symbol. Children represent a mysterious subculture in small southern towns.

At 5 p.m. on a Tuesday afternoon we drove down a side road into Ralph, Alabama. A sign told us that the ZIP was 35480, the pop. 50, and that the town included:

Bethel (Baptist)
Shiloh (Baptist)
Wesley Chapel
Post Office
School.

Ralph was also a Prize Winner for Cotton Improvement. Tiger lilies and no people, anywhere.

Off US 82-W, near Tuscaloosa, is Lake Lurleen. Bear

Bryant Volkswagen in Tuscaloosa. Rebel Oil. Bumper stickers: "Yahweh vs. Evolution / Don't Make a Monkey Out of Yourself." Tiger Lilies. Red Tide, Crimson Tide, Go Tide, Roll Tide.

At the Ramada Inn in Tuscaloosa I sat outside by the swimming pool about five o'clock one afternoon and read Sally Kempton's piece in *Esquire* about her father and other men she had known. There was no sun. The air was as liquid as the pool. Everything seemed to be made of concrete, and damp. A couple of men in short-sleeved nylon shirts sat at another metal table and drank beer from cans. Later we tried to find somewhere open to eat. I called a place on University Boulevard, and the owner said to turn left at the Skyline Drive-in. On the way we got lost and stopped in a gas station to ask directions. The attendant had no idea where University Boulevard was (the University of Alabama is on University Boulevard) but could give us directions to the Skyline.

Birmingham

When I called a friend in Birmingham to ask who I should see around the countryside, what was going on, and he asked me what I wanted to know and I explained, he said, "You want to see who's sitting around the Greyhound bus station and who's sitting around in a Packard car, is that right?" I said that was right.

The country way in which he gave me names: "There's ole Rankin Fife, Speaker of the state House of Representatives, he pretty much runs Winfield. Over to Boligee there's David Johnston, he's got a big farm. There's a union leader, the Haneys, they live outside Guin, and he's a farmer and a preacher and a union leader. There's the Hill family, they run the bank. There's Boyd Aman in Boligee, number one hunter and fisherman—I reckon you could find him at the general store. And if you get in any trouble up there, you be sure to call me."

The sense of sports being the opiate of the people. In all the small towns the high school gymnasium was not only the most resplendent part of the high school but often the most solid structure in the town, redbrick, immense, a monument to the hopes of the citizenry. Athletes who were signing "letters of intent" were a theme in the local news.

At dinner one night in Birmingham there were, besides us, five people. Two of the men had gone to Princeton and the third was, when he was traveling on business, a habitué of Elaine's in New York and the Beverly Hills Hotel in California. They talked with raucous good humor about "seein' those X-rated movies" when their wives were out of town. This was a manner of speaking, a rococo denial of their own sophistication, which I found dizzying to contemplate.

"You could almost say that all the virtues and all the limitations of the South are a function of low population," someone said at lunch in Birmingham. "Cities, well, cities *are* melting pots. What we've had here was an almost feudal situation." We had been in places in Mississippi and Alabama where there had been virtually no ethnic infusion.

"Leave 'em to their stamps," someone said at dinner about the white tenants on his father's place.

Southern houses and buildings once had space and windows and deep porches. This was perhaps the most beautiful and comfortable ordinary architecture in the United States, but it is no longer built, because of air-conditioning.

NOTE: The curious ambivalence of the constant talk about wanting industry. Is not wanting industry the death wish, or is wanting it?

Talking about "a gentleman of the old school," there was the familiarity with generations of eccentric behavior, scandals and arrangements, high extramarital drama played out against the Legion parade.

It is said that the dead center of Birmingham society is the southeast corner of the locker room at the Mountain Brook country club. At Mountain Brook everyone goes to St. Luke's Episcopal Church or Briarwood Presbyterian, and it is hard to make the connection between this Birmingham and that of Bull Connor, and Birmingham Sunday.

Lunch with Hugh Bailey at the club, up high enough to see the smoke haze. "We got a pollution count in Birmingham now, which I guess you could say is a sign of progress." On that day the *Birmingham Post-Herald* (June 18) reported the downtown pollution count at 205, or over the U.S. Public Health Service's critical level, and the number of respiratory deaths in Jefferson County that week at six. There did not seem to be much pollution in Mountain Brook.

In Birmingham at dinner they were talking about catching rattlesnakes. "You take a hose, and go out in the fields, and take a few drops of gasoline down the hose into a hole—any hole—and that makes the rattlesnakes kind of drunk, and they come out for some air."

At every social level, the whole quality of maleness, the concentration on hunting and fishing. Leave the women to their cooking, their canning, their "prettifying."

A sign in a trailer camp in Walker County, Alabama: YOUR VOTE AND SUPPORT APPRECIATED/WALLACE FOR GOVERNOR. The thought that the reason Wallace has never troubled me is that he is a totally explicable phenomenon.

Most southerners are political realists: they understand and accept the realities of working politics in a way we never did in California. Graft as a way of life is accepted, even on the surface. "You get somebody makes eight hundred dollars a month as state finance director, he's only got four years to make his stake."

Inscriptions on gravestones:

THE ANGELS CALLED HIM
DYING IS BUT GOING HOME

MOORE
ELLIE   JESSIE T.
1888–19   1887–1952

SANDLIN
RAND IDA M.
1871–1952 1873–19

JENNIE B., *wife of J. R. Jones.*
She was a kind and affectionate wife,
a fond aunt, and a friend to all.

In so many family plots there was someone recently dead—dead after World War II—who remembered the Civil War. This was in a graveyard in a harsh red-dirt hill town, plastic flowers on the plots, overlooking the bright lights of the ballpark.

At the St. Francis Motel in Birmingham I went swimming, which occasioned great notice in the bar. "Hey, look, there's somebody with a bikini on."

Winfield

Maybe the rural South is the last place in America where one is still aware of trains and what they can mean, their awesome possibilities.

I put my clothes in the laundromat and walked on down the dirt at the side of the road to the beauty shop. A girl with long straight blond hair gave me a manicure. Her name was Debby.

"I got one more year at Winfield High," Debby said, "then I'm getting out."

I asked her where she would get out to.

"Birmingham," she said.

I asked what she would do in Birmingham.

"Well, if I keep on working while I'm in school, I'll have enough hours for my cosmetologist's license. You need three thousand, I got twelve hundred already. Then I'll go to modeling school." Debby reflected a moment. "I hope I will."

An electric fan hummed in the small shop. The smell of hair conditioners, shampoos, warm and sticky. The only other person there was the daughter of the proprietress. I asked her if she was still in school. She giggled as if she did not believe anyone could ask such a silly question.

"I been *married* three years," she said.

"You don't look old enough," I said.

"I'm *twenty*."

She lives in a trailer with her husband, Scott, who operates a power saw. Trailers got hot, we all agreed. They cool down at night, Debby suggested. "Oh, sure," the twenty-year-old said, "it cools down at night." Her mother, who owned the beauty shop, was home "doing her bookwork." She was in charge, and bossing Debby slightly. "You didn't get her *name*? She couldn't come any other *time*?"

They revert to the theme of the heat. The trailer does cool down at night, they agreed.

"Last night it was cool," the twenty-year-old said.

"I didn't think so," Debby said.

"I don't mean when we went to *bed*, I mean late. I woke up, it was almost cool. 'Course I'd had the *conditioning* on in the trailer all day."

Debby looked impassively out the open door. "So hot, Daddy had to come out from the bedroom to sleep on the couch."

"Cooler in than out."

Debby dried my hands. "I guess," she said idly.

At the little concrete pool between the motel and the creek, two teenage girls in two-piece bathing suits were lying in the sun on the stained pavement. They had come in a pickup truck and a transistor radio on the seat of the pickup played softly. There was algae in the pool, and a cigarette butt. "ABC," the Jackson 5.

I bought a large paper cup full of cracked ice in the drugstore (Hollis Pharmacy) for a nickel and walked back down the road to the laundromat eating it. Nothing had changed in the laundromat in the hour or so I had been gone: the same women, most with rollers in their hair, sat and stared and folded frayed flower-printed towels and sheets. There were two men in the laundromat, a repairman and an officious young man, straw-haired and rednecked, who seemed to be the owner. He regarded the women with contempt and the women regarded him in sullen impassivity.

"Hot 'nough for you?" a middle-aged woman said to me. I said it was. There was no hostility toward or even curiosity about me in the laundromat: by virtue of spending a summer afternoon in this steaming bleak structure I had moved into a realm where all women are sisters in misery. "Use this one," the woman said a while later, pointing out a dryer to me. "This one's dried her clothes and mine both, and she just put in one dime." The woman glanced furtively at the repairman as she spoke, and at the owner, as if fearful that they might fix the machine, deprive us of our jackpot.

On weekday afternoons in towns like Winfield one sees mainly women, moving like somnambulists through the days of their lives. The men work out at plants somewhere, or on farms, or in lumber. When I left the laundromat there was a boy in a bike helmet working on the road. Bike helmets had come to seem a normal mode of dress. *How the West Was Won* was playing at the movie house.

In the Angelyn Restaurant in Winfield at lunchtime a number of men, among the few I saw in town in the daytime, sat around and watched *General Hospital* on the television.

Guin

A traveler in the rural South in the summertime is always eating dinner, dispiritedly, in the barely waning heat of the day. One is a few hundred miles and a culture removed from any place that serves past 7:30 or 8 p.m. We ate dinner one night at a motel on the road between Winfield and Guin. The sun still blazed on the pavement outside, and was filtered only slightly by the aqueous blue-green Pliofilm shades on the windows inside. The food seemed to have been deep-fried for the lunch business and kept lukewarm on a steam table. Eating is an ordeal, as in an institution, something to be endured in the interests of survival. There are no drinks to soften the harshness of it. Ice is begrudged. I remember in one such place asking for iced coffee. The waitress asked me how to make it. "Same way as iced tea," I said. She looked at me without expression. "In a cup?" she asked.

The waitress in the place in Guin trailed me to the cash register. She was holding a matchbook I had left on the table. "I was looking at your matchbook," she said. "Where's it from?" I said it was from Biloxi. "Biloxi, *Mississippi*?" she said, and studied the matchbook as if it were a souvenir from Nepal. I said yes. She tucked the matchbook in her pocket and turned away.

On the outskirts of Guin the sign says GU-WIN/CITY LIMIT. At the Wit's Inn in Guin, an MYF (I think) coffeehouse, there were a couple of kids with guitars entertaining. They were billed as Kent and Phil, and their last engagement had been at Tuscaloosa. They sang "Abraham, Martin and John" and "Bridge over Troubled Water," and the children in the place joined in when asked, in clear sweet voices.

Some of the boys were wearing Guin baseball uniforms and one beautiful boy about sixteen was wearing a tie-dyed shirt and pants. Kids would drink Cokes and then drift out to the street and talk to somebody idling by in a car and then drift back in. The night was warm and there was fresh corn growing high along the road just past town. It seemed a good and hopeful place to live, and yet the pretty girls, if they stayed around Guin, would end up in the laundromat in Winfield, or in a trailer with the air-conditioning on all night.

When the program ended about ten kids all stood around in the street, making idle connections. A half an hour later the only people seen on the streets of Guin were twelve-year-olds wearing baseball uniforms. We drove between Guin and Hamilton on the George C. Wallace White Way, four lanes to nowhere, brightly lit. In Hamilton the street lights were turned off. We were getting Fort Worth and San Antonio on the car radio, gospel stations, "Rock of Ages" and "Lonesome Valley." Drove into a drive-in to see the end of *The Road Hustlers*, starring Jim Davis, Andy Devine, and Scott Brady. *The Losers* was the next bill at the drive-in. We followed *The Losers* all over the South. Outside Guin the night shift was working at the 3M plant.

Grenada, Mississippi

Driving over from Oxford to Grenada to have dinner one night with Bob Evans, Jr., and his wife, I noticed the shadows on the kudzu vine, the vine consuming trees, poles, everything in its range. The kudzu makes much of Mississippi seem an ominously topiary landscape. And the graveyards everywhere, with plastic sweet peas on the graves of infants. Death is still natural and ever present in the South, as it is no more in those urbanized parts of the country where graveyards are burial parks and relegated to unused or unusable land far from sight.

On Highway 7, Buck Brown & Son filling station. The rifles slung across the back cab windows of pickups. The Yalobusha Country Club just south of Water Valley. In Water Valley, blacks hanging around the main street, the highway, leaning on cars, talking across the street, the highway. In Coffeeville, Miss., at 6 p.m., there was a golden light and a child swinging in it, swinging from a big tree, over a big lawn, back and forth in front of a big airy house. To be a white middle-class child in a small southern town must be on certain levels the most golden way for a child to live in the United States.

On Margin Street in Grenada, as we drove in, a girl in a yellow bridesmaid's dress and a tulle headpiece, her husband in a cutaway, walked home from a wedding carrying their daughter, a baby two or three.

At the Evanses' house, there was a framed Christmas card from The President and Mrs. Nixon, and what appeared to be a framed slave deed. We had drinks, and after a while we took our drinks, our road glasses, and went for a drive through town. Mrs. Evans had grown up in Grenada, had been married once before, and now she and her second husband—who was from Tupelo—lived in her mother's old house. "Look at all those people standing around in front of that motel," she said once on the drive. "That's a cathouse," her husband told her. We went out to a lake, and then to dinner at the Holiday Inn, this being another of those towns where the Holiday Inn was the best place to eat. We brought our drinks and a bottle in with us, because there was no liquor served, only setups. I am unsure whether the bottle was legal. The legality or illegality of liquor in the South seems a complication to outsiders, but is scarcely considered by the residents. At dinner some people were watching us, and later came over to say hello to the Evanses. They introduced us as friends from California. "We were wondering where you were from," one of them said.

On our drive we passed a five-year-old in baseball pajamas playing catch with a black maid in a white uniform, the ball going back and forth, back and forth, suspended in amber.

The Evanses had a little baby, their child, and a sixteen-year-old daughter, her child. "She only comes out of her room when it's time to eat or time to go out," he said about her.

About the bottle at dinner: actually we brought three bottles, Scotch, bourbon, and vodka, and it was not legal to bring them inside in this dry county, because Mrs. Evans had them in a large handbag she carried exactly for this purpose.

About the cathouse: the notion that an accepted element in the social order is a whorehouse goes hand in hand with the woman on a pedestal.

Oxford

In the student union at Ole Miss they were watching *General Hospital* on the TV, just as they had been in the Angelyn Restaurant in Winfield.

In the student union there was an official calendar for May, on which was printed "May 28—Vacation—Raise Hell." Below this someone had scribbled, "An appropriate preoccupation for an Ole Miss student." The self-image of the Southern Blood as Cavalier very apparent here.

In the university bookstore, which appeared to be the one place in Oxford to buy a book (with the exception of a drugstore on the square which had several racks of paperbacks), the only books available other than assigned texts were a handful of popular bestsellers and a few (by no means all) novels by William Faulkner.

At the swimming pool at the Holiday Inn, the musical dialogue:

"Get that penny, it's down there yonder."

"Hurt my toe."

"I hurt *my* toe climbing a plum tree."

"*How'd* you hurt your toe?"

"Climbed a plum tree."

"Why."

"Get a plum."

"Hey, Bruiser, drop my sneaks down?"

"OK, Goose."

In the parking lot at the Holiday Inn one afternoon a police car was parked, its door open, the police radio breaking the still afternoon air the whole time I was sitting by the pool. Later when I was swimming a little girl pointed out to me that by staying underwater one could hear, by some electronic freak, a radio playing. I submerged and heard news of the Conservative victory in Great Britain, and "Mrs. Robinson."

When I was driving in the afternoon alone on the Ole Miss campus the wind came up, sudden and violent, and the sky darkened and there was thunder but no rain. I was afraid of a tornado. The suddenness and unpredictability of this shocked me. The weather around here must shape ideas of who and what one is, as it does everywhere.

On the same afternoon I saw a black girl on the campus: she was wearing an Afro and a clinging jersey, and she was quite beautiful, with a NY-LA coastal arrogance. I could not think what she was doing at Ole Miss, or what she thought about it.

At dinner in the Holiday Inn, overhearing an academic foursome: two teachers, the wife of one of them, and a younger woman, perhaps a graduate student or a teaching assistant. They were talking about how the SAEs and the Sigma Nus and the Sigma Chis used to "control politics." The break in this situation had come when Archie Manning, who was I believe a Sigma Nu, had run for something and either lost, or just barely won, which went to prove. There had been "a little article in the *Mississippian* about this," about the way the Greeks used to run things, and, said one of the men, "it said they did no more, but it upset my wife and daughter. Why did that have to be?"

The others added that the piece had been "trivial," "not very well done," but they did not address themselves to their colleague's plaintive question.

At one point during dinner the younger woman stated in a spirit of reckless defiance, "I don't care what the student union looks like, I couldn't care less." At another point she said that she believed the FBI had her "staked out," because she had two friends who used drugs. She did not and would not use drugs herself, she added: "My mind's expanded enough."

When I think about Oxford now I think about Archie Manning, the Sigma Nu, and all the bumper stickers that read ARCHIE and ARCHIE'S ARMY, with a Rebel flag, and about the immense and beautifully landscaped fraternity and sorority houses that surround the campus, and about boys and girls who in 1970 come out of the pinewoods to sing "White Star of Sigma Nu" at dances after football games. I had telephoned someone I knew in the English Department at Berkeley to ask if he knew anyone on any faculty in any department at any college in Mississippi to whom I should talk, anyone noted in any field he knew about, but he did not, and could only suggest that I call up Miss Eudora Welty, in Jackson.

As a matter of fact I had intended to, if ever I got near Jackson, but I was afraid to get too near Jackson because planes left from Jackson for New York and California, and I knew I would not last ten minutes in Jackson without telephoning Delta or National and getting out. All that month I hummed in my mind "Leavin' on a Jet Plane," Peter, Paul and Mary, and every night in our motel room we got out the maps and figured out how many hours' driving time to Jackson, to New Orleans, to Baton Rouge, to the closest place the planes left from.

We drove out on Old Taylor Road at night to look for Rowan Oak, William Faulkner's house. There were fireflies, and heat lightning, and the thick vines all around, and we could not see the house until the next day. It was large and private, secluded, set back from the road. I read a book about Faulkner in Oxford, interviews with his fellow citizens in Oxford, and I was deeply affected by their hostility to him and by the manner in which he had managed to ignore it. I thought if I took a rubbing from his gravestone, a memento from this place, I would know every time I looked at it that the opinion of others counted for not much one way or another.

So we went out to the graveyard, the Oxford cemetery, to look for the grave. Under a live oak tree a black kid sat in a parked two-tone salmon Buick, the door open. He was sitting on the floorboard with his feet outside, and while I was there several cars with Ole Miss and Archie's Army stickers came winding up the cemetery road, and boys would get out, and they would have some dealing with the black kid and drive away. He seemed to be dealing marijuana, and his car had a Wayne State sticker. Other than that there was nobody, just rabbits and the squirrels and the hum of bees and the heat, dizzying heat, heat so intense I thought of fainting. For several hours we looked for the grave, found the Faulkner plot and a number of other Faulkner/Falkner graves, but we never found William Faulkner's grave, not in that whole graveyard full of Oxford citizens and infant sons.

The way in which all the reporting tricks I had ever known atrophied in the South. There were things I should do, I knew it: but I never did them. I never made an appointment with the bridal consultant of the biggest department store in any town I was in. I never made the Miss Mississippi Hospitality Contest Semi-Finals, although they were being held in little towns not far from where we were, wherever we were. I neglected to call the people whose names I had, and hung around drugstores instead. I was underwater in some real sense, the whole month.

I kept talking to Mrs. Frances Kirby by telephone in Jackson. Mrs. Kirby was in charge of the Miss Hospitality contests, in Bay Springs, Cleveland, Clinton, Greenwood, Gulfport, Indianola, Leland, Lewisville. I was within a few miles of Cleveland on the day that contest would be held, and I called the sponsors, the chamber of commerce, and they said to come on "up at the country club" and watch, but I never even did that.

A Sunday Lunch in Clarksdale

One day we drove from Oxford over to Clarksdale, to have Sunday lunch with Marshall Bouldin and his wife, Mel. Lunch was served promptly at noon, a few minutes after our arrival. There was fried chicken and gravy, white rice, fresh green peas, and a peach pie for dessert. The heat was so intense that the ice was already melted in the Waterford water goblets before we sat down at the table. Grace was said. The children were allowed to speak on topics of interest, but not to interrupt. I have never eaten so long or heavy a meal. I was in a place where "Sunday" still existed as it did in my grandmother's house, a leadening pause in the week, a day of boredom so extreme as to be exhausting. It was the kind of Sunday to make one ache for Monday morning.

After lunch we sat in the living room of the small house in town the Bouldins were using while their plantation house was being remodeled. Marshall Bouldin talked, and here are some of the things he said:

"The money and the power in the South have traditionally been in the hands of the people who plant. The Delta, because of that, is rich. There are rich people in the Delta. You don't get governors from the Delta, but you do get the money and the power to elect them. Governors come from the hills, and from Hattiesburg. There's a lieutenant governor now from Clarksdale, but that's unusual. There are fewer blacks in the hill sections. The Delta, which is more affluent, has a higher black population. The third part of Mississippi, besides the hills and the Delta, is the coastal area, which is really an isolated phenomenon.

"I'm so glad to see what has happened in Mississippi. The thinking has come so far in just these twenty years. The hill country is certainly more reactionary. The Delta's still conservative, yes, but people here have money, and people who have money can be exposed to new ideas.

"Mainly we plant cotton here, soybeans are replacing truck crops. We tried cattle, but the soil here is too rich for cattle, the flat land ends at Vicksburg. The Delta is maybe fifty miles wide, and was all overflow land until after the Civil War when the levees were built. Around 1870, then, people began to move in, they had this rich land, all river silt. What size is the average Delta farm? Well, fourteen thousand acres would be a large one, and two hundred to three hundred acres would be a small one, the average is said to be seven hundred seventy, but that would be small for cotton or beans.

"Thirty years ago my dad and my Mel's dad led the ideal planter's life. Now it's more of a business, it's not the same. It was a series of small towns then, there were great social functions, and you went from town to town for your social functions, and this held the country together.

"What you have here is the last of the feudal system. It's an area where you have plenty of servants. We're fortunate to have Charles and Frances here, they were on my dad's place. What you had around here until very lately was mainly the tenant system. Each black family was responsible for the ten or fifteen acres around his cabin. The owner supervised and provided food, and provided anything else the family needed, and these were sizable families, but they'd say, 'Mr. Marshall, take care of me,' and we would. That's part of the change here. Mel's brother is not on the tenant system.

"My dad never put anyone off. And Mel, your dad never did either. Some planters, they abused the tenant system. There was one planter around here, on payday he used to make them smile, he'd hand out silver dollars when he got the smile, but that was just some, and maybe it was condoned but it was never approved of. Mel's daddy kept *books*, and settled with every tenant. The community knew who these people were who took advantage, and frowned on them. Of course, nobody put them in jail, which is maybe what we should've done.

"Automation changed things, the cotton picker meant we didn't need so many. We never put anybody off the land, they just gradually left for Detroit or they moved into town. A few planters told people to get off, but on the whole there was not much dispossessing of the black man.

"The big change, I do think, was when television came. The kids could see the way other people lived, other lives. It has been the greatest educational system in the county.

"My dad's main job was just talking to John, seeing if he needed anything (John was the overseer or foreman). Mel's brother, on the other hand, he runs—I don't want to say it's a factory, but it turns out cotton. He has about three thousand acres in three pieces. In 1950 I farmed like my daddy farmed, on a horse. Now you need to have a manager on each place, in his pickup. You need to have a personal radio, to be able to reach a man you've got in town and tell him to get that part out here in fifteen minutes. You used to be able to have a good time farming. When you got the cotton picked in the fall you read books, went hunting, sat around the fire and socialized. Now, they're working on the machinery all winter. Maybe if you can get the repair work done in January, you can take a month or six weeks off in February, but that's it." He paused, and looked at his wife. "Isn't that right, Mel?"

Mel shrugged. "It's still the good life," she said.

"The black population is still high here," he went on. "In the schools right now it's 80 percent black and 20 percent white, now that we're integrated. We have tortured and tortured over what to do with our children, and our tentative decision for now is to send them to private schools, even though that is against our ideals. I can't sacrifice my child to my ideal. They had to force the black to integrate. Basically I know that the people who are pushing it are right, but they seem so precipitous. They say we had to integrate on February 2. Now, why couldn't they have waited 'til September? It hardened attitudes, is what it did. There are people in this community who might have been showing signs of opening up their minds, and then a parent finds out that as of next week his kid is going to be over in Higgins High—that door is closed, and when it's going to open again nobody knows.

"They say around here it takes three generations to make a gentleman, and yet if I was about a sixteen-year-old black boy I'll be damned if I'd want to wait three generations. All over this area we still have these large maternal families, families with no daddy, nobody to say if you're going to reap the benefits, you've got to put in the work.

"I'm a middle-of-the-roader, and like the majority, we're trying to do the easiest thing that will get us all by happily. There are five or six houses in Clarksdale right now where this conversation could take place. That may not seem like many but when I was growing up there were none.

"The best thing we can do is raise our children differently, and add four people to the community who can come home from this little Episcopal school and think differently. When the integration orders were flying around Mississippi last year it was hard to think what to do, and it still is."

Charles and Frances came out from the kitchen, to say goodbye. They were on their way to church. Marshall Bouldin beamed as he introduced them. "Charles and Frances were on my daddy's place, isn't that right, Frances?" Frances bobbed her head. "That's right, surely is," she said. "Mr. Marshall and us, we were little itty-bittys together."

There was news of a tornado somewhere near the Delta, although not in Coahoma County, and a telephone call to inform Marshall Bouldin that "a black man died on the place last night."

We drove out to the plantation, where the house was being remodeled. He pointed out the tenant cabins standing empty. "When I was little we farmed it all with mules," he said. "When I went off to college we had four-row equipment. Now we have six-row equipment." He pointed out the tractors, which cost $15,000 apiece, and added that there were $60,000 worth of tractors alone in the shed. He pointed out what had been his father's payoff office, and one tenant cabin which was occupied. "This is one of the tenant cabins still occupied by my old fishing buddy, Ernie." Ernie calls the Bouldins Miss Mel and Mister Marshall.

"That's cotton," he said, "far back as the cypress break." I asked what was beyond the cypress break. "Some more of our place."

Mel Bouldin, for a southern woman of her age and class, had done an extraordinary thing: she had gone to medical school after the birth of her children, and now practiced ob-gyn in Memphis, in partnership with three men. She flew to Memphis from "the place" in a private plane. "I can't stand to sit around the country club and *talk*," she said by way of explanation.

She was, at the time we visited her, taking a year off her practice to supervise the reconstruction of the house. The house was to be "a boys' house, everything rough and ready." "I love boys," she kept saying. In certain ways she seemed to have been affected by the great leap she had taken out of her time and place: in order to be her own woman she had found it necessary to vehemently reject many of the things which traditionally give women pleasure, cooking (" 'Course I hate to cook, I'd walk a mile and a half to avoid it"), any vanity about her own appearance, any interest in having her house reflect her own tastes. Her mother's house reflected her mother: Mel's house would reflect "the boys," and her greatest delight was in secret stairways and hideaways she was having built into the walls for the children.

At lunch, or just before, the seven-year-old had been asked to perform, and did so with pleasure, playing "Joy to the World" on the piano, a peculiar melody on this steaming June day in the Delta. Everyone held hands during the blessing at table. The four boys were dressed in matching blue mandarin shirts. The family had just come from church services, at the Presbyterian church. When I called the day before from Oxford and Marshall Bouldin suggested we come to lunch, he had said, "Come after church." The idea of "church" as a Sunday morning donnée has not existed for a couple of generations in the Protestant societies I know, but it exists in the South.

On our drive, we passed Delta Road, where there live

"nothing but blacks, or if there were any whites, I wouldn't want to meet them."

Out behind the house, the immense Sears, Roebuck swimming tank, raised five or six feet above the lawn. "Keeps the snakes and frogs out," Mel said.

Clarksdale calls itself "The Golden Buckle on the Cotton Belt." At parties in the Delta they say to one another: "How yo' cotton coming?" And then: "Yeah? What's wrong?"

On Silk Stocking Row in Clarksdale there live a few planters, a lawyer, and the cotton broker. Many of the planters live in town. There is one plantation around Clarksdale owned by an English syndicate.

Down the Delta to Greenville

Outside the Bolivar County Courthouse in Rosedale, an old policeman, his collar loosened around his thick neck, sat in his car with the motor idling in the Sunday twilight.

Outside Rosedale, on the sign for a RR crossing, the letters KKK had been painted.

All the billboards were for cotton and soybean insecticides and fertilizers.

In Benoit, the town where *Baby Doll* was shot, people hanging around with that remarkable "vacant" look which people in the South always mention before you do and then become defensive about. ("Ever look on a subway in Detroit, Michigan?")

The endless green of the Delta, the flatness, the haze in the mornings. The algae-covered ditches alive with mosquitoes.

In Greenville, the presence of the levee, a high wall at the end of every street downtown. We ate dinner out on the pier at a place that had good gumbo, and I was glad to be on the river (actually we were on a slough), glad to be in a place with good food, glad to be, I suppose, so very close to the place where the National and Delta flights left for California.

We went to have dinner with Hodding Carter III and his wife, Peggy, and with Lew Powell, the city editor of the paper, and his girl. Hodding picked us up and there was the ubiquitous glass on the dashboard, the road glass, in this instance a martini.

We went to dinner at Boyt's, a roadhouse in the next crossroads over. On Boyt's menu: "Italian or Wop Salad."

Hodding Carter III: "The blacks who leave the Delta say they'd come back if there were just something here—this is a place with a strong pull."

He spoke about New Orleans as the place you cop out to, "you go down there with the eleven-and-a-half-month debutante season." His wife came from New Orleans, went to Miss McGehee's and to Sophie Newcomb, and now, he implied, she lives on the frontier.

It would be a while, he thought, before automation came to southern agriculture. Its arrival in California was "speeded up by labor problems." He saw an industrial New South as a kind of pipe dream, the difficulty being an unskilled labor force. "They talk about cheap labor in the South, but cheap labor is a myth for a national company, for any company with labor contracts. So that's no advantage, and another disadvantage here for industry, we've got social problems you don't have in the North."

"The FBI" as a leitmotif in the South. I had heard it in Biloxi, in Oxford, in Grenada, in Greenville.

The time warp: the Civil War was yesterday, but 1960 is spoken of as if it were about three hundred years ago.

Downriver and Home

The names of plantations going south on 61: Baconia, Lydia, and Evanna. On the billboards: PESTICIDE DYANAP. A plantation south of Onward: Reality Plantation. The Yazoo County Bookmobile, a cropduster releasing sprays of yellow haze. A Greyhound bus with CHICAGO emblazoned over the window hurtling north on 61 through Warren County.

Outside Vicksburg is a shopping center, with a mall named Battlefield Village. In Port Gibson there is a Presbyterian church with, instead of a cross on top of the steeple, a gold finger, pointing heavenward. The kudzu.

Fayette had the aspect of a set from *Porgy and Bess*, in that there were only blacks to be seen on the street and behind windows. The only white I saw as we drove through was wearing a blue work shirt and had a Zapata mustache.

"The Interstate" as a phrase, and a concept. The great pulsing links between there and everywhere else.

On the window of a coffee shop in South McComb, SUPPORT YOUR CITIZEN'S COUNCIL and STATES RIGHTS – RACIAL INTEGRITY, which pretty much laid it right where it was. (Actually I think the restaurant—Boyt's—with Wop Salad on the menu was in McComb, not in Greenville.)

We stopped at Walker Percy's in Covington, Louisiana. We sat out in back by the bayou and drank gin and tonics and when a light rain began to fall, a kind of mist, Walker never paid any mind but just kept talking, and walking up to the house to get fresh drinks. It was a thunderstorm, with odd light, and there were occasional water-skiers on the black bayou water. "The South," he said, "owes a debt to the North . . . tore the Union apart once . . . and now only the South can save the North." He said he had not wanted to see us in New Orleans, at Ben C.'s, because at Ben C.'s he was always saying things he would not ordinarily say, playing a role. Greenville, he said, was a different kind of town. He had spent some time in Los Angeles once but could not face it. "It was the weather," his wife said mildly. "The weather was bad." "It wasn't the weather," he said, and he knew exactly what it was.

Crossing the Pontchartrain bridge, the gray water, the gray causeway, the gray skyline becoming apparent in the far distance just about the time you lose sight of the shore behind you. The sight of New Orleans coming up like a mirage from about the midway point on the Lake Pontchartrain Causeway.

Sycamores and pit vipers. From Audubon, 1830:

Deep morasses, overshadowed by millions of gigantic dark cypresses, spreading their sturdy moss-covered branches . . . Would that I could represent to you the dangerous nature of the ground, its oozing, spongy, and miry disposition . . .

A senseless disagreement on the causeway, ugly words and then silence. We spent a silent night in an airport motel and took the 9:15 National flight to San Francisco. I never wrote the piece.

CALIFORNIA NOTES

I had told Jann Wenner of Rolling Stone *that I would cover the Patty Hearst trial, and this pushed me into examining my thoughts about California. Some of my notes from the time follow here. I never wrote the piece about the Hearst trial, but I went to San Francisco in 1976 while it was going on and tried to report it. And I got quite involved in uncovering my own mixed emotions. This didn't lead to my writing the piece, but eventually it led to—years later—*Where I Was From *(2003).*

When I was there for the trial, I stayed at the Mark. And from the Mark, you could look into the Hearst apartment. So I would sit in my room and imagine Patty Hearst listening to Carousel. *I had read that she would sit in her room and listen to it. I thought the trial had some meaning for me—because I was from California. This didn't turn out to be true.*

The first time I was ever on an airplane was in 1955, and flights had names. This one was *The Golden Gate*, American Airlines. Serving Transcontinental Travelers Between San Francisco and New York. A week before, twenty-one years old, I had been moping around Berkeley in my sneakers and green raincoat, and now I was a Transcontinental Traveler, Lunching Aloft on Beltsville Roast Turkey with Dressing and Giblet Sauce. I believed in Dark Cottons. I believed in Small Hats and White Gloves. I believed that Transcontinental Travelers did not wear white shoes in the City. The next summer I went back on *The New Yorker*, United Airlines, and had a Martini-on-the-Rocks and Stuffed Celery au Roquefort over the Rockies.

The image of the Golden Gate is very strong in my mind. As unifying images go, this one is particularly vivid.

At the *Sacramento Union* I learned that Eldorado County and Eldorado City are so spelled but that regular usage of El Dorado is two words; to UPPERCASE Camellia Week, the Central Valley, Sacramento Irrigation District, Liberator bombers and Superfortresses, the Follies Bergere [*sic*], the Central Valley Project, and "such nicknames as Death Row, Krauts or Jerries for Germans, Doughboys, Leathernecks, Devildogs."

Arden School class prophecy:

> *In Carnegie Hall we find Shirley Long*
> *Up on the stage singing a song.*
> *Acting in pictures is Arthur Raney's job,*
> *And he is often followed by a great mob.*
> *As a model Yavette Smith has achieved fame,*
> *Using "Bubbles" as her nickname . . .*
> *We find Janet Haight working hard as a missionary,*

Smart she is and uses a dictionary . . .
We find Joan Didion as a White House resident
Now being the first woman president.

Looking through the evidence I find what seems to me now (or rather seemed to me then) an entirely spurious aura of social success and achievement. I seem to have gotten my name in the paper rather a lot. I seem to have belonged to what were in context the "right" clubs. I seem to have been rewarded, out of all proportion to my generally undistinguished academic record, with an incommensurate number of prizes and scholarships (merit scholarships only: I did not qualify for need) and recommendations and special attention and very probably the envy and admiration of at least certain of my peers. Curiously, I only remember failing, failures and slights and refusals.

I seem to have gone to dances and been photographed in pretty dresses, and also as a pom-pom girl. I seem to have been a bridesmaid rather a lot. I seem always to have been "the editor" or "the president."

I believed that I would always go to teas.

This is not about Patricia Hearst. It is about me and the peculiar vacuum in which I grew up, a vacuum in which the Hearsts could be quite literally king of the hill.

I have never known deprivation.

"How High the Moon," Les Paul and Mary Ford. *High Noon.*

I have lived most of my life under misapprehensions of one kind or another. Until I was in college I believed that my father was "poor," that we had no money, that pennies mattered. I recall being surprised the first time my small brother ordered a dime rather than a nickel ice cream cone and no one seemed to mind.

My grandmother, who was in fact poor, spent money: the Lilly Daché and Mr. John hats, the vicuña coats, the hand-milled soap and the $60-an-ounce perfume were to her the necessities of life. When I was about to be sixteen she asked me what I wanted for my birthday and I made up a list (an

Ultra-Violet lipstick, some other things), meaning for her to pick one item and surprise me: she bought the list. She gave me my first grown-up dress, a silk jersey dress printed with pale blue flowers and jersey petals around the neckline. It came from the Bon Marché in Sacramento, and I knew what it cost ($60) because I had seen it advertised in the paper. I see myself making many of the same choices for my daughter.

At the center of this story there is a terrible secret, a kernel of cyanide, and the secret is that the story doesn't matter, doesn't make any difference, doesn't figure. The snow still falls in the Sierra. The Pacific still trembles in its bowl. The great tectonic plates strain against each other while we sleep and wake. Rattlers in the dry grass. Sharks beneath the Golden Gate. In the South they are convinced that they have bloodied their place with history. In the West we do not believe that anything we do can bloody the land, or change it, or touch it.

How could it have come to this?

I am trying to place myself in history.

I have been looking all my life for history and have yet to find it.

The resolutely "colorful," anecdotal quality of San Francisco history. "Characters" abound. It puts one off.

In the South they are convinced that they are capable of having bloodied their land with history. In the West we lack this conviction.

Beautiful country burn again.

The sense of not being up to the landscape.

There in the Ceremonial Courtroom a secular mass was being offered.

I see now that the life I was raised to admire was infinitely romantic. The clothes chosen for me had a strong element of the Pre-Raphaelite, the medieval. Muted greens and ivories. Dusty roses. (Other people wore powder blue, red, white, navy, forest green, and Black Watch plaid. I thought of them as "conventional," but I envied them secretly. I was doomed to unconventionality.) Our houses were also darker than other people's, and we favored, as a definite preference, copper and brass that had darkened and greened. We also let our silver darken carefully in all the engraved places, "to bring out the pattern." To this day I am disturbed by highly polished silver. It looks "too new."

This predilection for "the old" carried into all areas of our domestic life: dried flowers were seen to have a more lasting charm than fresh, prints should be faded, a wallpaper should be streaked by the sun before it looks right. As decorative touches went, our highest moment was the acquisition of a house (we, the family, moved into it in 1951 at 22nd and T in Sacramento) in which the curtains had not been changed since 1907. Our favorite curtains in this house were gold silk organza on a high window on the stairwell. They hung almost two stories, billowed iridescently with every breath of air, and crumbled at the touch. To our extreme disapproval, Genevieve Didion, our grandmother, replaced these curtains when she moved into the house in the late 1950s. I think of those curtains still, and so does my mother (domestic design).

Oriental leanings. The little ebony chests, the dishes. Maybeck houses. Mists. The individual raised to mystic level, mysticism with no religious basis.

When I read Gertrude Atherton* I recognize the territory of the subtext. The assemblies unattended, the plantations abandoned—in the novels as in the dreamtime—because of high and noble convictions about slavery. Maybe they had convictions, maybe they did not, but they had also worked out the life of the farm. In the novels as well as the autobiography of Mrs. Atherton we see a provincial caste system at its most malign. The pride in "perfect taste," in "simple frocks."

In the autobiography, page 72, note Mrs. Atherton cutting snakes in two with an axe.

* Gertrude Atherton (1857–1948) was born in San Francisco and became a prolific and at times controversial writer of novels, short stories, essays, and articles on subjects that included feminism, politics, and war. Many of her novels are set in California.

When I read Gertrude Atherton I think not only of myself but of Patricia Hearst, listening to *Carousel* in her room on California Street.

The details of the Atherton life appear in the Atherton fiction, or the details of the fiction appear in the autobiography: it is difficult to say which is the correct construction. The beds of Parma violets at the Atherton house dissolve effortlessly into the beds of Parma violets at Maria Ballinger-Groome Abbott's house in Atherton's *The Sisters-in-Law*. Gertrude's mother had her three-day "blues," as did one of the characters in *Sleeping Fires*. Were there Parma violets at the Atherton house? Did Gertrude's mother have three-day blues?

When I contrast the houses in which I was raised, in California, to admire, with the houses my husband was raised, in Connecticut, to admire, I am astonished that we should have ever built a house together.

Climbing Mount Tamalpais in Marin County, a mystical ideal. I never did it, but I did walk across the Golden Gate Bridge, wearing my first pair of high-heeled shoes, bronze kid De Liso Debs pumps with three-inch heels. Crossing the Gate was, like climbing Tamalpais, an ideal.

Corte Madera. Head cheese. Eating apricots and plums on the rocks at Stinson Beach.

Until I read Gertrude Atherton I had never seen the phrase "South of Market" used exactly the way my grandmother, my mother, and I had always used it. Edmund G. "Pat" Brown was South of Market.

My father and brother call it "Cal" (i.e., the University of California at Berkeley). They were fraternity men, my father a Chi Phi, my brother a Phi Gamma Delta. As a matter of fact I belonged to a house too, Delta Delta Delta, but I lived in that house for only two of the four years I spent at Berkeley.

There used to be a point I liked on the Malibu Canyon road between the San Fernando Valley and the Pacific Ocean, a point from which one could see what was always called "the Fox sky." Twentieth Century–Fox had a ranch back in the hills there, not a working ranch but several thousand acres on which westerns were shot, and "the Fox sky" was simply that: the Fox sky, the giant Fox sky scrim, the Big Country backdrop.

By the time I started going to Hawaii, the Royal Hawaiian was no longer the "best" hotel in Honolulu, nor was Honolulu the "smart" place to vacation in Hawaii, but Honolulu and the Royal Hawaiian had a glamour for California children who grew up as I did. Little girls in Sacramento were brought raffia grass skirts by returning godmothers. They were taught "Aloha 'Oe" at Girl Scout meetings, and to believe that their clumsiness would be resolved via mastery of the hula. For dances, later, they wanted leis, and if not leis, bracelets of tiny orchids, "flown in" from Honolulu. I recall "flown in" as a common phrase of my adolescence in Sacramento, just "flown in," the point of origin being unspoken, and implicit. The "luau," locally construed as a barbecue with leis, was a favored entertainment. The "lanai" replaced the sunporch in local domestic architecture. The romance of all things Hawaiian colored my California childhood, and the Royal Hawaiian seemed to stand on Waikiki as tangible evidence that this California childhood had in fact occurred.

I have had on my desk since 1974 a photograph that I cut from a magazine just after Patricia Campbell Hearst was kidnapped from her Berkeley apartment. This photograph appeared quite often around that time, always credited to Wide World, and it shows Patricia Hearst and her father and one of her sisters at a party at the Burlingame Country Club. In this photograph it is six or seven months before the kidnapping, and the three Hearsts are smiling for the camera, Patricia, Anne, and Randolph.

The father is casual but festive—light coat, dark shirt, no tie; the daughters flank him in long flowered dresses. They are all wearing leis, father and daughters alike, leis quite clearly "flown in" for the evening. Randolph Hearst wears two leis, one of maile leaves and the other of orchids strung in the tight design the lei-makers call "Maunaloa." The daughters each wear pikake leis, the rarest and most expensive kind of leis, strand after strand of tiny Arabian jasmine buds strung like ivory beads.

Sometimes I have wanted to know what my grandmother's sister, May Daly, screamed the day they took her to the hospital, for it concerned me, she had fixed on me, sixteen, as the source of the terror she sensed, but I have refrained from asking. In the long run it is better not to know. Similarly, I do not know whether my brother and I said certain things to each other at three or four one Christmas morning or whether I dreamed it, and have not asked.

We are hoping to spend part of every summer together, at Lake Tahoe. We are hoping to reinvent our lives, or I am.

The San Francisco Social Register. When did San Francisco become a city with a Social Register? How did this come about? The social ambitiousness of San Francisco, the way it has always admired titles, even bogus titles.

All my life I have been reading these names and I have never known who they were or are. Who, for example, is Lita Vietor?

C. Vann Woodward: "Every self-conscious group of any size fabricates myths about its past: about its origins, its mission, its righteousness, its benevolence, its general superiority." This has not been exactly true in San Francisco.

SOME WOMEN:

Gertrude Atherton
Julia Morgan
Lillie Coit
Jessica Peixotto
Dolly Fritz MacMasters Cope
Lita Vietor
Phoebe Apperson Hearst
Patricia Campbell Hearst
Jessie Benton Frémont

Part of it is simply what looks right to the eye, sounds right to the ear. I am at home in the West. The hills of the coastal ranges look "right" to me, the particular flat expanse of the Central Valley comforts my eye. The place names have the ring of real places to me. I can pronounce the names of the rivers, and recognize the common trees and snakes. I am easy here in a way that I am not easy in other places.

LET ME TELL YOU
WHAT I MEAN

Contents

359
Alicia and the Underground Press

363
Getting Serenity

366
A Trip to Xanadu

370
On Being Unchosen by the College of One's Choice

374
Pretty Nancy

378
Fathers, Sons, Screaming Eagles

382
Why I Write

389
Telling Stories

400
Some Women

405
The Long-Distance Runner

410
Last Words

422
Everywoman.com

LET ME TELL YOU
WHAT I MEAN

Alicia and the Underground Press

The only American newspapers that do not leave me in the grip of a profound physical conviction that the oxygen has been cut off from my brain tissue, very probably by an Associated Press wire, are *The Wall Street Journal*, the Los Angeles *Free Press*, the Los Angeles *Open City*, and the *East Village Other*. I tell you that not to make myself out an amusing eccentric, perverse and eclectic and, well, groovy in all her tastes; I am talking here about something deadening and peculiar, the inability of all of us to speak to one another in any direct way, the failure of American newspapers to "get through." *The Wall Street Journal* talks to me directly (that I have only a minimal interest in much of what it tells me is beside the point), and so does the "underground" press.

The *Free Press*, the *EVO*, the *Berkeley Barb*, all the other tabloid-sized papers that reflect the special interests of the young and the disaffiliated: their particular virtue is to be devoid of conventional press postures, so many of which rest on a quite factitious "objectivity." Do not misread me: I admire objectivity very much indeed, but I fail to see how it can be achieved if the reader does not understand the writer's particular bias. For the writer to pretend that he has none lends the entire venture a mendacity that has never infected *The Wall Street Journal* and does not yet infect the underground press. When a writer for an underground paper approves or disapproves of something, he says so, quite often in lieu of who, what, where, when, how.

Of course there is nothing particularly underground about the underground papers. New York south of Thirty-fourth Street is papered with the *EVO*; Los Angeles accountants pick up the *Free Press* at lunch on the Strip. It is a commonplace to complain that the papers are amateurish and badly written (they are), that they are silly (they are), that they are boring (they are not), that they are not sufficiently inhibited by information. In fact, the information content of an underground paper is low in the extreme. News of a peace march or of the defection of a rock group to the forces of exploitation (the group released a record, say, or accepted an engagement to play at Cheetah), advice from Patricia Maginnis on what to tell the admitting intern if you start hemorrhaging after a Mexican abortion ("Feel perfectly free to tell them that Patricia Maginnis and/or Rowena Gurner assisted you to get your abortion. Please don't incriminate anyone else. We are trying to get arrested. Other people aren't"), second thoughts from a fifteen-year-old narcotics dealer ("You have to have a commitment to dealing as a lifestyle, or you can't do it well"), admonitions that Speed Kills: one issue of, say, the *Free Press* is very like the next five issues of the *Free Press*, and, to anyone who follows only casually the various schisms among drug users and guerrilla revolutionaries, indistinguishable from the *EVO*, the *Barb*, the *Fifth Estate*, the Washington *Free Press*. I have never read anything I needed to know in an underground paper.

But to think that these papers are read for "facts" is to misapprehend their appeal. It is the genius of these papers that they talk directly to their readers. They assume that the reader is a friend, that he is disturbed about something, and that he will understand if they talk to him straight; this assumption of a shared language and a common ethic lends their reports a considerable cogency of style. A recent *Free Press* carried an analysis of Ann Arbor by a reader named "Alicia," who said all there was to say about a university community in three lines of haiku-like perfection: "The professors and their wives are ex-Beatniks (Berkeley, Class of '57), and they go on peace marches and bring daffodils to U Thant. Some of the kids still believe in Timothy Leary and Kahlil Gibran. Some of their parents still believe in the Kinsey Report."

These papers ignore the conventional newspaper code, say what they mean. They are strident and brash, but they do not irritate; they have the faults of a friend, not of a monolith. ("Monolith," of course, is a favorite underground-press word, one of the few with three syllables.) Their point of view is clear to the densest reader. In the best of the traditional press there exist very strong unspoken attitudes indeed, and the fact that those attitudes remain unspoken, unadmitted, comes between the page and the reader like so much marsh gas. *The New York Times* brings out in me only unpleasant agrarian aggressions, makes me feel like the barker's barefoot daughter in *Carousel*, watching the Snow children prance off to Sunday dinner with McGeorge Bundy, Reinhold Niebuhr, Dr. Howard Rusk. The cornucopia overflows. The Cross of Gold gleams. The barker's daughter dreams of anarchy and would not trust the Snow children to tell her that last night it was dark. Below the level of the New York or the Los Angeles *Times*, the problem is not so much whether one trusts the news as whether one finds it; quite often a monkey seems to have taken the entire bewildering affair from the teletype, throwing in a totem report here, a press release there. The summer I was seventeen I worked on a paper where the major thrust of each day's effort was to clip and rewrite the opposition paper ("Check it out if it looks like a plant," I was advised my first day); I have the impression that this kind of thing remains a lively local industry: County Board of Supervisors Lauds North Area Realtors for Plan to Raze Slum, Construct Howard Johnson's. Charity-minded Debutantes Inspect Recently Purchased Machine for Treatment of Terminal Cancer. Dear Abby. Mirror of Your Mind. The tongue lolls, reality recedes. "Seminary Sounds Like Boy Needs Dictionary," one reads on page 35. "PADUCAH, KY. (AP)—"When Kay Fowler asked her Sunday-school class to describe a seminary, one little fellow piped up: 'That's where they bury people.'" Tell me that on page 35, and I am not likely to believe you on page one.

Monkeys on the lower levels, code on the higher. It is a comment on our press conventions that we are considered "well-informed" to precisely the extent that we know "the real story," the story not in the newspaper. We have come to expect newspapers to reflect the official ethic, to do the "responsible" thing. The most admired newspapermen are no longer adversaries but confidants, participants; the ideal is to advise Presidents, dine with Walter Reuther and Henry Ford, and dance with the latter's daughters at Le Club. And then, heavy with responsibility, to file their coded reports. Alicia is not long on responsibility. Alicia never goes to Le Club. Alicia probably doesn't know anything about anything outside of Ann Arbor. But she tells me all she knows about that.

1968

Getting Serenity

"Speaking for myself," the young woman said, "in the seven months since I been on the program it's been real good. I was strictly a Gardena player, lowball. I'd play in the nighttime after I got my children to bed, and of course I never got home before five a.m., and my *problem* was, I couldn't sleep then. I'd replay every single hand, so the next day I'd be, you know, tired. Irritable. With the children."

Her tone was that of someone who had adapted her mode of public address from analgesic commercials, but she was not exactly selling a product. She was making a "confession" at a meeting of Gamblers Anonymous I attended not long ago: nine o'clock on a winter evening in a bungalow neighborhood clubhouse in Gardena, California. Gardena is the draw-poker capital of Los Angeles County (no stud, no alcoholic beverages, clubs closed between 5:00 a.m. and 9:00 a.m. and all day on Christmas Day; this is not Nevada but California, where there is only draw poker and that only on local option), and the seductive proximity of the poker clubs hung over this particular meeting like a paraphysical substance, almost as palpable as the portraits of Washington and Lincoln, the American flag, the plastic hydrangeas, and the table laid by the Refreshments Committee. Just around the corner waiting for someone, there it was, the action, and there in that overheated room, shifting uneasily on folding chairs and blinking against the cigarette smoke, were forty people who craved it. "This Gardena," a young man breathed softly. "She destroyed me." The young man, who said he had done OK in mechanical drawing at Van Nuys High School, was twenty-two years old and wore his hair in a sharp 1951 ducktail, which perhaps suggests the extent to which he, like everyone else in the room, heard a different drummer. "I didn't lose no fortune," he said, "but I lost all the money I could get my hands on, it began in the Marine Corps, I met a lot of pigeons in Vietnam, I was making easy money and it was, you might say, this period in my life that, uh, led to my downfall."

The smoke grew thicker, the testimony more intense. I had not heard so many revelations of a certain kind since I used to fall into conversations on Greyhound buses under the misapprehension that it was a good way to learn about life. "See, I had just got through embezzling a large sum of money from my employer," they were saying to one another, and "I started out for a Canoga Park meeting and turned around on the freeway, that was last Wednesday. I ended up in Gardena and now I'm on the verge of divorce again." *Mea culpa*, they appeared to be crying, and many of them had cried it the night before and the night before that: every night there is a Gamblers Anonymous meeting somewhere around Los Angeles, somewhere like Long Beach or Canoga Park or Downey or Culver City, and the ideal is to attend five or six a week. "I never made this Gardena meeting before," someone explained, "for one simple reason only, which is I break out in a cold sweat every time I pass Gardena on the freeway even, but I'm here tonight because every night I make a meeting is a night I don't place a bet, which with the help of God and you people is 1,223 nights now."

There were certain curiosities in the way they talked to one another. As if they were casters of horoscopes (and perhaps some of them were), they kept fanatical track not only of their own but of everyone else's important "dates" ("December third, '65, that was a bad date for me because that was the night I wrote the first phony check in the amount of $343, but it was an important date for Frank L., that date one year later made eight months on the same job for Frank L., even though he subsequently lost it, which shows that some of us are struggling on the same date when others of us are slipping, which is the miracle of G.A."); they spoke in general as if from some subverbal swamp, snatching at phrases as they floated by. "Now that I'm on the program I have the togetherness with my family," someone said, and "the most important thing I've gotten out of the program at the present time is my, uh, mental thinking."

"As you all know I reached my bottom that night of November twenty-eighth over at the Normandie Club," another said, "and after that I got serenity." "That's my ideal," someone added. "Getting serenity."

There was nothing particularly wrong with any of it, and yet there was something not quite right, something troubling. At first I thought that it was simply the predilection of many of the members to dwell upon how "powerless" they were, how buffeted by forces beyond their control. There was a great deal of talk about miracles, and Higher Presences, and a Power Greater Than Ourselves; the Gamblers Anonymous program, like that of Alcoholics Anonymous, tends to reinforce the addict's own rather passive view of his situation. (The first of the G.A. "Twelve Steps" involves admitting that one's life "has become" unmanageable. Five steps further, and still being acted upon, one avers that one is ready to "have these defects of character removed.") "My neighbor introduced me to Hollywood Park, big favor he did me," someone said that night. "They oughta bomb this Gardena," a young man whispered to me fervently. "A kid goes in one of those places, he's hooked for life."

But of course, *mea culpa* always turns out to be not entirely *mea*. Still, there was coffee to be drunk, a cake to be cut: it was Frank L.'s "birthday" in Gamblers Anonymous. After six years on the program he had finally completed a full year without placing a bet, and was being honored with a one-year pin ("Frank L., I want you to remember just one thing, the one-year pin is just a leafmark, just a bookmark in the book of life") and a cake, a white cake with an inscription in pink icing: MIRACLES STILL HAPPEN, the cake read. "It hasn't been easy," Frank L. said, surrounded by his wife, his children, and his wife's parents. "But in the last three, four weeks we've gotten a . . . a *serenity* at home." Well, there it was. I got out fast then, before anyone could say "serenity" again, for it is a word I associate with death, and for several days after that meeting I wanted only to be in places where the lights were bright and no one counted days.

1968

A Trip to Xanadu

It has been for almost half a century a peculiar and affecting image in the California mind: San Simeon, "*La Cuesta Encantada*," the phantasmagoric barony that William Randolph Hearst made for himself on the sunburned hills above the San Luis Obispo County coast. California children used to hear about San Simeon when they were very small (I know because I was one of them), used to be told to watch for it from Highway 1, quite far in the distance, crested on the hill, the great Moorish towers and battlements shimmering in the sun or floating fantastically just above the coastal fog; San Simeon was a place which, once seen from the highway, was ever in the mind, a material fact which existed in proof of certain abstract principles. San Simeon seemed to confirm the boundless promise of the place we lived. The gates were always barred on that road up the hill, and yet there was a kind of frontier accessibility about the Hearsts; the Hearst money was Western money, money that had come originally from a silver strike in Nevada, money made and spent in a singularly Western spirit of luck, imagination, irresponsibility, and general flamboyance. If a Hearst could build himself a castle, then every man could be a king.

San Simeon was, moreover, exactly the castle a child would build, if a child had $220 million and could spend $40 million of it on a castle: a sand castle, an implausibility, a place swimming in warm golden light and theatrical mists, a pleasure dome decreed by a man who insisted, out of the one dark fear we all know about, that all the surfaces be gay and brilliant and playful. More than any other place ever built in this country, San Simeon was dedicated to the proposition that all the pleasures of infinity are to be found in the here and the now. The leaves never fell at San Simeon, nothing went bare or died. All year long the roses and fuchsia and the bougainvillea blossomed, half a million gallons of water glittered in the great pools, zebras and eland roamed the golden hills. The carillon bells could be heard for thirty miles. Brilliant Sienese flags fluttered over the long refectory dining tables. The guests ate pressed duck and wiped their hands on paper napkins: again, a child's fantasy, every meal a picnic. The spirit of San Simeon was uninhibited by nervous adult distinctions about what was correct and what was not, what was good and what was less good, what was "art" and what not: if William Randolph Hearst liked something he bought it, and brought it to San Simeon. And a child would people his castle with exactly the same cast: there was the omnipotent King, the spurned Queen, the captive Princess from another land. There were the ambitious underlings, bearing dispatches from the capitals of the earth. And of course there were the courtiers, the decorative courtiers, some of whom came for the weekend and stayed for months, because no one was banished from this court unless he drank too much, or mentioned death. There were to be no shadows at all in this fairy tale: San Simeon was to be the kingdom where nobody dies.

And there it all was, floating on the hill for any child to see. I actually saw it there only three or four times, but I heard about it, and I remembered it, and San Simeon was an imaginative idea that affected me, shaped my own imagination in the way that all children are shaped by the actual and emotional geography of the place in which they grow up, by the stories they are told and the stories they invent. Because that was so, I made a trip not long ago to San Simeon, which since 1958 has been a state monument (the King did die, of course, in 1951, and his sons gave the castle to the state). I joined one of the daily tours through certain of the 147 rooms in the Great House and the guest houses.

It was what I had expected, and it was not. In most ways, most of the physical ways, San Simeon now looks precisely as it was supposed to have looked when William Randolph Hearst was alive: the ranch has dwindled from 275,000 to 85,000 acres, but it remains a working cattle ranch, and 85,000 acres is still pretty much as far as one can see from the broad tiled terraces. The private zoo is gone, the gnu and the sloth bears and the elephant, but a few zebras still graze in the stands of bay laurel on the hill. The art historians who visit the place now and then complain that the tapestries are fading, the paintings cracking and the polychrome wooden statuary flaking, the carved wooden ceilings being destroyed by insects; except for such incursions of time, however, and except for the absence of cut flowers, the state maintains the houses just as Hearst last saw them. The roses still blossom outside, and the sun glistens on the palm fronds, and the yellow hills running down to the sea absorb the light in that way peculiar to the California countryside. Nothing seems to have changed, and yet everything has, for in a way the state has made San Simeon what it never was, just another rich man's estate. The visitors come, as many as four million a year, in slacks and straw hats and hair rollers; they pay their three dollars and walk through on strips of protective nylon carpeting. They advise one another on snapshot angles, and speculate about how much it costs to heat the place. In the peak seasons the state hires eighty-nine civil-service guides and tour aides; some of them live in the servants' quarters, all of them swim in the Neptune Pool between six and eight each evening. They have barbecues on the terraces, and after-hours discussion groups, with such topics as "The Generation Gap." The guides wear khaki uniforms and are treasuries of fact: *2,144 rose bushes in Mr. Hearst's gardens, 5,400 volumes in Mr. Hearst's private library, at one time Mr. Hearst was noted for buying up one quarter of the world's art objects, in 504 categories of art.* "If you'd been a guest of Mr. Hearst's . . . ," they say, over and over again. If you'd been a guest of Mr. Hearst's, you could have played the Wurlitzer baby grand before dinner. If you'd been a guest of Mr. Hearst's, you could have seen a movie after dinner, *and actually sat next to the cast of the movie in the projection room*. It is a reverence which extends unto the Hearst sons, who occasionally stay at San Simeon, in a twenty-room guest house reserved for their use. "If you saw them, you probably wouldn't recognize them," the guide advises, "because they wouldn't be dressed any differently from you." I listened to the guides for a long while, and had a hard time getting the tone. And then I recognized it: it was a tone reflecting the idolatry of the rich that so often accompanies the democratization of things, the flattening out. I had taken a child up there with me, a niece from Connecticut who had never before heard of San Simeon, and she liked the flowers and the pools and the ornate ceilings, but it occurred to me as we left that she would have found it more affecting had she only glimpsed it from Highway 1, the gates barred, the castle floating in the distance. Make a place available to the eyes, and in certain ways it is no longer available to the imagination.

1968

On Being Unchosen
by the College of One's Choice

"Dear Joan," the letter begins, although the writer did not know me at all. The letter is dated April 25, 1952, and for a long time now it has been in a drawer in my mother's house, the kind of back-bedroom drawer given over to class prophecies and dried butterfly orchids and newspaper photographs that show eight bridesmaids and two flower girls inspecting a sixpence in a bride's shoe. What slight emotional investment I ever had in dried butterfly orchids and pictures of myself as a bridesmaid has proved evanescent, but I still have an investment in the letter, which, except for the "Dear Joan," is mimeographed. I got the letter out as an object lesson for a seventeen-year-old cousin who is unable to eat or sleep as she waits to hear from what she keeps calling the colleges of her choice. Here is what the letter says:

> The Committee on Admissions asks me to inform you that it is unable to take favorable action upon your application for admission to Stanford University. While you have met the minimum requirements, we regret that because of the severity of the competition, the Committee cannot include you in the group to be admitted. The Committee joins me in extending you every good wish for the successful continuation of your education. Sincerely yours, Rixford K. Snyder, Director of Admissions.

I remember quite clearly the afternoon I opened that letter. I stood reading and re-reading it, my sweater and my books fallen on the hall floor, trying to interpret the words in some less final way, the phrases "unable to take" and "favorable action" fading in and out of focus until the sentence made no sense at all. We lived then in a big dark Victorian house, and

I had a sharp and dolorous image of myself growing old in it, never going to school anywhere, the spinster in *Washington Square*. I went upstairs to my room and locked the door and for a couple of hours I cried. For a while I sat on the floor of my closet and buried my face in an old quilted robe and later, after the situation's real humiliations (all my friends who applied to Stanford had been admitted) had faded into safe theatrics, I sat on the edge of the bathtub and thought about swallowing the contents of an old bottle of codeine-and-Empirin. I saw myself in an oxygen tent, with Rixford K. Snyder hovering outside, although how the news was to reach Rixford K. Snyder was a plot point that troubled me even as I counted out the tablets.

Of course I did not take the tablets. I spent the rest of the spring in sullen but mild rebellion, sitting around drive-ins, listening to Tulsa evangelists on the car radio, and in the summer I fell in love with someone who wanted to be a golf pro, and I spent a lot of time watching him practice putting, and in the fall I went to a junior college a couple of hours a day and made up the credits I needed to go to the University of California at Berkeley. The next year a friend at Stanford asked me to write him a paper on Conrad's *Nostromo*, and I did, and he got an A on it. I got a B- on the same paper at Berkeley, and the specter of Rixford K. Snyder was exorcised.

So it worked out all right, my single experience in that most conventional middle-class confrontation, the child vs. the Admissions Committee. But that was in the benign world of country California in 1952, and I think it must be more difficult for children I know now, children whose lives from the age of two or three are a series of perilously programmed steps, each of which must be successfully negotiated in order to avoid just such a letter as mine from one or another of the Rixford K. Snyders of the world. An acquaintance told me recently that there were ninety applicants for the seven openings in the kindergarten of an expensive school in which she hoped to enroll her four-year-old, and that she was frantic because none of the four-year-old's letters of recommendation had mentioned the child's "interest in art." Had I been raised under that pressure, I suspect I would have taken the codeine-and-Empirin on that April afternoon in 1952. My rejection was different, my humiliation private: no parental hopes rode on whether I was admitted to Stanford, or anywhere. Of course my mother and father wanted me to be happy, and of course they expected that happiness would necessarily entail accomplishment, but the terms of that accomplishment were my affair. Their idea of their own and of my worth remained independent of where, or even if, I went to college. Our social situation was static, and the question of "right" schools, so traditionally urgent to the upwardly mobile, did not arise. When my father was told that I had been rejected by Stanford, he shrugged and offered me a drink.

I think about that shrug with a great deal of appreciation whenever I hear parents talking about their children's "chances." What makes me uneasy is the sense that they are merging their children's chances with their own, demanding of a child that he make good not only for himself but for the greater glory of his father and mother. Of course it is harder to get into college now than it once was. Of course there are more children than "desirable" openings. But we are deluding ourselves if we pretend that desirable schools benefit the child alone. ("I wouldn't care at all about his getting into Yale if it weren't for Vietnam," a father told me not long ago, quite unconscious of his own speciousness; it would have been malicious of me to suggest that one could also get a deferment at Long Beach State.) Getting into college has become an ugly business, malignant in its consumption and diversion of time and energy and true interests, and not its least deleterious aspect is how the children themselves accept it. They talk casually and unattractively of their "first, second, and third choices," of how their "first-choice" application (to Stephens, say) does not actually reflect their first choice (their first choice was Smith, but their adviser said their chances were low, so why "waste" the application?); they are calculating about the expectation of rejections, about their "backup" possibilities, about getting the right sport and the right extracurricular activities to "balance" the application, about juggling confirmations when their third choice accepts before their first choice answers. They are wise in the white lie here, the small self-aggrandizement there, in the importance of letters from "names" their parents scarcely know. I have heard conversations among sixteen-year-olds who were exceeded in their skill at manipulative self-promotion only by applicants for large literary grants.

And of course none of it matters very much at all, none of these early successes, early failures. I wonder if we had better not find some way to let our children know this, some way to extricate our expectations from theirs, some way to let them work through their own rejections and sullen rebellions and interludes with golf pros, unassisted by anxious prompting from the wings. Finding one's role at seventeen is problem enough, without being handed somebody else's script.

1968

Pretty Nancy

Pretty Nancy Reagan, the wife of the governor of California, was standing in the dining room of her rented house on Forty-fifth Street in Sacramento listening to a television newsman explain what he wanted to do. She was listening attentively. Nancy Reagan is a very attentive listener. The television crew wanted to watch her, the newsman said, while she was doing precisely what she would ordinarily be doing on a Tuesday morning at home. Since I was also there to watch her doing precisely what she would ordinarily be doing on a Tuesday morning at home, we seemed to be on the verge of exploring certain media frontiers: the television newsman and the two cameramen could watch Nancy Reagan being watched by me, or I could watch Nancy Reagan being watched by the three of them, or one of the cameramen could step back and do a *cinéma vérité* study of the rest of us all watching and being watched by one another. I had the distinct sense that we were on the track of something revelatory, the truth about Nancy Reagan at twenty-four frames a second, but the television newsman opted to overlook the moment's peculiar essence. He suggested that we watch Nancy Reagan picking some flowers in the garden. "That's something you might ordinarily do, isn't it?" he asked. "Indeed it is," Nancy Reagan said with spirit. Nancy Reagan says almost everything with spirit, perhaps because she was an actress for a couple of years and has the beginning actress's habit of investing even the most casual lines with a good deal more dramatic emphasis than is ordinarily called for on a Tuesday morning on Forty-fifth Street in Sacramento.

"Actually," she added then, with the air of someone about to disclose a delightful surprise, "actually, I really *do* need flowers."

She smiled at each of us, and I smiled back. We had all been smiling quite a bit that morning. "And then," the television newsman said thoughtfully, surveying the dining room table, "even though you've got a beautiful arrangement right now, we could set up the pretense of your arranging, you know, the flowers."

We all smiled at one another again, and then Nancy Reagan walked resolutely into the garden, equipped with a decorative straw basket about six inches in diameter. "Uh, Mrs. Reagan," the newsman called after her. "May I ask what you're going to select for flowers?"

"Why, I don't know," she said, pausing with her basket on a garden step. The scene was evolving its own choreography.

"Do you think you could use rhododendrons?"

Nancy Reagan looked critically at a rhododendron bush. Then she turned to the newsman and smiled. "Did you know there's a Nancy Reagan rose now?"

"Uh, no," he said. "I didn't."

"It's awfully pretty, it's kind of, oh, a kind of coral color."

"Would the . . . the Nancy Reagan rose be something you might be likely to pick now?"

A silvery peal of laughter. "I could certainly pick it. But I won't be *using* it." A pause. "I *can* use the rhododendron."

"Fine," the newsman said. "Just fine. Now I'll ask a question, and if you could just be nipping a bud as you answer it . . ."

"Nipping a bud," Nancy Reagan repeated, taking her place in front of the rhododendron bush.

"Let's have a dry run," a cameraman said.

The newsman looked at him. "In other words, by a dry run, you mean you want her to fake nipping the bud."

"Fake the nip, yeah," the cameraman said. "Fake the nip."

I tell you about all that because whenever I think of Nancy Reagan now I think of her just so, the frame frozen, pretty Nancy Reagan about to pluck a rhododendron blossom too large to fit into her decorative six-inch basket. Nancy Reagan has an interested smile, the smile of a good wife, a good mother, a good hostess, the smile of someone who grew up in comfort and went to Smith College and has a father who is a distinguished neurosurgeon (her father's entry in the 1966–67 *Who's Who* runs nine lines longer than her husband's) and a husband who is the definition of Nice Guy, not to mention governor of California, the smile of a woman who seems to be playing out some middle-class American woman's daydream, circa 1948. The set for this daydream is perfectly dressed, every detail correct. There in the rental house on Forty-fifth Street the white matchbooks read EXECUTIVE MANSION, but it is not hard to imagine them reading NANCY AND RONNIE, and there on the coffee table in the living room lie precisely the right magazines for the life being portrayed: *Town & Country*, *Vogue*, *Time*, *Life*, *Newsweek*, *Sports Illustrated*, *Fortune*, *ARTnews*. There are two dogs, named Lady and Fuzzy, and there are two children, named Pattie and Ronnie. Pattie, fifteen, is described as artistic, and she goes to a boarding school in Arizona. Ronnie, ten, is referred to as a regular boy, and he goes to a private school in Sacramento. He is also referred to as "the Skipper." Everyone on the set smiles, the social secretary, the state guard, the cook, the gardeners. And, out there in the garden, Nancy Reagan smiles, about to pluck the rhododendron blossom. "Oh, no, no, *no*," she is saying to the television newsman, who seems to have asked his question. "There's been no difference at all as far as our friends are concerned." She studies her basket. "If there was a difference, why, they just wouldn't be friends. Your friends are . . . your *friends*."

It is later the same day. Nancy Reagan has plucked and arranged the rhododendron blossoms several times, and the television crew has gone. Nancy Reagan has shown me the game room, where the governor and the Skipper and some of the state legislators like to play with electric trains. She has shown me the original drawings for some *Peanuts* cartoon strips, which Charles Schulz gave to the governor after the governor declared a Happiness-Is-Having-Charles-Schulz-as-a-California-Resident Day. She has shown me a photograph of the governor jumping a horse. ("His horse Nancy D," she mused, "who died the day we came to Sacramento.") She has told me that the governor never wore makeup even in motion pictures, and that politics is rougher than the picture business because you do not have the studio to protect you. We have gone downtown, and she has shown me how she replaced the old padded leather walls in the State Capitol ("dark, horrible, shabby") with beige burlap and carpeted the floors in a pleasing shade of green. "Having a pretty place to work is important to a man," she has advised me. She has shown me the apothecary jar of hard candies she keeps filled on the governor's desk. She has shown me how she says hello to Girl Scouts when she comes across them in the Capitol corridors.

She has shown me all those things, and now we are back in the living room of the rented house on Forty-fifth Street, waiting for the Skipper to come home from school. The Skipper's arrival is, I have been told, the pivotal point of Nancy Reagan's day.

The Skipper is expected at 3:20. He goes to a private school and comes home in a car pool. On this day Ronald Azavedo, a State Highway Patrol officer assigned to the Reagans, is driving the car in the pool. We wait awhile longer, but don't hear the car drive up. Nancy Reagan goes to the stairway and listens a moment. "I believe he slipped up the back stairway," she says. "Ronnie? Ronnie?"

Ronnie does not seem to be planning an appearance. "Bye," he says from somewhere.

"Come in for just a minute, Ronnie."

"Lo," he says, appearing in the doorway.

"How's Chuck's cold?" Nancy Reagan asks.

"Chuck doesn't have a cold."

"Chuck doesn't have a cold?"

"No. Bruce has braces."

"Bruce has braces," Nancy Reagan repeats.

"Bye," the Skipper says.

"Bye," I say.

Nancy Reagan smiles radiantly at me, and calls Ronald Azavedo to drive me back downtown. "I don't believe in being an absentee mother," she says to me. "I just don't."

1968

Fathers, Sons, Screaming Eagles

"I hope you don't think I'm a hippie," said the man to whom I was talking in the Crown Room of the Stardust Hotel on the Las Vegas Strip in Las Vegas, Nevada. "I'm just kind of, you know, growing this beard." His name tag said Skip Skivington. He was probably in his early forties and he had been at Bastogne with the 101st Airborne Division in 1944 and his voice was gentle and apologetic and I had not thought him a hippie. It was the first evening of the 101st Airborne Association's twenty-third annual reunion, one weekend in Las Vegas not long ago. Outside the late-summer sky burned all day and all night and inside it was perpetually cold and carpeted and no perceptible time of day or night, and here, in the Crown Room of the Stardust, along with a great many wives and a few children, were a couple of hundred survivors of Normandy, Bastogne, the Battle of the Bulge. I had come over from Los Angeles to find them and knew that I had found them when I walked into the Stardust bar and saw a couple of men in sport shirts and overseas caps. "Just wait a minute," one of them had been saying. "I gotta finish this brew." In the afternoon they had commandeered the Stardust swimming pool for a beer party, and now they were lining up for a buffet dinner (roast beef, ham, coleslaw, sliced beets, sliced tomatoes, American cheese, and dinner rolls), filling plates and finding tables and snapping the toy metal crickets that had been the 101st's identification code on D-day. "General McAuliffe. *General*," called a weathered man in an overseas cap as he threaded his way through the tables with a small child, two or three years old, by the hand. "Look at the boy. I wanted to show you the boy."

Almost everyone else had found friends and a table by then, but Skip Skivington still stood with me. He was telling me about his son. His son, he said, had been missing in Vietnam since Mother's Day. I did not know what to say, but because Skip Skivington was active in the 101st Airborne Association, I asked if his son had belonged to the 101st. The father looked at me and then away. "I talked him out of it," he said finally. He reached into his coat pocket then and brought out a newspaper clipping, preserved in clear plastic, a story about his son: where he had gone to high school, the report that he was missing, the action in which he had last been seen. There was a snapshot of the boy, his face indistinct in the engraving dots, a blond eighteen-year-old sitting on a rock and smiling. I gave the clipping back to Skip Skivington, and before he put it in his pocket again he looked at it a long while, smoothed out an imagined crease, and studied the fragment of newsprint as if it held some answer.

The indistinct face of the boy and the distinct face of the father stayed in my mind all that evening, all that weekend, and perhaps it was their faces that made those few days in Las Vegas seem so charged with unspoken questions, ambiguities only dimly perceived. In most ways the reunion was a happy occasion. The wives had pretty dresses, and everyone liked Las Vegas, agreed that it was definitely the place for the reunion ("I've been to every reunion and I never saw so many guys as right here in Vegas, Vegas is definitely the place to have it"), agreed that the Stardust's Lido Revue was—well, bare breasts are risqué, but the girls were just lovely and the whole thing was tastefully done, especially the ice-skating sequence, which was a work of art. There were meetings to be held, Gold Star Mothers, like Mrs. C. J. (Mom) Miller, to be recognized. There was a new president of the association to be installed. "Thanks, Bernie, fellow Screaming Eagles," said the new president, "men of the 101st, our wives, our friends, our Gold Star Mothers . . ."

There was a wives' luncheon, a hospitality suite. "I'll be floatin' around the hotel in the afternoon. I'm not gonna *touch* that hospitality suite till after two," said someone to whom I was talking. There were Army movies, and I sat with a sprinkling of wives in the cool darkness and learned about the future of the Weapons Command, the function of Procurement. The wives slipped off their shoes and consulted slips of paper. "Not counting a couple of quarters at the airport," one of them said, "we were down twenty-seven dollars yesterday and up twelve dollars today. That's not bad, that's *net*." There were telegrams to be sent, to the 101st in Vietnam ("Keep that Eagle Screaming"), and telegrams to be read, from Hubert Humphrey ("We are not a nation that has lost its way, but a nation seeking a better way"). There was even a Teen Room, where a handful of children sat on folding chairs and regarded a Wurlitzer in sullen ennui.

And of course there were speeches. Maxwell Taylor came, to point out similarities between the Battle of the Bulge and the Tet Offensive. "By the way these things were reported, many of the people at home had the impression that we were losing the Bulge, just as they now have the impression that . . ." A colonel from Vietnam came, flown in to assure the guests that operations there were characterized by high *esprit*, rugged determination, that "the men in Vietnam are exactly like you were, and I was, twenty, twenty-five years ago." Gen. Anthony McAuliffe came, the man who said "Nuts" when the Germans asked for a surrender at Bastogne, and he said that he would be with the group in Holland next year to commemorate the twenty-fifth anniversary of the European invasion. "We'll visit our Dutch friends," he said, "and revive memories of that great adventure we had there."

And of course there it was, that was it. They had indeed had a great adventure, an essential adventure, and almost everyone in the room had been nineteen and twenty years old when they had it, and they had survived and come home and their wives had given birth to sons, and now those sons were nineteen, twenty, and perhaps it was not such a great adventure this time. Perhaps it was hard to bring quite the same urgency to holding a position in a Vietnamese village or two that they had brought to liberating Europe. On the night of the speeches I sat with a man named Walter Davis and his wife, a soft-faced woman in a good black dress. Walter Davis jumped into Holland in 1944, and now he works for the Metropolitan Life in Lawndale, California, and has three children, a daughter of eighteen, a son of fourteen, and a daughter of three. There was a Dutch girl at the table, and Mrs. Davis asked her to write a message in Dutch to their son. "Eddie's at that age where he's interested in everything his father did when he was a teenager, everything about the war and Holland," Mrs. Davis said. We talked awhile, and I mentioned, because those faces were very much with me, that I had met someone whose son was missing in Vietnam. Walter Davis said nothing for a moment. "I never thought of dying then," he said suddenly, after a while. "I see it a little differently now. I didn't look at it from the parents' point of view then. I was eighteen, nineteen. I wanted to go, couldn't stand not to go. I got to see Paris, Berlin, got to see places I'd heard about but never dreamed I'd see. Now I've got a boy, well, in four years maybe he'll have to go." Walter Davis broke open a roll, buttered it carefully, and put it down again, untouched. "I see it a little differently now," he said.

1968

Why I Write

Of course I stole the title for this talk, from George Orwell. One reason I stole it was that I like the sound of the words: Why I Write. There you have three short unambiguous words that share a sound, and the sound they share is this:

I

I

I

In many ways, writing is the act of saying I, of imposing oneself upon other people, of saying *listen to me, see it my way, change your mind*. It's an aggressive, even a hostile act. You can disguise its aggressiveness all you want with veils of subordinate clauses and qualifiers and tentative subjunctives, with ellipses and evasions—with the whole manner of intimating rather than claiming, of alluding rather than stating—but there's no getting around the fact that setting words on paper is the tactic of a secret bully, an invasion, an imposition of the writer's sensibility on the reader's most private space.

I stole the title not only because the words sounded right but because they seemed to sum up, in a no-nonsense way, all I have to tell you. Like many writers I have only this one "subject," this one "area": the act of writing. I can bring you no reports from any other front. I may have other interests: I am "interested," for example, in marine biology, but I don't flatter myself that you would come out to hear me talk about it. I am not a scholar. I am not in the least an intellectual, which is not to say that when I hear the word "intellectual" I reach for my gun, but only to say that I do not think in abstracts. During the years when I was an undergraduate at Berkeley I tried, with a kind of hopeless late-adolescent energy, to buy some temporary visa into the world of ideas, to forge for myself a mind that could deal with the abstract.

In short I tried to think. I failed. My attention veered inexorably back to the specific, to the tangible, to what was generally considered, by everyone I knew then and for that matter have known since, the peripheral. I would try to contemplate the Hegelian dialectic and would find myself concentrating instead on a flowering pear tree outside my window and the particular way the petals fell on my floor. I would try to read linguistic theory and would find myself wondering instead if the lights were on in the Bevatron up the hill. When I say that I was wondering if the lights were on in the Bevatron you might immediately suspect, if you deal in ideas at all, that I was registering the Bevatron as a political symbol, thinking in shorthand about the military-industrial complex and its role in the university community, but you would be wrong. I was only wondering if the lights were on in the Bevatron, and how they looked. A physical fact.

I had trouble graduating from Berkeley, not because of this inability to deal with ideas—I was majoring in English, and I could locate the house-and-garden imagery in *The Portrait of a Lady* as well as the next person, "imagery" being by definition the kind of specific that got my attention—but simply because I had neglected to take a course in Milton. For reasons which now sound baroque I needed a degree by the end of that summer, and the English department finally agreed, if I would come down from Sacramento every Friday and talk about the cosmology of *Paradise Lost*, to certify me proficient in Milton. I did this. Some Fridays I took the Greyhound bus, other Fridays I caught the Southern Pacific's City of San Francisco on the last leg of its transcontinental trip. I can no longer tell you whether Milton put the sun or the earth at the center of his universe in *Paradise Lost*, the central question of at least one century and a topic about which I wrote ten thousand words that summer, but I can still recall the exact rancidity of the butter in the City of San Francisco's dining car, and the way the tinted windows on the Greyhound bus cast the oil refineries around Carquinez Strait into a grayed and obscurely sinister light. In short my attention was always on the periphery, on what I could see and taste and touch, on the butter, and the Greyhound bus. During those years I was traveling on what I knew to be a very shaky passport, forged papers: I knew that I was no legitimate resident in any world of ideas. I knew I couldn't think. All I knew then was what I couldn't do. All I knew then was what I wasn't, and it took me some years to discover what I was.

Which was a writer.

By which I mean not a "good" writer or a "bad" writer but simply a writer, a person whose most absorbed and passionate hours are spent arranging words on pieces of paper. Had my credentials been in order I would never have become a writer. Had I been blessed with even limited access to my own mind there would have been no reason to write. I write entirely to find out what I'm thinking, what I'm looking at, what I see and what it means. What I want and what I fear. Why did the oil refineries around Carquinez Strait seem sinister to me in the summer of 1956? Why have the night lights in the Bevatron burned in my mind for twenty years? *What is going on in these pictures in my mind?*

When I talk about pictures in my mind I am talking, quite specifically, about images that shimmer around the edges. There used to be an illustration in every elementary psychology book showing a cat drawn by a patient in varying stages of schizophrenia. This cat had a shimmer around it. You could see the molecular structure breaking down at the very edges of the cat: the cat became the background and the background the cat, everything interacting, exchanging ions. People on hallucinogens describe the same perception of objects. I'm not a schizophrenic, nor do I take hallucinogens, but certain images do shimmer for me. Look hard enough, and you can't miss the shimmer. It's there. You can't think too much about these pictures that shimmer. You just lie low and let them develop. You stay quiet. You don't talk to many people and you keep your nervous system from shorting out and you try to locate the cat in the shimmer, the grammar in the picture.

Just as I meant "shimmer" literally I mean "grammar" literally. Grammar is a piano I play by ear, since I seem to have been out of school the year the rules were mentioned. All I know about grammar is its infinite power. To shift the structure of a sentence alters the meaning of that sentence, as definitely and inflexibly as the position of a camera alters the meaning of the object photographed. Many people know about camera angles now, but not so many know about sentences. The arrangement of the words matters, and the arrangement you want can be found in the picture in your mind. The picture dictates the arrangement. The picture dictates whether this will be a sentence with or without clauses, a sentence that ends hard or a dying-fall sentence, long or short, active or passive. The picture tells you how to arrange the words and the arrangement of the words tells you, or tells me, what's going on in the picture. *Nota bene:*

It tells you.

You don't tell it.

Let me show you what I mean by pictures in the mind. I began *Play It as It Lays* just as I have begun each of my novels, with no notion of "character" or "plot" or even "incident." I had only two pictures in my mind, more about which later, and a technical intention, which was to write a novel so elliptical and fast that it would be over before you noticed it, a novel so fast that it would scarcely exist on the page at all. About the pictures: the first was of white space. Empty space. This was clearly the picture that dictated the narrative intention of the book—a book in which anything that happened would happen off the page, a "white" book to which the reader would have to bring his or her own bad dreams—and yet this picture told me no "story," suggested no situation. The second picture did. This second picture was of something actually witnessed. A young woman with long hair and a short white halter dress walks through the casino at the Riviera in Las Vegas at one in the morning. She crosses the casino alone and picks up a house telephone. I watch her because I have heard her paged, and recognize her name: she is a minor actress I see around Los Angeles from time to time, in places like Jax and once in a gynecologist's office in the Beverly Hills Clinic, but have never met. I know nothing about her. Who is paging her? Why is she here to be paged? How exactly did she come to this? It was precisely this moment in Las Vegas that made *Play It as It Lays* begin to tell itself to me, but the moment appears in the novel only obliquely, in a chapter which begins:

> Maria made a list of things she would never do. She would never: walk through the Sands or Caesar's alone after midnight. She would never: ball at a party, do S-M unless she wanted to, borrow furs from Abe Lipsey, deal. She would never: carry a Yorkshire in Beverly Hills.

That is the beginning of the chapter and that is also the end of the chapter, which may suggest what I meant by "white space."

I recall having a number of pictures in my mind when I began the novel I just finished, *A Book of Common Prayer*. As a matter of fact one of these pictures was of that Bevatron I mentioned, although I would be hard put to tell you a story in which nuclear energy figures. Another was a newspaper photograph of a hijacked 707 burning on the desert in the Middle East. Another was the night view from a room in which I once spent a week with paratyphoid, a hotel room on the Colombian coast. My husband and I seemed to be on the Colombian coast representing the United States of America at a film festival (I recall invoking the name Jack Valenti a lot, as if its reiteration could make me well), and it was a bad place to have fever, not only because my indisposition offended our hosts but because every night in this hotel the generator failed. The lights went out. The elevator stopped. My husband would go to the event of the evening and make excuses for me and I would stay alone in this hotel room, in the dark. I remember standing at the window trying to call Bogotá (the telephone seemed to work on the same principle as the generator) and watching the night wind come up and wondering what I was doing eleven degrees off the equator with a fever of 103. The view from that window definitely figures in *A Book of Common Prayer*, as does the burning 707, and yet none of these pictures told me the story I needed.

The picture that did, the picture that shimmered and made these other images coalesce, was of the Panama airport at

6:00 a.m. I was in this airport only once, on a plane to Bogotá that stopped for an hour to refuel, but the way it looked that morning remained superimposed on everything I saw until the day I finished *A Book of Common Prayer*. I lived in that airport for several years. I can still feel the hot air when I step off the plane, can see the heat already rising off the tarmac at 6:00 a.m. I can feel the skirt damp and wrinkled on my legs. I can feel the asphalt stick to my sandals. I remember the big tail of a Pan American plane floating motionless down at the end of the tarmac. I remember the sound of a slot machine in the waiting room. I could tell you that I remember a particular woman in the airport, an American woman, a *norteamericana*, a thin *norteamericana* about forty who wore a big square emerald in lieu of a wedding ring, but there was no such woman there.

I put this woman in the airport later. I made this woman up, just as I later made up a country to put the airport in, and a family to run the country. This woman in the airport is neither catching a plane nor meeting one. She is ordering tea in the airport coffee shop. In fact she is not simply "ordering" tea but insisting that the water be boiled, in front of her, for twenty minutes. Why is this woman in this airport? Why is she going nowhere, where has she been? Where did she get that big emerald? What derangement, or disassociation, makes her believe that her will to see the water boiled can possibly prevail?

> She had been going to one airport or another for four months, one could see it, looking at the visas on her passport. All those airports where Charlotte Douglas's passport had been stamped would have looked alike. Sometimes the sign on the tower would say "BIENVEN-IDOS" and sometimes the sign on the tower would say "BIENVENUE," some places were wet and hot and others were dry and hot, but at each of these airports the pastel concrete walls would rust and stain and the swamp off the runway would be littered with the fuselages of cannibalized Fairchild F-227s and the water would need boiling.

> I knew why Charlotte went to the airport even if Victor did not.
>
> I knew about airports.

These lines appear about halfway through *A Book of Common Prayer*, but I wrote them during the second week I worked on the book, long before I had any idea where Charlotte Douglas had been or why she went to airports. Until I wrote these lines I had no character called Victor in mind: the necessity for mentioning a name, and the name Victor, occurred to me as I wrote the sentence. *I knew why Charlotte went to the airport* sounded incomplete. *I knew why Charlotte went to the airport even if Victor did not* carried a little more narrative drive. Most important of all, until I wrote these lines I did not know who "I" was, who was telling the story. I had intended until that moment that the "I" be no more than the voice of the author, a nineteenth-century omniscient narrator. But there it was:

"I knew why Charlotte went to the airport even if Victor did not."

"I knew about airports."

This "I" was the voice of no author in my house. This "I" was someone who not only knew why Charlotte went to the airport but also knew someone called Victor. Who was Victor? Who was this narrator? Why was this narrator telling me this story? Let me tell you one thing about why writers write: had I known the answer to any of these questions I would never have needed to write a novel.

1976

Telling Stories

In the fall of 1954, when I was nineteen and a junior at Berkeley, I was one of perhaps a dozen students admitted to the late Mark Schorer's English 106A, a kind of "writers' workshop" which met for discussion three hours a week and required that each student produce, over the course of the semester, at least five short stories. No auditors were allowed. Voices were kept low. English 106A was widely regarded in the fall of 1954 as a kind of sacramental experience, an initiation into the grave world of real writers, and I remember each meeting of this class as an occasion of acute excitement and dread. I remember each other member of this class as older and wiser than I had hope of ever being (it had not yet struck me in any visceral way that being nineteen was not a long-term proposition), not only older and wiser but more experienced, more independent, more interesting, more possessed of an exotic past: marriages and the breaking up of marriages, money and the lack of it, sex and politics and the Adriatic seen at dawn; the stuff not only of grown-up life itself but, more poignantly to me at the time, the very stuff which might be transubstantiated into five short stories. I recall a Trotskyist, then in his forties. I recall a young woman who lived, with a barefoot man and a large white dog, in an attic lit only by candles. I recall classroom discussions which ranged over meetings with Paul and Jane Bowles, incidents involving Djuna Barnes, years spent in Paris, in Beverly Hills, in the Yucatán, on the Lower East Side of New York and on Repulse Bay and even on morphine. I had spent seventeen of my nineteen years in Sacramento, and the other two in the Tri Delt house on Warring Street in Berkeley. I had never read Paul or Jane Bowles, let alone met them, and when, some fifteen years later at a friend's house in Santa Monica Canyon, I did meet Paul Bowles, I was immediately rendered as dumb and awestruck as I had been when I was nineteen and taking English 106A.

In short I had no past, and, every Monday-Wednesday-Friday at noon in Dwinelle Hall, it seemed increasingly clear to me that I had no future. I ransacked my closet for clothes in which I might appear invisible in class, and came up with only a dirty raincoat. I sat in this raincoat and I listened to other people's stories read aloud and I despaired of ever knowing what they knew. I attended every meeting of this class and never spoke once. I managed to write only three of the required five stories. I received—only, I think now, because Mr. Schorer, a man of infinite kindness to and acuity about his students, divined intuitively that my failing performance was a function of adolescent paralysis, of a yearning to be good and a fright that I never would be, of terror that any sentence I committed to paper would expose me as *not good enough*—a course grade of B. I wrote no more stories for exactly ten years.

When I say I wrote no more stories for exactly ten years I do not mean that I wrote nothing at all. In fact I wrote constantly. I wrote, once I left Berkeley, for a living. I went to New York and I wrote merchandising copy for *Vogue* and I wrote promotion copy for *Vogue* (the distinction between the two was definite but recondite, and to try to explain it would be like giving the AFL-CIO definition of two apparently similar jobs on the line at the Ford assembly plant in Pico Rivera, California) and after a while I wrote editorial copy for *Vogue*. A sample of the last: "Opposite, above: All through the house, colour, verve, improvised treasures in happy but anomalous coexistence. Here, a Frank Stella, an art nouveau stained-glass panel, a Roy Lichtenstein. Not shown: a table covered with frankly brilliant oilcloth, a Mexican find at fifteen cents a yard."

It is easy to make light of this kind of "writing," and I mention it specifically because I do not make light of it at all: it was at *Vogue* that I learned a kind of ease with words, a way of regarding words not as mirrors of my own inadequacy but as tools, toys, weapons to be deployed strategically on a page. In a caption of, say, eight lines, each line to run no more or less than twenty-seven characters, not only every word but every letter counted. At *Vogue* one learned fast, or one did not stay, how to play games with words, how to put a couple of unwieldy dependent clauses through the typewriter and roll them out transformed into one simple sentence composed of precisely thirty-nine characters. We were connoisseurs of synonyms. We were collectors of verbs. (I recall "to ravish" as a highly favored verb for a number of issues and I also recall it, for a number of issues more, as the source of a highly favored noun: "ravishments," as in "tables cluttered with porcelain tulips, Fabergé eggs, other ravishments.") We learned as reflex the grammatical tricks we had learned only as marginal corrections in school ("there were two oranges and an apple" read better than "there were an apple and two oranges," passive verbs slowed down sentences, "it" needed a reference within the scan of the eye), learned to rely on the *OED*, learned to write and rewrite and rewrite again. "Run it through again, sweetie, it's not quite there." "Give me a shock verb two lines in." "Prune it out, clean it up, make the point." Less was more, smooth was better, and absolute precision essential to the monthly grand illusion. Going to work for *Vogue* was, in the late 1950s, not unlike training with the Rockettes.

All of this was tonic, particularly to someone who had labored for some years under the delusion that to set two sentences side by side was to risk having the result compared widely and unfavorably to *The Golden Bowl*. Gradually I began, in the evenings and between deadlines and in lieu of lunch, to play with words not for *Vogue* but for myself. I began to make notes. I began to write down everything I saw and heard and remembered and imagined. I began to write, or so I thought, another story. I had in mind a story about a woman and a man in New York:

> She could no longer concentrate on what he was saying, for she had thought of something that happened in California, the winter she was fifteen. There was no reason why she should remember it this afternoon, yet the recollection carried all that urgent, shining clarity peculiar

to things that happened a long time ago in another part of the country. There had been a week of heavy rain that December, and the valley rivers were nearing flood stage. She had been on Christmas vacation, and every morning she would get up to find the house colder and damper than it had been the day before. She and her mother would have breakfast together, looking out the kitchen window into the rain and watching the water swirl through the gully which separated their property from Dr. Wood's. "All the fruit's going," her mother would say dispassionately every morning at breakfast. "All the fruit, shot right to hell." Then she would pour another cup of coffee and remark resignedly that it was obvious to her, even if it was not to the army engineers, that the levees could not hold much longer. Every fifteen minutes the two of them listened to ominous bulletins on the radio, telling when and where the rivers were expected to crest. One morning the Sacramento crested at thirty-one feet, and when they announced that it would crest the next day at thirty-eight, the engineers began to evacuate the ranches upstream. Sometime during that next morning a levee gave way forty miles upstream from Sacramento, and the papers on Christmas Eve showed aerial photographs of the levee crumbling under sheets of muddy water, and of families huddled in their bathrobes on the tops of houses. The evacuees were streaming into town all that night, to sleep in school gymnasiums and the parish halls of churches.

"What are you going to do," he asked, quite as interested as if he were watching an intensely absorbing play.

"Go to California and work in the fruit," she said dully.

Raining: wet leaves, black streets.

Driving past the Horst ranch, hop strings limp in the rain.

Fulton strip wet and cheap. Fire in Mrs. Miles's: buying a dress to wear to parties.

Watching the rain from windows all over.

On dining room table, silver and linen lying after parties. Dances.

Bars in the rain where the fire never works.
Any place I hang my hat is home sweet home to me.

So went the "beginning" of this story I had in mind, this story I believed to be about a woman and a man in New York—I use the word "beginning" only as shorthand, since nothing so rough and inchoate can be said to have a true beginning—and so went some of the notes I made in an attempt to get down on paper some of the things I wanted in the story. The notes, tellingly, have nothing to do with a woman and a man in New York. The notes—that silver lying on the dining room table after parties, those bars in the rain where the fire never worked, those figures about when and where the Sacramento River would crest—say simply this: *remember.* The notes reveal that what I actually had on my mind that year in New York—had *on my mind* as opposed to *in mind*—was a longing for California, a homesickness, a nostalgia so obsessive that nothing else figured. In order to discover what was on my mind I needed room. I needed room for the rivers and for the rain and for the way the almonds came into blossom around Sacramento, room for irrigation ditches and room for the fear of kiln fires, room in which to play with everything I remembered and did not understand. In the end I wrote not a story about a woman and a man in New York but a novel about the wife of a hop grower on the Sacramento River. The novel was my first and it was called *Run River* and I did not have it clearly in mind until five years later, when I was finishing it. I suspect that writers of short stories know their own minds rather better than that.

Short stories demand a certain awareness of one's own intentions, a certain narrowing of the focus. Let me give you an example. One morning in 1975 I found myself aboard the 8:45 a.m. Pan American from Los Angeles to Honolulu. There were, before take-off from Los Angeles, "mechanical difficulties," and a half-hour delay. During this delay the stewardesses served coffee and orange juice and two children played tag in the aisles and, somewhere behind me, a man began screaming at a woman who seemed to be his wife. I say that the woman seemed to be his wife only because the tone of his invective sounded practiced, although the only words I heard clearly were these: "You are driving me to murder." After a moment I was aware of the door to the plane being opened a few rows behind me, and of the man rushing off. There were many Pan American employees rushing on and off then, and considerable confusion. I do not know whether the man reboarded the plane before take-off or whether the woman went on to Honolulu alone, but I thought about it all the way across the Pacific. I thought about it while I was drinking a sherry on the rocks and I thought about it during lunch and I was still thinking about it when the first of the Hawaiian Islands appeared off the left wing-tip. It was not until we had passed Diamond Head and were coming in low over the reef for landing at Honolulu, however, that I realized what I most disliked about this incident: I disliked it because it had the aspect of a short story, one of those "little epiphany" or "window on the world" stories, one of those stories in which the main character glimpses a crisis in a stranger's life—a woman weeping in a tea room, quite often, or an accident seen from the window of a train, "tea rooms" and "trains" still being fixtures of short stories although not of real life—and is moved to see his or her own life in a new light. Again, my dislike was a case of needing room in which to play with what I did not understand. I was not going to Honolulu because I wanted to see life reduced to a short story. I was going to Honolulu because I wanted to see life expanded to a novel, and I still do. I wanted not a window on the world but the world itself. I wanted everything in the picture. I wanted room for flowers, and reef fish, and people who might or might not have been driving one another to murder but in any case were not impelled, by the demands of narrative convention, to say so out loud on the 8:45 a.m. Pan American from Los Angeles to Honolulu.

By way of explaining what moved me to write three short stories in 1964 and none at all—if we except classroom assignments—in any other year, I can suggest only that my first novel had just been published, and I was suffering a fear common among people who have just written a first novel: the fear of never writing another. (As a matter of fact this fear is also common among people who have just written a second novel, a third novel, and, for all I know, a forty-fourth novel, but at the time I considered it a unique affliction.) I sat in front of my typewriter and believed that another subject would never present itself. I believed that I would be forever dry. I believed that I would "forget how." Accordingly, as a kind of desperate finger exercise, I tried writing stories.

I had, and have, no talent for it, no feel for the particular rhythms of short fiction, no ability to focus the world in the window. The first of these stories, "Coming Home," is cast in an extremely simple and highly conventional form: it is one of those stories in which the lives of the characters are meant to be revealed through a single dialogue, a dialogue apparently overheard by a neutral recorder. This form demands absolute control—consider Hemingway's "Hills Like White Elephants" and you will see the form at its best—and "Coming Home" illustrates no control at all. One whole section of the story resembles nothing so much as a studio synopsis of a novel. What is that Kentucky coal mine doing in the story? Who saw those Impressionist paintings? Who is telling the story? Why was I trying to write this kind of story if I didn't know enough to stick to the rules, do it right, let the dialogue do all the work? My impatience with "Coming Home" applies equally to "The Welfare Island Ferry," a story which differs in technique from "Coming Home" but is, again, a very familiar kind of story. "The Welfare Island Ferry" is a "shock of recognition" story, a story in which the reader is meant to apprehend, late on and quite suddenly, something of which the characters remain unaware. There is in this story a single withheld revelation: one of the characters is demented. My instinct now—and it is an instinct fatal to the story-telling impulse—would be to say, up front, "This girl has gotten herself mixed up with somebody crazy as a loon," and get on with it.

Actually, I am not at all impatient with the third of these stories, "When Did Music Come This Way? Children Dear, Was It Yesterday?" I do not mean to say that I think it is a successful short story: it works not at all as a story. It is instead a kind of extended notation for an unwritten novel, an exercise in the truest sense. It was in "When Did Music" that I taught myself—or began to teach myself—how to use the first person. It was in "When Did Music" that I taught myself—or began to teach myself—how to make narrative tension out of nothing more than the juxtaposition of past and present. I should have known what I learned in this story before I ever wrote my first novel. Had I never written this story I would have never written a second novel. As crude and imperfect as the story is, it seems to me by far the most interesting of the three.

It was also the most difficult of the three to place. "Coming Home" appeared in *The Saturday Evening Post*. "The Welfare Island Ferry" appeared in *Harper's Bazaar*. "When Did Music Come This Way?" appeared nowhere at all for a long, long time. It was written, curiously enough, "on commission" from Rust Hills, who was then the fiction editor at the *Post*. He had called or written me—I forget which—to say that the *Post* was planning a "theme" issue about children, an issue in which every article and story would have to do—however peripherally—with children. A number of writers had been asked to submit stories for this issue. Each would receive a "guarantee," or minimum payment. Not all of the stories would be accepted. I wrote the story and submitted it. I was represented at the time by the William Morris Agency, and these letters from the Morris office in New York to me in California suggest the troubled course of the story:

> *October 9, 1964:* "As you probably know, Rust wrote to a great many writers regarding stories for a children's issue, and the guarantee for everyone is a flat $200. On the price for the story itself, they will pay $1750, or a $250 increase over your last price. Please let me know whether this is agreeable and if so we'll confirm the terms on your behalf . . ."

> *November 30, 1964:* "I'm really disappointed not to have better news for you, but Rust Hills has returned WHEN

DID MUSIC COME THIS WAY? CHILDREN DEAR, WAS IT YESTERDAY? . . . We'll of course send the guarantee check off to you just as soon as we receive it. Since you indicated that you wanted to do some further work on the story, I am wondering whether you would like the manuscript returned to you at this point . . ."

December 8, 1964: ". . . I am looking forward to receiving the revised copies of THE WELFARE ISLAND and WHEN DID MUSIC COME THIS WAY . . ."

December 11, 1964: ". . . The revised versions of both stories have gone out—WELFARE ISLAND to *Bazaar* and WHEN DID MUSIC COME THIS WAY to *The New Yorker* . . ."

April 13, 1965: ". . . The manuscript is now at *Esquire* and I will let you know as soon as we hear anything further . . ."

June 2, 1965: "I'm really sorry there isn't any good news yet on WHEN DID MUSIC COME THIS WAY? CHILDREN DEAR, WAS IT YESTERDAY? Since I wrote you last it has been declined by *Esquire* and *Harper's Bazaar*. *Bazaar* commented that they love the way you write, but feel MUSIC is not as good as THE WELFARE ISLAND FERRY . . ."

August 2, 1965: "As you know, we've been submitting WHEN DID MUSIC COME THIS WAY? CHILDREN DEAR, WAS IT YESTERDAY? to the magazines, and the following is a list of places where it's been seen. *Saturday Evening Post*: 'Many of us read it and a great many were excited and insistent in their admiration of it. Others, and they include Bill Emerson who has the final vote, also admired it but felt that it was wrong for the *Post*, not so much because of its subject matter, but also because of the oblique method of narration.' *The New Yorker:* 'as a whole it just isn't effective enough.' *Ladies' Home Journal:* 'too negative for us.' *McCall's:* 'I feel very bad about rejecting this story—not because I think it's really a well worked-out story but because the writing is so awfully good. She has a very special way of involving the reader . . . but I'm turning this down, reluctantly, because I don't think it's a successful story in the end.' *Good Housekeeping:* 'marvelously written, very real, and so utterly depressing that I'm going to sit under a cloud of angst and gloom all afternoon . . . I'm sorry we are seldom inclined to give our readers this bad a time.' *Redbook:* 'just too brittle.' *Atlantic Monthly:* 'I hope you'll be sending us more of Joan Didion's work, but this didn't make it, so back to you.' *Cosmopolitan:* (sent twice due to change in editorial staff) 'too depressing.' *Esquire:* no comment. *Harper's Bazaar:* 'While THE WELFARE ISLAND FERRY is almost my favorite among the stories we have published . . . I feel that WHEN DID MUSIC COME THIS WAY? is not quite as good.' *Vogue:* 'not quite right for us.' *Mademoiselle:* 'unable to use this particular story.' *The Reporter:* 'alas, not right for *The Reporter.*' I'm afraid that at this point we can think of no other markets to which we can submit it other than the reviews. I would like to try the story at some of the reviews, unless you have some other ideas. Would you let me know, please."

November 7, 1966: ". . . I had sent it . . . to the *Denver Quarterly* who write that they would like to use it in their fourth issue, which is due shortly after the first of the year. Their rate is a minuscule $5 per page and since the story would run about 10 pages for them, they would pay $50. Please let me know whether or not you'd like us to go ahead with this on your behalf. For the record, the story was submitted to the following markets before going to *Denver: Saturday Evening Post, New Yorker, Ladies' Home Journal, Cosmopolitan, McCall's, Good Housekeeping,*

Redbook, Atlantic Monthly, Cosmopolitan (resubmitted), *Esquire, Harper's Bazaar, Vogue, Mademoiselle, Reporter, Harper's Hudson Review, Kenyon Review, Virginia Quarterly, Ladies' Home Journal* (resubmitted), *Paris Review, Yale Review* and *Sewanee Review.* All best . . ."

All best indeed. The story appeared in the winter 1967 issue of *The Denver Quarterly.* By winter 1967 I had begun a second novel, and never wrote another story. I doubt that I ever will.

1978

Some Women

Some years ago I had a job, at *Vogue*, which involved going to photographers' studios and watching women being photographed. These were photographs meant not for the fashion but for the "feature" pages of *Vogue*, portraits of women celebrated for one reason or another, known (usually) because they were starring in a movie or appearing in a play or known (less often) because they had pioneered a vaccine or known (more often than we pretended) just because they were known. "Anything at all you're comfortable in," we were instructed to say if the subject ventured to ask what she should wear for the sitting; "We only want you to be yourself." We accepted without question, in other words, the traditional convention of the portrait, which was that somehow, somewhere, in the transaction between artist and subject, the "truth" about the latter would be revealed; that the photographer would penetrate and capture some "essence," some secret of personality or character not apparent to the naked eye.

In fact what occurred in these sittings, as in all portrait sittings, was a transaction of an entirely opposite kind: success was understood to depend on the extent to which the subject conspired, tacitly, to be not "herself" but whoever and whatever it was that the photographer wanted to see in the lens. Of those long mornings and afternoons in the studio (whether the studio was uptown or downtown, whether it belonged to Irving Penn or to Bert Stern or to Duane Michals or to one of a dozen other photographers then shooting features for *Vogue*, it was referred to always as just "the studio," a generic workspace, a syntactical reflex left from the years when all *Vogue*'s contract photographers worked in the magazine's own studio) I recall mainly little tricks, small improvisations, the efforts required to ensure that the photographer was seeing what he wanted. I remember one sitting for which the lens was covered with black chiffon. I remember another during which, after the "anything at all" in which the subject had apparently believed herself comfortable had been seen in the Polaroids and declared not what was wanted, I lent the subject my own dress, and worked the rest of the sitting wrapped in my raincoat. Here, then, was an early lesson: there would be in each such photograph a "subject," the woman in the studio, and there would also be a subject, and the two would not necessarily intersect.

This business of the subject is tricky. Whether they are painters or photographers or composers or choreographers or for that matter writers, people whose work it is to make something out of nothing do not much like to talk about what they do or how they do it. They will talk quite freely about the technical tricks involved in what they do, about lighting and filters if they are photographers, about voice and tone and rhythm if they are writers, but not about content. The attempt to analyze one's work, which is to say to know one's subject, is seen as destructive. Superstition prevails, fear that the fragile unfinished something will shatter, vanish, revert to the nothing from which it was made. Jean Cocteau once described all such work as deriving from "a profound indolence, a somnolence in which we indulge ourselves like invalids who try to prolong dreams." In dreams we do not analyze the action, or it vanishes. Gabriel García Márquez once spoke to *The New York Times* about the "bad luck" that would befall him were he to discuss the novel he was then writing; he meant of course that the novel would go away, lose its power to compel his imagination. I once knew I "had" a novel when it presented itself to me as an oil slick, with an iridescent surface; during the several years it took me to finish the novel I mentioned the oil slick to no one, afraid the talismanic hold the image had on me would fade, go flat, go away, like a dream told at breakfast. "If you say too much you lose some of that mystery," Robert Mapplethorpe once told a BBC interviewer who wanted to talk about his work. "You want to be able to pick up on the magic of the moment. That's the rush of doing photography. You don't know why it's happening but it's happening."

One question: If Robert Mapplethorpe's "subjects" here are women, what then is his subject? One answer: His subject is the same as it was when his "subjects" were the men in leather, or the flowers, or the Coral Sea on a low horizon. *You don't know why it's happening but it's happening.* "I was a Catholic boy," he also told the BBC. "I went to church every Sunday. The way I arrange things is very Catholic. It's always been that way when I put things together. Very symmetrical."

Of the women Robert Mapplethorpe chose to photograph during the course of his career, most were well known, figures of considerable celebrity or fashion or achievement. There were models and there were actresses. There were singers, dancers, choreographers; makers of art and dealers in art. Most were New York women, with the familiar New York edge. Most were conventionally "pretty," even "beautiful," or rendered so not only by the artifices of light and makeup but by the way they presented themselves to the camera: They were professional women, performers before the camera. They were women who knew how to make their way in the world. They were women who knew a lot of things, and what they knew did not, on the evidence, encourage certainty. Some met the camera with closed eyes, as in a carnal swoon, or Victorian faint. Others confronted it so directly as to seem startled into a fleeting madness; these would seem to have been inhabitants of a world in which survival depended on the ability to seduce, beguile, conspire, deceive. *Sing for your supper,* something in these photographs tells us, *and you'll get breakfast.*

Songbirds always eat: this is not a "modern" idea, nor did the women in Mapplethorpe photographs present themselves to us as modern women. There were in some of his photographs the familiar nineteenth-century images of domination and submission, the erotic discomforts of straps and leather and five-inch heels, of those shoes that cause the wearer's flesh to wrinkle at the instep. There were doomed virgins (downcast eyes, clasped hands), and intimations of mortality, skin like marble, faces like masques, a supernatural radiance, the phosphorescent glow we sometimes attribute to angels, and to decaying flesh.

The idealization here was never of the present. Mapplethorpe photographs meant to sell bathing suits suggested not the athleticism associated with an idealized present, not freedom of movement at all, but bondage, and spanking, the sexual dreams of imperial England. The familiar face of Grace Jones, as photographed by Mapplethorpe, suggested not the androgynous future for which it had come to stand but the nineteenth-century passion for the exotic, the romance with Africa, with Egypt. A Mapplethorpe fashion photograph, the naked black "Thomas" dancing with the spectrally white "Dovanna," suggested classical ballet, the pas de deux in which the betrayer courts the betrayed, back from the grave, the prima ballerina from the dance of the shades.

Even little girls, as photographed by Mapplethorpe, seemed Victorian, not children in the modern sense but sentient beings, creatures with barrettes and bunnies but nonetheless grave with responsibility; small adults, who gazed at us with the utter clarity of what they knew and did not yet know. Perversely, of all the women Robert Mapplethorpe photographed, perhaps only Yoko Ono presented herself as "modern," entirely in charge of herself, a woman who had negotiated the demands of sex and celebrity to appear before us as a middle-aged survivor, with sensible lapels, clear eyes, blown hair. There was something interesting in all of this, and willful, and the will was not that of the "subjects."

There was always about Robert Mapplethorpe an astonishing convergence of quite romantic impulses. There was the romance of the apparently unconventional. There was the romance of art for its own sake. There was the willingness to test the outer reaches of the possible, to explore the "interesting" ("I just thought it would be an interesting idea, having a ring through your tit," he told the BBC about the early film *Robert Having His Nipple Pierced*, the romance of the edge). There was the romance of the Catholic boy from the lower-middle-class reaches of Queens ("It wasn't what I wanted," he once said about that) who came to the city and broke on through to the other side, reinvented himself as a Rimbaud of the baths.

That romantic agony should have been revived as the downtown style in the greatest bourgeois city in the modern world at the moment of its decline was, in any historical sense, predictable, and yet Robert Mapplethorpe's work has often been seen as an aesthetic sport, so entirely outside any historical or social context, and so "new," as to resist interpretation. This "newness" has in fact become so fixed an idea about Mapplethorpe that we tend to overlook the source of his strength, which derived, from the beginning, less from the shock of the new than from the shock of the old, from the rather unnerving novelty of exposure to a fixed moral universe. There was always in his work the tension, even the struggle, between light and dark. There was the exaltation of powerlessness. There was the seductiveness of death, the fantasy of crucifixion.

There was, above all, the perilous imposition of order on chaos, of classical form on unthinkable images. *It's always been that way when I put things together. Very symmetrical.* "I don't like that particular word, 'shocking,'" Robert Mapplethorpe told *ARTnews* in late 1988, when he was struggling with illness and was asked one more time to discuss the famous leather photographs. "I'm looking for the unexpected. I'm looking for things I've never seen before. But I have trouble with the word 'shocking' because I'm not really shocked by anything—I was in a position to take those pictures. I felt an obligation to do them." This is the voice of someone whose subject was finally that very symmetry with which he himself had arranged things.

1989

The Long-Distance Runner

There are in my husband's and my house two photographs of Tony Richardson. In the earlier of the two, taken in what must have been 1981, he is riding a dolly on which is mounted a Panaflex camera, somewhere near El Paso, a man deliriously engaged by—besotted by, transformed by—the act of making a picture, in this instance a "big" picture, the kind of picture on which every day the camera rolls costs tens of thousands of dollars, the kind of picture on which the dailies get flown to the studio every night and everyone in the projection room tenses a little when the take numbers flash on the screen, a picture with a big crew and a bankable star, Jack Nicholson, *The Border*. The more recent photograph was taken on an exterior location in Spain during the late fall of 1989. What appears to be a master shot is in progress. We see the camera operator, the sound boom, the reflector. We see the actors, James Woods and Melanie Griffith. And, over in the far left of the frame, in jeans and tennis shoes and a red parka, we see the director, a man visibly less well than he seemed riding the dolly outside El Paso but just as deliriously engaged by—besotted by, transformed by—the act of making a picture, in this case a twenty-one-minute film for television, an adaptation of Ernest Hemingway's "Hills Like White Elephants" for HBO.

I never knew anyone who so loved to make things, or anyone who had such limited interest in what he had already made. What Tony loved was the sheer act of doing it: whether what he was making was a big picture or theater or twenty-one minutes for television, its particular nature or potential success or potential audience was to him irrelevant, of no interest, not in the least the point. The purity of his enthusiasm for making, say, an *As You Like It* to run for a few nights at a community theater in Long Beach, or an *Antony and Cleopatra* starring television actors at a theater in downtown Los Angeles, was total: the notion that these projects might have less intrinsic potential than the productions of the same plays he had done in London with Vanessa Redgrave remained alien to him. "Something absolutely magical happens at the end," I remember him promising about the downtown *Antony and Cleopatra*. He was talking not about his work but about *working*, about everyone making the moment together in some larger proscenium. "Everything is magic, a dream," I remember him announcing when he called from Spain to ask for a minor adjustment (the script, which my husband and I had written, called for the principals to wade in a stream, but the available stream was too cold) on "Hills Like White Elephants." He was talking, again, not about his work but about working, about that suspended state of being in which the cold stream and the olive grove and the not entirely well man in the red parka could be composed and recomposed, controlled, remembered just that way.

"Magic" was what Tony always wanted, in life as in work, and, like most people who love what they do, he made no distinctions between the two. "I want it to be magic," he would say, whether he was planning a picture or an improvised theatrical at his house or a moonlight picnic on the beach: he wanted magic, and he made it, and in the interests of making it he would mortgage his house, put up his own completion bonds, start shooting on the eve of an actors' strike. When he was not making a picture or theater he would make the same kind of magic happen at home: a lunch or a dinner or a summer was for him raw footage, something to shoot and see how it printed. His house was a set, filled with flowers and birds and sunlight and children, with old loves and current loves, with every conceivable confrontational possibility; forests of Arden, Prospero's island, a director's conceit. "Come to France with me in July," I recall him saying one night at dinner, and when my husband and I said we could not, he turned to our daughter, then fourteen, and announced that in that case she would come alone. She did. There seemed to be dozens of people in Tony's conceit that July, and by the time we arrived to pick up Quintana she was swimming topless in St. Tropez, dancing all night, speaking French, and was being courted by two Italians under the misapprehension that she was on vacation from UCLA. "This has been absolutely magical," Tony said.

It was also in the interests of making this magic that Tony could be so famously dogmatic, contrary, relentlessly ready to strand himself on whatever limb seemed likely to draw lightning. Quite often, for example, I heard him speak emphatically and enthusiastically about the virtues of "colorizing" black-and-white motion pictures, in each case to someone who had just signed a letter or written an op-ed piece or obtained an injunction opposing colorization. "If they had had color, they would have shot color," he would say, emphasizing each syllable equally, the declarative enunciation that gave him what John Osborne once described as "the most imitated voice in his profession." "*That is just pretentious nonsense. Color is better.*" On two occasions I heard him rise to a passionate defense of the tennis player John McEnroe, who had done, Tony declared, "the most glorious thing" by throwing down his racket in a match at Wimbledon; the case Tony made derived partly, of course, from his quite fundamental anarchism, his essential loathing of the English class system and attendant sporting rituals.

Yet it derived equally from a simple wish to provoke the listener, structure the evening, make the scene work. Tony thrived on the very moments most of us try to avoid. Social consensus was to him unthinkable, stifling, everything he had left behind. Raised voices were the stuff of theater, of freedom. I remember him calling on the morning after a dinner in Beverly Hills that had abruptly become a shambles when my husband and an old friend, Brian Moore, began shouting at each other. There had been eight at the table (six, after my husband walked out and I fled), including Tony, whose delight in the turn the dinner had taken seemed absolute: the fight was the unexpected "magic" of the evening, the quiet dinner among friends dissolving into peril, the dramatic possibility realized.

> I thought of the first sheep I ever remember seeing—hundreds of them, and how our car drove suddenly into them on the back lot of the old Laemmle studio. They

were unhappy about being in pictures, but the men in the car with us kept saying:

"Is that what you wanted, Dick?"

"Isn't that swell?" And the man named Dick kept standing up in the car as if he were Cortez or Balboa, looking over that gray fleecy undulation.

—F. SCOTT FITZGERALD, *The Last Tycoon*

Tony died, of a neurological infection resulting from AIDS, at St. Vincent's Hospital in Los Angeles on the fourteenth of November, 1991. He had begun this book some years before, during one of the many periods when he was waiting for one or another script or element or piece of financing to fall into place so that he could once again stand up in the car as if he were Cortez or Balboa and look out over whatever it was he wanted to make. Most people who make pictures learn to endure these periods of enforced idleness, some better than others, and since Tony was one of the others, he tended during such periods to multiply whatever balls he had in the air, commission a new script, meet one last time with the moneyman, undertake some particularly arduous excursion ("You just don't like to have fun," he said accusingly when I declined to consider a weekend trip that involved cholera shots), *improve the moment*. Writing this book, he said on the evening he first mentioned it, was "something to do," and then he did not mention it again. When we asked, some time later, he said that he had abandoned it. "It is worthless," I remember him saying. "Absolutely worthless." Whether he believed that the book was worthless, or that the act of writing it was worthless, or that looking back itself was worthless, I never knew.

Nor did I know, until the afternoon of the day he died, when someone who had typed for him gave his daughters this manuscript, that he had finished the book, and I am still not at all sure when he finished it. The book does not deal with the work he did during the seven years between *The Hotel New Hampshire* and the time he died, and he mentions in the closing pages that he is fifty-seven, which would seem to suggest that he wrote them six years before he died, yet there is about those closing pages a finality, an uncharacteristic sense of *adieu*. This was not a man who had much interest in looking back. Nor was this a man afflicted by despair; the only time I ever saw him wretched was when he perceived a sadness or pain or even a moment of fleeting uncertainty in one of his daughters. And yet he wrote:

> Snapshots of my three daughters look directly at me from a bulletin board as I'm writing. And as one of their gazes makes contact they seem to be asking the one question—what's ahead? In the theatre just as there's a well-known superstition you can't ever quote or mention "the Scottish play" *Macbeth* without bringing bad luck, there's also a superstition that you should never say the last word or the last couplet of a Restoration play until the first night. I'm finding this as hard to finish as to say that last word. I can say to Natasha and Joely and Katharine I love them very much, but I sense they want more.

Did he know for six years that he was dying? Or would he say that to speak of "dying" in that sense is sentimental nonsense, since we are all dying? "There isn't an answer," he wrote earlier in this book about learning something he had not known about someone he loved. "Just a kind of spooky sadness—angels passing over us, or like that moment in Act II of *The Cherry Orchard* when Madame Ranevsky hears a distant sound like the string of a violin snapping." I suppose there were not many weeks during those six years when we did not talk or have lunch or spend an evening together. We spent holidays together. His daughter Natasha was married in our house. I loved him. And yet I have no idea.

1993

Last Words

In the late summer of that year we lived in a house in a village that looked across the river and the plain to the mountains. In the bed of the river there were pebbles and boulders, dry and white in the sun, and the water was clear and swiftly moving and blue in the channels. Troops went by the house and down the road and the dust they raised powdered the leaves of the trees. The trunks of the trees too were dusty and the leaves fell early that year and we saw the troops marching along the road and the dust rising and leaves, stirred by the breeze, falling and the soldiers marching and afterward the road bare and white except for the leaves.

So goes the famous first paragraph of Ernest Hemingway's *A Farewell to Arms*, which I was moved to re-read by the recent announcement that what was said to be Hemingway's last novel would be published posthumously next year. That paragraph, which was published in 1929, bears examination: four deceptively simple sentences, 126 words, the arrangement of which remains as mysterious and thrilling to me now as it did when I first read them, at twelve or thirteen, and imagined that if I studied them closely enough and practiced hard enough I might one day arrange 126 such words myself. Only one of the words has three syllables. Twenty-two have two. The other 103 have one. Twenty-four of the words are "the," fifteen are "and." There are four commas. The liturgical cadence of the paragraph derives in part from the placement of the commas (their presence in the second and fourth sentences, their absence in the first and third), but also from that repetition of "the" and of "and," creating a rhythm so pronounced that the omission of "the" before the word "leaves" in the fourth sentence ("and we saw the troops marching along the road and the dust rising and leaves, stirred by the breeze, falling") casts exactly what it was meant to cast, a chill, a premonition, a foreshadowing of the story to come, the awareness that the author has already shifted his attention from late summer to a darker season. The power of the paragraph, offering as it does the illusion but not the fact of specificity, derives precisely from this kind of deliberate omission, from the tension of withheld information. In the later summer of *what* year? *What* river, *what* mountains, *what* troops?

We all know the "life" of the man who wrote that paragraph. The rather reckless attractions of the domestic details became fixed in the national memory stream: *Ernest and Hadley have no money, so they ski at Cortina all winter. Pauline comes to stay. Ernest and Hadley are at odds with each other over Pauline, so they all take refuge at Juan-les-Pins. Pauline catches cold, and recuperates at the Waldorf-Astoria.* We have seen the snapshots: the celebrated author fencing with the bulls at Pamplona, fishing for marlin off Havana, boxing at Bimini, crossing the Ebro with the Spanish loyalists, kneeling beside "his" lion or "his" buffalo or "his" oryx on the Serengeti Plain. We have observed the celebrated author's survivors, read his letters, deplored or found lessons in his excesses, in his striking of attitudes, in the humiliations of his claim to personal machismo, in the degradations both derived from and revealed by his apparent tolerance for his own celebrity.

"This is to tell you about a young man named Ernest Hemingway, who lives in Paris (an American), writes for the *transatlantic review* and has a brilliant future," F. Scott Fitzgerald wrote to Maxwell Perkins in 1924. "I'd look him up right away. He's the real thing." By the time "the real thing" had seen his brilliant future both realized and ruined, he had entered the valley of extreme emotional fragility, of depressions so grave that by February of 1961, after the first of what would be two courses of shock treatment, he found himself unable to complete even the single sentence he had agreed to contribute to a ceremonial volume for President John F. Kennedy. Early on the Sunday morning of July 2, 1961, the celebrated author got out of his bed in Ketchum, Idaho, went downstairs, took a double-barrelled Boss shotgun from a storage room in the cellar, and emptied both barrels into the center of his forehead. "I went downstairs," his fourth wife, Mary Welsh Hemingway, reported in her 1976 memoir, *How It Was*, "saw a crumpled heap of bathrobe and blood, the shotgun lying in the disintegrated flesh, in the front vestibule of the sitting room."

The didactic momentum of the biography was such that we sometimes forgot that this was a writer who had in his time made the English language new, changed the rhythms of the way both his own and the next few generations would speak and write and think. The very grammar of a Hemingway sentence dictated, or was dictated by, a certain way of looking at the world, a way of looking but not joining, a way of moving through but not attaching, a kind of romantic individualism distinctly adapted to its time and source. If we bought into those sentences, we would see the troops marching along the road, but we would not necessarily march with them. We would report, but not join. We would make, as Nick Adams made in the Nick Adams stories and as Frederic Henry made in *A Farewell to Arms*, a separate peace: "In the fall the war was always there, but we did not go to it any more."

So pervasive was the effect of this Hemingway diction that it became the voice not only of his admirers but even of those whose approach to the world was in no way grounded in romantic individualism. I recall being surprised, when I was teaching George Orwell in a class at Berkeley in 1975, by how much of Hemingway could be heard in his sentences. "The hills opposite us were grey and wrinkled like the skins of elephants," Orwell had written in *Homage to Catalonia* in 1938. "The hills across the valley of the Ebro were long and white," Hemingway had written in "Hills Like White Elephants" in 1927. "A mass of Latin words falls upon the facts like soft snow, blurring the outlines and covering up all the details," Orwell had written in "Politics and the English Language" in 1946. "I was always embarrassed by the words sacred, glorious, and sacrifice and the expression in vain," Hemingway had written in *A Farewell to Arms* in 1929. "There were many words that you could not stand to hear and finally only the names of places had dignity."

This was a man to whom words mattered. He worked at them, he understood them, he got inside them. When he was twenty-four years old and reading submissions to Ford Madox Ford's *Transatlantic Review* he would sometimes try rewriting them, just for practice. His wish to be survived by only the words he determined fit for publication would have seemed clear enough. "I remember Ford telling me that a man should always write a letter thinking of how it would read to posterity," he wrote to Arthur Mizener in 1950. "This made such a bad impression on me that I burned every letter in the flat including Ford's." In a letter dated May 20, 1958, addressed "To my Executors" and placed in his library safe at La Finca Vigía, he wrote, "It is my wish that none of the letters written by me during my lifetime shall be published. Accordingly, I hereby request and direct you not to publish or consent to the publication by others of any such letters."

His widow and executor, Mary Welsh Hemingway, describing the burden of this restriction as one that "caused me continuous trouble, and disappointment to others," eventually chose to violate it, publishing excerpts from certain letters in *How It Was* and granting permission to Carlos Baker to publish some six hundred others in his *Ernest Hemingway: Selected Letters, 1917–1961*. "There can be no question about the wisdom and rightness of the decision," Baker wrote, for the letters "will not only instruct and entertain the general reader but also provide serious students of literature with the documents necessary to the continuing investigation of the life and achievements of one of the giants of twentieth-century American fiction."

The peculiarity of being a writer is that the entire enterprise involves the mortal humiliation of seeing one's own words in print. The risk of publication is the grave fact of the life, and, even among writers less inclined than Hemingway to construe words as the manifest expression of personal honor, the notion that words one has not risked publishing should be open to "continuing investigation" by "serious students of literature" could not be calculated to kindle enthusiasm. "Nobody likes to be tailed," Hemingway himself had in 1952 advised one such investigator, Charles A. Fenton of Yale, who on the evidence of the letters was tormenting Hemingway by sending him successive drafts of what would be *The Apprenticeship of Ernest Hemingway: The Early Years*. "You do not like to be tailed, investigated, queried about, by any amateur detective no matter how scholarly or how straight. You ought to be able to see that, Fenton." A month later Hemingway tried again. "I think you ought to drop the entire project," he wrote to Fenton, adding, "It is impossible to arrive at any truth without the co-operation of the person involved. That co-operation involves very nearly as much effort as for a man to write his autobiography." A few months later, he was still trying:

> In the first page or pages of your Mss. I found so many errors of fact that I could spend the rest of this winter re-writing and giving you the true gen and I would not be able to write anything of my own at all. . . . Another thing: You have located unsigned pieces by me through pay vouchers. But you do not know which pieces were changed or re-written by the copy desk and which were not. I know nothing worse for a writer than for his early writing which has been re-written and altered to be published without permission as his own.
>
> Actually I know few things worse than for another writer to collect a fellow writer's journalism which his fellow writer has elected not to preserve because it is worthless and publish it.
>
> Mr. Fenton I feel very strongly about this. I have written you so before and I write you now again. Writing that I do not wish to publish, you have no right to publish. I would no more do a thing like that to you than I would cheat a man at cards or rifle his desk or wastebasket or read his personal letters.

It might seem safe to assume that a writer who commits suicide has been less than entirely engaged by the work he leaves unfinished, yet there appears to have been not much question about what would happen to the unfinished Hemingway manuscripts. These included not only "the Paris stuff" (as he called it), or *A Moveable Feast* (as Scribner's called it), which Hemingway had in fact shown to Scribner's in 1959 and then withdrawn for revision, but also the novels later published under the titles *Islands in the Stream* and *The Garden of Eden*, several Nick Adams stories, what Mrs. Hemingway called the "original treatment" of the bullfighting pieces published by *Life* before Hemingway's death (this became *The Dangerous Summer*), and what she described as "his semi-fictional account of our African safari," three selections from which she had published in *Sports Illustrated* in 1971 and 1972.

What followed was the systematic creation of a marketable product, a discrete body of work different in kind from, and in fact tending to obscure, the body of work published by Hemingway in his lifetime. So successful was the process of branding this product that in October, according to the House & Home section of *The New York Times*, Thomasville Furniture Industries introduced an "Ernest Hemingway Collection" at the International Home Furnishings Market in High Point, North Carolina, offering "96 pieces of living, dining and bedroom furniture and accessories" in four themes, "Kenya," "Key West," "Havana," and "Ketchum." "We don't have many heroes today," Marla A. Metzner, the president of Fashion Licensing of America, told the *Times*. "We're going back to the great icons of the century, as heroic brands." Ms. Metzner, according to the *Times*, not only "created the Ernest Hemingway brand with Hemingway's three sons, Jack, Gregory and Patrick," but "also represents F. Scott Fitzgerald's grandchildren, who have asked for a Fitzgerald brand."

That this would be the logical outcome of posthumous marketing cannot have been entirely clear to Mary Welsh Hemingway. During Hemingway's lifetime, she appears to have remained cool to the marketing impulses of A. E. Hotchner, whose thirteen-year correspondence with Hemingway gives the sense that he regarded the failing author not as the overextended and desperate figure the letters suggest but as an infinite resource, a mine to be worked, an element to be packaged into his various entertainment and publishing "projects."

The widow tried to stop the publication of Hotchner's *Papa Hemingway*, and, although the correspondence makes clear that Hemingway himself had both trusted and relied heavily on its author, presented him in her own memoir mainly as a kind of personal assistant, a fetcher of manuscripts, an arranger of apartments, a Zelig apparition in crowd scenes: "When the *Ile de France* docked in the Hudson River at noon, March 27, we were elated to find Charlie Sweeny, my favorite general, awaiting us, together with Lillian Ross, Al Horowitz, Hotchner and some others."

In this memoir, which is memorable mainly for the revelation of its author's rather trying mixture of quite striking competence and strategic incompetence (she arrives in Paris on the day it is liberated and scores a room at the Ritz, but seems bewildered by the domestic problem of how to improve the lighting of the dining room at La Finca Vigía), Mary Welsh Hemingway shared her conviction, at which she appears to have arrived in the face of considerable contrary evidence, that her husband had "clearly" expected her to publish "some, if not all, of his work." The guidelines she set for herself in this task were instructive: "Except for punctuation and the obviously overlooked 'ands' and 'buts' we would present his prose and poetry to readers as he wrote it, letting the gaps lie where they were."

Well, there you are. You care about the punctuation or you don't, and Hemingway did. You care about the "ands" and the "buts" or you don't, and Hemingway did. You think something is in shape to be published or you don't, and Hemingway didn't. "This is it; there are no more books," Charles Scribner III told *The New York Times* by way of announcing the "Hemingway novel" to be published in July of 1999, to celebrate the centennial year of his birth. This piece of work, for which the title *True at First Light* was chosen from the text ("In Africa a thing is true at first light and a lie by noon and you have no more respect for it than for the lovely, perfect weed-fringed lake you see across the sun-baked salt plain"), is said to be the novel on which Hemingway was trying intermittently to work between 1954, when he and Mary Welsh Hemingway returned from the safari in Kenya which provides its narrative, and his suicide in 1961.

This "African novel" seems to have presented at first only the resistance that characterizes the early stage of any novel. In September of 1954, Hemingway wrote to Bernard Berenson from Cuba about the adverse effect of air conditioning on this thing he was doing: "You get the writing done but it's as false as though it were done in the reverse of a greenhouse. Probably I will throw it all away, but maybe when the mornings are alive again I can use the skeleton of what I have written and fill it in with the smells and the early noises of the birds and all the lovely things of this finca which are in the cold months very much like Africa." In September of 1955, he wrote again to Berenson, this time on a new typewriter, explaining that he could not use his old one "because it has page 594 of the [African] book in it, covered over with the dust cover, and it is unlucky to take the pages out." In November of 1955, he reported to Harvey Breit, of *The New York Times*, "Am on page 689 and wish me luck kid." In January of 1956, he wrote to his attorney, Alfred Rice, that he had reached page 810.

There then falls, in the *Selected Letters*, a certain silence on the matter of this African novel. Eight hundred and ten pages or no, there comes a point at which every writer knows when a book is not working, and every writer also knows when the reserves of will and energy and memory and concentration required to make the thing work simply may not be available. "You just have to *go on* when it is worst and most helpless—there is only one thing to do with a novel and that is go straight on through to the end of the damn thing," Hemingway had written to F. Scott Fitzgerald in 1929, when Fitzgerald was blocked on the novel that would be published in 1934 as *Tender Is the Night*.

In 1929, Hemingway was thirty. His concentration, or his ability to "*go on* when it is worst and most helpless," was still such that he had continued rewriting *A Farewell to Arms* while trying to deal, in the aftermath of his father's suicide in December of 1928, with the concerns of his mother, his sixteen-year-old sister, and his thirteen-year-old brother. "Realize of course that thing for me to do is not worry but get to work—finish my book properly so I can help them out with the proceeds," he had written to Maxwell Perkins within days of his father's funeral, and six weeks later he delivered the finished manuscript. He had seen one marriage destroyed, but not yet three. He was not yet living with the residue of the two 1954 plane crashes that had ruptured his liver, his spleen, and one of his kidneys, collapsed his lower intestine, crushed a vertebra, left first-degree burns on his face and head, and caused concussion and losses of vision and hearing. "Alfred this was a very rough year even before we smashed up in the air-craft," he wrote to Alfred Rice, who had apparently questioned his tax deductions for the African safari:

> But I have a diamond mine if people will let me alone and let me dig the stones out of the blue mud and then cut and polish them. If I can do it I will make more money for the Government than any Texas oilman that gets his depreciation. But I have been beat-up worse than you can be and still be around and I should be working steadily on getting better and then write and not think nor worry about anything else.

"The literal details of writing," Norman Mailer once told an interviewer, "involve one's own physiology or metabolism. You begin from a standing start and have to accelerate yourself to the point of cerebration where the words are coming—well, and in order. All writing is generated by a certain minimum of ego: you must assume a position of authority in saying that the way I'm writing it is the only way it happened. Writer's block, for example, is simply a failure of ego." In August of 1956, Hemingway advised Charles Scribner, Jr., that he had "found it impossible to resume work on the Africa book without some disciplinary writing," and so was writing short stories.

In November of 1958, he mentioned to one of his children that he wanted to "finish book" during a winter stay in Ketchum, but the "book" at issue was now "the Paris stuff."

In April of 1960, he told Scribner to scratch this still untitled Paris book from the fall list: "Plenty of people will probably think that we have no book and that it is like all the outlines that Scott had and borrowed money on that he never could have finished but you know that if I did not want the chance to make it even better it could be published exactly as you saw it with a few corrections of Mary's typing." Ten months later, and five months before his death, in a letter written to his editor at Scribner's between the two courses of shock treatment administered to him at the Mayo Clinic in Rochester, Minnesota, the writer tried, alarmingly, to explain what he was doing:

> Have material arranged as chapters—they come to 18—and am working on the last one—No *19*—also working on title. This is very difficult. (Have my usual long list—something wrong with all of them but am working toward it—Paris has been used so often it blights anything.) In pages typed they run 7, 14, 5, 6, 9½, 6, 11, 9, 8, 9, 4½, 3½, 8, 10½, 14½, 38½, 10, 3, 3: 177 pages + 5½ pages + 1¼ pages.

I recall listening, some years ago at a dinner party in Berkeley, to a professor of English present *The Last Tycoon* as irrefutable proof that F. Scott Fitzgerald was a bad writer. The assurance with which this judgment was offered so stunned me that I had let it slip into the *donnée* of the evening before I managed to object. *The Last Tycoon*, I said, was an unfinished book, one we had no way of judging because we had no way of knowing how Fitzgerald might have finished it. But of course we did, another guest said, and others joined in: We had Fitzgerald's "notes," we had Fitzgerald's "outline," the thing was "entirely laid out." Only one of us at the table that evening, in other words, saw a substantive difference between writing a book and making notes for it, or "outlining it," or "laying it out."

The most chilling scene ever filmed must be, for a writer, that moment in *The Shining* when Shelley Duvall looks at the manuscript on which her husband has been working and sees, typed over and over again on each of the hundreds of pages, only the single line: "All work and no play makes Jack a dull boy." The manuscript for what became *True at First Light* was, as Hemingway left it, some 850 pages long. The manuscript as edited for publication is half that. This editing was done by Hemingway's son Patrick, who has said that he limited his editing to condensing (which inevitably works to alter what the author may have intended, as anyone who has been condensed knows), changing only some of the place names, which may or may not have seemed a logical response to the work of the man who wrote, "There were many words that you could not stand to hear and finally only the names of places had dignity."

This question of what should be done with what a writer leaves unfinished goes back to, and is conventionally answered by, citing works we might have lost had the dying wishes of their authors been honored. Virgil's *Aeneid* is mentioned. Franz Kafka's *The Trial* and *The Castle* are mentioned. In 1951, clearly shadowed by mortality, Hemingway judged that certain parts of a long four-part novel on which he had been working for a number of years were sufficiently "finished" to be published after his death, and specified his terms, which did not include the intrusion of any editorial hand and specifically excluded the publication of the unfinished first section. "The last two parts need no cutting at all," he wrote to Charles Scribner in 1951. "The third part needs quite a lot but it is very careful scalpel work and would need no cutting if I were dead. . . . The reason that I wrote you that you could always publish the last three parts separately is because I know you can in case through accidental death or any sort of death I should not be able to get the first part in proper shape to publish."

Hemingway himself, the following year, published the fourth part of this manuscript separately, as *The Old Man and the Sea*. The "first part" of the manuscript, the part not yet "in proper shape to publish," was, after his death, nonetheless published, as part of *Islands in the Stream*. In the case of the "African novel," or *True at First Light*, 850 pages reduced by half by someone other than their author can go nowhere the author intended them to go, but they can provide the occasion for a chat-show hook, a faux controversy over whether the part of the manuscript in which the writer on safari takes a Wakamba bride does or does not reflect a "real" event. The increasing inability of many readers to construe fiction as anything other than roman à clef, or the raw material of biography, is both indulged and encouraged. *The New York Times*, in its announcement of the publication of the manuscript, quoted Patrick Hemingway to this spurious point: " 'Did Ernest Hemingway have such an experience?' he said from his home in Bozeman, Montana. 'I can tell you from all I know—and I don't know everything—he did not.' "

This is a denial of the idea of fiction, just as the publication of unfinished work is a denial of the idea that the role of the writer in his or her work is to make it. Those excerpts from *True at First Light* already published can be read only as something not yet made, notes, scenes in the process of being set down, words set down but not yet written. There are arresting glimpses here and there, fragments shored against what the writer must have seen as his ruin, and a sympathetic reader might well believe it possible that had the writer lived (which is to say had the writer found the will and energy and memory and concentration) he might have shaped the material, written it into being, made it work as the story the glimpses suggest, that of a man returning to a place he loved and finding himself at three in the morning confronting the knowledge that he is no longer the person who loved it and will never now be the person he had meant to be. But of course such a possibility would have been in the end closed to this particular writer, for he had already written that story, in 1936, and called it "The Snows of Kilimanjaro." "Now he would never write the things that he had saved to write until he knew enough to write them well," the writer in "The Snows of Kilimanjaro" thought as he lay dying of gangrene in Africa. And then, this afterthought, the saddest story: "Well, he would not have to fail at trying to write them either."

1998

Everywoman.com

According to "The Web Guide to Martha Stewart—The UNOFFICIAL Site!," which was created by a former graduate student named Kerry Ogata as "a thesis procrastination technique" and then passed on to those who now maintain it, the fifty-eight-year-old chairman and CEO of Martha Stewart Living Omnimedia LLC ("MSO" on the New York Stock Exchange) needs only four hours of sleep a night, utilizes the saved hours by grooming her six cats and gardening by flashlight, prefers Macs in the office and a PowerBook for herself, commutes between her house in Westport and her two houses in East Hampton and her Manhattan apartment in a GMC Suburban ("with chauffeur") or a Jaguar XJ6 ("she drives herself"), was raised the second-oldest of six children in a Polish-American family in Nutley, New Jersey, has one daughter, Alexis, and survived "a non-amicable divorce" from her husband of twenty-six years, Andrew Stewart ("Andy" on the site), who then "married Martha's former assistant who is 21 years younger than he is."

Contributors to the site's "Opinions" page, like good friends everywhere, have mixed feelings about Andy's defection, which occurred in 1987, while Martha was on the road promoting *Martha Stewart Weddings*, the preface to which offered a possibly prescient view of her own 1961 wedding. "I was a naïve nineteen-year-old, still a student at Barnard, and Andy was beginning Yale Law School, so it seemed appropriate to be married in St. Paul's Chapel at Columbia in an Episcopalian service, mainly because we didn't have anyplace else to go," she wrote, and included a photograph showing the wedding dress she and her mother had made of embroidered Swiss organdy bought on West Thirty-eighth Street. Online, the relative cases of "Martha" and of "Andy" and even of "Alexis," who originally took her mother's side in the divorce, get debated with startling familiarity. "BTW: I don't blame Andy," one contributor offers. "I think he took all he could. I think it's too bad that Alexis felt she had to choose." Another contributor, another view: "I work fifty hours a week and admit sometimes I don't have time to 'be all that I can be' but when Martha started out she was doing this part-time and raising Alexis and making a home for that schmuck Andy (I bet he is sorry he ever left her)."

Although "The UNOFFICIAL Site!" is just that, unofficial, "not affiliated with Martha Stewart, her agents, Martha Stewart Living Omnimedia, LLC or any other Martha Stewart Enterprises," its fairly lighthearted approach to its subject's protean competence ("What can't Martha do? According to Martha herself, 'Hang-gliding, and I hate shopping for clothes'") should in no way be construed as disloyalty to Martha's objectives, which are, as the prospectus prepared for Martha Stewart Living Omnimedia's initial public offering last October explained, "to provide our original 'how-to' content and information to as many consumers as possible" and "to turn our consumers into 'doers' by offering them the information and products they need for do-it-yourself ingenuity 'the Martha Stewart way.'" The creators and users of "The UNOFFICIAL Site!" clearly maintain a special relationship with the subject at hand, as do the creators and users of other unofficial or self-invented sites crafted in the same spirit: "My Martha Stewart Page," say, or "Gothic Martha Stewart," which advises teenagers living at home on how they can "goth up" their rooms without alarming their parents ("First of all, don't paint everything black") by taking their cues from Martha.

"Martha adores finding old linens and gently worn furniture at flea markets," users of "Gothic Martha Stewart" are reminded. "She sews a lot of her own household dressings. She paints and experiments with unusual painting techniques on objects small and large. She loves flowers, live and dried . . . and even though her surroundings look very rich, many of her ideas are created from rather simple and inexpensive materials, like fabric scraps and secondhand dishes." For the creator of "My Martha

Stewart Page," even the "extremely anal" quality of Martha's expressed preoccupation with the appearance of her liquid-detergent dispenser can be a learning experience, a source of concern that becomes a source of illumination: "It makes me worry about her. . . . Of course it is just this strangeness that makes me love her. She helps me know I'm OK—everyone's OK. . . . She seems perfect, but she's not. She's obsessed. She's frantic. She's a control freak beyond my wildest dreams. And that shows me two things: A) no one is perfect and B) there's a price for everything."

There is an unusual bonding here, a proprietary intimacy that eludes conventional precepts of merchandising to go to the very heart of the enterprise, the brand, what Martha prefers to call the "presence": the two magazines (*Martha Stewart Living* and *Martha Stewart Weddings*) that between them reach 10 million readers, the twenty-seven books that have sold 8.5 million copies, the weekday radio show carried on 270 stations, the syndicated "AskMartha" column that appears in 233 newspapers, the televised show six days a week on CBS, the weekly slot on the CBS morning show, the cable-TV show (*From Martha's Kitchen*, the Food Network's top-rated weekly show among women aged twenty-five to fifty-four), the website (www.marthastewart.com) with more than one million registered users and 627,000 hits a month, the merchandising tie-ins with Kmart and Sears and Sherwin-Williams (Kmart alone last year sold more than a billion dollars' worth of Martha Stewart merchandise), the catalogue operation (Martha by Mail), from which some 2,800 products (Valentine Garlands, Valentine Treat Bags, Ready-to-Decorate Cookies, Sweetheart Cake Rings, Heart Dessert Scoops, Heart Rosette Sets, Heart-Shaped Pancake Molds, and Lace-Paper Valentine Kits, to name a few from the online "Valentine's Day" pages) can be ordered either from the catalogues themselves (eleven annual editions, 15 million copies) or from webpages with exceptionally inviting layouts and seductively logical links.

These products are not inexpensive. The Lace-Paper Valentine Kit contains enough card stock and paper lace to make "about forty" valentines, which could be viewed as something less than a buy at forty-two dollars plus time and labor. On the "Cakes and Cake Stands" page, the Holiday Cake-Stencil Set, which consists of eight nine-inch plastic stencils for the decorative dusting of cakes with confectioner's sugar or cocoa, sells for twenty-eight dollars. On the "marthasflowers" pages, twenty-five tea roses, which are available for eighteen dollars a dozen at Roses Only in New York, cost fifty-two dollars, and the larger of the two "suggested vases" to put them in (an example of the site's linking logic) another seventy-eight dollars. A set of fifty Scalloped Tulle Rounds, eight-and-three-quarter-inch circles of tulle in which to tie up wedding favors, costs eighteen dollars, and the seam binding used to tie them ("sold separately," another natural link) costs, in the six-color Seam-Binding Ribbon Collection, fifty-six dollars. Seam binding sells retail for pennies, and, at Paron on West Fifty-seventh Street in New York, not the least expensive source, 108-inch-wide tulle sells for four dollars a yard. Since the amount of 108-inch tulle required to make fifty Scalloped Tulle Rounds would be slightly over a yard, the online buyer can be paying only for the imprimatur of "Martha," whose genius it was to take the once familiar notion of doing-it-yourself to previously uncharted territory: somewhere east of actually doing it yourself, somewhere west of paying Robert Isabell to do it.

This is a billion-dollar company the only real product of which, in other words, is Martha Stewart herself, an unusual business condition acknowledged in the prospectus prepared for Martha Stewart Living Omnimedia's strikingly successful October IPO. "Our business would be adversely affected if: Martha Stewart's public image or reputation were to be tarnished," the "Risk Factors" section of the prospectus read in part. "Martha Stewart, as well as her name, her image, and the trademarks and other intellectual property rights relating to these, are integral to our marketing efforts and form the core of our brand name. Our continued success and the value of our brand name therefore depends, to a large degree, on the reputation of Martha Stewart."

The perils of totally identifying a brand with a single living and therefore vulnerable human being were much discussed around the time of the IPO, and the question of what would happen to Martha Stewart Living Omnimedia if Martha Stewart were to become ill or die ("the diminution or loss of the services of Martha Stewart," in the words of the prospectus) remained open. "That was always an issue for us," Don Logan, the president of Time Inc., told the *Los Angeles Times* in 1997, a few months after Stewart managed to raise enough of what she called "internally generated capital," $53.3 million, to buy herself out of Time Warner, which had been resisting expansion of a business built entirely around a single personality. "I think we are now spread very nicely over an area where our information can be trusted," Stewart herself maintained, and it did seem clear that the very expansion and repetition of the name that had made Time Warner nervous—every "Martha Stewart" item sold, every "Martha Stewart Everyday" commercial aired—was paradoxically serving to insulate the brand from the possible loss of the personality behind it.

The related question, of what would happen if "Martha Stewart's public image or reputation were to be tarnished," seemed less worrisome, since in any practical way the question of whether it was possible to tarnish Martha Stewart's public image or reputation had already been answered, with the 1997 publication and ascension to the *New York Times* best-seller list of *Just Desserts*, an unauthorized biography of Martha Stewart by Jerry Oppenheimer, whose previous books were unauthorized biographies of Rock Hudson, Barbara Walters, and Ethel Kennedy. "My investigative juices began to flow," Oppenheimer wrote in the preface to *Just Desserts*. "If her stories were true, I foresaw a book about a perfect woman who had brought perfection to the masses. If her stories were not true, I foresaw a book that would shatter myths."

Investigative juices flowing, Oppenheimer discovered that Martha was "driven." Martha, moreover, sometimes "didn't tell the whole story." Martha could be "a real screamer" when situations did not go as planned, although the case Oppenheimer makes on this point suggests, at worst, merit on both sides. Martha was said to have "started to shriek," for example, when a catering partner backed a car over the "picture-perfect" Shaker picnic basket she had just finished packing with her own blueberry pies. Similarly, Martha was said to have been "just totally freaked" when a smokehouse fire interrupted the shooting of a holiday special and she found that the hose she had personally dragged to the smokehouse ("followed by various blasé crew people, faux-concerned family members, smirking kitchen assistants, and a macho Brazilian groundskeeper") was too short to reach the flames. After running back to the house, getting an extension for the hose, and putting out the fire, Martha, many would think understandably, exchanged words with the groundskeeper, "whom she fired on the spot in front of everyone after he talked back to her."

Other divined faults include idealizing her early family life (p. 34), embellishing "everything" (p. 42), omitting a key ingredient when a rival preteen caterer asked for her chocolate-cake recipe (p. 43), telling readers of *Martha Stewart Living* that she had as a young girl "sought to discover the key to good literature" even though "a close friend" reported that she had "passionately devoured" the Nancy Drew and Cherry Ames novels (p. 48), misspelling "villainous" in a review of William Makepeace Thackeray's *Vanity Fair* for the Nutley High School literary magazine (p. 51), having to ask what Kwanza was during a 1995 appearance on *Larry King Live* (p. 71), and not only wanting a larger engagement diamond than the one Andy had picked out for her at Harry Winston but obtaining it, at a better price, in the diamond district (p. 101). "That should have set off an alarm," a "lifelong friend" told Oppenheimer. "How many women would do something like that? It was a bad omen."

This lumping together of insignificant immaturities and economies for conversion into character flaws (a former assistant in the catering business Martha ran in Westport during the 1970s presents the damning charge "Nothing went to waste. . . . Martha's philosophy was like someone at a restaurant who had eaten half his steak and tells the waiter 'Oh, wrap it up, and I'll take it home'") continues for 414 pages, at which point

Oppenheimer, in full myth-shattering mode, reveals his trump card, "an eerie corporate manifesto" that "somehow slipped out of Martha's offices and made its way from one Time Inc. executive's desk to another and eventually from a Xerox machine to the outside world. . . . The white paper, replete with what was described as an incomprehensible flow chart, declared, in part":

> In Martha's vision, the shared value of the MSL enterprises are highly personal—reflecting her individual goals, beliefs, values and aspirations. . . . "Martha's Way" can be obtained because she puts us in direct touch with everything we need to know, and tells/shows us exactly what we have to do. . . . MSL enterprises are founded on the proposition that Martha herself is both leader and teacher. . . . While the ranks of "teaching disciples" within MSL may grow and extend, their authority rests on their direct association with Martha; their work emanates from her approach and philosophies; and their techniques, and products and results meet her test. . . . The magazine, books, television series, and other distribution sources are only vehicles to enable personal communication with Martha. . . . She is not, and won't allow herself to be, an institutional image and fiction like Betty Crocker. . . . She is the creative and driving center. . . . By listening to Martha and following her lead, we can achieve real results in our homes too—ourselves—just like she has. . . . It is easy to do. Martha has already "figured it out." She will personally take us by the hand and show us how to do it.

Oppenheimer construes this purloined memo or mission statement as sinister, of a piece with the Guyana Kool-Aid massacre ("From its wording, some wondered whether Martha's world was more gentrified Jonestown than happy homemaker"), but in fact it remains an unexceptionable, and quite accurate, assessment of what makes the enterprise go. Martha Stewart Living Omnimedia LLC connects on a level that transcends the absurdly labor-intensive and in many cases prohibitively expensive table settings and decorating touches (the "poinsettia wreath made entirely of ribbon" featured on one December show would require of even a diligent maker, Martha herself allowed, "a couple of hours" and, "if you use the very best ribbon, two or three hundred dollars") over which its chairman toils six mornings a week on CBS. Nor is the connection about her recipes, which are the recipes of Sunbelt Junior League cookbooks (Grapefruit Mimosas, Apple Cheddar Turnovers, and Southwestern Style S'Mores are a few from the most recent issue of *Martha Stewart Entertaining*), reflecting American middle-class home cooking as it has existed pretty much through the postwar years. There is in a Martha Stewart recipe none of, say, Elizabeth David's transforming logic and assurance, none of Julia Child's mastery of technique.

What there is instead is "Martha," full focus, establishing "personal communication" with the viewer or reader, showing, telling, leading, teaching, "loving it" when the simplest possible shaken-in-a-jar vinaigrette emulsifies right there onscreen. She presents herself not as an authority but as the friend who has "figured it out," the enterprising if occasionally manic neighbor who will waste no opportunity to share an educational footnote. "True," or "Ceylon," cinnamon, the reader of *Martha Stewart Living* will learn, "originally came from the island now called Sri Lanka," and "by the time of the Roman Empire . . . was valued at fifteen times its weight in silver." In a television segment about how to serve champagne, Martha will advise her viewers that the largest champagne bottle, the Balthazar, was named after the king of Babylon, "555 to 539 B.C." While explaining how to decorate the house for the holidays around the theme "The Twelve Days of Christmas," Martha will slip in this doubtful but nonetheless useful gloss, a way for the decorator to perceive herself as doing something more significant than painting pressed-paper eggs with two or three coats of white semigloss acrylic paint, followed by another two or three coats of yellow-tinted acrylic varnish, and finishing the result with ribbon and beads: "With the egg so clearly associated with new life, it is not surprising that the six geese a-laying represented the six days of Creation in the carol."

*

The message Martha is actually sending, the reason large numbers of American women count watching her a comforting and obscurely inspirational experience, seems not very well understood. There has been a flurry of academic work done on the cultural meaning of her success (in the summer of 1998, *The New York Times* reported that "about two dozen scholars across the United States and Canada" were producing such studies as "A Look at Linen Closets: Liminality, Structure and Anti-Structure in Martha Stewart Living" and locating "the fear of transgression" in the magazine's "recurrent images of fences, hedges and garden walls"), but there remains, both in the bond she makes and in the outrage she provokes, something unaddressed, something pitched, like a dog whistle, too high for traditional textual analysis. The outrage, which reaches sometimes startling levels, centers on the misconception that she has somehow tricked her admirers into not noticing the ambition that brought her to their attention. To her critics, she seems to represent a fraud to be exposed, a wrong to be righted. "She's a shark," one declares in *Salon*. "However much she's got, Martha wants more. And she wants it her way and in her world, not in the balls-out boys' club realms of real estate or technology, but in the delicate land of doily hearts and wedding cakes."

"I can't believe people don't see the irony in the fact that this 'ultimate homemaker' has made a multi-million dollar empire out of baking cookies and selling bed sheets," a posting reads in *Salon*'s "ongoing discussion" of Martha. "I read an interview in *Wired* where she said she gets home at 11pm most days, which means she's obviously too busy to be the perfect mom/wife/homemaker—a role which many women feel like they have to live up to because of the image MS projects." Another reader cuts to the chase: "Wasn't there some buzz a while back about Martha stealing her daughter's BF?" The answer: "I thought that was Erica Kane. You know, when she stole Kendra's BF. I think you're getting them confused. Actually, why would any man want to date MS? She is so frigid looking that my television actually gets cold when she's on." "The trouble is that Stewart is about as genuine as Hollywood," a writer in *The Scotsman* charges. "Hers may seem to be a nostalgic siren call for a return to Fifties-style homemaking with an updated elegance, but is she in fact sending out a fraudulent message—putting pressure on American women to achieve impossible perfection in yet another sphere, one in which, unlike ordinary women, Stewart herself has legions of helpers?"

This entire notion of "the perfect mom/wife/homemaker," of the "nostalgic siren call for a return to Fifties-style homemaking," is a considerable misunderstanding of what Martha Stewart actually transmits, the promise she makes her readers and viewers, which is that know-how in the house will translate to can-do outside it. What she offers, and what more strictly professional shelter and food magazines and shows do not, is the promise of transferred manna, transferred luck. She projects a level of taste that transforms the often pointlessly ornamented details of what she is actually doing. The possibility of moving out of the perfected house and into the headier ether of executive action, of doing as Martha does, is clearly presented: "Now I, as a single human being, have six personal fax numbers, fourteen personal phone numbers, seven car-phone numbers, and two cell-phone numbers," as she told readers of *Martha Stewart Living*. On October 19, the evening of her triumphant IPO, she explained, on *The Charlie Rose Show*, the genesis of the enterprise. "I was serving a desire—not only mine, but every homemaker's desire, to elevate that job of homemaker," she said. "It was floundering, I think. And we all wanted to escape it, to get out of the house, get that high-paying job and pay somebody else to do everything that we didn't think was really worthy of our attention. And all of a sudden I realized: it was terribly worthy of our attention."

Think about this. Here was a woman who had elevated "that job of homemaker" to a level where even her GMC Suburban came equipped with a Sony MZ-B3 Minidisc Recorder for dictation and a Sony ICD-50 Recorder for short messages and a Watchman FDL-PT22 TV set, plus phones, plus PowerBook.

Here was a woman whose idea of how to dress for "that job of homemaker" involved Jil Sander. "Jil's responded to the needs of people like me," she is quoted as having said on "The UNOFFICIAL Site!" "I'm busy; I travel a lot; I want to look great in a picture." Here was a woman who had that very October morning been driven down to the big board to dispense brioches and fresh-squeezed orange juice from a striped tent while Morgan Stanley Dean Witter and Merrill Lynch and Bear Stearns and Donaldson, Lufkin & Jenrette and Banc of America Securities increased the value of her personal stock in the company she personally invented to $614 million. This does not play into any "nostalgic siren call" for a return to the kind of "homemaking" that seized America during those postwar years when the conversion of industry to peacetime production mandated the creation of a market for Kelvinators, yet Martha was the first to share the moment with her readers.

"The mood was festive, the business community receptive, and the stock began trading with the new symbol MSO," she confided in her "Letter from Martha" in the December *Martha Stewart Living*, and there between the lines was the promise from the mission statement: *It is easy to do. Martha has already "figured it out." She will personally take us by the hand and show us how to do it.* What she will show us how to do, it turns out, is a little more invigorating than your average poinsettia-wreath project: "The process was extremely interesting, from deciding exactly what the company was (an 'integrated multimedia company' with promising internet capabilities) to creating a complicated and lengthy prospectus that was vetted and revetted (only to be vetted again by the Securities and Exchange Commission) to selling the company with a road show that took us to more than twenty cities in fourteen days (as far off as Europe)." This is getting out of the house with a vengeance, and on your own terms, the secret dream of any woman who has ever made a success of a PTA cake sale. "You could bottle that chili sauce," neighbors say to home cooks all over America. "You could make a fortune on those date bars." You could bottle it, you could sell it, you can survive when all else fails: I myself believed for most of my adult life that I could support myself and my family, in the catastrophic absence of all other income sources, by catering.

The "cultural meaning" of Martha Stewart's success, in other words, lies deep in the success itself, which is why even her troubles and strivings are part of the message, not detrimental but integral to the brand. She has branded herself not as Superwoman but as Everywoman, a distinction that seems to remain unclear to her critics. Martha herself gets it, and talks about herself in print as if catching up her oldest friend. "I sacrificed family, husband," she said in a 1996 *Fortune* conversation with Charlotte Beers, the former CEO of Ogilvy & Mather and a member of Martha Stewart Living Omnimedia's board of directors, and Darla Moore, the president of Richard Rainwater's investment firm and the inventor of "debtor in possession" financing for companies in bankruptcy. The tone of this conversation was odd, considerably more confessional than the average dialogue among senior executives who know they are being taped by *Fortune*. "Not my choice," Martha confided about her divorce. "His choice. Now, I'm so happy that it happened. It took a long time for me to realize that it freed me to do more things. I don't think I would have accomplished what I have if I had stayed married. No way. And it allowed me to make friends that I know I never would have had."

Martha's readers understand her divorce, both its pain and its upside. They saw her through it, just as they saw her through her dealings with the SEC, her twenty-city road show, her triumph on Wall Street. This relationship between Martha and her readers is a good deal more complicated than the many parodies of and jokes about it would allow. "While fans don't grow on fruit trees (well, some do), they can be found all over America: in malls, and Kmarts, in tract houses and trailer parks, in raised ranches, Tudor condos and Winnebagos," the parody Martha is made to say in HarperCollins's *Martha Stuart's Better Than You at Entertaining*. "Wherever there are women dissatisfied with how they live, with who they are and who they are not, that is where you'll find potential fans of mine." These parodies are themselves interesting: too broad, misogynistic in a cartoon way (stripping Martha to her underwear has been a reliable motif of countless online parodies), curiously nervous ("Keeping Razors Circumcision-Sharp" is one feature in *Martha Stuart's Better Than You at Entertaining*), oddly uncomfortable, a little too intent on marginalizing a rather considerable number of women by making light of their situations and their aspirations.

Something here is perceived as threatening, and a glance at "The UNOFFICIAL Site!," the subliminal focus of which is somewhere other than on homemaking skills, suggests what it is. What makes Martha "a good role model in many ways," one contributor writes, is that "she's a strong woman who's in charge, and she has indeed changed the way our country, if not the world, views what used to be called 'women's work.'" From an eleven-year-old: "Being successful is important in life. . . . It is fun to say 'When I become Martha Stewart I'm going to have all the things Martha has.'" Even a contributor who admits to an "essentially anti-Martha persona" admires her "intelligence" and "drive," the way in which this "supreme chef, baker, gardener, decorator, artist, and entrepreneur" showed what it took "to get where she is, where most men aren't and can't. . . . She owns her own corporation in her own name, her own magazine, her own show."

A keen interest in and admiration for business acumen pervades the site. "I know people are threatened by Martha and Time Warner Inc. is going to blow a very 'good thing' if they let Martha and her empire walk in the near future," a contributor to "The UNOFFICIAL Site!" wrote at the time Stewart was trying to buy herself out of Time Warner. "I support Martha in everything she does and I would bet if a man wanted to attach his name to all he did . . . this wouldn't be a question." Their own words tell the story these readers and viewers take from Martha: Martha is *in charge*, Martha is *where most men aren't and can't*, Martha has *her own magazine*, Martha has *her own show*, Martha not only has *her own corporation* but has it *in her own name*.

This is not a story about a woman who made the best of traditional skills. This is a story about a woman who did her own IPO. This is the "woman's pluck" story, the dust-bowl story, the burying-your-child-on-the-trail story, the

I-will-never-go-hungry-again story, the Mildred Pierce story, the story about how the sheer nerve of even professionally unskilled women can prevail, show the men; the story that has historically encouraged women in this country, even as it has threatened men. The dreams and the fears into which Martha Stewart taps are not of "feminine" domesticity but of female power, of the woman who sits down at the table with the men and, still in her apron, walks away with the chips.

2000

ACKNOWLEDGMENTS

Grateful acknowledgment is made to the following for permission to reprint previously published material.

THE YEAR OF MAGICAL THINKING
Columbia University Press: Excerpt from "Re-Grief Therapy" by Dr. Volkan from *Bereavement: Its Psychosocial Aspects*, edited by Schoenberg, Gerber, Wiener, Kutscher, Peretz, and Carr. Copyright © 1975 by Columbia University Press. Reprinted by permission of Columbia University Press. *Harcourt, Inc. & Faber and Faber Ltd.:* Excerpt from "East Coker" in *Four Quartets* by T. S. Eliot. Copyright © 1940 by T. S. Eliot and renewed 1968 by Esme Valerie Eliot. Reprinted by permission of Harcourt, Inc. and Faber and Faber Ltd. *Eugene Kennedy:* Excerpt from a letter written by Eugene Kennedy to Joan Didion. Reprinted by permission of the author. *Liveright Publishing Company:* Excerpt from "Buffalo Bill's." Copyright 1923, 1951, © 1991 by the Trustees for the E. E. Cummings Trust. Copyright © 1976 by George James Firmage, from *Complete Poems: 1904–1962* by E. E. Cummings, edited by George J. Firmage. Reprinted by permission of Liveright Publishing Company. *Massachusetts Medical Society:* Excerpt from "Out-of-Hospital Cardiac Arrest – The Solution Is Shocking" by David J. Callans from *The New England Journal of Medicine* (August 12, 2004). Copyright © 2004 by Massachusetts Medical Society. Reprinted by permission of Massachusetts Medical Society. *Earl McGrath:* Excerpt from a poem written by Earl McGrath. Reprinted by permission of the author. *New Directions Publishing Corp.:* Excerpt from "Calmly We Walk Through This April's Day" by Delmore Schwartz from *Selected Poems: Summer Knowledge*. Copyright © 1959 by Delmore Schwartz. Reprinted by permission of New Directions Publishing Corp. *The New York Times Agency:* Excerpt from "Death Comes Knocking" by Bob Herbert from *The New York Times* (November 12, 2004). Copyright © 2004 by The New York Times Co. Reprinted by permission of The New York Times Agency. *Oxford University Press:* Excerpt from "Spring and Fall," "Heaven-Haven," "No Worst," and "I Wake and Feel" by Gerard Manley Hopkins from *The Poems of Gerard Manley Hopkins*, 4th ed., edited by W. H. Gardner and N. H. MacKenzie (1970). Reprinted by permission of Oxford University Press on behalf of the British Province of the Society of Jesus. *Random House, Inc.:* Excerpt from "Funeral Blues," copyright 1940 and renewed 1968 by W. H.

Auden from *Collected Poems* by W. H. Auden. Reprinted by permission of Random House, Inc. *Viking Penguin:* Excerpt from "Self-Pity" by D. H. Lawrence from *The Complete Poems of D. H. Lawrence* by D. H. Lawrence, edited by V. de Sola Pinto & F. W. Roberts. Copyright © 1964, 1971 by Angelo Ravagli and C. M. Weekley, Executors of the Estate of Frieda Lawrence Ravagli. Reprinted by permission of Viking Penguin, a division of Penguin Group (USA) Inc.

BLUE NIGHTS

Alfred Music Publishing Co., Inc.: Excerpt from "Hotel California," words and music by Don Henley, Glenn Frey, and Don Felder, copyright © 1976, copyright renewed by Cass County Music (BMI), Red Cloud Music (BMI), and Fingers Music (ASCAP). All print rights for Cass County Music and Red Cloud Music administered by Warner-Tamerlane Publishing Corp. All rights reserved. Reprinted by permission of Alfred Music Publishing Co., Inc., on behalf of Don Henley and Glenn Frey, and Don Felder. Random House, Inc., and Curtis Brown, Ltd.: "Funeral Blues," copyright © 1940, copyright renewed 1968 by W. H. Auden; excerpt from "Many Happy Returns," copyright © 1945, copyright renewed 1973 by W. H. Auden, from *Collected Poems of W. H. Auden* by W. H. Auden (currently published by Modern Library, a division of Random House, Inc.). Reprinted by permission of Random House, Inc. on behalf of print rights and Curtis Brown, Ltd. on behalf of audio and electronic rights. Russell & Volkening, Inc.: Excerpt from "what i thought i'd never lose & did/what i discovered when i didn't know i cd" by Ntozake Shange, copyright © 1993 by Ntozake Shange, from *In the Fullness of Time: 32 Women on Life after 50* (New York: Atria/Simon & Schuster, 2010). Reprinted by permission of Russell & Volkening as agents for the author.

LET ME TELL YOU WHAT I MEAN

Little, Brown and Company: "Some Women" originally published as the introduction to *Some Women* by Robert Mapplethorpe. Introduction copyright © 1989 by Joan Didion. Reprinted by permission of Little, Brown and Company, an imprint of Hachette Book Group, Inc. HarperCollins Publishers: "The Long-Distance Runner" originally published as the introduction to *The Long-Distance Runner* by Tony Richardson. Introduction copyright © 1993 by Joan Didion. Reprinted by permission of HarperCollins Publishers. The following essays first appeared in the *Saturday Evening Post:* "Alicia and the Underground Press," "Getting Serenity," "A Trip to Xanadu," "On Being Unchosen by the College of One's Choice," "Pretty Nancy," "Fathers, Sons, Screaming Eagles." "Why I Write" first appeared in *The New York Times*

Magazine; "Telling Stories" first appeared in *New West*; "Last Words" and "Everywoman.com" first appeared in *The New Yorker*. A shortened version of "Pretty Nancy" subsequently appeared in *The White Album*, published by Simon & Schuster, New York, in 1979. "Why I Write" subsequently appeared in the anthology *The Writer on Her Work*, edited by Janet Sternberg and published by W. W. Norton & Company, New York, in 1980.